THE SPIRIT OF THE BLITZ

THE spirit OF THE BLITZ

Home Intelligence and British Morale

September 1940–June 1941

EDITED BY

PAUL ADDISON & JEREMY A. CRANG

OXFORD
UNIVERSITY PRESS

OXFORD
UNIVERSITY PRESS

Great Clarendon Street, Oxford, OX2 6DP,
United Kingdom

Oxford University Press is a department of the University of Oxford.
It furthers the University's objective of excellence in research, scholarship,
and education by publishing worldwide. Oxford is a registered trade mark of
Oxford University Press in the UK and in certain other countries

Published in the United States of America by Oxford University Press
198 Madison Avenue, New York, NY 10016, United States of America

British Library Cataloguing in Publication Data
Data available

Library of Congress Control Number: 2020931695

ISBN 978–0–19–884850–9

Printed in Great Britain by
Bell & Bain Ltd., Glasgow

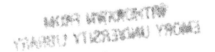

ACKNOWLEDGEMENTS

In editing this volume we have accumulated a number of debts. We are grateful to the Arts and Humanities Research Council for awarding Jeremy Crang a period of sabbatical leave to undertake research for the book. Thanks are also due to Andrew Gordon at David Higham, and to Luciana O'Flaherty, Kizzy Taylor-Richelieu, and Christina Fleischer at Oxford University Press, for their indispensable advice and guidance in the construction of the volume. We are further indebted to the staffs of the United Kingdom National Archives and the Mass Observation Archive for their unfailing courtesy and helpfulness, to Lucy Metzger, Dawn Preston, Martin Noble, and Jayashree Thirumaran, for their invaluable assistance in preparing the Home Intelligence reports for publication, and to Naomi Walker in the School of History, Classics and Archaeology at the University of Edinburgh for her expert help with the administration of the project. The Home Intelligence reports are reproduced here under the Open Government Licence whilst material drawn from the Mary Adams papers appears courtesy of the Mass Observation Archive. Last but not least we owe an enormous debt of gratitude to our respective spouses, Rosy and Fiona, for their unstinting support during our collaboration over many years.

CONTENTS

LIST OF FIGURES

Map Ministry of Information Regions 1940

HOME INTELLIGENCE, THE BLITZ, AND THE BRITISH

Paul Addison and Jeremy A. Crang

During the Second World War the morale of the British people was clandestinely monitored by Home Intelligence (HI), a unit of the Ministry of Information (MOI) that kept watch on the behaviour of the public and eavesdropped on their conversations. Intelligence from a wide range of sources and every region of the United Kingdom (UK) was collected and analysed by a small team of officials, based at the Senate House of the University of London, who compiled regular reports on the state of popular morale. Issued daily from May to September 1940, and weekly thereafter until HI closed down in December 1944, they provide us with a unique and extraordinary window into the thoughts and emotions of the British at war. This treasure trove of reports reads like the collective diary of a nation.

In *Listening to Britain: Home Intelligence Reports on Britain's Finest Hour, May to September 1940* (2010) we edited and published an unabridged set of the daily reports covering the period of the Dunkirk evacuation, the Battle of Britain, and the start of the Blitz. In the present volume, a sequel, we have published a complete set of the reports and appendices for the period of the Blitz, which is usually reckoned to have begun with the massed air attacks on London on 7 September 1940, and petered out in May 1941 as Hitler transferred the Luftwaffe to the east in preparation for the assault on the Soviet Union. In order to ensure full coverage of the subject we have included the first three weeks of the reports already published in *Listening to Britain*. We have extended the period a little to include the transition from the Blitz to Barbarossa in June 1941.

HI was set up for the purpose of monitoring the state of popular morale in wartime. This led the staff, with the aid of their regional officers and other contacts, to enquire into almost every aspect of life on the home front. The Blitz, therefore, was only one of many subjects on which they reported between September 1940 and June 1941. They monitored popular reactions to major events in the war: the defeat of the Italians in the western desert, the loss of Crete, the sinking of the *Bismarck*, and so on. They examined popular attitudes towards rationing and shortages and investigated the extent of anti-war feeling and anti-Semitism. And when Hitler's deputy Rudolf Hess flew to Scotland in May 1941, they recorded the rumours and speculation that followed. These were very eventful months but running like a connecting thread through them all was the ever present menace of the Blitz.

Prior to 7 September, the Luftwaffe's bombing offensive consisted mainly of daylight attacks on the Royal Air Force and its airfields. The assault on London marked the beginning of a sustained campaign of night bombing in which ports, industrial centres, and the capital itself were the main targets. With the exception of the night of 3 November, London was subjected to heavy raids every night from 7 September to 13 November. The bombing of Coventry on 14 November marked the start of a second phase in which the Luftwaffe fanned out to attack a range of provincial targets, among them Portsmouth, Plymouth, Cardiff, Bristol, Birmingham, Merseyside, Hull, Belfast, and Clydeside. Raids on London were now intermittent but more destructive than ever. The total number of those killed across the UK is often estimated at around 43,000, but if we define the Blitz as beginning on 7 September 1940 and ending on 31 May 1941, the total is slightly lower at just under 40,000. The higher figure might be the result of including the casualty figures for the first few days of September, as well as the figures for the second half of 1941.[1] Nearly half of the Blitz deaths were in London.[2]

Contrary to British assumptions at the time, the German offensive was never primarily intended as an exercise in the terror bombing of civilians. The strategic objective was to disrupt the supply of essential imports and impede war production, and the bombers were under orders to attack specific targets. Collateral damage was, however, inevitable, and the intimidation of civilians a welcome bonus from the German point of view. Although the Blitz was not therefore an attempt to terrorize the British into surrender, it was an effort to wreck the war economy and undermine morale to the point at which the government might sue for peace.

In Britain between the wars, airmen, politicians, and civil servants had all tended to assume that the bombing of British cities would indeed have devastating effects. In the 1930s officials had been haunted by fears of a bloodbath that might kill 600,000 people in the first sixty days,[3] leading to mass panic and a collapse in morale. In particular, they expected that the enemy would attempt to launch a knock-out blow against London. With the development in the late 1930s of a system of air defence against the bomber—secret of course but hinted at in government publicity—and the establishment of the civil defence services, Britain was better prepared to defend itself, but no one on 7 September 1940 could predict the effects heavy raids would have on popular morale. Nor did HI, or Whitehall in general, have a clear definition of what they meant by morale or how it could be measured.

Two stories are interwoven here. One is the story, as told in the HI reports, of the British during the Blitz. The other is the story of HI itself, the little group of wartime civil servants, housed in the Senate House, who pieced together the data and compiled the reports. In retrospect it can be seen as a bold and imaginative exercise in bridging the gap between government and people. But in seeking to articulate popular complaints against the authorities they made enemies in Whitehall who sabotaged and all but wrecked their activities.

THE ORIGINS OF HOME INTELLIGENCE

In the twenty-first century we take for granted the fact that we are under continuous surveillance by numerous agencies: social surveys, opinion pollsters, market researchers, and social media. Trends in opinion and fashions in lifestyle are monitored twenty-four hours a day. The situation in 1939 was very different. Two organizations, Mass Observation (MO) and the British Institute of Public Opinion (BIPO), were pioneers in the field, but MO's methods were often censured as unscientific, and the political world paid little if any attention to the poll results regularly published by BIPO in the *News Chronicle*. The political class relied mainly on the press, a highly unreliable source, as a guide to the state of public opinion. When, however, it was decided in the 1930s that in the event of a new great war there would have to be another MOI, it was also decided that it should be equipped with its own independent source of intelligence on the state of popular morale.

Unlike Joseph Goebbels's Ministry of Propaganda, set up in 1933, the MOI only came into existence at the outbreak of war. The first blueprint of its activities, drawn up by a sub-committee of the Committee of Imperial Defence in July 1936, envisaged that it would pursue two main objectives on the domestic front: the censorship of news and information, and the dissemination of propaganda intended to sustain popular support for the war. There was no specific mention of the word 'morale' but its importance was taken so much for granted that no explicit reference was needed. In practice the planners paid far more attention to the question of censorship than they did to the cloudy topics of propaganda and morale. Nevertheless, some preparations were made.[4]

It was recognized that the MOI would need some kind of machinery for gauging the public's response to publicity campaigns, as well as the assessment of morale in general. The planners proposed a Collecting Division to gather intelligence about public opinion from sources such as the press and government departments. The secretary of the University Grants Committee, John Beresford, a former Treasury official and well-known man of letters, was appointed as its provisional director in June 1937.[5] As Ian McLaine explains, Beresford planned to expand the range of sources to include 'Rotary Clubs, Chambers of Commerce, the Federation of British Industry, Workers' Educational Associations, school inspectors, teachers' organisations, the Ministry's Regional Information Offices (RIOs), the Labour movement, and even "Communist cells", the latter contact to be explored "as discreetly as possible"'.[6] Beresford also made tentative plans to engage the services of MO and BIPO.[7] 'I should like to point out,' he wrote to a Treasury official, 'that the Collecting Division is an entirely new and pioneering experiment. No division with similar duties as far as I am aware existed in the last war. It is impossible to foresee before the event precisely how it will actually develop.'[8]

An essential adjunct of HI's activities was the ministry's regional machinery, which enabled it to set up listening posts in all parts of the country. At the outbreak of war eleven regional offices, corresponding to the civil defence regions of the UK but excluding London, were established under the direction of regional information officers (RIOs), whose task was to organize publicity and propaganda at the local level. They included offices for Wales in Cardiff and Scotland in Edinburgh. Regional offices for London and Northern Ireland (which was not a civil defence region) were added in 1940.[9] In every region the RIO was to be assisted by Local Information Committees made up of representatives drawn from the three main political parties—a rule inapplicable to Northern Ireland—businesses, trade unions, voluntary bodies, and other local interest groups.[10]

Almost before it started, the machinery ground to a halt. The ministry proved to be an administrative shambles presided over by an ineffectual minister, Lord Macmillan. In October 1939 it was stripped of its censorship functions, which were transferred to a Press and Censorship Bureau. The rest of the ministry was subjected to draconian economies imposed by Lord Camrose, the proprietor of the *Daily Telegraph*, who was brought in as chief assistant to the minister. Beresford, who had been appointed as one of the ministry's directors, resigned and the experiment of a Collecting Division appears to have been abandoned. The regional machinery was cut back and a number of RIOs stepped down.[11]

It soon became evident that domestic publicity would be unworkable without the regional apparatus and it was gradually restored.[12] Meanwhile, due largely to the efforts of John Hilton, the ministry's director of home publicity, a unit with objectives similar to those of the Collecting Division was created under the title of Home Intelligence. Hilton, the child of working-class parents from Bolton, was one of the many temporary civil servants who brought a breath of fresh air to wartime Whitehall. A popular broadcaster of the 1930s, and pre-war professor of industrial relations at Cambridge, he understood the value of market research and pressed for its introduction into the MOI. Coincidentally, a request arrived from the Ministry of Food for the creation of a market research agency.[13] Hilton's proposal to set up HI was agreed and in December 1939 he secured the appointment of his friend Mary Adams as its director.[14]

THE ACHIEVEMENTS OF MARY ADAMS

The archetypal civil servant of the administrative class was male, upper-middle class, ex-public school, ex-Oxbridge, and a graduate in the humanities. Adams, a scholarship girl from a modest background, was a graduate in botany from the University of Cardiff. After joining the Talks Department of the BBC in 1930, she became the first woman television producer in 1937, broadcasting from Alexandra Palace at a time when the infant service was still confined to the London area. When it closed down at the outbreak of war she was free to take on a new challenge. 'In appearance,' her daughter recalled, 'Mary Adams was small, birdlike, always well dressed, with bright blue eyes and, in public, a knowing confidence. She was a socialist, a romantic communist…a fervent atheist and advocate of humanism and common sense.'[15] Despite her left-wing convictions she was married to the Conservative member of parliament (MP), Vyvyan Adams, a strong opponent of appeasement.

Adams proposed that the existence of HI should be made public and its rationale explained. 'All super-imposed intelligence services,' she wrote, 'run the risk of being represented as part of a disguised espionage system organised by the Government for political purposes and, as such, contraventions of the rules of democratic society.' Much future embarrassment, she argued, could be avoided by a publicity campaign explaining the necessity of keeping the government in touch with public opinion.[16] She was to be overruled, a sign of the embarrassment felt by the government at 'snooping' on the political opinions of private citizens. Except for very occasional references in Parliament and the press, HI was concealed from the public gaze throughout the war.

Adams pressed ahead with the building up of her department. She won the approval of the Treasury for the establishment of a headquarters staff which consisted, by July 1940, of nine people assisted by four shorthand typists and two clerks.[17] One of the first of her recruits was the artist and illustrator Nicolas Bentley, who had appeared on some of the television programmes she produced at Alexandra Palace. Having trained as an auxiliary fireman before the war, he went on to serve, on temporary leave from the

MOI, as a fire-fighter during the London Blitz.[18] Another Adams protégé, the poet and writer Winifred Holmes, belonged to a literary circle that included T. S. Eliot, W. H. Auden, Christopher Isherwood, and Edith Sitwell.[19] In order, perhaps, to balance the artistic abilities of Bentley and Holmes with a more scientific mind she also recruited Stephen Taylor, an ambitious young psychiatrist whom she had invited on to the radio during her time as a talks producer at the BBC. 'Had the war not come,' she noted in March 1940, 'he would have been selected for a production post in Television.'[20] During the phoney war Taylor was working in a naval hospital in Bristol and months passed before she could persuade the admiralty to release him. Eventually, however, she prevailed and Taylor joined the department with the rank of 'Specialist' in May 1940.[21]

HI was tasked with the collection of data on morale and public opinion, but how and where was it to be found? Adams could draw on in-house sources in the shape of reports from the MOI's regional officers, but she was sceptical of their ability to report objectively on the response to campaigns run by their own ministry.[22] For harder evidence she turned to the Postal and Telegraph Censorship, which agreed to supply HI with regular summaries of its findings. Shortly afterwards, in April 1940, responsibility for this censorship was transferred from the War Office to the MOI.[23]

Outgoing mail from the UK was scrutinized, but censorship of internal mail was applied to areas like the north of Scotland, where key defence facilities were sited.[24] The postal censorship correspondents, Adams noted, were predominantly lower-middle class, and 'not of an unintellectual type', and their letters were not always a reliable indicator of morale: 'Experience has shown that some writers feel it their duty to act a propagandist role when painting a picture of wartime England for foreign consumption.' Nevertheless, she concluded that postal censorship was a valuable source.[25] By October 1940, when the first of the weekly reports was produced, 120,000 letters a week were being opened and read.[26]

HI, however, was founded on the assumption that no single source could be relied upon as an accurate measure of opinion. The aim was to create a broad stream of evidence from numerous tributaries. The Home Office supplied summaries of morale drawn from the police duty-room reports of chief constables. The BBC made available the findings of Robert Silvey's Listener Research Department. A number of voluntary organizations like the Women's Institute, the Women's Voluntary Service, and the Citizens' Advice Bureau responded to requests for information. The managers of the Odeon cinema chain sent in reports (presumably on audience reactions to newsreels), but the arrangement was broken off at the request of MI5. Another unusual source was the railway bookstalls of W. H. Smith's, whose travelling superintendents filled in questionnaires based on discussions with bookstall managers.[27]

The most important of Adams's sources was MO. In the course of her work at the BBC she had commissioned Tom Harrisson, a self-taught social anthropologist and brilliant, buccaneering self-publicist, to broadcast for her. An upper-class misfit, Harrisson had dropped out of university at Cambridge after twelve months and embarked on a life of adventure. At an age when other young men of his background were making a career for themselves in the Army or the City, he was taking part in expeditions to the South Seas and making friends with cannibals. In 1937 he and the poet Charles Madge co-founded MO with the aim of creating a social anthropology of the British, observing them as though they were a hitherto unknown tribe. Harrisson set up a branch in Bolton ('Worktown' in MO's publications) and began to study behaviour in all manner of social contexts from pubs to dance halls and wrestling matches. He was assisted by a small team of full-time investigators whose task was to research the multitude of topics inspired by his fertile brain. Madge, who was based in London, was in charge of a nationwide panel of volunteers who responded by post to requests for their observations and opinions. At first Madge and Harrisson worked well together but tensions arose and the relationship degenerated to the point at which Madge was forced out. By June 1940 Harrisson was in sole charge of MO.[28]

Harrisson was continuously engaged in scraping enough money together to pay his full-time investigators. With the approach of war he saw the chance of attaching MO to the government payroll, a stroke of opportunism allied to the conviction that his organization alone could bridge the gulf of mutual incomprehension between the rulers and the ruled. The appointment of Adams to HI seemed providential and she soon arranged for Harrisson to be employed on the study of opinion at by-elections, the main purpose of which was to gauge the strength of anti-war feeling. In April 1940 she obtained approval for a three-month contract under which MO was employed on a full-time basis. The ministry, however, kept the employment of MO secret. So great was the fear that the government would be charged with spying on its own people that MO's full-time investigators were instructed never to mention, even when questioned by the police, that they were working for the MOI.[29]

Although she was a great admirer of Harrisson's work, Adams was well aware that he was a controversial figure. Among the career civil servants in the ministry there was a 'lingering suspicion' that his organization 'was heavily inclined towards the left'.[30] This was true in the sense that the majority of MO's voluntary panel were on the left, and several of its full-time investigators pacifists or communists. But Harrisson himself was robustly pro-war, a liberal in politics, and quite indifferent to Marxist theory or sociological concepts of class. In the academic world his reliance on methods that were both intuitive and impressionistic was regarded as unscientific and some thought him a charlatan. MO's paid observers conducted daily face-to-face interviews with men and women in the street, and attempts were made to quantify the findings, but Harrisson was convinced that opinions expressed in public, in response to questions framed by pollsters, often concealed the opinions they expressed in private. One of the main objectives of MO, therefore, was to document spontaneous opinion by eavesdropping on people whose unguarded remarks were recorded by investigators as 'overheards'.

Adams recognized that HI needed objective statistical data, based on a representative sample of the population, to act as a counterweight to the impressionism of MO. No organization was fully capable of this at the time but the best qualified was Henry Durant's BIPO. It had, however, been ruled out as a specialist source for HI in the early weeks of the war, and Adams made no attempt to reinstate it, although some of its findings were to feature in HI reports. In contrast, the BBC, the Board of Trade, and the Ministry of Food were all subsequently to commission the BIPO to undertake surveys.[31] Adams decided instead to set up a new organization, the War-Time Social Survey (referred to here as 'the Social Survey'). Established in April 1940, it was separate from HI, but run by the same director. In contrast with MO, it was an academically respectable body, supervised by Professor Arnold Plant of the London School of Economics and operating under the aegis of the National Institute of Social and Economic Research. The Social Survey employed house-to-house interviews in which respondents replied to a standardized list of questions. Adams hoped that it would provide HI with a statistically reliable 'barometer of public opinion'.[32]

In mid-May 1940, with the Germans advancing rapidly towards the Channel, Adams was instructed by her superiors at the MOI to produce a daily report on the state of morale. The RIOs, who were asked to telephone in each day between 12.00pm and 2.30pm, had little evidence to offer beyond impressions gathered from casual conversations or 'a hurried series of visits to public houses'.[33] Other sources like the Social Survey produced more reliable findings but at longer intervals. Only Harrisson's full-time observers could provide survey data on a daily basis. The first of the daily reports, on 18 May 1940, seems to be virtually a carbon copy of a report written by Harrisson. So MO became even more indispensable to HI—for the time being.

HI was never likely to engage in the kind of surveillance practised by police states. As a general rule neither MO nor HI disclosed the names of individuals in their reports. When Winifred Holmes wrote to the Home Office about communism at an air-raid wardens' post, and mentioned the name of the well-known children's writer Noel Streatfeild, she was roundly rebuked by Adams: 'Only under the most exceptional circumstances should it be necessary for any information about individuals to be lodged with another Ministry, especially with the Home Office.'[34]

If HI did not 'snoop' on individuals, it nonetheless supplied the Home Office with a series of special reports on the activities of communists, fascists, pacifists, and other anti-war groups. They may therefore have been of some use to the intelligence services in providing background information on dissident organizations. 'Most RIOs,' recorded a circular in January 1941, 'send to Home Intelligence leaflets and notes of the activities of such groups.'[35]

THE DOWNFALL OF MARY ADAMS

Adams had constructed an ingenious mechanism whereby the swift impressionism of MO was to be counterbalanced by the slower but more scientific methods of the Social Survey. Both halves of the machinery were destined to buckle. The Social Survey fell victim to attacks in Parliament and the press, as a result of which its staff were cut and its enquiries restricted. Adams's contract with MO continued for the time being, but Harrisson now had an enemy inside HI in the person of Stephen Taylor. The conflict between the two, laid bare in James Hinton's book *The Mass Observers*, was eventually resolved when Taylor succeeded Adams as director of HI in April 1941, and began to disentangle himself from MO's embrace.[36]

When Churchill became prime minister in May 1940 he appointed his friend and ally Alfred Duff Cooper as Minister of Information. The Social Survey, meanwhile, was venturing into politically sensitive territory. People were asked not only whether they had heard or read about Churchill's broadcast speeches, but also whether they *approved* of them. Fifty per cent approved his first broadcast on 19 May, 78.5 per cent his second on 16 June. Early in July, when fears of invasion were widespread, people were asked whether they believed that Britain was adequately prepared for the dangers. Seventy-six per cent were satisfied that the preparations were adequate but 16 per cent were dissatisfied. 'The survey,' it was contended by HI, 'can help to reveal unsuspected weak spots in morale—grumbles, worries, dangers and the like—which if not righted or explained may lead to more serious troubles.'[37]

The Social Survey then got caught up in the ongoing crossfire between the press and the MOI. Inevitably, as its interviewers went from door to door, explaining that they were from the Social Survey, the press got wind of their activities and launched an attack on 'Cooper's Snoopers'. The government was accused of invading privacy, spying on the public, and imitating the methods of totalitarian states.[38] From the point of view of the MOI, the attack on the survey had the advantage of distracting attention from the activities of HI. The Social Survey's enquiries were defensible on the grounds that they were openly conducted with the knowledge and

consent of householders. More positively, they could be justified as a contribution to the workings of a democracy. The case of HI was quite different. It really *was* 'snooping'—eavesdropping on people who were unaware
that their views were being reported, albeit anonymously. Some MPs suspected that something of the kind was going on with the aid of MO. In the
feverish political atmosphere of the summer of 1940 the revelation of the
extent of MO's involvement would have caused a political storm. Duff
Cooper concluded that he would have to be highly economical with the
truth. When the topic was debated in the House of Commons on 1 August he
mounted a strong defence of the Social Survey while misleading MPs about
the role of MO. 'Mass Observation', he declared, 'is, I understand, privately
run and controlled. We have once or twice applied to it for statistical information on certain subjects which it has been able to furnish.'[39]

While the Social Survey took the flak HI remained largely invisible and
immune from public scrutiny. 'The Government and the Civil Service',
wrote Taylor, 'were provided with a guide to the changing moods of public
opinion; yet the Minister of Information was never called upon to justify
this activity in public. Had he been asked to do so, pressure from Press and
Parliament might have forced him to discontinue the service.'[40]

Like Adams, Taylor was a socialist. He combined his work for HI with a
low-profile campaign for a National Health Service in the columns of the
Lancet and the *Spectator*.[41] As a post-war Labour MP he was to be a strong
supporter of Aneurin Bevan's reforms. Robustly patriotic, with an Orwellian
mistrust of the progressive intelligentsia, he encountered Tom Harrisson
at one of Mary Adams's parties before the war but was unimpressed. 'I did
not take to him,' he wrote, 'if only because he seemed to be a journalist mas-
querading as a scientist.'[42] Taylor was sceptical of MO's methodology, sus-
pecting that Harrisson interpreted his results 'with greater enthusiasm
than accuracy',[43] and believed that its reports were tendentious. Arriving at
HI he found that 'alarm and despondency were the order of the day.
Defeatism was reported to be rife. The war was as good as lost. These were
the conventional attitudes of the intellectual left at that time.'[44]

Taylor warned Adams not to place too much reliance on reports from
MO, but she was not persuaded. In his memoirs he described her as 'a

sweet, energetic, liberal minded but muddled lady...For a rational scientist (which she was), reason seemed to play little part in her thinking.'[45] Yet as he explained in a brief, unpublished history of HI, written at the end of the war, some action was taken in the summer of 1940 to address the problem:

> Those in Home Intelligence who were doubtful about the representa-
> tiveness of Mass Observation reports were anxious to provide some
> system of studying the feelings of the public more directly and impar-
> tially. So it was decided to make contact with a number of people in
> London, in all strata of society, who would be prepared, in response to
> a telephone call or a personal visit, to report the feelings of those with
> whom they came in contact...The types of people approached were
> doctors, dentists, parsons, publicans, small shopkeepers, newsagents,
> trades union officials, factory welfare officers, shop stewards, Citizens'
> Advice Bureau secretaries, hospital almoners, business men, and local
> authority officials.[46]

It seems likely that HI's assessments of morale would have been more pessimistic but for the presence of Taylor.

The Social Survey had survived the 'Cooper's Snoopers' row but was now under scrutiny and vulnerable to criticism. Heedless of the critics, in September 1940 Adams instructed it to go ahead with an even more con-
tentious project. A team of psychiatric social workers was hired to assess the general morale of interviewees on a five-point scale. The National Institute of Social and Economic Research, which believed that the psy-
chological measurement of morale was beyond its expertise, withdrew from its supervisory role. Fortunately for Adams the scheme quickly proved unworkable and was abandoned.[47] In the meantime the MOI had acquired a new director-general, Frank Pick, the former chief executive of London Transport. Sceptical of the value of the Social Survey he cut staff numbers from sixty to twenty and decreed that in future it should concentrate on 'purely factual' investigations for other government departments.[48] This dealt a severe blow to Adams's attempts to employ the Social Survey as a source for HI. She did, however, continue to direct it as a separate entity.

For data on morale and opinion Adams was now more dependent than ever on Harrisson and MO. Nor was her faith in him diminished. In October 1940 she extended MO's contract for a further period of six months.[49] Meanwhile, the Blitz had plunged Adams into fresh difficulties. The main problem was the mounting tension between HI and the MOI on the one hand, and the Home Office, one of the most powerful of Whitehall departments, on the other.[50] During the summer of 1940, the two had shared intelligence on the effects of air raids. The Home Office intelligence reports, however, were based on information supplied by the civil defence services. As Adams and Harrisson saw it, one of the main functions of HI was to report on public attitudes *towards* the civil defence services. When the victims of raids complained that public air-raid shelters were damp, overcrowded, and unhygienic, Adams's department reported their views. Although the organization of air-raid precautions was largely in the hands of local authorities, the overall responsibility lay with the Home Office and its officials were angered by the tone of the HI reports.[51] As Hinton comments: 'The Home Office was never able to understand that MO was dealing not in authenticated fact about official performance but in popular perceptions.'[52]

Up to this point the daily reports had been circulated to ministers and officials outside the MOI at Adams's discretion. Under pressure from the Home Office Pick now decreed that in future they were to be circulated only within the ministry.[53] She was also instructed to replace daily with weekly reports.[54] As the new format enabled HI to draw more considered conclusions from a larger body of data, this probably marked an improvement in the quality of HI's findings. Throughout the Blitz, however, the weekly reports were withheld from home front ministries like Food, Labour, or the Board of Trade, whose interactions with the public were key determinants of morale. They were, therefore, largely irrelevant to government policy at the time, although invaluable to future historians.

Adams's difficulties were not confined to the turf war with the Home Office. 'Naturally,' she wrote to R. J. Silvey of BBC Listener Research, 'everyone is frightened of the work of our department, regard it with suspicion, and many senior civil servants do their utmost to bring about a standstill. I needn't tell you that techniques of social research are so little understood, and I might add so little authenticated, that ignorance, misunderstanding and suspicion abound.'[55] Pouring out her troubles to Harold Nicolson, the junior minister at the MOI, she complained bitterly of the obstruction she faced:

> My Department has been charged with the task of documenting morale and assessing changes in public opinion, but there has never been any clearly defined policy about the use to which the reports might be put. For example, at the present moment, I've got excellent detailed material about the Glasgow and Clydeside situation but no one is really interested in considering it. There's such departmental jealousy and a staggering sensitivity to criticism that this Ministry would never dream of forwarding these reports (containing as they must do indirect criticism of the work of other Government Departments) to the Ministry of Labour, the Regional Commissioner or the Ministry of Health . . .
>
> Naturally if our reports are to be of the slightest use they must be completely frank and not be eternally concerned with conciliating other interests...There is, of course, terrific pressure everywhere to *say* (especially in cold print) that everything is alright, that morale is splendid, that people are taking it, etc. We are subject to the same pressure. It's in the air.[56]

Adams was distraught. 'Never in my wildest dreams,' she wrote to Julian Huxley, 'had I believed such inefficiency and inability existed. No one seems ever to make up their minds about anything.'[57] The situation, she confided to another correspondent, was 'unadulterated hell'.[58] Her isolation seems to have been the consequence of a general loss of confidence in her judgement. Convinced that she was right, she expected the logic of her arguments to prevail, but the only response from Whitehall was an ominous silence. In a desperate bid to gain her independence she sent Walter Monckton, who had succeeded Pick as director-general of the MOI at the end of 1940, a memorandum suggesting that HI should be transferred to the Cabinet Office,[59] but nothing came of this. For his part, Duff Cooper seems to have ignored the existence of HI altogether. 'The Minister has never considered it proper', she complained, 'to make use of our reports in any policy decisions that affect morale.'[60]

What exacerbated matters was that in March 1941 R. H. Parker, a former Indian civil service judge and Home Office official of strongly right-wing views, was drafted in to the MOI as director of the Home Division and placed in authority over her.[61] Parker had previously headed the Home Office's intelligence branch,[62] whose reports during the Blitz have been described as reading 'like morale-boosting propaganda'.[63] Whilst at the Home Office in the summer of 1940 he had been scathing about Adams's organization:

> It will suffice to say that, after three months' co-operation with the Intelligence Department of Ministry of Information and study of its methods, I am of [the] opinion that it is without reliable information upon national reactions and morale; that it is not so managed as to obtain any; that its opinions are without judgement, and that its sources reside in small and eccentric classes unrepresentative of the Nation. In my opinion this is due to the Ministry possessing neither the system, the machinery, nor the methods to produce a comprehensive survey of the spirit, the reactions, or the courage of the Nation. I believe this view will be endorsed by all who have read their daily reports on morale.[64]

It was thus no surprise that Adams found herself in an increasingly untenable position. Harrisson urged her to quit: 'Let not our new battle cry be: "Parker must go". Let it instead be: "WE MUST GO". Go somewhere with some lieberstraum and leave after the end of March, if you cannot take it before!'[65] In a last futile attempt to force the issue, Adams tried to persuade her staff to resign with her. They refused to do so and she departed in April 1941, taking up a post in the North American service of the BBC.[66]

Stephen Taylor was now put in charge but for the time being HI remained a branch of the Home Division under Parker's direction. When Plymouth suffered a series of heavy air raids between 21 and 29 April, Parker instructed Taylor himself to visit the city and report on conditions—thus bypassing MO and asserting his own authority over HI.[67] Harrisson got the impression that he was being frozen out by the MOI and when he wrote to Taylor in July asking for some regular contact he not did receive a response.

He would henceforth be forced to look outside of government for alternative patronage and funding for MO.[68]

In the weekly reports HI continued as before to rely mainly on qualitative judgements, but Adams's desire to create a 'barometer of morale' lingered on and found expression in a curious in-house method of quantifying 'public feeling'. The opening paragraph of each of the weekly reports was translated by HI into a number on a scale from 0 to 20. On the basis of the weekly figures a chart was then compiled showing fluctuations in 'public feeling' from March 1941.[69] As neither the figures nor the chart were referred to in the weekly reports, they appear to have been for internal guidance only, although it was observed with cool understatement that 'no absolute validity' could be claimed for the graph.[70]

Meanwhile, Taylor, step by step, rescued HI from its plight. He reorganized its intelligence-gathering machinery, freed it from the supervision of Parker, distanced it from MO, won the support of top officials, and ensured that its reports were circulated throughout Whitehall. The story of how he achieved all this, however, belongs to a later chapter of history. We now turn from the history of HI itself to the history of Britain during the Blitz as HI reported it.

THE DISCONTENTS OF THE BLITZ

In reading the reports it is easy to slip into the habit of treating them as a factual record. They were not. The methods by which intelligence was collected were unscientific and in some instances plainly unreliable. The qualitative judgements of the data made by Adams and her staff were, inevitably, subjective. Given the fact that working-class views were, for the most part, reported indirectly through the medium of middle-class informants, aspects of the truth may have been lost in translation.

While the reports have to be read with such reservations in mind they also had their strengths. In spite of the fact that Adams and Taylor were both socialists, they sought to describe and inform, not to indoctrinate. They recognized that public opinion was never monolithic and tried to reflect the diversity of viewpoints. Although they claimed no scientific authority for their judgements, their methods were transparent and evidence-based. Every report contained a full reference apparatus documenting the sources from which information had been obtained. (After considering the many pros and cons involved in retaining that apparatus in our reproduction of the reports, we concluded that it would be an impediment for readers and decided, with some reluctance, to omit. But, for illustrative purposes, we have included the reference apparatus for two reports in early January 1941.) Whatever their limitations, the reports are the closest we are ever likely to get to the truth about morale and public opinion in wartime Britain.

The first few days of the London Blitz gave rise, in HI's words, to 'shock amongst all classes and in all districts'. In the eye of the storm the people of the Docklands showed 'visible signs of nerve cracking from constant ordeals',[71] but there was no mass panic, no breakdown of order, and no collapse of morale. Nor did it collapse in any of the other towns and cities bombed by the Luftwaffe. Beyond this point, however, it is difficult to generalize about the impact of the Blitz. Responses to bombing depended on many different factors including the resilience of individuals, the frequency and intensity of raids, the efficiency or otherwise of the civil defence measures, and the size and topography of the towns and cities concerned.

London stood out from everywhere else by virtue of the number of times it was bombed. Whereas Cardiff suffered one 'major' night-time raid, Hull three, and Birmingham eight, London suffered seventy-one such attacks.[72] In the capital the Blitz became a way of life to which its inhabitants became adapted over a nine-month period. As it was by far the largest of the blitzed cities, it was also to some extent cushioned by the fact that bombed areas could draw upon help and resources from neighbouring boroughs. In a small industrial town like Coventry, a major raid could strike a savage psychological blow against the whole population.

While the Blitz was initially concentrated on London, the bombing of Coventry in November 1940 marked the point at which the Luftwaffe began to broaden the scope of the offensive to encompass the industrial towns and major ports of provincial Britain. Although the staff of HI were based in London, their sensitivity to the wider Blitz was evident in both the weekly reports and the special reports they commissioned into the effects of raids on Coventry, Clydebank, Hull, Barrow-in-Furness, Plymouth, Merseyside, and Portsmouth. Morale, it appeared, was more robust in some places than others. After the Clydebank raid in March 1941 the Edinburgh office reported: 'It is agreed by all observers that the bearing of the people in Clydeside was beyond praise. They are of a high moral and intellectual calibre.'[73] The following month, however, a special report on Plymouth read more like the obituary of a town:

> For the present, Plymouth as a business and commercial centre of a prosperous countryside has ceased to exist…It would be wrong to assume that the people are broken. But equally it would be suicidal to ignore the implications and symptoms of the actual state of affairs, and to avoid probing the disturbing causes of the aftermath of some of the fiercest raids yet made upon a provincial centre.[74]

Levels of morale could also vary between one part of town and another. In the case of Hull, which suffered heavy raids in March 1941, the local Information Committee painted a sombre picture of the St Paul's district, where the immediate post-raid reaction was one of 'complete helplessness and resignation'. This they attributed to pre-war social conditions of poverty and bad housing. The North Hull Estate, by contrast, 'gave a remarkable demonstration of high morale…We can frankly state that in not one single case did we see any undue fear or weakening of morale.'[75]

While HI consistently reported high levels of popular support for the war, they were nonetheless vigilant for signs of anti-war feeling in the aftermath of bombing. In December 1940 the RIO in Bristol reported that

> in the poorer districts (particularly Knowle West, Bedminster, and South Mead) there is much talk of having been let down by the Government, and of the possibility of a negotiated peace. These reports come from such divergent sources as university lecturers, social workers, company directors and doctors. The feeling is said to be particularly marked among the women.[76]

With the Soviet Union neutral, the Communist Party of Great Britain was pursuing an ambiguous line of exploiting popular grievances against the government—notably the absence of deep shelters in the Blitz—and calling for a 'People's Peace'. The shelters, in fact, gave the Communists the opportunity of organizing shelter committees and distributing propaganda.

At HI Mary Adams and her staff were particularly worried about the damage communist propaganda might do to war production in the ship-building and engineering industries of the west of Scotland, as well as the Scottish coalfields. In January 1941 the government, having con-cluded that the communist aim was to subvert the war effort, suppressed the party newspaper, the *Daily Worker*—though not the Communist Party itself.

No one imagined that casualties could be prevented altogether, but much could be done to minimize the death toll and mitigate the hardship and suf-fering that ensued. Both local authorities and central government bore a heavy weight of responsibility and found themselves under attack for the inadequacy of their preparations. In the wake of raids, HI recorded com-plaints about the shortcomings of rest centres, the inadequacy of shelters, the confusing character of air-raid warnings, and the absence of fighter protection and anti-aircraft guns. The reporting of raids was also a conten-tious issue: 'From all parts of the country there are reports of "indignation and exasperation" at recent broadcasts and official communiques about the bombing of large provincial towns…People fail to understand why the names of some towns are announced, while others are suppressed, even when they have been mentioned on the German radio.'[77]

In the early stages of the Blitz HI reported that there were calls for reprisal raids against German civilians, with the demand coming mainly from parts of Britain which had not experienced bombing. By the end of 1940, however, HI was indicating a growing demand for reprisals across the wider country. 'Increasing bitterness towards the whole German race is still reported…,' it was remarked in December. 'It is again suggested that the time has come to stop the slogan "Britain can take it". The public is now more concerned about "giving it".'[78] In March 1941 reports from seven regions expressed a ferocious demand for revenge: 'Our bombing policy is described as "flabby". More and more it is being suggested that we should "lay off" military objectives for a few nights and instead annihilate one or more German towns—preferably Berlin.'[79]

BEYOND THE BLITZ: THE HOME FRONT

While the Blitz remained a constant theme of the weekly reports, it ceased, as the months passed, to be the dominant one. The bombing offensive continued to kill and destroy but came to be seen as a failed strategy that exposed the impotence of the Luftwaffe. Once they had survived the first heavy raid or series of raids on their home town, most inhabitants of blitzed areas proved remarkably resilient and adaptable. As HI noted in January 1941: 'Reports continue to point out that heavy raids increase rather than diminish the determination of the people in the blitzed towns.'[80] Also, of course, for much of the time most people were not being bombed, while small-town and rural Britain rarely witnessed an air raid. Meanwhile, other topics clamoured for attention and an opinion poll in March 1941 found that only 8 per cent of respondents thought air raids the most important war problem.[81]

On the home front everyday life was beginning to reflect the slow but steady transition from a peacetime to a wartime economy, with voluntary effort increasingly replaced by compulsion. In March 1941 the Minister of Labour, Ernest Bevin, issued an order compelling all women aged twenty and twenty-one to register for employment. This gave him the power, should he wish to use it, to direct women to whatever type of work best served the needs of the war economy. 'Registration of women has been more discussed than any other subject on the home front this week,' HI observed. While opinion was generally in favour, there was strong opposition to conscripting women with young children into industry until all other available women had been called up.[82]

The following month it was the turn of the Chancellor of the Exchequer, Kingsley Wood, to crank up the war effort. In his budget he raised the standard rate of income tax by 1/6d to 10s in the pound and reduced personal and earned income allowances and exemption limits, so bringing millions of new workers into the scope of the tax. 'The middle classes', HI commented, 'are glad that direct taxation is at last to affect the labouring classes, whose incomes in munitions factories and on Government contracts the middle classes regard as excessive.'[83]

By the spring of 1941 one of the main topics of discussion on the home front was food. In this respect the British were relatively fortunate. While the wartime diet could be drab and monotonous, they always had enough to eat and food rationing itself commanded almost universal support as a means of ensuring 'fair shares' for all. Another positive feature was the success of the Minister of Food, Lord Woolton, in communicating with the public and establishing himself as the housewife's favourite uncle. As a broadcaster his popularity rivalled that of Churchill.

Yet a multitude of petty grievances continued to flourish around the topic of food. In its report for the week of 5–12 March 1941 HI listed no fewer than eight flashpoints. Among the complaints was a perceived unfairness in the rations allotted to civil defence workers and those working in heavy industry, as compared to service personnel, the opportunity for evacuees with time on their hands to obtain more items off the ration than local residents, and 'back-of-the-shop' sales for favoured customers.[84] Shortages were a frequent problem. One of the consequences of this was the reappearance of queueing, last seen in the First World War. When a shopkeeper obtained a supply of some scarce item, the competition to obtain it would lead to the formation of a queue in which customers might stand for hours, only to find that stocks had run out by the time they got to the counter. In February 1941 the mayors of Bewdley, Stourport, Stafford, West Bromwich, and Dudley declared that 'food queues are a bigger menace to public morale than several serious German air raids'.[85] By June HI reported that the problem was becoming more acute:

> Considerable evidence has been received to suggest that queues are becoming more frequent, and more widespread, and that they are being formed for a far greater number of commodities than before. There are queues for saccharine, cakes, sweets, biscuits, eggs, sausages, cooked meats, dog and cat food, and tobacco, and for rationed goods such as butter and meat. In one place they are said to start at seven in the morning . . .
>
> The main result of queues is that only those who have plenty of time on their hands derive any benefit from them, while war-workers, mothers with babies, and the old and infirm are unable to compete. A typical case is that of a bus-conductress who works 8 to 10 hours a

day and has her house-work to do, and asks how she is to feed her children.[86]

Grumbles about food reflected the broader reality of society in wartime as described by HI. In some respects the British were more united than they ever had been before. As Taylor put it in October 1941:

> Schisms and party distinctions have largely disappeared. In their place there is a new sense of purpose in life with a clear-cut objective in view—winning the war. Class distinctions among men have also greatly declined.
>
> Thanks to air-raids, rationing, war industrialisation, and civil defence, everyone has some sense of personal participation in the work of the country.[87]

Nothing demonstrated the extent of that solidarity more than the remarkably high level of public approval for Churchill as prime minister. HI quoted the verdict of a special postal censorship report for October 1940: 'The one desire of the British Public seems to be: Government of the people, for the people, by Mr Churchill.'[88]

In other respects, as Taylor knew better than anyone, the British were full of grumbles and complaints, partly against the authorities, and partly against one another. There were many signs of resentment against the privileges, real or imagined, of the wealthy, and in factories, mines, and shipyards the class divide was still deeply entrenched. But, as the HI reports indicate, class was only one source of discontent and not necessarily the most important. For all its solidarity, the home front was riddled with petty rivalries, disputes, and tensions between civilians and servicemen, shopkeepers and customers, evacuees and locals, adults and adolescents, the skilled and less skilled, non-Jews and Jews, natives and foreigners.

BEYOND THE BLITZ: THE WIDER WAR

On 17 September 1940 Hitler instructed that preparations for the invasion of Britain should be postponed indefinitely, after which they were never resumed. No one in Britain, however, knew this at the time. With the approach of wintry weather, and the dispersal of the invasion barges, it seemed likely that there was no immediate threat, but Churchill and the chiefs of staff could not rule out the possibility of a renewed attempt, possibly in the spring. Preparations against invasion continued, with occasional reminders to the public that it might still happen. Perhaps this was the reason why HI commissioned a number of reports on opinion in Eire, which it was thought might be the springboard for a German invasion of Britain. In December 1940 the postal censor reported:

> It is useless to expect rational or logical thought or sentiment in Eire. The historical, the religious, the mythical, and the frankly ridiculous continually obtrude themselves. Hopes that a Hitler victory will settle partition are expressed in the same town in which a Spitfire fund is organised; the wife of a German embassy official wins a fur coat in a raffle in aid of another Spitfire fund; and the Local Security Force refuse to patrol a certain beach in Donegal after 12 at night 'because they are afraid of the fairies'.[89]

Few people in Britain, HI concluded in February 1941, were thinking seriously about invasion:

> It is still treated rather as an exciting and thrilling kind of game in which we may soon be involved. People are impatient at the delay, they talk of fighting with any weapon which comes to hand (kettles of hot water, shot-guns etc.), and they boast that every German will be cut to pieces.[90]

The early months of 1941 appear to have been a time of optimism about the war in general. In January, HI noted, 'reports continue to stress that, associated with the New Year and helped on by Cabinet speeches, there is a widespread belief that victory will be achieved this year'.[91] 'The tide of battle is fast changing,' wrote a correspondent quoted by the postal censor, 'and this year will see old England on top of the lot.'[92]

Optimism was fuelled by the news of British victories in North Africa. In September 1940 an Italian army under Marshal Graziani had invaded Egypt. In December British and Commonwealth forces launched a successful counterattack, driving the Italians back into Libya. In early February the remnants of the Italian army in Libya surrendered. By May the Italian empire in East Africa—Eritrea, Abyssinia, and Italian Somaliland—had been overrun by British and imperial forces converging from Anglo-Egyptian Sudan and Kenya.

British euphoria was tempered by the knowledge that the main enemy, Germany, had yet to be dealt with. The arrival of General Rommel's Afrika Korps in Libya led to a swift reversal of fortunes and the retreat of the British back to the frontiers of Egypt. 'Some are saying', HI noted in April, 'that whenever we meet the Italians we advance, but whenever we meet the Germans we retreat.'[93] Meanwhile, Hitler's armies drove south-east into the Balkans, conquering Greece and expelling the expeditionary force Britain had sent to its aid.

On 10 May Hitler's deputy, Rudolf Hess, flew to Scotland on a mission to make peace. HI reported 'amazement at what was regarded as the most astonishing event of the war...Strangers spoke to one another with animation in trains and buses on the way to work. The romantic, unexpected and comic elements of the situation alike caught the public fancy.'[94] HI judged that on balance it was good for morale,[95] though it also prompted some speculation about the continued existence of a peace party in 'high society'.[96]

A significant blow was, however, about to fall. The German conquest of Crete in late May 1941 was a particularly humiliating defeat for the British, whose forces had been in occupation of the island for several months. In its report for the week of 4–11 June, HI reported that

> The most striking feature of public feeling during the week has been a decline in expressed confidence in the Government—both national and local. The trigger which fired off this feeling was the evacuation of Crete...
>
> Now there is anger as well as apprehension; the main line of criticism is that 'we were seven months in the island; what were we doing? Why were our airfields not properly defended?'[97]

In response, HI's in-house index of 'public feeling', which had indicated dips in morale in reaction to heavy air raids in March and April, plunged briefly to a rating of 3 out of 20 in late May and early June, the lowest point it ever reached with the exception of a similar rating in February 1942 after the fall of Singapore. Thereafter it climbed to 15 by the end of June as the bombing receded, British military intervention in Syria and Lebanon to forestall German plans to create a base there made encouraging progress, and Hitler invaded the Soviet Union.[98]

TAYLOR ON MORALE AND NATIONAL IDENTITY

As the Blitz wound down Taylor's thoughts turned towards an assessment of popular morale during the raids. In May 1941 the HI report incorporated an overview of the key factors on which morale was deemed to depend:

> It is now possible to postulate some general if tentative conclusions about the spirit of the public under the Air War. In the past months it has become increasingly noticeable that the morale of the civilian population depends more upon material factors, acutely involving their lives, than upon the ebb and flow of the events of war beyond these islands. Good or bad news produces, as it were, only ripples on the surface of morale, though these ripples may sometimes gather into an appreciable peak or trough.[99]

Among the material factors identified as important were 'a secure base' (the availability of a safe refuge); 'fatigue' (the opportunity to catch up on lost sleep); 'conditioning' (a gradual familiarization with the effects of bombing); 'personal blitz experiences' (near misses or the death of friends or relatives); and 'food' (in particular, hot cooked food). It was accepted, however, that a number of less material factors were also relevant. These included a 'belief in equality of sacrifice'; 'trust in leadership'; 'assurance of ultimate victory'; and 'belief in a better world after the war'.[100]

In October 1941 Taylor reflected on the conclusions of a year of HI weekly reports and elaborated on the theme of home morale. '*Good war morale* of the British public,' he opined, 'is conduct and behaviour indicating that they are prepared to go through with the war to final victory, whatever the cost to the individual or the group.'[101] The factors which determined morale, he reiterated, were 'material and mental', but 'since most British people are, on the whole, practical and unimaginative, the material factors appear to be more important than the mental ones'.[102] He did, however, note that this generalization was subject to one qualification:

> Certain of the mental factors are so strongly ingrained in the average British man and woman that they are not shaken by the ordinary processes of argument and reason. If, in some as yet unforeseen situation, they *were* shaken the results might well be more disastrous than the most dire material upset. So far, even the most calamitous events have been turned to a mental profit by the British public. Thus, the collapse of France was treated along these lines: 'At last, we're on our own and there's no-one else to let us down; now we've really got to get on with the job.' Again, the blitz was converted from a thing of terror to a symbol of pride and toughness. 'Our blitz was worse than yours— and look at us!'[103]

Such observations inevitably led Taylor into deeper assessments of the character—or as we now say, the national identity—of the British people. The public, he remarked, were 'pragmatic' and displayed a high degree of 'common-sense' and 'stability of temperament, with a slightly gloomy tinge'.[104] But these traits were accompanied by a series of caveats:

> A determination not to be 'put upon', or 'messed about' except by their own consent. In fact, a deep rooted belief in the liberty of the subject.
>
> A determination not to allow others to be 'put upon' similarly, *provided* the 'others' concerned are reasonably near the British Isles geographically, or in the British Empire. Thus, the butchering of a thousand Chinese creates far less indignation than the shooting of twenty Belgians.
>
> A sense of 'fair play' inside our own team. Outside 'the public school' classes, 'dirty tricks' on the enemy are, however, regarded as most desirable and very funny . . .

A tendency to smell out and voice grumbles loudly. The volume of grumbling varies inversely with the severity of the war situation.

A distrust of excessive enthusiasm, and a delight in 'knowing the worst'. With this is coupled a strange anxiety about not being told 'the worst'.

A tendency to doubt rather than believe any new information, unless gloomy, and particularly, a suspicion of 'newspaper talk'.[105]

Hand in hand with this, Taylor continued, was a 'righteous indignation when things go wrong' and a propensity 'not to blame the enemy, but to blame some section of those in authority'.[106] 'A fundamental tenet of the British public's creed,' he added, 'is that all in authority, above all "officials", are inefficient.'[107]

Delving further into the national psyche, Taylor judged that his compatriots were not only 'unimaginative'—a characteristic which found expression in the supposition that despite their perilous situation 'the possibility of defeat is neither imagined, nor imaginable'[108]—but also 'lazy':

The English public is basically lazy, with, in consequence, a very large reserve and capacity for effort on the rare occasions when it considers this vitally necessary. This does not apply to Scotland, Wales or Northern Ireland. This innate laziness leads secondarily to a high degree of tolerance, coupled with an apparent indifference to unpleasant environments.[109]

In fact, he went as far as to surmise that 'the public, as a whole, is happier, since the war, than it was in the peace'. This he put down to a combination of enhanced social solidarity, the smoothing out of gross inequalities of income, an improvement in general health as a result of higher wages, rationing, evacuation, and milk schemes for children, and the fact that 'the predicted picture of war on the home front was fortunately far more terrible than the real thing turned out to be'.[110] Taylor's overall conclusion was stark and defiant: 'There is, at present, no evidence to suggest that it is possible to defeat the people of Britain by any means other than extermination.'[111]

NOTE ON THE TEXT

A few explanatory words are required on the editing of the documents. The text published here is based predominantly on the set of weekly HI reports and appendices located in The National Archives at INF 1/292. But some gaps have been filled by another set of reports among the Mary Adams papers at the Mass Observation Archive. We have corrected mistakes in spelling and punctuation, omitted headings where they seemed superfluous, and made some other minor presentational changes in order to create a more consistent house style. As noted above, we have excluded the reference apparatus. We have incorporated the appendices attached to the reports in the sequence we think they would have originally appeared but have included an additional appendix on Merseyside that falls slightly outside our time frame as it features material on the aftermath of the Blitz. In all other aspects the text of the original documents has been reproduced in its original form.

To assist readers we have grouped the reports together into three periods and have provided brief introductory time lines for each period. We have also attached a list of abbreviations and a glossary identifying, as appropriate, individuals and terms referred to in the text.

NOTES

1. Richard Overy provides monthly casualty figures from September 1940 to May 1941 extracted from Home Office records. These give us a total of 41,480 killed. Meanwhile, O'Brien notes that 1,698 people were killed between 3 and 6 September. Deducting this figure from Overy's total, we reach a revised calculation of 39,782. See Richard Overy, *The Bombing War: Europe 1939–1945* (London: Allan Lane, 2013), p. 187, and Terence H. O'Brien, *Civil Defence* (London: HMSO, 1955), p. 677. It is unlikely that any of the statistics are entirely correct.

2. This figure is calculated using the breakdown of deaths by civil defence region in the following document: The National Archives, Kew (hereafter TNA), Home Office papers (hereafter HO), 191/11, 'Statement of civilian casualties in the United Kingdom (viz: Gt. Britain and Northern Ireland) resulting from enemy

action from the outbreak of war to 31 May 1945', Ministry of Home Security, 31 July 1945.

3. Richard M. Titmuss, *Problems of Social Policy* (London: HMSO, 1950), p. 13.

4. On pre-war preparations see Ian McLaine, *Ministry of Morale: Home Front Morale and the Ministry of Information in World War II* (London: George Allen and Unwin, 1979), pp. 12–33.

5. Ibid., p. 22. Beresford was the editor of the diaries of Parson Woodforde: *The Diary of a Country Parson: The Reverend James Woodforde 1758–1802* (London: Oxford University Press, 5 volumes, 1924–31). It was a minor literary classic of the interwar years.

6. Quoted in McLaine, *Ministry of Morale*, pp. 22–3.

7. Ibid., p. 23.

8. Ibid., p. 24.

9. TNA, Ministry of Information papers (hereafter INF), 1/296, Mr Rhodes to Mr Balfour, 11 June 1940.

10. McLaine, *Ministry of Morale*, p. 46.

11. Ibid., pp. 41–2, 49. A list of headquarters staff circulated by the ministry on 9 October shows that Beresford was still in post as 'Director' at that date: see *The Times*, 10 October 1939, p. 4. When Beresford was killed in the Blitz in October 1940 the *New York Times* reported that he had resigned as 'Director of Intelligence' at the MOI 'about a year ago'. See *New York Times*, 22 October 1940, p. 4. *The Times*'s obituary made no mention of his work for the MOI: see *The Times*, 22 October 1940, p. 7.

12. McLaine, *Ministry of Morale*, p. 46. The Oxford historian, A. J. P. Taylor, became a member of a MOI Local Information Committee and in October 1940 found himself at the centre of controversy after he made a speech in which he was reported to have claimed that a British withdrawal from Egypt would not be a major disaster. Although it was said that he had made it clear he was speaking in a private capacity, his critics argued that he had no right to make such an 'irresponsible and ridiculous' statement whilst holding this 'public position'. See *The Times*, 25 October 1940, p. 9.

13. TNA INF 1/290, 'The work of Home Intelligence Division 1939–44', p. 1. This short history of HI was unsigned and undated but almost certainly the work of Stephen Taylor, the director of HI from 1941 to 1945.

14. McLaine, *Ministry of Morale*, p. 50; James Hinton, *The Mass Observers: A History, 1937–1949* (Oxford: Oxford University Press, 2013), p. 144.

15. Sally Adams, 'Adams [née Campin], Mary Grace Agnes (1898–1984)', *Oxford Dictionary of National Biography* (online edition, 2004).

16. TNA INF 1/472, 'Home Intelligence and the censorship', no author, 23 January 1940.

17. TNA INF 1/101, 'Home Intelligence: Organisation and staffing', Mary Adams to Mr Bamford, 17 July 1940.

18. Nicolas Bentley, *A Version of the Truth* (London: Andrew Deutsch, 1960), pp. 173–80, 197.

19. *The Times*, 20 September 1995, p. 18.

20. Mass Observation Archive, The Keep, Brighton (hereafter MOA), Mary Adams papers, SxMOA4/1/2/1, Mary Adams to Mr Waterfield, 9 March 1940.

21. Lord Taylor of Harlow, *A Natural History of Everyday Life: A Biographical Guide for Would-Be Doctors of Society* (London: British Medical Journal/Memoir Club, 1988), p. 261; Hinton, *The Mass Observers*, p. 180.

22. TNA INF 1/290 'The work of Home Intelligence Division', p. 2.

23. Philip M. Taylor, *British Propaganda in the Twentieth Century: Selling Democracy* (Edinburgh: Edinburgh University Press, 1999), p. 160. The Press and Censorship Bureau was also restored to MOI control in April 1940.

24. TNA, Ministry of Defence papers (DEFE), 1/333, 'History of the Postal and Telegraph Censorship Department 1938–1946', vol. 1, Home Office, 1952, pp. 50–1, 272.

25. TNA INF 1/472, 'Assessment of Home Intelligence sources', no author, undated. A draft of this note is to be found in MOA, Mary Adams papers, SxMOA4/1/2/2.

26. TNA INF 1/292, weekly report by HI, [no. 1], 30 September–9 October 1940. See note above the source list on the final page. (9 October, rather than 7 October, is given in the heading of the main report. This appears to be an error.)

27. TNA INF 1/47, 'Home Intelligence machinery', memorandum by Home Intelligence, 16 July 1940; TNA INF 1/290, 'The work of Home Intelligence Division', p. 4; MOA, Mary Adams papers, SxMOA4/1/1, 'Weekly report by Home Intelligence: Special report on methods of compilation', memorandum by HI, undated.

28. For Harrisson's background and his role in the founding of MO, see Hinton, *The Mass Observers*, and Judith M. Heimann, *The Most Offending Soul Alive: Tom Harrisson and His Remarkable Life* (Honolulu: University of Hawaii Press, 1999).

29. Hinton, *The Mass Observers*, pp. 143–4, 152–9.

30. McLaine, *Ministry of Morale*, p. 52.

31. Ibid., p. 50; Mark Roodhouse, '"Fish–and–Chip Intelligence": Henry Durant and the British Institute of Public Opinion, 1936–63', *Twentieth Century British History*, vol. 24, no. 2 (2013), p. 244.

32. Hinton, *The Mass Observers*, pp. 179–80; McLaine, *Ministry of Morale*, p. 53.

33. TNA INF 1/290, 'The work of Home Intelligence Division', p. 3.

34. MOA, Mary Adams papers, SxMOA4/1/2/2, Mary Adams to Mrs W. Holmes, 2 November 1940. Noel Streatfeild was an air-raid warden but the context in which Holmes was referring to her is not clear from Adams's note.

35. TNA HO 262/1, HI to all RIOs, 6 January 1941. HI also made extensive enquiries into anti-Semitism. See, for example, TNA HO 262/9. TNA HO 262/13, on Jehovah's Witnesses, is closed until 2021.

36. Hinton, *The Mass Observers*, pp. 180–1, 184, 190, 212–13.

37. 'Results of the War-Time Social Survey', *The Lancet*, 7 September 1940, p. 305.

38. MO online, MO file report no. 325, 'Report on the "Cooper's Snoopers" press campaign', 5 August 1940, pp. 1–3, 5.

39. *House of Commons Debates*, vol. 763, 1 August 1940, col. 1555.

40. TNA INF 1/290, 'The work of Home Intelligence Division', p. 2.

41. Taylor, *A Natural History of Everyday Life*, p. 216.

42. Ibid., p. 260.

43. Quoted in Hinton, *The Mass Observers*, p. 181.

44. Taylor, *A Natural History of Everyday Life*, p. 261.

45. Ibid., pp. 259–60.

46. TNA INF 1/290, 'The work of Home Intelligence Division', p. 3.

47. TNA INF 1/273, Mr Parker to DG, 8 September 1941; TNA INF 1/290, 'The work of Home Intelligence Division', p. 2; TNA INF 1/273, 'Suggested press handout: Wartime Social Survey', by Stephen Taylor, 4 September 1941.

48. Hinton, *The Mass Observers*, pp. 188–90.

49. Ibid., p. 190.

50. On the outbreak of war a Ministry of Home Security was carved out of the Home Office with specific responsibility for civil defence. This, however, maintained close relations with its parent ministry, shared the same ministerial head, and had some overlapping staff and functions. We use the term Home Office here as shorthand for both ministries.

51. Hinton, *The Mass Observers*, pp. 200–1.

52. Ibid., p. 201.

53. TNA INF 1/290, 'The work of Home Intelligence Division', p. 4; Hinton, *The Mass Observers*, p. 201.

54. MOA, Mary Adams papers, SxMOA4/2/4/1, Mary Adams to 'Julian', 3 October 1940. Julian Huxley was the head of an advisory committee on HI which Adams had set up in April 1940 and there is little doubt that the 'Julian' in question was Huxley. Adams had already planned to introduce a weekly report as a supplement to the daily report.

55. MOA, Mary Adams papers, SxMOA4/1/2/2, Mary Adams to Mr Silvey, 28 February 1941.

56. MOA, Mary Adams papers, SxMOA4/1/2/2, Mary Adams to 'Harold', 15 March 1941. It is unlikely that her correspondent can have been anyone else but Harold Nicolson, who was parliamentary secretary at the MOI.

57. MOA, Mary Adams papers, SxMOA4/2/4/1, Mary Adams to 'Julian', 15 March 1941.

58. MOA, Mary Adams papers, SxMOA4/2/4/1, Mary Adams to Dr Glover, 15 March 1941.

59. TNA, INF 1/101, 'Memorandum on the present position of Home Intelligence with recommendations for its reorganisation', no author, 11 March 1941. A draft of this memorandum is to be found in MOA, Mary Adams papers, SxMOA4/1/1.

60. MOA, Mary Adams papers, SxMOA4/1/1, 'HI notes on the present position for the DG', 7 February 1941.

61. Taylor, *A Natural History of Everyday Life*, p. 261; Hinton, *The Mass Observers*, p. 212; *The Times*, 18 March 1941, p. 4.

62. TNA, HO 199/16, 'Scheme for Intelligence Branch, Home Security', by R. H. Parker, 27 July 1940.

63. Edgar Jones, Robin Woolven, Bill Durodié, and Simon Wessely, 'Civilian Morale during the Second World War: Responses to Air Raids Re-examined', *Social History of Medicine*, vol. 17, no. 3 (2004), p. 468.

64. TNA HO 199/16, note by R. H. Parker, 29 June 1940.

65. MOA, Mary Adams papers, SxMOA4/4/7/1, Tom Harrisson to Mary Adams, 15 March 1941.

66. Taylor, *A Natural History of Everyday Life*, p. 261; Hinton, *The Mass Observers*, p. 212. Adams returned to television after the war and was responsible for putting *Muffin the Mule* and *Andy Pandy*, as well as a young zoologist, David Attenborough, on the screen.

67. TNA INF 1/292, 'Report on conditions in Plymouth following the severe raids', appendix to weekly report by Home Intelligence, no. 32, 7–14 May 1941, p. 1.

68. Hinton, *The Mass Observers*, pp. 212–13, 215.

69. TNA, INF 1/291, 'Graph showing fluctuations in public feeling during the past three years and ten months', HI, 29 December 1944. Starting in May 1940, and continuing until VE Day, MO compiled a parallel index of morale based, according to circumstances, on daily, twice-weekly, or weekly samples of opinion, and a scale ranging from –100 to +100. Unlike the HI figures, MO's were based on a question put by investigators to passers-by in London: 'What do you think of the news today?'. See MO online, 'War morale chart I', MO file report no. 2346,

6 February 1946 (but listed as file report 2332, January 1946, in online MO catalogue).

70. TNA, INF 1/291, 'Graph showing fluctuations in public feeling during the past three years and ten months', HI, 29 December 1944.

71. TNA INF 1/292, daily report on morale, Monday, 9 September 1940.

72. Basil Collier, *The Defence of the United Kingdom* (London: HMSO, 1957), p. 506.

73. TNA INF 1/292, 'Clydebank raid—public behaviour', appendix to weekly report by HI, no. 25, 19–26 March 1941, p. 1.

74. TNA INF 1/292, 'The Plymouth raids, April 1941', appendix to weekly report by HI, no. 31, 30 April–7 May 1941, p. 2.

75. TNA INF 1/292, 'Effects of enemy air raids upon Hull, on the nights of Thursday 13 March, Friday 14 March, and Tuesday 18 March, 1941. Report by Hull and East Riding Information Committee', appendix to weekly report by HI, no. 27, 2 April–9 April 1941, pp. 1–2.

76. TNA INF 1/292, weekly report by HI, no. 10, 4–11 December 1940, p. 1.

77. TNA INF 1/292, weekly report by HI, no. 9, 25 November–4 December 1940, pp. 5–6.

78. TNA INF 1/292, weekly report by HI, no. 12, 18–24 December 1940, p. 1.

79. TNA INF 1/292, weekly report by HI, no. 25, 19–26 March 1941, p. 3.

80. TNA INF 1/292, weekly report by HI, no. 15, 8–15 January 1941, p. 2.

81. Overy, *The Bombing War*, p. 172.

82. TNA INF 1/292, weekly report by HI, no. 25, 19–26 March 1941, p. 5.

83. TNA INF 1/292, weekly report by HI, no. 28, 9–16 April 1941, p. 3.

84. TNA INF 1/292, weekly report by HI, no. 23, 5–12 March 1941, p. 4.

85. TNA INF 1/292, weekly report by HI, no. 20, 12–19 February 1941, p. 4.

86. TNA INF 1/292, weekly report by HI, no. 36, 4-11 June 1941, p. 5.

87. TNA INF 1/292, 'Home morale and public opinion: A review of some conclusions arising out of a year of Home Intelligence weekly reports', by Stephen Taylor, 1 October 1941, p. 7, appendix to weekly report by HI, no. 53, 29 September–6 October 1941, p. 7.

88. TNA INF 1/292, weekly report by HI, no. 6, 4–11 November 1940, p. 5.

89. TNA INF 1/292, weekly report by HI, no. 12, 18–24 December 1940, p. 2.

90. TNA INF 1/292, weekly report by HI, no. 20, 12–19 February 1941, p. 1.

91. TNA INF 1/292, weekly report by HI, no. 15, 8–15 January 1941, p. 1.

92. TNA INF 1/292, weekly report by HI, no. 17, 22–29 January 1941, p. 1.

93. TNA INF 1/292, weekly report by HI, no. 27, 2–9 April 1941, p. 1.

94. TNA INF 1/292, weekly report by HI, no. 32, 7–14 May 1941, p. 3.

95. TNA INF 1/292, weekly report by HI, no. 33, 14–21 May 1941, p. 2.

96. TNA INF 1/292, weekly report by HI, no. 34, 21–28 May 1941, p. 2.

97. TNA INF 1/292, weekly report by HI, no. 36, 4–11 June 1941, p. 1.

98. TNA, INF 1/291, 'Graph showing fluctuations in public feeling during the past three years and ten months', HI, 29 December 1944.

99. TNA INF 1/292, weekly report by HI, no. 32, 7–14 May 1941, p. 1.

100. Ibid., pp. 1–2.

101. TNA INF 1/292, 'Home morale and public opinion: A review of some conclusions arising out of a year of Home Intelligence weekly reports', by Stephen Taylor, 1 October 1941, p. 1, appendix to weekly report by HI, no. 53, 29 September–6 October 1941, p. 1.

102. Ibid.

103. Ibid.

104. Ibid., p. 6.

105. Ibid.

106. Ibid.

107. Ibid., p. 7.

108. Ibid.

109. Ibid.

110. Ibid.

111. Ibid., p. 8.

UNIVERSITY OF LONDON: SENATE HOUSE
TOWER FLOODLIT

1. The Senate House, University of London, where the Home Intelligence unit was based

2 Mary Adams, director of Home Intelligence, 1939–41

3. Tom Harrisson, co-founder of the social research organization Mass Observation

4. Stephen Taylor, who took over as director of Home Intelligence in 1941

I

SEPTEMBER TO DECEMBER 1940

---

7 SEPTEMBER Air raids on London by 570 German bombers kill 430 people. Subsequently the city is bombed every night until 3–4 November, with intermittent heavy raids continuing until May 1941.

13 SEPTEMBER Italian forces invade Egypt.

15 SEPTEMBER The Battle of Britain reaches a climax in a daylight air battle over London in which the Luftwaffe sustains heavy losses. Two days later Hitler postpones invasion plans indefinitely.

18 SEPTEMBER *SS City of Benares* sunk by a German U-boat en route to Canada. Among the dead are seventy-seven child evacuees.

23 SEPTEMBER British and Free French forces launch ill-fated operation to secure the port of Dakar in French West Africa.

3 OCTOBER Herbert Morrison is appointed Home Secretary. Ernest Bevin, the Minister of Labour, is promoted to the War Cabinet.

9 OCTOBER Winston Churchill succeeds Neville Chamberlain as leader of the Conservative Party.

13 OCTOBER Princess Elizabeth, aged fourteen, broadcasts to evacuee children.

28 OCTOBER Italian forces invade Greece.

5 NOVEMBER Franklin D. Roosevelt is re-elected President of the United States.

11–12 NOVEMBER The Fleet Air Arm inflicts heavy damage on Italian warships at the Battle of Taranto.

14 NOVEMBER Coventry suffers heavy raid. Notable attacks follow on Southampton (17, 23, 30 November and 1 December), Birmingham (19, 20, 22 November and 3, 4, 11 December), Bristol (24 November and 2, 6 December), Plymouth (27 November), Liverpool-Birkenhead (28 November and 20, 21 December), Portsmouth (5 December), Sheffield (12, 15 December), Manchester (22, 23 December).

9 DECEMBER General Sir Archibald Wavell, commander-in-chief of British and Commonwealth forces in the Middle East, launches a counter-offensive against the Italians in the Western Desert.

25 DECEMBER In his Christmas Day broadcast King George VI says that 'we are all in the front line and the danger together'.

29 DECEMBER In the United States President Roosevelt foreshadows his proposal for Lend-Lease in a 'fireside chat' to the American people; and in a further major raid on the capital eight Wren churches are burnt out in the 'Second Great Fire of London'.

31 DECEMBER Herbert Morrison announces that the government has approved in principle the compulsory recruitment of males for civil defence duties.

MONDAY 9 SEPTEMBER 1940

In the areas which have been most heavily raided there has been little sign of panic and none of defeatism, but rather of bitterness and increased determination to 'see it through'. There is widespread and deeply felt apprehension, which is apparent mostly in the London dock area, of a continuation of raids, and much anxiety about the chaos in domestic affairs which has resulted from the activities of the last few nights.

As far as the East End is concerned, this is beginning to show itself in an aimless evacuation to what are believed to be safer places, e.g. the St James's Park shelters and Paddington Station. It appears that this exodus is caused by greater fear than the actual circumstances justify, and it might be a good thing if loudspeaker vans, giving encouragement and instructions, could circulate in the streets. There is at present very little official reassurance being given to the public, and it is to some extent this lack of guidance which is causing them to leave their homes. There seems evidence that unless some immediate steps of this sort are taken to check this movement, it is likely to grow.

Men working in factories in the East End are encouraging their wives and families in this haphazard escape, but express their own willingness to stay and face further raids if they can be sure that their relations are in comparative safety.

Owing to the behaviour of the Jews, particularly in the East End where they are said to show too great a keenness to save their own skins and too little consideration for other people, there are signs of anti-Semitic trouble. It is believed locally that this situation may at any moment become extremely serious. This is put forward as an additional reason for a planned dispersal of East End families to be carried out with all speed.

Unsatisfactory reports about shelter conditions continue to be received. Those in the London area and in Birmingham show a state of affairs which from the point of view of health alone is highly undesirable. The practice of carrying bedding, prams, etc. into shelters causes much indignation among people who are thus denied accommodation.

Although it seems to be fairly well understood that for security reasons it is not possible to give many details about the activities of the RAF and AA units, there is a good deal of comment on what are believed in some places to be inadequate precautions, though the gallantry of both the RAF and the AA crews continues to receive great praise.

There is continued criticism of the BBC's method of announcing casualties and raid details. Special exception was taken to Charles Gardner's broadcast on Saturday, and it is suggested that what is wanted by the public in its present frame of mind is the kind of encouragement which can only be given by a real working-class man who has himself been through the worst of the recent raids.

POINTS FROM REGIONS

NORTHERN (Newcastle) Reports from many centres indicate that enemy news bulletins are receiving progressively less attention. Exaggerated rumours of damage due to raids are still widespread. There is much interest in the speed of our aircraft production, and further facts are eagerly awaited.

NORTH MIDLAND (Nottingham) The impression of Hitler's speech is that it was 'that of a frustrated criminal'. There is a complaint from Chesterfield that details of the damage to Ramsgate should not have been delayed until the Premier's speech. In Grimsby it is suggested that daily reports of damage and casualties would be less alarming than monthly reports. It is felt in Rutland that householders who have had evacuees since war broke out are now tired of them, and would welcome a shuffle round to other householders. Complaints have been received that the fixed price for plum jam is excessive.

SOUTH-WESTERN (Bristol) Rumours of invasion are rife in the Region today following the ringing of church bells and the calling out of the Home Guard. The raid on London has been appreciated as serious, and it is realised that though casualties were high, they were not more than was to be expected from a severe attack. It is reported from Plymouth that people consider the BBC tends to gloss over damage by enemy aircraft.

MIDLAND (Birmingham) There are reports from Birmingham, Wolverhampton and Black Country towns that householders are going to public shelters and taking their bedding with them. It is 'getting round' that many middle-class people leave Birmingham at night by road and sleep in country districts, and many more are doing this at weekends; this is causing some annoyance among the working class.

NORTHERN IRELAND (Belfast) Some surprise is felt at the extensive casualties and damage in London due to raids, and although bearing in mind the devastation wrought by the RAF in Germany, it is being asked whether the British defences are as effective as has been supposed. It is felt that an invasion of south-east England may soon be attempted. There are reports of airmen talking freely about Belfast defences. Householders in provincial areas with whom evacuated children are billeted complain that they have to buy clothes for them, and that the parents do not realise their responsibilities.

LONDON

Strongest feeling one of shock amongst all classes and in all districts as people have lulled themselves into a state of false security saying: 'London is the safest place', and 'they'll never get through the London defences'. No signs of defeatism except among small section of elderly women in 'front line' such as East Ham who cannot stand constant bombing. Districts sustaining only one or two shocks soon rally, but in dockside areas the population is showing visible signs of nerve cracking from constant ordeals. Old women and mothers are undermining morale of young women and men by their extreme nervousness and lack of resilience. Men state they cannot sleep because they must keep up the morale of their families and express strong desire to get families away from danger areas. Families clinging together, however, and any suggestions of sending children away without mothers and elderly relations considered without enthusiasm. People beginning to trek away from Stepney and other dockside areas in families and small groups. Many encountered in City today with suitcases or belongings. Some make for Paddington without any idea of their destination. All dockland people afraid large fires will attract German raiders each night and queue up long before dusk to get places in large underground shelters. Many expressions of bitterness at apparent impossibility of stopping German raiders doing what they like and opinion that anti-aircraft gunfire is astonishingly small. This latter point is bewildering and frightening people more than anything else. Lack of sleep already showing signs of undermining morale and working capacity of population. Young black-coated workers in City depressed about news from Africa and express the hope that we can take the offensive there. There is urgent need in Rest Centres for people rendered homeless for toys, etc. for the children, and workers are needed to organise games.

TUESDAY 10 SEPTEMBER 1940

Morale remains unchanged today. Voluntary and unplanned evacuation of East End families continues, and although it is largely confined to women and children, some men are also going. Families in the Deptford area are making for the hopfields in Kent, taking with them such of their belongings as they can carry, while those further west are making for the main line stations, though without any other apparent object than 'to get away from it all'. There is, however, little evidence that these efforts to escape are due to defeatist feelings, but are simply because the people are thoroughly frightened.

Now that they are beginning to feel, and are being referred to, as 'soldiers in the front line', everything should be done to encourage this opinion of themselves. It would undoubtedly help if the public were made to feel that their friends and relations had died for their country, in the same sense as if they were soldiers, sailors or airmen. It might be a small but extremely telling point if, for instance, the dead were buried with Union Jacks on their coffins, or if the Services were represented at their funerals. Attentions of this kind would undoubtedly mean much at the moment.

Among other suggestions that have been made for the alleviation of the difficulties of those in the bombed areas is that field service postcards for civilians should be issued in the areas which have suffered the worst damage, so that the poor can inform their distant relatives of their safety and thus avoid overloading the telegram and telephone services.

The need for mobile canteens in bombed areas is urgent. Certain voluntary societies are already doing their best to provide these facilities, but are quite unable to cope with the immense demands which are made upon them.

The foregoing conclusions naturally reflect the conditions in the London area more than elsewhere, and today's reports from Regions show that their spirits also are steady and confident. Much sympathy is felt with London's sufferings, but confidence is everywhere expressed in the ability of the metropolitan population to stand up to what they are going through.

POINTS FROM REGIONS

NORTH-EASTERN (Leeds) Morale and confidence are unchanged. Keen interest is centred on events in London. Many people feel there should be a curfew in large towns, and a curfew on motoring also has been suggested. There has been a considerable increase in absenteeism at the pits in Rother Valley, and there is much local feeling about the need for better shelters for miners' families, which may explain the increased number of absentees. A report from Ecclesfield states that there is much feeling that communal brick shelters, which are to replace Anderson shelters, do not afford the same protection as steel.

EASTERN (Cambridge) Raids on London are the chief topic of conversation. There is a growing feeling that severe reprisals should be taken on Berlin, although the intensity of this feeling diminishes in proportion to the distance from London.

SOUTHERN (Reading) The view is commonly expressed that the only way to stop the Germans is to bomb Berlin even more extensively than they bomb London. Rumours due to Saturday night's invasion alarm have decreased. The sound of the tocsin brought people out into the streets. People are disconcerted by the late arrival of daily papers, and the revival of the mid-morning BBC news is suggested to meet this need.

WALES (Cardiff) The comparative quietness of the last three days in this Region has left everyone refreshed. The progress of attacks on the Thames Estuary has been watched with anxiety. The continued success of our fighters and the nightly activity of our bombers have raised hopes very high.

South Wales coalpits are now mostly working short-time, and there is disappointment that the effort to secure distribution to home markets to fill gaps caused by the loss of continental trade has so far been unsuccessful. Delays in publication, and the nebulous character of our reports on raids on this country is encouraging increasing numbers to tune in to German stations.

NORTH-WESTERN (Manchester) A peaceful night has strengthened the spirit of those who grumbled at the supposed lack of defences. There is a general feeling that if London can stick it, so can Manchester. There is a query from Salford as to why national leaders do not speak to the public at the present time. There is depression in St Helens through the closing down of a colliery employing more than 1,000 hands.

SOUTH-EASTERN (Tunbridge Wells) Lorry drivers are coming into the Region with harrowing tales of damage and panic in London. Morale is extremely high in the Region, and everyone is full of praise for the RAF. People are still going out into the streets to witness thrilling dog-fights overhead. Residents of Shoreham Beach Bungalow Town were recently ordered to leave by military authorities, and it seems that distress has been caused as many of the bungalows were built as an investment by elderly people, and it is reported that no provision has been made to look after them.

LONDON

Exodus from East End growing rapidly. Taxi drivers report taking party after party to Euston and Paddington with belongings. Hundreds of people leaving Deptford for Kent. Increased tension everywhere and when siren goes people run madly for shelter with white faces. Contact spending night in West Ham reports loyalty and confidence in ultimate issue unquenched but nerves worn down to fine point. Conditions of living now almost impossible and great feeling in dockside areas of living on island surrounded by fire and destruction. Urgent necessity of removing women and children and old and crippled people today is reported from all sources – official and unofficial. Extreme nervousness of people rendered homeless at being herded together in local schools with inadequate shelters. West Ham school filled to bursting point from Saturday night onwards blown up by HE bomb with many casualties. This has caused great shock in district. People angry at inadequacy of compensation of wrecked and burnt-out houses; grumbling and dissatisfaction openly voiced, states Deptford contact. Civil Defence services receiving much praise but growing exceedingly tired in heavily bombed areas. Class feeling growing because of worse destruction in working-class areas; anti-Semitism growing in districts where large proportion of Jews reside owing to their taking places in public shelters early in the day. People in target areas living in shelters; women emerging for short time to do shopping and bolting back again. Many reported going into Tubes to shelter in spite of instructions to contrary. Dismay and wonder at apparent inadequacy of London defences reported from most districts especially in East End, and intense disgust at hospital bombing. Districts less regularly bombed, such as Lewisham and Chelsea, report great neighbourly feeling. Bermondsey Citizens' Advice Bureau inundated with mothers and young children, hysterical and asking to be removed from district. Reports from Woolwich and Eltham that people are saying our searchlights are being used to guide German planes at night – suspicion of Fifth Column activity. Gravesend seriously disturbed that bombs are dropped without warning as planes pass over; London sirens go and then the sirens at Gravesend; when the 'All Clear' goes they know that they will get more bombs dropped on the planes' return journey. People feel that Gravesend is not given adequate consideration by the authorities.

WEDNESDAY 11 SEPTEMBER 1940

Reports now received make it possible to assess critically the effects of continued bombing in the East End. Morale is rather more strained than the newspapers suggest, whereas the damage to property seems to be less than is reported by them. The pictures of devastation and accounts of destruction weaken the resolve of people to stay put.

Organised evacuation is necessarily a slow business but is proceeding uninterruptedly. Voluntary evacuation also continues fairly steadily, though there is a tendency for those who work in badly-affected districts to evacuate themselves during the night and to return in the daytime.

Factors which contribute to the strain on morale are, of course, as much psychological as material. Listening tension (e.g. anticipation of planes and bombs) is one to which little official notice has been paid. Few people are using ear pads or understand that the diminution of noise can do much to lessen their state of anxiety. Nor does there seem to have been enough encouragement for people to try and sleep as and when they can. The fear, mostly among men, that they may lose their jobs, as has already happened in many cases in the Silvertown district, is an added anxiety, and if it were possible for some reassurance to be given that speedy efforts will be made to find other work for them this would undoubtedly have a good effect.

The need for mobile canteens is still urgent, as is the necessity for providing a hot meal every day for families evacuated from their homes.

An increase is reported in the number of people listening to Haw-Haw, and rumours, mostly exaggerated accounts of raid damage and casualties, have also increased considerably.

A certain amount of anti-Semitism in the East End still persists, but this is not so much on account of a marked difference in conduct between Jews and Cockneys, but because the latter, seeking a scapegoat as an outlet for emotional disturbances, pick on the traditional and nearest one. Though many Jewish people regularly congregate and sleep in the public shelters, so also do many of the Gentiles, nor is there any evidence to show that one or other predominates among those who have evacuated themselves voluntarily through fear or hysteria.

Reports from the Regions show that their attention is directed mainly towards London's sufferings and consequently their own troubles are to some extent diminished. Shelter problems are common to many districts as are also the various types and causes of anxiety associated with raids. There is, however, no sign of morale weakening, or that powers of resistance and determination are deteriorating.

POINTS FROM REGIONS

NORTHERN (Newcastle) Inability to obtain the necessary material for the completion of shelters and their protection against damp is causing public dissatisfaction; the habit of sleeping in shelters is growing and anxiety is expressed by local authorities with regard to the danger of epidemics with the approach of bad weather. The lighting of road blocks is reported in many cases to be unsatisfactory. It is suggested that when enemy planes are overhead people are opening their doors to go to shelter, and many shafts of light are shown at critical moments.

NORTH MIDLAND (Nottingham) A report from Nottingham rural areas shows no weakening of morale, and defeatism which was apparent earlier in the war is disappearing. It is suggested that lights on railways near centres of population should be masked with cowls. Complaints are general that public shelters are being abused by a few people. There is loss of interest in salvage in some villages because dumps have not been collected. The schemes of insurance against property damage have caused widespread interest.

SOUTH-WESTERN (Bristol) The new siren recommendations are widely approved. There is a demand for the continued bombing of Berlin. Evacuees from London are spreading exaggerated stories of London raids. People in Exeter were much impressed by the keenness of the Home Guard to get to grips with the reported invaders during the weekend. There is a current rumour in Bristol that sirens will not sound during the day, and it is reported that women are keeping their children away from school on this account.

MIDLAND (Birmingham) The apparent absence of fighter planes against night raiders is still worrying many people. Local air raids are causing a crop of rumours as to the places and amount of damage caused.

SCOTLAND (Edinburgh) People are watching what is happening in London and forgetting their own grievances. Considerable talk among the Home Guard in the West about the call-out over the weekend is reported, and some say they will refuse to 'turn out on a fool's errand again'. People are quite uncertain as to what they are supposed to do when they hear church bells. The opinion is held in Montrose that the military authorities should release a suitable hall for entertaining the troops.

NORTHERN IRELAND (Belfast) Much indignation is felt at the indiscriminate bombing of London, and a consequent satisfaction at the success of

RAF raids on Germany, and keen interest in news of the new incendiary weapon. The demand continues for more war industries to absorb the 70,000 unemployed. Farmers continue to protest against reductions in pork and beef prices, and the low prices generally allowed for agricultural produce.

THURSDAY 12 SEPTEMBER 1940

In London particularly morale is high: people are much more cheerful today.

The dominating topic of conversation today is the anti-aircraft barrage of last night. This greatly stimulated morale: in public shelters people cheered and conversation shows that the noise brought a shock of positive pleasure. It made people feel that 'all the time we had a wonderful trick up our sleeves ready to play when the moment came'.

The increased noise kept people awake but tiredness is offset by the stimulus which has been created.

The Prime Minister's speech was well received but not so enthusiastically as usual. The speech was admired for its plain speaking, but there is evidence that many people, having convinced themselves that invasion is 'off', disliked being reminded of it again. Some people remarked that he sounded 'tired'. In Wales people were surprised that Wales was omitted as a possible point of invasion. The speech nowhere created alarm.

There is still a good deal of unplanned evacuation from London, and there is evidence that small batches of refugees arriving without money at provincial stations are creating anxiety and some alarm. There are exaggerated stories of the damage to London circulating in the provinces. These reports are partly due to the stories told by these refugees, but there is also evidence that Haw-Haw rumours have greatly increased.

A reliable observer just returned to London from the North reports that press and radio have given an account of London damage which has an exaggerated effect. Many people appear to think that London is 'in flames'. There is great sympathy for London and on the whole a belief that 'London will see it through'.

Attached are two reports from London for September 11th & 12th.

POINTS FROM REGIONS

NORTH-EASTERN (Leeds) There is intense sympathy with London and a general confidence that the capital will stand up to the present strain. The way in which the King and Queen freely visited the bombed areas is the subject of much favourable comment. Many people still believe that the civilian population in Germany should be bombed. The new warning system for factories is welcomed amongst men, and women are pleased that the sirens are still to be sounded.

EASTERN (Cambridge) News of evacuation plans for Colchester and Ipswich has spread to towns outside the new evacuation area, and there is some speculation as to whether Norwich and other towns are to be included. A rumour gained currency along the Essex and Herts border to the effect that parachutists had descended; this was apparently due to puffs of smoke being seen from AA guns.

WALES (Cardiff) Morale is still very good. Interest still centres on action in the Thames Estuary and London and news is awaited with anxiety. Widespread sympathy is expressed for those in congested areas. The continued bombing of Berlin is a source of general satisfaction. Opinion is widespread that more details of provincial bombing should be released. The procedure for obtaining relief in respect of raid damage is becoming more generally known but there are complaints that official assessment of damage is based on figures below the present cost of replacement. Stirrup pumps are now in great demand following 'Self-help' propaganda, but they are extremely difficult to obtain. Little interest is evinced by news from Italy and Africa due to events at home.

NORTH-WESTERN (Manchester) Shortage of shelters is a predominant topic at the moment, and many people realise that they should have planned their protection sooner. Authorities everywhere are pushing on with schemes for erection of shelters, and the sight of bricks and mortar is having a good effect. There was a feeling of anger when it was learned that Buckingham Palace had been bombed.

SOUTH-EASTERN (Tunbridge Wells) In view of the fact that the heavy raids on London indicate that the war is entering a new stage, some people believe that it will be over soon with an Allied victory. There is a complaint from Brighton of lack of synchronisation in sounding 'Raiders Passed'. There is still some grumbling over the fact that RAF bombers sometimes return from Germany without unloading their bombs.

LONDON

Morale high in most districts in spite of damage and casualties. Pessimism reported among business men owing to discovery that weather conditions suit German bombers. People worried about possible further breakdown of public utility services and its effect on a population used to 'all modern conveniences'. Traffic difficulties in city causing great irritation and nervous exhaustion among workers travelling in overcrowded trains. City contacts suggest working hours might be staggered or clerks allowed to work half week as little business is transacted. Crowds of sightseers might also be discouraged. Lewisham reports overcrowding of Rest Centres and people growing extremely tired from lack of sleep; workers complaining they cannot concentrate in day time. Latter condition also reported by brain workers who complain particularly of noise and talk in large shelters, especially in blocks of luxury flats, by people who have little work to do by day. Wish expressed that noise and talk in shelters could be branded as 'Fifth Column' activities. Reports from East End show people to be evacuating themselves from heavily bombed areas. In Isle of Dogs those who cannot evacuate themselves reported to be growing angry with authorities, stating they have been forgotten and are on an island which may at any moment be cut off and ringed with fire. Many shelters in district too badly damaged for use; gas and electricity are cut off; there is little water – all this has led to talk today of marching to West End to commandeer hotels and clubs. This type of talk reported also from Stepney, but in lesser degree. Bermondsey reports women and children, old people and invalids impatient to escape to less vulnerable area. Class bitterness expressed there and in Fulham by some individuals. Bermondsey Rest Centres overcrowded, with many people there since Saturday night. People in these centres nervous of remaining there as local school used for same purpose was badly bombed last week. Re-billeting is proceeding.

11 September

LONDON

Morale has jumped to new level of confidence and cheerfulness since tremendous AA barrage. This is true of every district contacted, including East End and areas badly hit yesterday such as Woolwich and Lewisham. 'We'll give them hell now' is a typical working-class comment today. City far more cheerful and less crowded with sightseers than yesterday. Kensington people rendered homeless in night joking when taken in by neighbours. In spite of little sleep, factory workers are turning up as usual and working well; employers reported to be very accommodating about time. Traffic dislocations causing delay and annoyance; people passing in empty cars are much grumbled at by queues of workers waiting for buses who would like to be offered lifts. Unofficial walk-out from dock areas still going on; people from Greenwich reported to be taking buses to Bromley from where they hope to go to the west; others going to Bucks and Herts. A few have any but vaguest ideas as to where they are going and how they will fare there. Many people taking rugs and cushions from poor districts to spend nights in West End shelters: fear of great dockside fires appears to be chief motivating force. Stoke Newington and other boroughs not close to docks report most people 'sticking to their homes' as long as they can. Re-billeting of homeless people proceeding, but many Rest Centres still overcrowded. As they are not provided with shelters adequate for number of people in them are rousing apprehension in districts such as Bermondsey as two Rest Centres have been bombed with great loss of life. Stoke Newington now reported to be fitting public shelters with bunks for children.

12 September

FRIDAY 13 SEPTEMBER 1940

In London the anti-aircraft barrage continues to stimulate morale. People are sleeping better in spite of increased noise, and reports show there is an increased feeling of security based on the psychological knowledge that we are hitting back.

People living near guns are suffering from serious lack of sleep: a number of interviews made round one gun in West London showed that people were getting much less sleep than others a few hundred yards away. Very few used ear plugs, and many of those interviewed were still relying on deck chairs instead of mattresses. There is little complaint about lack of sleep, mainly because of the new exhilaration created by the barrage. Nevertheless this serious loss of sleep needs watching.

There is a growth of anger against the Germans and growing demands for 'reprisals on civilians'.

Reports continue to show a great increase in rumours about damage and casualties ('They say the casualties are really ten times bigger than we are told').

Motorists do not appear to give lifts willingly and there is considerable criticism of 'the rich in their cars'.

POINTS FROM REGIONS

SOUTHERN (Reading) The Prime Minister's speech has been received 'with approbation and quiet confidence'. There are some signs of a recrudescence of Fifth Columnist rumours, some of which are attributed to Haw-Haw. Exaggeration of the casualties on a recent raid on Southampton gives rise to a suggestion that the BBC should give a reminder that gossip about air-raid damage 'can be just as dangerous as the spreading of totally unfounded rumours'.

NORTH MIDLAND (Nottingham) Leicestershire IC has received 'urgent representations' about the delay in supplying the Civil Defence services with uniform and equipment. The Nottingham IC would like an explanation of the variation of the Ministry of Labour Gazette's cost of living index. The decrease of two points during August seems to be doubted.

SOUTH-WESTERN (Bristol) Mr. Churchill's speech has had 'a stimulating effect'. A demand for reprisal raids on Berlin is made in various parts of the Region. Concern is expressed about the way in which the King and Queen and Prime Minister are visiting the bombed areas, although the effect of their behaviour on public morale is fully appreciated.

MIDLAND (Birmingham) There has been an enthusiastic reception for the Prime Minister's speech. This applies also to the new raid warning system. Various Information Committees have commented upon the display of car lights which are to be seen on trunk roads throughout the Region.

SCOTLAND (Edinburgh) Full approval is given to the Prime Minister's speech. It has enhanced the expectation of invasion, but the public are nevertheless confident about the outcome of such an enterprise. There are many rumours dealing with this subject.

NORTHERN IRELAND (Belfast) Investigations are being made into the accommodation available for the reception of Londoners rendered homeless through air raids. This problem is being considered by the Northern Ireland Cabinet. The local press alleges that the voluntary recruiting system has been unsatisfactory and that young men prefer the dole.

LONDON

Majority carrying on with calmness and courage even in heavily bombed areas. Most prevalent emotion anger with Germans and irritation over constant raids. Real hatred and savagery flash out at times from those who have come in contact with actual tragedies: 'we must wipe them off the face of the earth' is working man's comment heard today. AA barrage continues to be encouraging. Much talk today of invasion; expectancy but not fear expressed. Croydon contact reports local people 'determined to see it through' but that defeatist sentiments are voiced by isolated members of the middle class. Noticeable friendliness everywhere among all classes and types of people. Everybody is trying to help everybody else – except motorists who are rousing angry bitterness at not offering lifts with empty cars to long queues of tired workers. Even when Home Guard asked motorists to give lifts in Balham to stranded workers they refused. Misuse of public shelters in Wandsworth reported; people push in with bedding and prevent strangers from getting a place; conditions described as dirty and unhygienic. Borough of Finsbury keeps its public shelters in excellent condition; result is that people come to large underground shelter from other boroughs in cars and crowd it out. Authorities feel they cannot turn people away as in present state of nervous tension there would be angry scenes.

SATURDAY 14 SEPTEMBER 1940

People in London are slightly less cheerful today. The decline in the activity of the anti-aircraft barrage has caused comment, and there are many questions about the effect of cloud and rain on the barrage.

Unplanned evacuation from London is continuing. Most people leave without giving any indication of their destination. A report on the reception of refugees in Oxford and Buckinghamshire will be provided on Monday.

Conditions in many shelters are still unsatisfactory. Complaints are mainly about insanitary conditions, lack of ventilation and overcrowding.

Many of our reports show criticism of the Lord Mayor's 'charitable appeal' for relief and consider the charge should properly be carried by the Government.

Exaggerated stories of damage and Haw-Haw rumours continue to circulate.

There is little interest in the possibility of invasion, nor does the prospect alarm people.

Public opinion about the bombing of Buckingham Palace is divided: most people feel a fresh bond with their leaders, others think that 'the King and Queen ought not to be exposed to such danger'.

POINTS FROM REGIONS

NORTH-EASTERN (Leeds) All eyes are still on London, and newspaper accounts of the behaviour of Londoners have stiffened public resolve in the North. Despite warnings about invasion, it cannot be said that most people take the threat seriously. The War Weapons Week has had a brilliant send-off in Leeds. Although morale is high, more people than for some time past are listening to Haw-Haw, and it seems that people hope to pick up hints about coming events. There is strong feeling because bombs fell again this week and there were no sirens sounded or AA fire.

EASTERN (Cambridge) The chief reactions to the bombing of London appear to be anxiety concerning communications. The accounts of the bombing of Buckingham Palace have captured public imagination. There has been an increase in rumours although not of an unduly alarmist nature. Complaints of non-arrival of postal packets sent to the USA have caused a suspicion that certain letters are being systematically stopped.

SOUTHERN (Reading) There is some anxiety as to the possibility of continued night raiding through the winter. An authoritative statement on the damage which is being done to Germany would undoubtedly have a tonic effect on many people. Although the public is alive to the possibilities of invasion, there is a general feeling that it can only be a disaster for the Germans. There is a feeling in some quarters that there is too much emphasis placed on damage by press photographs, and the attitude that 'we can take it', which suggests our ability to suffer rather than our power to hit back.

WALES (Cardiff) Interest is centred on activities in south-east England, the prospect of invasion, and additions or improvements to shelters to meet winter conditions. The continued presence of the King and Queen in London and their tours has enhanced the respect felt by all. There is some call for reprisals by random bombing in Germany.

NORTH-WESTERN (Manchester) Today's topic of conversation is surprise at getting through a whole night without an alarm. There are fresh reports that Liverpool dockers are not co-operating and are far too ready to stop work for alarms. The deliberate bombing of Buckingham Palace is thought to be a blunder by Hitler.

SOUTH-EASTERN (Tunbridge Wells) Tunbridge Wells suffered considerable damage on Thursday as a result of a lightning raid. No siren was sounded but members of the Civil Defence behaved splendidly, but soon after the streets became full of curious sightseers who interfered with the work of the fire services. If the raider had returned there might have been many casualties.

MONDAY 16 SEPTEMBER 1940

Yesterday's aerial successes have produced enthusiastic praise for the RAF. There is, however, comment that the AA barrage last night seemed less intense than usual. This may be due to nothing more than people becoming used to it.

Most people anticipate an invasion within a few days, and are very confident that it will be a failure. Rumours that it has already been attempted and has failed are reported from many quarters. From the Northern Region it is stated that there are many requests for a public denial or an explanatory statement. From Nottingham comes the rumour that hundreds of German bodies have been floating in the Channel. In north Nottinghamshire the invasion is said to have been attempted on Lincolnshire and the south coast. In Northampton it is said that the attack was launched on the west coast. Invasion rumours are also reported in the South-Western Region and Scotland.

The people of London are in the great majority more optimistic, but unplanned evacuation of the 'jittery' to Bucks, Berks, Herts, Oxford and Kent continues. These evacuees magnify their adventures and the amount of destruction in London, thus alarming people in reception areas. Nightly migrations to public shelters which people regard as safe in the West End and elsewhere are now routine events. Tubes are also being used as shelters.

There is still criticism of lack of washing and other facilities at Rest Centres, and suggestions are made that these centres should co-operate more closely with the public baths.

The Lord Mayor's Fund for Air Raid Relief is criticised on two scores: first that the matter is really a Government concern, and secondly that many towns have suffered considerably already but that no national fund has been opened for them.

In the excitement of aerial battles, air raids, and invasion threats, the situation in Egypt is being allowed to pass by the public with little comment.

POINTS FROM REGIONS

NORTHERN (Newcastle) Rumours of an attempted invasion which failed are widespread. There is much evidence that public feeling against the

German people is rapidly hardening as a result of the more intensive raids. Complaints have been made that many people fail to hear the one-minute warning when asleep, and it has been urged that after 10.30 p.m. the sirens should be sounded for at least two minutes. The heating of shelters is becoming a major concern for many people. Feeling is growing in working-class circles that certain classes are not pulling their weight in the financing of the war, in view of big interest-free loans made by working-class organisations.

NORTH MIDLAND (Nottingham) Widespread rumours are prevalent that an invasion has already been attempted. The continued presence of the King, Queen and Government in London is appreciated. More news of our air raids on Germany is still desired, as there is a feeling that we can stand bombing better if the Germans are getting the same treatment. In Northamptonshire some workers express concern at the sparing use of alarms; they do not mind working through so long as they can feel their families can take cover in good time. War investments have increased in Nottingham mining areas as a result of local bombing.

MIDLAND (Birmingham) The relative calm of the past few nights is creating a belief that invasion is imminent and there is absolute confidence in the outcome. People are less worried by siren warnings than formerly, and go to bed until bombs are dropped. Licensing Justices of Birmingham are to consider the earlier closing of public houses in view of the disorderly behaviour of intoxicated people in public shelters.

NORTHERN IRELAND (Belfast) There is enthusiastic praise for the way in which the RAF has bombed enemy invasion bases, and brought down so many aircraft in London raids. There is some comment on the relatively small number of planes destroyed by AA fire. Anger is expressed at the renewed bombing of Buckingham Palace. The situation in Egypt is viewed with some uneasiness.

SOUTH-WESTERN (Bristol) Admiration is expressed for the exploits of the RAF in yesterday's raids, and many people are expressing the hope that retaliation will be made on Berlin. There are rumours of parachutists landing in Cornwall.

SCOTLAND (Edinburgh) In Dundee there is general scepticism about invasion, based on confidence in the Navy, but elsewhere there are vigorous rumours of an attempted invasion of north-east Scotland. There is little talk about the Italian moves on the Egyptian border and this campaign seems to be regarded as a side issue. It is reported that on receipt of an air-raid warning in Glasgow last night many lights became visible, and ARP workers complain that they have no power to take effective action.

LONDON

Big trek each evening to find shelter accommodation for the night – from such areas as Bermondsey, Canning Town, and Paddington. Numbers of people, including many children, shelter in Underground stations. In a West-End district, it is reported that people bombed out of a public shelter were refused admittance to the large private shelter of a big store. A Stepney observer reports: 'need for clothes for refugees at Rest Centres; Communal Feeding Centres working well, though many people ignorant of their existence, and uninformed of changed addresses as the result of fresh raids; many working men unable to obtain meal in evening owing to bombing of market, and lack of gas, electricity and water'; suggests temporary hostels for them. Watford observer reports that district is making London refugees welcome; some anxiety about getting in touch with relatives. Improvement in the offering of lifts by private cars reported from several areas.

TUESDAY 17 SEPTEMBER 1940

While many continue to anticipate invasion, and indeed hope that it will come within the next few days, reports show that some people are suggesting that its likelihood has diminished. Rumours that it has already been attempted and has failed continue to be reported.

Regional reports continue to state that there is an increase in the amount of listening to German broadcasts.

The great delay in the receipt of the national morning papers in many parts of the provinces has led to requests that the BBC should revive their Ten O'Clock Morning News.

Londoners whose families have been re-billeted or who have evacuated themselves are having great difficulty in making contact with them. Suggestions are made that Rest Centres should keep careful records of the destinations of those they house temporarily, and that anxious relatives should be instructed to apply at these centres to trace their families.

Descriptions of our retreat from Sollum are criticised for attempting to disguise bad news as good news.

POINTS FROM REGIONS

NORTH-EASTERN (Leeds) Confidence throughout the Region is very high. Rumours are rife that attempts at invasion have been made. More people are listening to Haw-Haw, and the New British Broadcasting Station appears to have a large number of listeners. Despite the bombing of London and local propaganda, there is no appreciable difference in the rate at which Leeds children are being registered for evacuation. Censorship of letters to Eire appears to cause some resentment. It is felt in some quarters that undue publicity has been given to the bombing of Buckingham Palace.

EASTERN (Cambridge) Morale still remains high, and once again some people feel the threat of immediate invasion has disappeared. New refugees from London are settling down, but it seems that billets earmarked for troops or compulsory evacuees are at present being occupied by them. There appears to be a slight increase in listening to German broadcasts. A number of stories are in circulation concerning alleged invasion, and it is said that isolated groups of vessels have been beaten off. There are increasing signs of a disposition to settle down to winter routine.

SOUTHERN (Reading) London's reaction to air raids, German air losses, and stories of the RAF attacks on invasion bases stimulate confidence and courage. Threatened cities such as Portsmouth and Southampton are effectively adapting themselves to war conditions. A fresh wave of evacuees from London is disquieting local authorities in the northern part of the Region, which already has refugees from coastal cities and evacuated children, and the billeting demands of the military are also increasing.

WALES (Cardiff) Air successes on Sunday and the bombing of the Channel ports has increased confidence in our ability to cope with the enemy. There is criticism of the report of the BBC observer in Egypt on our 'withdrawal' from Sollum: 'If we retreat, let us admit it.'

NORTH-WESTERN (Manchester) While Manchester and Liverpool have been heartened by London's resistance to a week of severe bombing, there is growing perturbation over stories of lack of shelters, and accommodation for those who have been bombed; many people are worried over lack of shelters in this Region, and in one or two housing estates rent strikes have been staged until shelters have been provided. Many people are urging that municipal transport should continue to run until danger is imminent.

SOUTH-EASTERN (Tunbridge Wells) Stories of damage to London brought by lorry drivers are becoming increasingly lurid, and demands for reprisals equally emphatic. More information regarding results of air raids is urged from many parts of the Region. There is a demand that the sounding of sirens should be entrusted to local authorities when lone raiders are overhead. There is some dissatisfaction among Kent members of the Home Guard because, although in the 'front line', they are without steel helmets and respirators. Many hop pickers arriving in a hurry from London are saying 'What is the good of going on?' A report from Folkestone says that morale is adversely affected by the exodus of a large number of well-off people from London, and others from Folkestone, including ARP and Red Cross personnel who should be in the front line.

LONDON

Morale steady; public on whole settling down to new air-raid life cheerfully and show fewer signs of tiredness. Small pockets of bad morale reported from different districts especially with regard to overcrowded Rest Centres (this is now being dealt with by London Region Ministry of Health). Bermondsey contact reports 'talk against Government on account of inadequate number and poor equipment of local shelters. Shelters under railway arches have insufficient seats and people are forced to sit and lie on pavement.' This and other 'target' areas of the docks still need some voluntary scheme of evacuation of mothers and children, also the old and infirm, state social workers and other responsible people. This less true of other bombed districts such as Lewisham, Stoke Newington, Finsbury, Battersea etc. where people cling to their homes at all costs. The Stoke Newington contact states bombed people in district very philosophical: 'majority set to work to clean up mess at once and say "it might have been worse"'. Same contact reports many people would like to get their old parents out but that the old people are difficult to move. South Kensington contact states roundsmen upsetting housewives by gossip of air-raid damage and numbers of customers leaving the district. Suggests propaganda to stop this. Rumours of unexploded bombs far outweigh their numbers and it is suggested that people should not believe such rumours but look only for police warnings. West End business woman states her own class feel that more generous treatment should be given to East-Enders who have lost homes or have to spend nights in shelters. Reports also 'bitterness against Government for not having built deep shelters to protect population'. Business circles ask for a definite lead on working hours and transport. Latter question increasingly difficult for workers although car drivers are giving lifts more readily than a few days ago. Working women reported to wish to use ground floors and basements of empty houses to sleep in to meet shelter difficulty. Day rest periods for workers, mentioned by Minister of Labour, being asked for by factory workers who are not sleeping well because of night raids.

WEDNESDAY 18 SEPTEMBER 1940

Provincial reports show that the bombardment of London is still the outstanding news interest. Sympathy for 'London's ordeal' is widely expressed, and there is reason to believe that the communiques describing detailed damage (but not the amount of London which still stands) and the newspaper pictures of ruined buildings are producing a greatly exaggerated picture in provincial minds. This is coupled with such expressions as 'if London can take it, so can we'. At the same time some people are beginning to wonder how long London will be able to go on taking it.

Rumours of damage to London, some accurate but many exaggerated, are common in the provinces and the Northern Region comments that the BBC's revelation on Saturday evening that a bomb fell on Madame Tussaud's was regarded as 'the most humorous remark on the wireless this year'; everyone had known about this for at least two days.

The rumour that invasion was attempted a few days ago and failed with considerable loss to the Germans is now reported to be causing excitement in the Midlands. There is also the rumour reported from the South-Western Region that British Marines have landed in Jersey.

It is again reported that listening to the German wireless is on the increase. This is attributed by many to the fact that when the Nine O'Clock News has to cut out on account of raids, the English News from Germany is often audible without re-tuning.

Though strong demands for reprisals on German civilians are still reported, there are many who are satisfied that the wisest policy is to continue attacking invasion objectives.

POINTS FROM REGIONS

NORTHERN (Newcastle) Expressions of sympathy with London are numerous, and there is an atmosphere of expectancy. In some centres local ARP wardens are anxious to go to London to relieve those on duty there. It has been suggested that more broadcasts from the Service ministers would be appreciated. There is little discussion of peace aims at present. Some complaints have been made by munitions contractors of the inexperience of Government inspectors.

NORTH MIDLAND (Nottingham) London casualties have caused anger, and there is a growing feeling in Notts that we ought 'to dose Hitler with his own medicine'. Official statements that if we hold out for a period of weeks the major crisis will pass, have been interpreted by some as meaning the war will end with the crisis. A report from Leicester states that benefits which can be immediately claimed by air-raid victims for material losses appear inadequate, and the replacement of furniture is said to be particularly difficult.

SOUTH-WESTERN (Bristol) People are facing the prospect of attempted invasion calmly, and are confident of the ultimate outcome. Three reliable contacts in Devon say that people with the least satisfactory attitude towards the war are mostly found in the income group from £250 to £750. Some dissatisfaction reported from Exeter and Penzance where bombs were dropped without the sirens being sounded. There are complaints from Weston-super-Mare that buses cease running in air raids. Evacuated Londoners are spreading highly coloured accounts of raids in Swindon. There is some speculation as to whether London can stand up to the bombing. The need for bombing barge concentrations is appreciated, and there is a decrease in demands for retaliations on Berlin.

MIDLAND (Birmingham) The rumour that an attempted German invasion last Sunday was frustrated with heavy losses is widespread. There is much feeling about lights on motor cars being left on after sirens are sounded. The question of earlier closing for public houses comes before the Justices tomorrow. There are complaints of lack of transport facilities for workers from Coventry.

SCOTLAND (Edinburgh) Middle-class people are beginning to ask 'What is going to be the end of this mutual bombing?' The chief reaction to the terror raids is one of anger with the enemy and admiration for those enduring the ordeal. There is some disquiet about the Italian advance. There is some adverse comment at the absence of AA fire in Glasgow, and the public would welcome some assurance that British fighters were up.

NORTHERN IRELAND (Belfast) There is some speculation as to the reason for the Secret Session in the House of Commons yesterday, although it is not presumed that the situation is more critical. It is generally felt that any attempt at invasion would be repulsed. In intellectual circles General Sir Alan Brooke's statement welcoming an invasion attempt is thought to be ill-advised. Ministry of Supply experts are investigating iron ore and bauxite sources in Ireland.

LONDON

Londoners still remain outwardly calm and are putting up with difficulties extremely well, but there are still numbers of people anxious to get out. One Earls Court Square has practically evacuated itself after bombing there; others in less fortunate position need scheme to help them. A certain amount of panic shown in individual cases where people have had horrible experiences but this is often due to temporary physical reaction. There are still criticisms about Rest Centres – inadequately staffed and equipped – although some districts report gradual improvement. Re-billeting of homeless still causing difficulties and organisation reported to be bad in some areas e.g. Chelsea, St. Pancras. ARP warden in West End and also social workers in East End feel Mayfair billeting does not solve the problems of homeless East-Enders – they feel homesick and lonely and food prices are beyond them. Still much criticism about inadequacy of shelter amenities. Many people have lost faith in surface shelters and now go to Tubes where atmosphere is reported to be bad; more supervision and help required here. Transport difficulties increasing and several observers comment on number of half-empty cars in congested streets. Harrow factory which carries on with production throughout the 'Alert' resents Government offices in the neighbourhood closing down; workers finding it more and more difficult to do essential shopping and transact necessary official business (Post Office, Labour Exchange, Stationery Office). Increase in unemployment reported in North London as many industries are without facilities for carrying on (water etc.), even where property remains undamaged; this is causing a certain amount of anxiety and distress.

THURSDAY 19 SEPTEMBER 1940

1. People are not so cheerful today. There is more grumbling. Elation over the barrage is not so strong: people wonder why it is not more effective in preventing night bombing and many avow it has decreased in intensity. There is also evidence that physical tiredness is beginning to have an effect on nerves.

2. There are increasing demands for reprisals and growing hatred against the Germans: wild suggestions are made, 'Fill Buckingham Palace with prisoners', 'Shoot all captured airmen', etc. These expressions are common in public shelters in specially heavily bombed areas.

3. In London the following tension points continue:

    Amenities of public shelters

    Inability of local authorities to remove people quickly from rest shelters

    Inadequate methods of evacuation to other parts of London and to the country

    Transport difficulties

    Curtailment of services, e.g. Post Offices, shops, Employment Exchanges, etc.

    Lack of a register of evacuated persons

    Determination of the public to use Underground stations as shelters

    Rigidity of compensation regulations

4. Last night the number of people taking shelter in Underground stations greatly increased.

5. Rumours and exaggerated stories circulate widely in London and the provinces. The most important subjects are

    Terrors of the new magnetic mines dropped by parachute

    Invasion (in progress, repulsed, etc.)

    Spies (Fifth Column activities in shelters, signalling with torches, etc.)

    Damage and casualties in London

    Today several people reported 'a petition for peace' sent to the Prime Minister from the East End. This may be due to the petitions which the People's Vigilance Committees, communist groups, etc. are organising in shelters.

6. Reports confirm that in the country outside London there is an exaggerated view of the damage and dislocation in London. 'Refugees' are spreading highly coloured stories and the press continues to devote itself almost exclusively to accounts of damage.

7. The situation in Egypt is not raising popular concern. On the other hand thoughtful people are disturbed and already speak of 'another Somaliland'.

POINTS FROM REGIONS

NORTH-EASTERN (Leeds) Some apprehension about events in Africa, and doubt as to whether the power of the Navy in the Mediterranean is enough to check the Italian advance. Expectations of invasion are diminishing. News reels and pictures in papers of damage to London have done much to improve black-out and civil defence precautions. Showing of King and Queen visiting the East End in news reels has brought cheers everywhere. LIC at Sowerby Bridge passed resolution urging need for discussion of war aims as a positive factor in morale. Much discussion of deep shelters and many urge the need for them.

EASTERN (Cambridge) Increasing belief that our strong defences and the weather will defer invasion. Some demand for press pictures of RAF damage to Germany, to offset continual pictures of damage here. Requests for more information about our AA defences and some anxiety at American statement that life of AA guns is very short. Complaints continue about German wireless monopolising ether. Some criticism of expense to local authorities of salvage schemes; contractors suspected of excessive profits, sometimes quite unfairly.

SOUTHERN (Reading) Local authorities faced by big problem of East End refugees. Towns affected are Oxford, Windsor, Banbury, Chipping Norton, Aylesbury, Newbury, etc. Refugees spread despondency by lurid accounts of bombing. Growing demand that large empty country houses should have been taken over for refugees. Official statements about 'no retaliation' creating discussion. Belief expressed that in absence of retaliation indiscriminate bombing will get progressively worse, while retaliation might stop it. Some argue that civilian bombing *has* military value and instance bombing of Rotterdam. Criticism that we have not convinced neutrals of our own certainty of ultimate victory.

WALES (Cardiff) Complaints that civil defence equipment is impossible to obtain in both north and south Wales. Much criticism of cars parked in rows with side lamps lit outside hotels. Public believe these can be seen from the air. Curfew on beaches accepted as a wise precaution. Much interest, coupled with uneasiness, about situation in Africa. Suggestion is made that BBC interviews of victims of bombing do not ring true, as persons interviewed sometimes have difficulty in reading their apparently carefully prepared scripts.

NORTH-WESTERN (Manchester) Indignation reported in Merseyside area at daylight bombing without apparent resistance from fighters, and that sirens sounded after raid had started. Liverpool considers that for its size its losses have been as heavy as London's, and that it should have appropriate fighter protection. Increasing optimism about results of possible invasion, but distinct uneasiness about Spain and Egypt; public sceptical when told of negligible value of abandoned territory. Growing anxiety about conditions which are likely if long winter nights have to be passed in cold shelters.

SOUTH-EASTERN (Tunbridge Wells) Some alarm expressed at German programmes overlapping and substituting BBC programmes on closely similar wave-lengths. Rumours that East-Enders have sent a petition to the Prime Minister to stop the war. Sarcastic comments at closing of Post Offices whenever warnings sound. Increasing irritation at apparent immunity of German bombers which are thought to 'circle over' individual towns for hours at night. Rumours persist that invasions have taken place and have been repulsed.

LONDON

Some dismay expressed today at heavy raid last night and apparent inability of AA barrage to prevent it. Fear of mines dropped by parachute and the extent of the damage they cause is also evident. No break in morale, however, can be seen. Extreme annoyance again expressed by business people and other workers at closing down of public utility services during warnings, especially Post Offices and banks. Welfare supervisor of large employing concern reports workers less worried over difficulty of transport than lack of sleep. 75% of these workers are sleeping in shelters where their rest is continually disturbed. Rest Centres and Communal Feeding Centres in heavily bombed areas now working far more smoothly but problem of re-billeting of homeless in East End districts still acute. People turned out of houses by time bombs are not catered for on regular system; one family in

Greenwich reported to have been living in dugout for ten days waiting to go home when time bomb had exploded, and voicing resentment as they say that 'in Mayfair bomb would have been dealt with after two days'. Urgent need for some machinery by which contact can be kept with people who have left London so that relations can get in touch with them. Air-raid casualties reported by hospital almoner to be extremely brave and cheerful but anxious over welfare of relations. Local machinery needed to find out and report on these relations to hospital patients. Middle classes reported to be concerned over question of compensation when houses have been damaged or demolished. Complaints voiced that nothing is being done for them although they are hard hit by taxation and loss of business. Grievance also that full rates are charged for houses half demolished. Motorists willing to give lifts complain of confusion and delay in picking up people wanting to go in the same direction. Wish request could be made that people wanting lifts should hold out notices with names of places they are going to clearly marked. Bad feeling growing in North London suburbs about numbers of 'aliens' who go into street shelters with mattresses early in evening and leave no room for passers-by.

FRIDAY 20 SEPTEMBER 1940

In general morale is excellent and in particular people are more cheerful today. The feeling of being in the front line stimulates many people and puts them on their mettle in overcoming transport and shelter difficulties. Several of our reports comment on this characteristic.

There is, however, evidence of increasing physical tiredness.

Although there is no general demand for evacuation from heavily bombed areas there is evidence that certain classes of the community would welcome arrangements for them to go, e.g. wives and children of men working or serving elsewhere, infirm or invalid persons, old couples, widows. It is emphasised by our observers, however, that willing co-operation could only be got for a carefully thought out scheme which took into consideration the special needs and problems of these classes. Women with husbands are not in general prepared to go although evidence suggests that they might do so if proper arrangements were made for the men left behind.

In east and south-east London there are many complaints that the whereabouts of evacuated persons are unknown.

Taking shelter in Underground stations continued last night. People were orderly but conditions were very insanitary. There is evidence that people do not intend to pay attention to official requests not to shelter there.

POINTS FROM REGIONS

NORTHERN (Newcastle) Many statements have been made expressing fear that Hitler will not attempt invasion; it is generally felt that any attempt is bound to be unsuccessful and would shorten the war. Criticism of the closing of Post Offices and banks for long periods during warnings is widespread. The method of deducting income tax at source appears popular, but there is some criticism that it gives the employer too much information as to the private income of the employee.

NORTH MIDLAND (Nottingham) There is a general feeling of admiration for the way in which 'the Cockneys are standing up to air raids'. The rumour that invasion has been attempted is prevalent. There are some complaints by Grimsby people who have evacuated themselves to the Lake District that they are being exploited by landladies and others. There is grumbling at the shortage of eggs in Nottinghamshire and Leicestershire, and annoyance at official announcements that eggs are plentiful; a shortage of bagged coal is also reported.

SOUTH-WESTERN (Bristol) Despite official denial, stories of attempted invasion still circulate. From Trowbridge and Weston come reports of a demand for the publication of pictures of damage done to German towns by RAF. Sympathetic concern for the bombing of London is shown everywhere. People in Exeter would like to be shown what damage has *not* been done to London, and to know how normal life continues despite the raids, as well as to learn of the damage effected. Evacuees from London and coastal towns are reported to be well received. After several days of comparative peace, people of Plymouth are expecting a big attack, but except for a feeling that deep shelters should be provided, there is little concern and no alarm.

MIDLAND (Birmingham) It is generally felt that the bombing of the invasion ports is preventing invasion, and that the bombing of London calls for reprisals on Berlin. There are many complaints about shortage of coal, and protests against the 'means test' for supplementary old age pensions.

SCOTLAND (Edinburgh) Italian moves in North Africa are discussed with some concern and the questions are asked: 'Are we going to hit Italy hard soon?' and 'Are our forces out there strong enough?' During a survey of 10 cinemas held during a warning last night only one person was seen to move from the gallery to the ground floor, and nobody left the building. The fact that buses in Midlothian stop when a warning is sounded is causing some interference with colliery work.

NORTHERN IRELAND (Belfast) The manner in which Londoners are standing up to bombing continues to be praised. The bombing of ports in enemy hands is taken as a sign that Britain can maintain this preventive offensive indefinitely. Precautions are being taken against the possible development of enemy air activity over Ulster, and Civil Defence services in urban areas are to be strengthened. The Belfast Spitfire fund has now reached £72,000. Efforts are to be made greatly to increase Ulster's flax acreage in 1941.

LONDON

Morale still steady with growing anger against Germans. Many East End workers and others qualified to speak still feel that dispersal of non-essential population would ease the difficulties of London authorities. Large crowds, mostly women and children, still congregate in most Tube stations for sleeping at night; little space left for travellers. Observer on Edgware line noticed quantities of rubbish still being swept up about nine o'clock this morning. Islington social workers report need for broadcasts in simple language informing people rendered homeless what they should do and what provisions are made for them; this need evident from criticism of lack of co-ordination between various services. Golders Green resident expresses concern at squads of cyclists on road showing too much light. Responsible official in Woolwich impressed by extraordinary determination of employers to carry on in spite of factories receiving repeated hits. Business and professional people now asking what compensation they will have when houses or business premises are damaged; big employers concerned not only about personal loss but about resulting unemployment among their workers. Rest Centres reported to be working more smoothly in many districts but more officials needed. Jewish social worker says spirit of the poor in East End not broken in spite of terrible ordeals; Westminster Council now helping to re-billet homeless East-Enders and records being kept. Many would like to move from London. Heston professional man reports anxiety of many people about situation in Mediterranean, but no loss of confidence in present Government is expressed.

SATURDAY 21 SEPTEMBER 1940

There is little change in morale: yesterday's cheerfulness is maintained.

In London conversation is almost exclusively about air raids; it is gossipy, not panicky, and is centred in personal matters. There appears to be very little relationship between 'the bomb at the corner of our street' and the war as a whole. Interest in the total aspect of the war is very low, although demands for reprisals continue.

The necessity for seeking night shelter is accepted with resignation, and there are many examples of the fine spirit with which difficulties are met and overcome. At the same time, there are criticisms of obvious defects: shelter amenities, evacuation facilities, lack of information.

Taking shelter in Underground stations is still on the increase. People are orderly, officials humane.

There are a number of reports showing that people are well aware of the damage and danger of 'land mines'. Terror stories are frequent. There are also tales of new weapons, e.g. plaster bombs, and evidence that people only begin to feel secure when they are below the surface: in Tubes, basements, underground trenches, etc.

Time bombs are not regarded with undue alarm. The public feels that officials of various kinds are well aware of their dangers. There are, however, a number of enquiries about the duration of their effectiveness; people are very vague, some think they may be effective for a fortnight or longer; others that they cannot last more than a few hours. Evacuation on account of time bombs has brought hardship, but not alarm.

The AA barrage continues to cause a certain amount of disappointment: 'It's all very well, but they aren't bringing them down.' The idea that there is no protection against night bombing has not yet been accepted by most people. Protection is expected 'in time'. Only a few appear to contemplate much intensified bombing.

The public is increasingly anxious about black-out offences and there are many complaints about traffic lights, side lights, matches, torches, railway signals, etc. Many people appear to think that all lights are visible from the air.

Cinema attendances are low, and evidence shows that leisure time is not being profitably used.

There are fewer complaints about the warning system although today's incident in Bethnal Green has greatly perturbed people there. Their confidence is again shaken.

From the provinces come reports that AA and fighter defences are considered inadequate.

POINTS FROM REGIONS

NORTH-EASTERN (Leeds) No change in confidence except a slightly growing feeling of stalemate. In view of recent rumours, people are asking for clear statements as to whether there has or has not been an attempted invasion. In an interview given to the *Yorkshire Post*, the Leeds City Engineer says that brickwork is being done on non-essential buildings and shelter contractors are unable to get the labour they require.

EASTERN (Cambridge) The extent of damaged property in London has been exaggerated by refugees, and it is thought that the East End has been laid waste. There are still complaints about the limited number of BBC stations broadcasting, and with the delay in the distribution of London papers, there is increasing support for a ten o'clock a.m. bulletin. Yesterday's announcement that Post Offices will remain open during warnings is welcomed. Complaints about the uncertain arrangements for running buses during air raids continues, particularly from country districts where services are few.

SOUTHERN (Reading) Many refugees from London have arrived in the Region, and in Oxford where the number is about 10,000, the problem of accommodation is serious. Although most of these people appear to be in good heart, a small minority who have suffered from a continued loss of sleep and are dazed by their experiences, have tended to spread a somewhat defeatist attitude. There is discussion on the question of reprisals, and the speech by the Air Minister does not appear to have satisfied public opinion. Most people seem to think that invasion will not now be attempted. The more thoughtful section of the public is anxious about the position in Egypt, and although appreciating the advantage of allowing the Italians to have several hundred miles of desert communications, it hopes that the press accounts are not too 'rosy'.

NORTH-WESTERN (Manchester) There is much feeling in the Liverpool area over the apparent absence of local defence against bombers, and the inadequacy of shelters is also a subject of comment; yesterday a meeting of Merseyside mayors was convened and a message sent to the Prime Minister on the latter subject. The news of heavy RAF raids on Germany and occupied areas causes great satisfaction.

SOUTH-EASTERN (Tunbridge Wells) People are much concerned about the problem of countering night bombers, and such questions as 'why can't Spitfires be armed with searchlights' are being asked. It is reported that people who left London on account of air raids and went hop-picking are now worried because they will have nowhere to go when the picking is finished.

LONDON

Great fear of land mines reported from many districts. For example, this fear has resulted in occupants of luxury flats in St. John's Wood using the Tube for shelter at night; also, after experiencing effects last night it is reported from Bethnal Green that many people wish to be evacuated. From Poplar and Bethnal Green it is stated that there is some ill-feeling because homeless are not re-billeted quickly enough and the Rest Centres are over-crowded. People feel that the victims of raids deserve the most generous treatment and that those who wish, homeless or otherwise, to leave London should be given facilities for doing so without delay. A Stoke Newington official points out the danger of fire in unoccupied houses if evacuation becomes too general in some districts. Observer in Islington says that undertakers are making excessive charges for funerals and a minimum charge should be instituted. Observation at different Tube stations reveals that the number of people sleeping there is increasing. It has been sug-gested that tunnels used as shelters should have baffle walls to break blast.

MONDAY 23 SEPTEMBER 1940

There is anger and indignation about the torpedoing of the child evacuee ship. The effect has been to increase the demand for 'reprisals on German civilians'. A number of enquiries have been received about the sea-vacuation scheme: Will it go on? Was the ship convoyed? etc. Many people appear to think that the scheme will be discontinued. This is the first piece of news for a fortnight which has deflected people's interest from air raids.

Further investigation into the situation in those places outside London where 'refugees' have gone shows that while there is much sympathy for these people, there is an increase of criticism about their dirty habits and inconsiderate behaviour. The exodus is still largely unorganised and is pro-ducing local irritation. Shortages of certain kinds of food have been reported and accounts of exaggerated stories continue.

People in London are cheerful but continue to enquire when there will be protection against night bombing.

POINTS FROM REGIONS

NORTHERN (Newcastle) There is evidence of growth in the demand for reprisals on the German civilian population, although more thoughtful people realise that no real military advantage can be secured thereby. News reels showing the King and Queen visiting victims of air raids have received unusually warm applause. There is a feeling that there is too much red tape and too little responsibility and encouragement given to local authorities when dealing with air-raid victims, and many quarters urge greater elasticity of administration. Complaints about the quality of reception of BBC programmes have noticeably increased during the last two weeks. The desire for a real military success against the Italians remains very strong.

SOUTH-WESTERN (Bristol) Bitter demands for reprisals against German civilians are reported as a result of the news of the sinking of the evacuee ship; Barnstaple reports that apprehension is felt as to the effect of the sinking on a scheme for transporting children to Barnstaple Massachusetts. Activity amongst troops and Home Guards during the weekend is said to have been responsible for a further crop of invasion rumours. In spite of wireless talks and press reports Salisbury states that the position of men working after the siren has sounded is still not clearly understood.

MIDLAND (Birmingham) The drowning of evacuee children due to U-boat action has evoked indignation throughout the Region. The fact that there have been no raids over the Region for the past two days has encouraged the belief that Hitler has abandoned his invasion plan. Rules for air-raid shelter conduct have been issued by the Chief Constable of Wolverhampton, and wardens may refuse permission to persons living near who have been provided with domestic shelters. Day nurseries for children of women engaged on war work are opening in Birmingham.

NORTHERN IRELAND (Belfast) There is deep indignation at the sinking of the evacuee ship bound for Canada. The public is watching developments in the Mediterranean, and there is speculation as to the future policy of Spain. The appeal by the Minister of Aircraft Production for continued work in factories after the sounding of sirens is welcomed here as encouraging workers to intensify their efforts.

LONDON

Londoners trying to carry on as cheerfully and normally as possible, but many asking 'Can nothing be done to stop this night bombing?' Main concern still centres round shelter arrangements and re-billeting the homeless. Criticism reported from Bethnal Green, Stepney and Bermondsey over Rest Centres and rehousing of homeless, but matters are improving, though somewhat slowly. Outer London boroughs coping with evacuees sent to their areas, but social workers feel that rehousing rather than billeting would be more acceptable; local Councils need to take more drastic steps about requisitioning empty premises. More workers of the right type still needed in Rest Centres and shelters. Great bitterness expressed over sinking of liner taking children to Canada; it is feared that this tragedy may upset the whole overseas evacuation scheme. Social worker visiting hop fields at weekend suggests that East-Enders might be allowed to stay in hop field hutments rather than return to devastated areas.

TUESDAY 24 SEPTEMBER 1940

1. In London people remain determined, but cheerfulness varies. People are anxiously considering night life in shelters under winter conditions.

2. The King's speech was generally praised, and the creation of the George Cross and Medal has been widely welcomed.

3. Reports show that most people feel that the evacuation of children to the Dominions should proceed. To many the torpedoing was felt as a challenge to go ahead.

4. Rumours and exaggerated stories continue: in particular there are stories of poisonous substances dropped from enemy planes and of 'secret weapons' with which we shall eventually stop night bombing.

5. There is a steady drift towards public and away from private shelters.

6. Except in certain areas invasion talk has receded into the background.

7. 'Refugees' continue to move into the country round London. Here a general comment is 'no one has learned anything from the problems and failures of last September'.

POINTS FROM REGIONS

NORTH-EASTERN (Leeds) The King's speech was widely listened to and has been the subject of much favourable comment; many people seem to have expected him to announce grave news, and so the speech came as a relief. The new George Cross undoubtedly meets a general demand for recognition of civilian heroism. The sinking of the 'Mercy' ship is much discussed and the questions 'Why was it not convoyed the whole way?' and 'Was it convoyed at all?' are being asked. There are rumours of poisonous substances being dropped by enemy planes.

EASTERN (Cambridge) The effect of the King's broadcast has been particularly marked on women. The news of the ship carrying evacuees to Canada has aroused considerable anger; one reaction is 'I thought it would happen.' The publication of pictures showing damage by the RAF to German-occupied territory has been effective, but there is criticism of the small number and poor quality of the photographs. Criticism that vivid pictures illustrating conditions in an Underground railway tunnel published in a Sunday picture paper are a useful gift to German propagandists.

SOUTHERN (Reading) The exodus of refugees from London continues, and although the great majority is far from defeatist their stories support newspaper criticism that ARP preparations have been unequal to the emergency. There is renewed criticism of Chamberlain's continued presence in the Government. Some resentment is felt among workers at the alleged unwillingness of the middle classes to receive refugees. There is keen satisfaction that we have taken the initiative at Dakar. Intellectual circles eagerly await news from Egypt. Reports from South Coast cities which have been bombed indicate that the exodus has been small. Rumour, which is rife, concentrates upon invasion and damage due to raids. The proportion of Jews among evacuees is causing anti-Semitic talk.

WALES (Cardiff) Interest still centres around the bombing of London, and admiration is expressed for the courage of Londoners. There is some exaggeration of damage in bombed areas by people enlarging upon their experiences. Reports from North Wales express uneasiness in regard to the slowness of civil defence preparations by local authorities. America's increased friendliness gives satisfaction, and there is hope that all efforts are being made to rally Morocco to de Gaulle. The recent broadcast talk on 'Rumour' was much appreciated and there is a call for similar talks in Welsh, and for talks on the Egyptian situation. Rumours of invasion persist. Haw-Haw's alleged references to local places have a disturbing effect.

SOUTH-EASTERN (Tunbridge Wells) Complaints of the immunity with which enemy bombers fly over towns by night are still on the increase. Despite denials of reports of attempted invasion, the belief in the attempts is still widespread. There is some uneasiness over the system of warnings, in view of the fact that this morning two fairly large formations of enemy bombers circled over the town some minutes after 'Raiders passed' had been given, and when hundreds of school children were setting off for school. People in Canterbury are asking for Anderson shelters left in evacuated coastal towns. There is some renewal of talk of the Government going to Canada.

LONDON

Morale still steady, but transport difficulties remain one of the greatest problems for London workers. West End staffs feel that Government does not cope with disrupted communications efficiently. Shelter problems still acute but Home Security's statement issued yesterday has given a certain amount of reassurance; Willesden contact, however, states that surface shelters in this area will not be blast-proof as poor material has been used. Tubes in some places said to be more crowded than ever. Rest Centres generally are said to be improving. Women with young children still asking to be sent to a safe area and seem to be unaware of the various Government schemes. Factory supervisor, Clerkenwell, with depots all over London reports that his Home Guard numbering 400 are still without uniforms and arms and are losing interest; he states that some large firms have disbanded their units because of this. Land mines are still giving rise to much talk and exaggerated stories about their effects are spreading. The question of liability for rents and rates by people whose homes are damaged or who must leave on account of time bombs is causing a good deal of anxiety in Willesden. Difficulty is experienced in getting hot meals in some districts in East End and more mobile canteens and kitchens would ease the situation considerably.

WEDNESDAY 25 SEPTEMBER 1940

POINTS FROM REGIONS

NORTHERN (Newcastle) As a result of the sinking of the *City of Benares* there have been a number of cancellations for overseas evacuation in Middlesbrough; on the other hand, one or two statements have been received that parents think there is serious risk for their children whether they go or stay. The news of General de Gaulle and Dakar is considered confusing. Criticism is voiced of the regular publication in the press of pictures showing widespread damage in London. There is said to be confusion in the minds both of people and traders as to the methods of imposition of the Purchase Tax. Rumours that the bodies of German soldiers are being washed up on the east coast are prevalent.

NORTH MIDLAND (Nottingham) As a result of hearsay, correspondence and newspaper pictures, exaggerated stories of damage to London are being spread. More complaints are received of the poor reception of broadcasts, and it is suggested that as a consequence people are inclined to listen to German stations which are clearly heard. There is dissatisfaction at COs being able to derive financial advantages through exemption. There are reports of the freedom with which soldiers speak in canteens and elsewhere.

MIDLAND (Birmingham) There is little to indicate that the torpedoing of the *City of Benares* has caused opposition to trans-Atlantic evacuation, and it is felt that such misfortunes are exceptional. A mutual fund for helping people suffering air-raid damage has been started at Rubery, near Birmingham; Coventry is also making good progress with a fund to provide supplementary assistance to that offered by the Government.

NORTHERN IRELAND (Belfast) It is generally thought that the RAF is inflicting heavier damage on Germany than is being received by London and south-east England. The possibility of invasion is still discussed. There is puzzlement over the situation at Dakar. The Belfast deputation which has been studying ARP organisation in London has returned full of praise for the fortitude of Londoners in air raids.

LONDON

Responsible people in the East End say emphatically that women, children and old people should be got out of the badly raided districts; many of the women already show signs of great nervousness and fatigue; there is a lot of bitter feeling about the Government's slowness in coping with the emergency, the enormous difficulties of which are not realised. Tremendous crowds again used Tube stations for sleeping last night. An observer remarked on orderliness of crowds; the obvious relief of mothers at feeling safe; that the kindness of LPTB workers was much appreciated. From Aldwych it is reported that though the tunnel is not yet officially opened, enormous crowds spent the night there, and the overflow was accommodated in Aldwych House. Observer visiting a Hackney Rest Centre reports that workers are worried about hygienic conditions, as people are not examined for contagion and infection, and bedding is used by different people on successive nights; also need for more workers as present system of two teams of three people on twenty-four-hour shifts is too exhausting. The need for keeping track of people who have evacuated or changed their address continues; Citizens' Advice Bureaux have many enquiries from men of the Services home on leave who are unable to trace their relatives; from Poplar a case is reported of nearly 1,000 people departing in charabancs from the West End to the country, and not even husbands knew where their wives were going.

THURSDAY 26 SEPTEMBER 1940

POINTS FROM REGIONS

NORTH-EASTERN (Leeds) Dakar has had an unsettling effect on morale, and among the questions which are being asked are: 'Is our Intelligence

Service any good?' and 'Are the Free French full of Fifth Columnists?' Londoners coming north are said to be spreading exaggerated reports of air-raid damage, and there is much talk of deep shelters. The butter ration cut is accepted philosophically. All the papers contain letters demanding reprisals on Berlin.

EASTERN (Cambridge) Although there is fatigue, the morale of the public remains high, but there is considerable disquiet over the incident at Dakar. There is a widespread feeling that the action has been a half-hearted one, and in some quarters it is felt that de Gaulle took the initiative without the full support of our Government. The general view is that it is high time to avoid military operations which will give repetitions of Dunkirk and Somaliland. The Dakar incident and the loss of the *City of Benares* has caused the first diversion from interest in London. At present people do not seem sufficiently confident to allow their children to take part in overseas evacuation.

SOUTHERN (Reading) The failure at Dakar commands public interest, and many feel that it will have a decisive effect on the attitude of North Africa and possibly the Arab world. 'Why did we allow the French ships through the Straits of Gibraltar?' 'Why attempt the Dakar expedition unless we are prepared to see it through?' are typical of the questions being asked. There is criticism of the Government in a number of quarters over the lack of deep shelters, and shelters suited to winter conditions. There seems to be some muddle in the public mind about the necessity for working after the sirens, and some parts of the Region, Eastleigh in particular, have apparently refused to do so.

SOUTH-WESTERN (Bristol) The sinking of the *City of Benares* has caused anger; there is report of some demand for better convoying from Weston-super-Mare, and the general attitude in Plymouth is that the risk is worth taking. News of raids on Berlin have been received with jubilation. West Cornwall complains that Nazi airmen have a free play over the district, and Exeter also alleges a lack of defence of the city. There is a complaint from Bristol of the inadequacy of supplies of commodities affected by the Limitation of Supplies Act, said to be due to the influx of evacuees.

NORTH-WESTERN (Manchester) There is general disgust over the failure at Dakar. Reports of 'beating off' raiders do not completely offset the deep impression produced by stories of the raids which are in circulation. Merseyside still wants to know why it cannot have its share of credit for standing up to night bombing. The cut in the butter ration is not too well received, and it is felt there is 'too much anxiety to sugar the pill'.

SOUTH-EASTERN (Tunbridge Wells) The King's broadcast and the announcement of the George Cross was warmly praised. The voluntary evacuation scheme from Eastbourne has worked well, and the task of feeding men left in the town without their families has been well tackled. The fixing of the curfew at a reasonable hour in Brighton has minimised objections. A report from Sheerness says that there was a shortage of many foodstuffs last week, particularly margarine. There seems to be a general demand for employers to pay wages not later than Thursday. The general opinion is that the reduced ration of butter is very small, although people are not unduly worried.

WALES (Cardiff) The failure at Dakar is felt to be the biggest blow since the fall of France, and in some quarters it is felt that the French contingent in this country is more of a liability than an asset. People are saying: 'the cruisers should never have been allowed to pass through the Straits of Gibraltar', and the resultant loss of prestige is causing concern. That there should be any consideration for the Vichy government is strongly criticised.

LONDON

Continued belief in many districts that public surface shelters are not safe and people use Tube stations instead; last night the Tubes are reported to have been as crowded as ever. It is felt by East End social workers that the Government's scheme should include the evacuation of old people. The work of voluntary organisations in stricken areas has done much to prevent the breaking down of morale. In Croydon, it is reported that as a result of constant bombing, many people are wanting to leave and already many mothers and children are taking advantage of the Government's scheme. Women with children of school age, who have made their own billeting arrangements, are refused free railway vouchers, and they feel that this is unfair. Despite recent damage which has left many Silvertown workers homeless, their morale has improved since they have been allowed to continue working after the 'Alert'. From many districts comes praise of the work of demolition squads; there is some public comment that their numbers are small and instruments primitive. In bombed areas of Kensington there is reported to have been much neighbourly help for raid victims. Some discontent is reported among black-coated workers over compensation allowed for clothes damaged through air raids. Resentment heard expressed against first class passengers who show displeasure when third class passengers overflow into their compartments. There are complaints that workers losing their jobs as a result of their place of employment being damaged by air raids cannot claim unemployment benefit for the first nine days.

FRIDAY 27 SEPTEMBER 1940

POINTS FROM REGIONS

NORTHERN (Newcastle) In some circles the strongest dissatisfaction is expressed over the Dakar incident; interest in Africa has been strong and with a victory eagerly awaited, disappointment is correspondingly acute. There is evidence of a steady growth in the demand for reprisals on the German civilian population, although the strength of the demand varies from one quarter to another. The danger of invasion is rapidly receding from public interest. The problem of earlier closing for cinemas and public houses appears to be solving itself as attendances thin out rapidly as the evening draws on.

NORTH MIDLAND (Nottingham) Operations at Dakar are being talked about in contemptuous terms in Nottingham. A Rutland report suggests that many people wish Hitler would try invasion soon, as it would greatly shorten the war. There is increasing evidence of public approval of raids on Berlin. Some complaints have been heard from farmers about officials giving instructions on the ploughing-up campaign, who appear to have little knowledge of practical farming. The hope is expressed that the King, Queen and the Prime Minister have adequate shelter accommodation.

SOUTH-WESTERN (Bristol) There is general feeling that we have suffered a loss of prestige through the Dakar affair. A report from Trowbridge suggests that the torpedoing of the *City of Benares* has reinforced the feeling that children going overseas run as much risk as those staying at home. Bristol stood up magnificently to the heavy raid on Wednesday, and there is warm praise for the defence and repair squads. The release of the name of Bristol in connection with the raid has had a good effect. Rumours about the result of the raid, particularly with regard to casualties and damage, are flourishing, but not as bad as might have been expected. The difficulties of marketing and the present downward trend of prices paid to farmers appear to be having a bad effect.

MIDLAND (Birmingham) Those who a few weeks ago were not in favour of bombing German towns unless they contained military objectives are now whole-heartedly in favour of reprisals for the wanton attacks on London. It is felt that the Assistance Board should make generous initial allowances to those whose furniture has been destroyed. It is generally considered that nothing should have stopped us from bringing the Dakar expedition to a proper conclusion.

NORTHERN IRELAND (Belfast) The rescue of young evacuees believed lost is welcomed enthusiastically. The Dakar incident is still discussed, but the statement by de Gaulle has in some measure allayed uneasiness. Talk of invasion possibilities is diminishing. There is great confidence in the effectiveness of RAF action over Germany.

LONDON

Reports from many districts still show the spirit of London is extremely good, even where people have suffered seriously. Urgent need for more Information Officers and Bureaux of Information such as CABs in bombed areas to set people's minds at rest about what help they can and should obtain if rendered homeless. Transport difficulties cause much inconvenience to workers, and also to housewives who live some distance from shopping centres, but these inconveniences are cheerfully faced. Air raids without warning are causing some dismay and discontent in Fulham. Several areas report that people still prefer to use Tubes or trench shelters in preference to nearer surface shelters provided for them. Hammersmith reports difficulties over rehousing East End homeless as most wish to go to country; men who have lost their jobs said to be particularly anxious to do this. Many enquiries of extension of evacuation for mothers and families in areas other than those for which provision is at present made, also for aged and crippled. Community centre in Westminster struggling to keep club facilities going for young people as long hours in shelters are tedious. Mill Hill reports excellent co-operation amongst various official and unofficial bodies in district tackling billeting of people from bombed areas; local officials apply to voluntary organisations for suitable workers; East-Enders rehoused in empty houses in preference to being billeted, with furniture etc. provided by residents; each house containing several families has a 'godmother' in charge to see that all works smoothly. Several districts report that many people who can are moving out of London, not from panic but because they feel it is the most sensible thing to do. North Kensington Community Centre communal kitchen now provides 600 mid-day dinners for workers and children in neighbourhood in spite of difficulties such as water being cut off temporarily. Of large communal shelters in Stepney, one (Fruit Exchange shelter – holding 5,000 people) is much improved with extra conveniences and small first-aid post set up by local initiative; Tilbury shelter remains unhealthy and insanitary.

NO 1: MONDAY 30 SEPTEMBER TO MONDAY 7 OCTOBER 1940

REPORTS RECEIVED ON GENERAL MORALE

1. GENERAL COMMENTS

Morale in general continues good. 'Londoners have been more cheerful than for many weeks, partly because the more depressed have evacuated themselves, partly because raids "are not so terrible once you have got used to them", and partly because invasion seems to be more remote and we are hitting Berlin hard.' At the same time, 'sleeplessness and difficulty in "standing" raids are correlated with poor morale', and 'in general women are taking raids worse than men'.

In Yorkshire 'a frequent comment is "We shall get it some day", and people are calmly prepared for trouble'. 'Letters from London, Lancashire and other parts show that morale is high among the people.' At Exeter 'there is some jumpiness, but no sign of defeatism', and 'morale is still good' in Wales. In Northern Ireland 'the general tone of confidence prevails', and letters out 'continue to show a smiling but grim determination to win the war'. In Aberdeen 'which has suffered more severely from raiders in the last few weeks than any other Scottish city, the people seem to think it wrong to complain about the little they have suffered compared with London'. In spite of 'the draining away of man-power into the Services from the Outer Isles (of Scotland) and the heavy casualties among them, there is no defeatism, but the people are dispirited and feel isolated'.

2. SPECULATION ABOUT THE FUTURE
(INCLUDING PEACE AIMS)

Discussion of *invasion* is receding. It was only mentioned twice in 300 reports on prominent topics of conversation over bookstalls. What talk there is follows the line that 'we are scotching the invasion threat'.

It is a notable fact that 'wherever air raids have intensified, people's attitude to the future has become a short-term one'. This applies not only to *peace aims*, which for the past week have hardly been mentioned at all, but also to the ultimate road to victory. There is still speculation about the unpleasantness, boredom and danger of the coming winter's black-out and bombing, but people seem now to be living from day to day.

One future event is widely desired – *reprisals*. 'The desire is much stronger than anything shown in the newspapers.' It is the third commonest subject discussed at bookstalls, the only commoner subjects being the London raids and RAF exploits. This feeling also comes out strongly in the Postal Censorship: 'Fury against the Germans is strongly expressed, and there are many demands for either indiscriminate bombing or invasion of that country.' At the same time, Regional Information Officers record little on the subject – suggesting that the feeling is common mainly among the lower levels of the people, while thinking people are satisfied with the official policy. The strength of the feeling must however be recognised.

3. ALARMIST AND DESPONDENT TALK

The alarmist stories of damage to London spread by refugees are declining. 'At first, they were led to do this so as to excuse and justify their flight from London, as the papers were speaking each day of their marvellous courage in staying put. But as the number of refugees swelled – it is now practically impossible to get a room anywhere within 70 miles of London – the need for self-justification vanished, and alarmist stories have become much less conspicuous.' Wild talk of devastation by refugees is still reported from Yeovil and Leeds.

4. RUMOURS

Rumour has been 'at a moderate level this week, tending to decrease towards the end of the week'. At only two out of 50 bookstalls has an increase been noted. Exaggerated versions of raid damage (apart from those spread by refugees) still circulate. The striking rumours have been:

(a) that Reginald Foort, Charlie King, Charlie Kunz, or some other popular musician, has been interned for signalling to the enemy through the medium of broadcast dance tunes. This rumour appears to be based directly on the theme of the George Formby film *Let George Do It* generally released this week.

(b) that the Germans have been dropping a poisoned cobweb substance from planes. This rumour is rapidly dying.

(c) that invasion has been attempted and failed. This also is declining, though it is 'still surprisingly widespread in the Northern Region', and is mentioned in Surrey.

(d) Haw-Haw rumours of places bombed or to be bombed.

(e) that a 'high official has said the war will probably be over by Christmas'.

5. ANTI-SEMITISM

At the beginning of the bombing of London, anti-Semitism was seen both in the East End, particularly in certain shelters, and in areas receiving evacuees. The Postal Censorship at Reading records it in Oxford. 'The Jews are well up in the front of the evacuees as usual.' More detailed studies showed that the feeling was out of all proportion to the Jews arousing it, and it is no longer on the increase. Further, there was no marked difference in behaviour between Jews and Cockneys; the Jews were, however, more conspicuous for obvious reasons. It is reported that 'in London bad bombing is sometimes followed by an increase in anti-Semitism – for example in the Kilburn area at the end of last week'.

REPORTED REACTIONS TO WAR EXPERIENCES

1. AIR RAIDS

(A) GENERAL REACTIONS

Raids continue to be faced bravely. They are the main subjects of comment both in postal intercepts and in bookstall conversations. The typical picture is shown in a report from Maidstone: 'The effects of Friday's very bitter raid when many were killed and more rendered homeless makes me say morale here is very high despite signs of physical exhaustion. Neighbourly generosity has been much in evidence.' 'The degree of nervous shock among those rendered homeless is extremely small. Many overcome the blow apparently by telling exciting tales of what happened and of their escape. Those who are depressed are so largely because of loved ones killed or injured.' 'Often Union Jacks, pictures of the King and Queen, heather, and horse-shoes are put up on damaged property.'

The overdrawn picture of 'stricken London' painted by the papers has now been partially corrected, as a result of the recent tour of London by provincial journalists, but not before the overdrawn picture had had one beneficial effect. The provinces had been prepared for the very worst and their attitude may be summed up in the phrase 'if London can take it, so can we'. From Dundee comes the sentiment – 'if only they would give us a turn, they might give London a night's rest'.

'A new and interesting tendency is that, in heavily raided areas, feelings have tended to become much more localised. Whereas two weeks ago, a raid on London upset the whole of London, today Streatham or Stepney scarcely worry at all if there have been a great many bombs dropped on Shoreditch or Lewisham.' Further, 'two or three calm nights in one area send morale right up in that area'.

Landmines are 'still much discussed and exaggerations of their effects are common'. The following is typical: 'Here at Greenford the "Load of Hay" Inn was demolished by a landmine. Another totally demolished 6 houses just off Western Avenue. But as I write, this cinema (the Granada) is still quite full, so the people here do not seem unduly disturbed. A few have left the town, but refugees from other districts have made up their number.' 'Landmines are said to have been dropped round Willesden, and last week some people coming out of a cinema thought one was a parachutist and rushed towards it with dire results.' The report goes on to ask for a public announcement, but there are apparently security reasons preventing this, and the knowledge of mines has been widely spread by police and wardens so that such a mistake is unlikely to recur. At the same time, the absence of mention of the mines in the press and on the radio is said to be 'reawakening a general suspicion about air raid and other news'.

(B) ATTITUDE TO AERIAL DEFENCE

The presence or absence of an AA barrage and obvious fighter defences contributes much to the attitude to bombing adopted by the public. A report from Luton says: 'It is the dropping of bombs without any retaliation by gunfire which is getting on people's nerves; one woman down from London told me she felt far safer in London with the guns going off than she does here "hearing German planes come and go as they please".' Again from Bristol: 'A large-scale air-battle over Bristol had a remarkably stimulating effect on the thousands who watched the enemy planes being routed by our fighters.' From Edinburgh comes the following report: 'Edinburgh has had raids by single bombers during the last two nights, and many are still unaware of the difficulties in dealing with night raiders. The absence of AA fire is commented on with indignation. Parents are alarmed at what they consider to be a failure to sound warnings in time (the night before last there was no warning, and last night the warning followed a few minutes after a bomb). It might be wise to make a special explanatory statement on the comparative absence of AA fire and fighters to the Scottish public, which has so far suffered comparatively little.' The increasing barrage in London is universally welcomed, and some actually complained of insomnia on Sunday night when both barrage and bombs were missing.

(C) SLEEP

Detailed studies on sleep in air raids have been made by the War-time Social Survey and Mass Observation. Their conclusions may be summarised thus:

From September 12th to October 3rd, the number of people who got no sleep at all has fallen from 31% to 3%. Approximately ⅔ of Londoners are now probably getting more than 4 hours' sleep, while ⅓ are getting less than 4 hours' sleep. In the poorer areas, for example Shoreditch, the figures are less satisfactory – ½ getting less than 4 hours' sleep, and only 21% getting more than 6 hours' sleep. The factors which enable people to get more than 6 hours' sleep are first a sense of security, and secondly proper beds or mattresses and bedding. These two are of approximately equal importance. Assuming 7½ hours to be the minimum period of combined sleep and rest which is compatible with health over a long period, 71% of the people of Shoreditch are getting too little of both. Misplaced chivalry is causing children (who sleep anywhere) and women (who can sleep during the day) to be given the best places for sleeping, while men (who have to work during the day) are still often left standing or sitting all night.

(D) SHELTERS

A detailed study on shelters has been made by Mass Observation. A few of the main points which emerge are as follows:

In early days of intensive bombing of London, the number of people going to outside shelters or Anderson shelters increased. It has now decreased again, and on September 26th, 71% slept in their own homes, 25% in their own shelters, and 4% in public shelters (4% is approximately equivalent to 250,000 people). The majority of those who stayed at home slept either on their ground floors or in their basements. (A repeat investigation on September 26th gave a similar result.) Anderson shelters were popular mainly because of their nearness to home, and their homeliness. Brick shelters are still much the most unpopular type, though in the East End their popularity is on the increase – perhaps because they are relatively substantial compared with the homes of the people themselves. The objections to brick shelters are mainly on the grounds that they are no better than ordinary houses. Trench shelters are popular, mainly because they are 'underground' and therefore, people think, safer. Tubes are considered completely safe. The absence of sound is welcomed. Those who do not use them give as their reasons, fear of panic and fear of being buried. The most popular reason for staying at home was that 'you were not safe anywhere'. People who use shelters at night tend to do so regularly and to use the same one. They take some bedding with them, but little food, and little to occupy their time.

(E) EAR PLUGS

Only 10% of those who have bought or made ear plugs use them. They are usually given up because the person feels shut off from the world, or because of physical discomfort. Those who use them regularly are enthusiastic. In view of the free distribution of plugs now in progress, it would seem that the public needs urging to give the plugs a fair trial if (but only if) sleep is not obtained without them.

(F) EVACUATION AND THE RETURN OF EVACUEES

A preliminary report of a detailed study by Mass Observation made in 50 towns and hamlets around London, with special reference to Oxford and Burford, reveals the following points:

The evacuees have been much more warmly received this time (as compared with a year ago). Not only were the hosts more sympathetic, but the evacuees were glad to be out of the heavily raided areas. Nevertheless there is friction between adults. There is much profiteering, especially in hotels and boarding houses. There is much less talk of the dirtiness

of the evacuees. Indeed, in some places, they are very favourably compared with the last lot (though in fact there is little difference). The billeting officers are much less criticised this time than last time. The
present relatively satisfactory situation needs watching, and above all
careful arrangements are needed in each home so that the evacuees
and hosts do not 'get on each others' nerves' as time goes on.

There is a steady trickle of people returning to London, including
the East End. The reasons given are: dislike of being away from home
and familiar surroundings, the decline in raids in London, the barrage
makes it easier to stick London, difficulty in getting good billets, and
difficulties with hosts. Those returning are mostly young people, but
not children.

A study by the Social Survey shows that the elderly and infirm need (and
want) special consideration in raids and evacuation.

(G) NEED FOR INFORMATION BUREAUX

Reports from social workers and intelligent observers in heavily raided
areas stress the need for centralised bureaux to supply information and
help to the homeless after air raids. A typical report says 'There is difficulty
here in obtaining the information needed by those who have lost their
homes through bombing. Here in Maidstone one woman with several children was rendered homeless and destitute. She went to the Town Hall and
was told that nothing could be done for her unless she went to the Ministry
of Labour. These offices were closed during the raid, so in desperation she
sought the help of the *Kent Messenger* newspaper; they promptly contacted
the WVS which rapidly came to the rescue...if our morale is to remain high,
the Authorities must act more quickly in giving help and information
should a similar disaster hit the town.' The report goes on to suggest an MOI
instructional film. The Maidstone woman's experience could be multiplied
(and lengthened) endlessly by reports from the East End of London. A careful study by the War-time Survey in Shoreditch confirms the great need for
more simple information as to what to do in specific difficulties. Information
Bureaux have already been set up at some Town Halls in London boroughs,
and the Citizens' Advice Bureaux continue to do valuable service, but more
centres still appear needed.

REPORTED REACTIONS TO NEWS

1. DAKAR AND DE GAULLE

The provinces, as reflected by reports from Regional Information Officers and Local Information Committees, indicate a violent reaction to the Dakar incident. A typical report comes in telegraphese from the Bury Information Committee: 'Local opinion gravely disturbed by events. Another victory for evacuation. Another muddle, lowering still further our prestige. Whatever explanations may be forthcoming, Dakar should have been taken. The "kid gloves" are still on and people here are very much *rattled and disgusted* by this latest *failure*. Ethical distinction between Frenchmen and Free Frenchmen must not be allowed to interfere with *War Effort*. To win this war we must take the *gloves off and fight*. "Those who are not for us are against us." Remember this and apply it.' The same types of report come from the Nottingham and Chesterfield Information Committees, and the latter adds 'it has been noticed that news of a success is attributed to military and naval sources, while news of a failure is attributed to the Ministry of Information', thus once again demonstrating the Ministry's value as a scapegoat for the public. From Wales comes the report that the public remembers the stress placed on the importance of the capture of Dakar *before* it was attempted, and it is hoped that we will not neglect to take strong measures when the appropriate time comes.

By contrast, London's public, fully occupied by their nightly blitzkrieg, have shown little interest in the whole matter. The same is true of the vast mass of largely inarticulate people throughout the country, as reflected by the Postal Censorship and Mass Observation. The week's Postal Censorship says 'almost no mention of the Dakar incident, or of General de Gaulle'. 'To the majority, Dakar is only a place somewhere in Africa which they have heard of now for the first time, so that it is of little real significance to most people...Most working-class people regard de Gaulle as a Frenchman who is therefore of less importance than English personalities...Women show a high degree of ignorance of the whole subject; a typical comment is "Oh, the Frenchman, where is he now? He failed, didn't he?"' From Reading, it is reported that 'Dakar seems to interest the white collar man rather than the worker.' Dakar is only mentioned twice as a subject of conversation at bookstalls.

The public reaction to the Dakar incident demonstrates certain important general principles. There is not one public opinion but several, and the cleavage is now much less on political lines than formerly. On the one hand, we have those who are acutely involved in war events, who are therefore little concerned with more remote happenings (in this case the Londoners). On the other hand, we have the vocal more intelligent sections of the provincial public (reflected by the reports from Regional Information Officers and Local Information Committees), and the great inarticulate mass whose thoughts and words only become apparent through the work of the Postal Censorship and Mass Observation. There is yet another cleavage – between men and women.

2. CABINET CHANGES

The Cabinet changes have aroused 'little spontaneous interest', though what interest there is shows satisfaction. 'The general opinion is that it is a good thing to have Morrison at the Home Office. Not much regret at Chamberlain's resignation. There is much discussion on Anderson's transfer. Has he been promoted or demoted?' (Wolsey, factory, Leicester). In Manchester 'the first reaction to the Cabinet changes is good. Public have lost confidence in Anderson and welcome Morrison. Duncan also popular. Most doubt about promotion of Sir Kingsley Wood.' Wales is hopeful that Halifax 'who has been living in a fool's paradise for years' will soon join Chamberlain. Some regret at Chamberlain's departure is reported only from Trowbridge and Birmingham. Bristol is naturally 'delighted at the inclusion of Bevin in the War Cabinet', as he is a Bristol man. Cambridge notes 'there is some increase in party consciousness as a result of the new appointments, and if Mr. Churchill takes over the leadership of the Conservative Party this is likely to be further accentuated'.

3. SINKING OF SEA-VACUEE SHIP

This news was received 'with a gasp of horror, particularly by women. It has appreciably strengthened hatred of the Germans.' In Scotland there was 'a wave of horror and indignation, but surprisingly little comment after the first shock'. 'Blame was sometimes attached to parents who let their children go.' A typical series of comments are reported from Leeds: 'Why don't they print the passenger list? Why were there so few children aboard? Why were there so few passengers in so large a boat? It looks as if there must have been cargo aboard. Why are they letting rich people get out of the country?' The feeling about the matter has now died down, and up to the present no public reaction to the closure of the sea-vacuee scheme has been reported.

4. JAPAN AND THE AXIS

'Absorption with home affairs, plus the difficulty many people have in understanding abstract foreign affairs, has resulted in the Axis–Japan pact having very little effect. It does not seem to change existing conditions at all.' Regional Information Officers confirm this statement. The public has failed to connect the pact with the United States embargo on exports of scrap metal to Japan. From Reading comes the following report: 'People think Japan will not force the pace until compelled to do so by American pressure. An early announcement that the Burma Road will be reopened and that China will be given all the assistance we can spare is hoped for. Any further attempt at appeasement would certainly meet with a very hostile reception.'

The Brenner meeting has created neither interest, alarm, nor despondency.

5. NEWS PRESENTATION

'There are persistent complaints that the news is too scanty and too general. Although it is generally regarded as accurate, it is criticised because it sometimes suppresses or tones down bad news, and does not tell us enough.' There is a strong demand for the naming of places raided in daylight and for exact figures of casualties, so as to discount rumours. 'There is some feeling in Leeds about the fact that official communiques no longer give the number of air-raid casualties.' The Chief Constable of Kent states: 'Censorship continues to be accepted as necessary, but when the name of a place bombed is mentioned in the news it reduces speculation and anxiety, whereas a vague reference naturally leads to large numbers of unnecessary enquiries by relatives and friends.'

As a result of intensive study of public reactions over the past 3 months, it is reported that 'the prestige of the press, which has been steadily falling for a long time, has steadied up in the past week or two. This is partly because it has not been running any campaign alleged to be on the behalf of the public though actually not in sympathy with their actual feelings; partly because it actually has represented public feeling over shelters and care of the homeless; and partly because the general tone of the news has been good (the public often tend to blame the press for bad news).'

NO 2: MONDAY 7 OCTOBER TO MONDAY 14 OCTOBER 1940

REPORTS RECEIVED ON GENERAL MORALE

1. GENERAL COMMENTS

Morale continues to be good, and its generally satisfactory state is shown by reports from many sources. There are, however, certain localised patches of depression, which are directly associated with heavy bombing and lack of aerial defences. 'Though morale maintains a very high standard, at the same time there is uneasiness and some degree of gloom in areas which have undergone persistent bombing.' 'Hastings people are depressed as the town is not defended, for it has no military importance. German planes often machine-gun the streets, and the town is half dead for hours at a time.'

In the first half of the week there was some complacency towards the war in general and towards night bombing. This attitude towards the war had been encouraged by certain official speeches (e.g. Mr. Attlee's), while the feeling about night bombing was influenced by newspaper suggestions that the defeat of the night bomber was 'only a matter of time'. Prof. Andrade, in the *Daily Telegraph*, suggested that 'there is good reason to believe that secret inventions are bringing us nearer the time when the Germans will lose so high a percentage of their night bombers that they may cease raiding'. Later in the week the intensified raids dissipated this complacency and people took a rather more gloomy view. Though a minority seem to believe the winter weather will prevent enemy raids, the coming long winter evenings ahead are being more discussed.

Three different Postal Censorship reports say that the bombing of London has increased pro-British feeling in Eire.

2. SPECULATION ABOUT THE FUTURE (INCLUDING PEACE AIMS)

Our generalisation last week that 'wherever air raids have intensified people's attitude to the future has become a short-term one' still holds good, but at the same time a higher proportion of people are reported to be expecting a long war. This is said to be due in part to Rumanian and Japanese events. A group of young men under calling-up age anticipated a war of 3 to 6 years, while a group of older men thought 2 to 3 years more likely. The view that intensive bombing produces short-term thought is supported by the report that black-out fears are greater in the provinces than in London.

An interesting comment on *peace aims* comes from a Ministry speaker, who says that audiences are determined to win the war but are apprehensive about what will happen when peace comes. Will there be more unemployment? Will everyone bear their fair share in the work of rehabilitation? Will the peace terms sow the seeds of another war? Will justice be done to ex-Service men and their dependents? Similar comments are reported by working men between the ages of 18 and 20 when asked what they will do after the war.

Most reports show distinctly less talk about *reprisals* this week. This is attributed to satisfaction with the Prime Minister's statement, and the belief that 'the RAF is delivering shrewder blows on Germany than they on us'. Our reports directly disagree with an analysis of the *Daily Express* postbag which is stated to show that 5 out of 6 people now want reprisals. At the same time, it is said that 'reprisals' are not an ethical problem; indiscriminate bombing has caused serious economic dislocation, and this has a real military value to the enemy. Many people feel that our pilots gaining experience over Germany might go in for the random bombing of large German towns, and that the loss of sleep and production would be well worth while. Another type of comment is: 'Just because I know some chap in Germany is being bombed in his bed, I don't enjoy being bombed in mine.'

3. ALARMIST AND DESPONDENT TALK

The alarmist stories of refugees continue to decline. The refugees seem to be recovering from their nervous strain, but some who have failed to 'get a rise' out of their hosts are now saying 'they don't know what it's like'.

In a heavy daylight raid on Bristol there were 90 fatalities, but in the official figures issued in the Bristol area only those dying in that area – 30 in number – were mentioned. Many more deaths occurred in the Filton area. As a result of the Bristol announcement, exaggerated figures were in general circulation and there was a belief that the facts had been deliberately suppressed. This clearly shows the kind of difficulties which the authorities have to anticipate.

4. RUMOURS

There is little change in the amount of rumour this week. Only from one bookstall out of 20 is an increase reported. The most significant rumour has been that thousands of people in East London or in Liverpool have signed a petition for immediate peace overtures. This rumour is reported from Kettering and Bristol, where it is said to be current among 'usually reputable people'. This story may have been based on the deep shelter petitions organised by the Communist Party, but it is also one of the rumours which the BBC monitoring service report as being instigated by the German radio. It is suggested from Bristol that listening to the German radio has increased because the BBC is so much off the air these days, but we have no certain knowledge of this.

Rumours of frustrated invasion are still current in many places – the Orkneys, the Shetlands, Brighton, Dover, Isle of Wight, Inverness – and letters with circumstantial accounts of thousands of bodies washed up on our shores contain abuse of the Ministry of Information for withholding the news. The enemy radio has tried very strongly to counter these rumours of frustrated invasion but without success.

There are still a number of the usual Haw-Haw rumours about places to be bombed, and a new version is that certain industrial concerns in Cardiff have not been bombed because of the German capital invested in them. There are also rumours that the AA defences of certain places, e.g. Falmouth, have been taken away to protect London.

5. ANTI-SEMITISM

Anti-Semitism is still reported in evacuation areas, even as far afield as Pembrokeshire and Cardiganshire. In the big area round London to which many East-Enders have evacuated, anti-Semitic remarks are common. A new development is that London Jews who have stayed behind are themselves showing signs of turning against the Jewish evacuees. In some evacuation areas people are refusing to give billets to Jews. In certain London shelters the Jews are segregated from the Cockneys, and remarks are made that the Jews arrive earliest at the shelters. Though the strong family and property ties of the Jews naturally cause comments, there is little evidence to suggest that *in fact* Jews are behaving any worse or better than Cockneys. If anything, the naturalised alien minorities tend to arrive at shelters before either Jews or Cockneys.

6. DRINK

The high wages of munition and other workers has aroused fears, particularly in Scotland, of excessive drinking. In bombed areas, however, the public houses are said to be much emptier at an early hour than formerly, and a detailed report on drink in Scotland shows that the position is not serious. There has been a slight but steady decrease in arrests for drunkenness in Scotland since war began but drink prices have increased considerably and it may be that the police are more lenient or more fully occupied than before. In the early days of 'Going to it' there was a good deal of extra drinking because of the high wages and overtime, and the extra strain of the work, but it was mainly among unskilled labourers who had been unemployed for a long time. In the great majority of cases the extra drinking did not last. It is stated that the number of women in Scottish bars (including many in uniform) has considerably increased, but that beer is replacing cocktails. There is some anxiety about alleged excessive drinking by troops in Scotland and there are said to be indications that this is leading to impropriety in a certain number of cases. There is no public agreement about the remedy for the situation; earlier closing has actually been found to increase sales and the 'no treating' rule would be very unpopular. The probable solution is propaganda in favour of mild drinking, and alternative recreations.

REPORTED REACTIONS TO WAR EXPERIENCES

1. AIR RAIDS

(A) GENERAL REACTIONS

This week's reports show that air raids are beginning to be accepted as part of an unpleasant routine. As one letter-writer puts it 'one gets used to everything, and we are no longer frightened; we turn over and go to sleep'. A few people are extremely frightened by the heavy night raids, but many show 'extraordinary resilience'. The behaviour of children is largely determined by that of the grown-ups around them.

A special study of the attitude of those whose homes have been destroyed shows 'an astonishing degree of readjustment, provided they were in a shelter and that none of the family were killed. After a short period of great depression and shock, they wash their hands of past responsibilities and think about starting again, unless they are weak types. But those who have left a habitable home behind find it difficult to start thinking of another; this is increased by the double responsibility.' LCC school teachers who have taken over Rest Centres from the PACs are doing magnificent work. Though untrained in welfare work they are showing initiative, energy and kindness, and the atmosphere of the centres is much improved.

Need for normal work and amusement is felt by many people. 'While we worked at our jobs nervousness and even the knowledge that a raid was on left us completely. But as soon as we dived into the shelters...a feeling of nervousness and danger quickly returned.' Among young people some reversion to normal amusements is shown by a slight increase in the numbers present at dance halls, whist drives etc., 'because it takes you out of yourself'. In London people are not using profitably what leisure they have: in shelters a majority of people do nothing.

There is satisfaction in places such as Manchester, where the AA barrage has improved, but the south coast towns such as Brighton, Hastings and Shoreham are anxious about the apparent absence of AA defences.

(B) SLEEP

The majority of people in heavily bombed areas are not receiving adequate sleep, but an improvement in the situation has been noticed. It seems that a 'genuine adaptation' is taking place. Lord Horder comments on the value of transferring workers to sleep in the country occasionally.

(C) SHELTERS

The press controversy about deep shelters continues, and both central and local authorities are receiving deputations to urge construction of deep shelters. Tenants' Defence Leagues, Vigilance Committees, etc. continue to press for 'better ARP'. Lack of occupation for children in shelters is having a bad effect on them and their mothers. Practical suggestions are urgently needed. The anxiety about the effects of cold and damp in Anderson shelters is still expressed.

2. EVACUATION

Official schemes of evacuation 'on the whole have worked well'. The daily registration of mothers and children in London is now at the rate of 8,000, although the numbers who actually travel are always considerably below full strength.

Much planless evacuation is still going on and causing a great deal of dislocation and some antagonism in many areas. This planless evacuation is largely westwards, particularly into Region VI. The billeting of penniless 'refugees' is made more difficult by the large numbers with money to spend who make their own arrangements.

The reception of evacuees and 'refugees' varies considerably. Local authorities, although complaining of the burden on them, have risen to the emergency with good will and often efficiency. The efforts of voluntary organisations are also highly praised.

Despite their eagerness for jobs, there is some prejudice against employing evacuees 'in case they re-evacuate', but in other areas they are settling down. 'Whatever happens to the majority it seems likely that many of those who have left London will not return to it after the war.'

Complaints about profiteering in billets are not confined to any particular district, but 'the richer type of refugee are mainly affected'. 'Some people with comparatively small incomes rent rooms in safe areas in case they have to evacuate, and so prevent the use of them by those in more urgent need. Residents as well as refugees complain of this.' There is a good deal of criticism that richer homes evade billeting. Arrangements in many rural Rest Centres are unsatisfactory.

3. TRADE AND COMMERCE

The public are still confused and the trade apprehensive about the Purchase Tax, and suggestions have been received that more should be said about its value, 'not only for raising money, but also for decreasing consumption'. 'There is still no significant interest in the tax among the mass of people.' Apprehension is reported in Northern Ireland about whether the people who are thrown out of work by the Purchase Tax will be reabsorbed into war and export industries. It is feared there may be serious unemployment there.

In reception areas in the Southern Region evacuation has caused a temporary shortage of retail goods. The attitude of small retail shop-keepers towards evacuees is not one of whole-hearted approval. Many of the evacuees are not registered for rationing in the shops of their new town. The tradesmen like to serve their regular customers first and the evacuees make this difficult. There are complaints that the quota for tobacconists and confectioners is based on last year's sales and that now the quota should be increased at the expense of some of the London shops.

4. LABOUR

The high wages of armament and defence workers are strongly criticised by some, 'owing to their lavish spending habits'. 'Though a fair proportion of these wages are saved, this is by no means universal.' Reports suggest that Sir Robert Kindersley's radio talks on saving do not mean much to this type of workers, and that influential labour leaders might have a greater appeal for them.

REPORTED REACTIONS TO NEWS

1. DAKAR AND DE GAULLE

Interest in Dakar and de Gaulle has greatly declined though there are a few comments about 'loss of prestige' and 'a shocking fiasco'. De Gaulle's prestige has apparently recovered a little, and some people, when specifically questioned, say that 'he can't be so bad if Churchill thinks he's a good man'. 'The Prime Minister's statement about Dakar seems to have satisfied much of the public.'

2. POLITICAL EVENTS

The only additional comment since last week on the Cabinet changes is surprise that Morrison was left out of the War Cabinet.

The Prime Minister's speech aroused less interest than usual; all comments, apart from those in the press, were favourable. The speech has received less publicity than any previous ones. The greatest interest was shown in the air-raid insurance scheme, but some small householders are worried as they fear the insurance money will not be paid until after the war. People felt that the gloomy tone of the peroration made it ring true, and this was much appreciated. For the first time sympathetic papers criticised a speech of the Prime Minister – the *Mirror*, for its too optimistic note, and the *Herald* 'for its unjustified rebuke of the press'.

3. THE NEAR EAST AND THE FAR EAST

There is but limited interest in Japan. Her attitude is not regarded as a direct threat, but people are concerned because it seems likely that the war will spread still wider in her direction.

Regional Information Officers' reports show public interest and some confusion and anxiety about the Near East. The confusion is confirmed from other sources.

Typical questions which people are asking are: 'Has Russia been squared, so that when the Axis gets to Turkey she will be too intimidated to resist?' 'The Fifth Column and propaganda conquered Rumania without a single shot; are we doing enough in Turkey, Iran and Iraq?' 'Once more we are leaving the initiative to the enemy; why are we not more aggressive towards Italy?' There is some demand for 'educative broadcasts' on the strategic, economic and political problems in the Near East; the public are said to be interested but ignorant.

NEWS PRESENTATION

There is still much criticism of the official air-raid bulletins. People still object to the phrase: 'A few people were killed'; and unnecessary anxiety, aroused when it is vaguely said that 'a large hospital in the London area' or 'a well-known public school in the Home Counties' has been bombed, is commented on in *The Times* and also by the headmaster of Rugby school.

The most severe criticism has been aroused in all parts of London by the official bulletin which stated 'that the raids on Monday night were on a somewhat smaller scale than the previous night', when in fact they were heavier.

Two reports from Scotland criticise a picture of Lambeth people dancing on the ruins of their homes. It is described as 'ghoulish' and 'in the very worst taste'. In general, criticism of the press has slightly increased this week. This is more probably due to bewilderment about the news rather than to antagonism.

NO 3: MONDAY 14 OCTOBER TO MONDAY 21 OCTOBER 1940

REPORTS RECEIVED ON GENERAL MORALE

1. GENERAL COMMENTS

Reports this week show a varying state of morale throughout the country; variations are also noticed among different groups of people in the same places. In Yorkshire, although confidence is strong, there is an 'almost dangerous complacency' (local Labour leader). This is attributed to the absence of raids in the area, and the unconcern of the great mass of people with matters abroad. The propaganda for 'the island fortress' has succeeded almost too well. In the same area intellectual people are said to be depressed because they do not see how bombing Germany can win the war for us, if bombing London cannot win it for the Nazis.

In rural districts and in country market towns, there is little talk of the war.

The big provincial towns, which have been bombed, continue to show determination. On the south coast there is no despondency but some lowering of morale, thought to be due to the cumulative effects of warnings, raids, prolonged tension, long hours of work, the coming of winter, and more indirectly the absence of any spectacular war success.

A lowering of morale is also recorded in London. People say that the barrage seems weaker or at least ineffectual, and, although they are alright now, in a few months' time there will be little left of London or its people. This undercurrent of despondency is recorded in many parts, for example Gillingham, Catford and Lewisham. The depression is often shown by an inability to see any end to the bombing of London. As already reported, local variations of feeling occur within London, and these depend on the severity of the bombing in each area. Thus Streatham, Kilburn and Paddington have been very depressed, while Fulham has been relatively cheerful. A growing concern about London is recorded from the provinces, and people are wondering whether the 'new weapons' so frequently hinted at in the press will really reduce the damage and casualties.

2. SPECULATION ABOUT THE FUTURE
(INCLUDING PEACE AIMS)

Though there have been many press mentions of peace aims, the public have shown little interest in the matter this week. Young people, however, are said to be anxious for an outline of peace aims, and to be assured that there will be no attempt to restore the 'bad old days'; 'they just laugh at Halifax's Crusade stuff – especially as he proceeded to close the Burma Road'. As we noted last week, people in heavily bombed areas tend to look at the present and not the future – 'It doesn't do to look too far forward.'

There is neither fear nor expectation of invasion. The demand for reprisals continues to decline and Beable's 'bomb Berlin' posters have aroused little interest. There are, however, strongly worded demands that we should bomb the Rumanian oil wells, and it is suggested that our hesitancy is due to fear of hurting international financial interests. People wonder also why we do not bomb Italy more heavily as the Italians are considered likely to 'crack' easily. There is criticism of the RAF's failure to raid Germany in bad weather, since this does not prevent the Germans raiding us.

3. RUMOURS

Invasion rumours seem to have ceased, but rumours of excessive air-raid damage are still very prevalent. There are several suggestions that listening to the German wireless is increasing, because the BBC is off the air so much nowadays. Haw-Haw rumours of places bombed or to be bombed are still common, but in no case do they bear any relation to the actual material broadcast from Germany. Rumours are common that certain objects, such as reservoirs, serve to guide German planes, and the public asks why barrages are not concentrated at these points.

4. ALLEGED FIFTH COLUMN ACTIVITIES

The belief that black-out infringements are due to Fifth Columnists is still prevalent, and penalties for the careless use of torches are widely approved. There are still complaints that the lighting of cars and railways is unnecessarily bright and there is even some anxiety about the modified street lighting. Many people contrast the severity shown towards householders with the apparent leniency towards motorists.

5. ANTI-SEMITISM

Anti-Semitism is reported from many places to which refugees have gone. The Jews are accused of booking the best places, paying excessive prices, and buying up businesses outside London.

REPORTED REACTIONS TO WAR EXPERIENCES

1. AIR RAIDS

(A) GENERAL REACTIONS

While the public continues to accept raids as something which, if they cannot be cured, must be endured, there is, particularly in London, a growing undercurrent of anxiety about the probability of continuous raids throughout the winter.

Help for those rendered homeless through raids is still incompletely organized. The first line of air-raid services – ARP, AFS, etc. – work admirably, but the second line has not received the same consideration. 'Too many agencies are concerned in re-billeting, house repairs, compensation, evacuation, pensions, etc., and there is not enough co-ordination between them. What is really required is a new service – Air-Raid Welfare' (Prof. Julian Huxley in a special report containing practical suggestions for the inauguration of such a service).

The expense of burying several members of one family is a very real problem in poor districts, despite the waiving of clergy's fees, etc. As a result, some relatives are refusing to claim bodies, whose burial thus becomes the responsibility of local authorities. The natural distress of relatives in these circumstances is increased by the fact that such burials are often made without coffins. Local Information Committees in London report 'that public feeling would be greatly relieved if local authorities were empowered to make grants in certain cases to those who wish to bury their own dead'.

(B) SLEEP

The improvement noted last week in the amount of sleep people are getting continues. But it is noticeable that few women who might do so make any attempt to sleep during the day.

(C) SHELTERS

Shelter conditions are still a major problem, and although things are getting better, there are still many shelters, particularly in the London area, with unsatisfactory sanitary arrangements and general conditions.

The strain of queuing up for shelters, particularly in wet weather, is noted in several areas, and people hope that it will be possible to allocate space to 'regulars' where this is practicable.

There is great difficulty in keeping track of people who live in shelters, and the NCSS is having much trouble in including these people in the register of evacuated persons which they are compiling. This register is nevertheless 'gathering momentum' gradually. 'On this point poster publicity in shelters would be invaluable.'

Interest in deep shelters has declined this week. There are, however, demands for them in certain quarters, mainly in Scotland, though the agitation here 'seems to be conducted by comparatively small groups'. The heating and damp-proofing of Anderson shelters is still much discussed. Complaints about lack of shelters is reported from Milford Haven, St. Ives and Penzance, Derby and in Ulster schools.

(D) CIVIL DEFENCE SERVICES

Reports show that air-raid wardens are beginning to feel the strain of their duties, although they themselves complain little. But the effect of long periods of duty is showing itself in 'quarrelling and occasional violent scenes'. It has also been pointed out that, although the rest of their equipment is free, no allowance is made for shoe leather, the expense of which is considerable. 'In the poorer parts of Bristol, wardens find the strain on their shoes something real.'

2. EVACUATION

Planned and voluntary evacuation still continues on a large scale. As the number of evacuees grows, difficulties of smooth organisation increase and 'This week the result seems to be more chaotic than ever, especially in South-East England.' A striking trend seems to be increased ill-feeling towards the upper classes 'who are accused of being the first to leave bombed districts, of taking the best places in reception areas, and of refusing to accommodate poorer evacuees'.

Other areas report 'mixed feelings' towards evacuees. Complaints come from both sides, and while 'overcharging for billets' is one source of friction, the refusal of evacuees 'to help in the house' is another.

Overcrowding is still a big difficulty. It is reported from a large number of places, especially the Home Counties.

There are complaints from the London area about the working of the Government scheme of private assisted evacuation, as many old and infirm people are precluded from it by their inability to look for their own billets. This acts as a deterrent to families who refuse to leave dependent relatives behind. Another brake on the process is the lack of hostels in London where the working members of a family may live.

Many unmarried women clerks and shop assistants are leaving their jobs, and are arriving as evacuees in the Eastern Region. Some are reported as saying untruthfully that they have been bombed out of their homes or businesses, and are therefore given free accommodation by the billeting officer. They cannot all be absorbed into local trade, and apply for unemployment benefit, or for help from the UAB or PAC.

3. HEALTH

Considerable anxiety has been shown both in the medical and lay press about the possibility of serious epidemics in shelters. 'Unless effective measures are promptly taken, we foresee that with the approach of winter contagious and infectious diseases may well prove more devastating than the blitzkrieg' (*British Medical Journal*). Illnesses attributed by the public to 'time spent in shelters' are reported from several areas; those mentioned include paratyphoid, typhoid, scarlet fever, and throat troubles. Other diseases which the medical press indicate as dangerous are influenza, pneumonia, diphtheria, poliomyelitis, dysentery, and cerebro-spinal fever. Experts point out that the whole population can easily be immunized against diphtheria and the typhoid group; further, the treatment of sore throats, influenza, pneumonia and cerebro-spinal fever is likely to be much more satisfactory than it used to be, thanks to the new drug, M&B 693, but institutional care, presumably outside London, will certainly be needed for all severe cases. A serious effect on morale may be produced when deep shelterers discover that they are in greater danger from disease than from bombs, since it is likely that the people who use deep shelters and Tubes are those with the poorest morale. The remedies for the situation which have been advocated in the press are as follows:

(i) Compulsory evacuation of all children, non-essential women, and old people. Prof. M. Greenwood in *The Times* stresses particularly the value of dispersal. This must be associated with communal feeding and hostel arrangements for those who remain.

(ii) Compulsory immunisation against diphtheria and typhoid.

(iii) Relief in the country for London's workers and ARP workers at the rate of 2 days and 3 nights per fortnight, as a minimum. (This is strongly stressed in Prof. Huxley's report.)

(iv) In shelters a minimum of 600 cubic feet of air per sleeper, and proper ventilation.

(v) Proper sanitary arrangements in shelters.

(vi) Medical inspection of entrants to shelters, and the isolation of those with temperatures, bad throats, and rashes.

Another shelter danger which is causing public anxiety is the presence of many chronic tuberculosis cases in public shelters. Such cases are often ambulatory and are therefore discharged from hospital when other patients are evacuated. Expert opinion says the close contact between such patients and young children is the most important cause of miliary tuberculosis, a universally fatal disease in children.

4. CIVILIANS AND THE SERVICES

A good many complaints have been made because the rations allowed to soldiers are so large compared with those of the civilians on whom they are billeted.

REPORTED REACTIONS TO NEWS

1. OFFICIAL COMMUNIQUES

There have been many complaints about the delay of the Admiralty in announcing the Mediterranean successes, and in contradicting Nazi claims. There is also some bewilderment about the alleged naval battle off the Isle of Wight, which was announced by the Germans and reported in the London papers, but neither confirmed nor denied officially.

Criticism and concern about official news of aerial warfare and bombing is reported. The fact that German losses are now approximating to those of the British has been realised by the public and they are asking for an explanation; this they would like to come from Joubert or Sinclair.

There are still many comments of the vague announcements of the effects of bombing. These excite both exaggeration and anxiety. It is described as illogical that Buckingham Palace should be named the day it is bombed, while University College has to remain anonymous for a fortnight. In some places, where the local press announces that raids have produced little damage, anxiety is expressed because people fear that this will be a sign for the Germans to pay them another visit.

2. GENERAL DE GAULLE

The feeling about General de Gaulle and the Free Frenchmen is still unenthusiastic. The strong reaction to Dakar has died down, but people are surprised and upset as they now think that the fault lay with the British Navy.

3. PRINCESS ELIZABETH'S SPEECH

About two-thirds of people with whom this has been discussed had heard the speech. The main reaction was mild praise. The outstanding comments were first that the speech had been written for her and was not at all like a child talking, and secondly that her voice was very similar to that of her mother. Her excellent delivery was praised, but the stilted language she used was criticised as stereotyped.

4. ATTITUDE TO POLITICAL LEADERS

A considerable decrease has been noticed in the amount of talk about Mr. Churchill. At one Postal Censorship Centre he is mentioned only one tenth as much as formerly, though, with one exception, all the remarks were favourable. The censor comments that 'whereas in June people seemed to feel that only Churchill stood between them and disaster, now the ordinary people of England have shown that they too could play just as stubborn and important a part. His tremendous popularity seems also to have been a little reduced by Dakar and its not altogether satisfactory explanation.'

There is a growing feeling against Lord Halifax; this has appeared without any fanning by the press. He is regarded as 'not strong enough for the job', 'only fit to be a bishop', 'an obstacle to improved relations with Russia', and 'the cause of our feeble policy in the Balkans, Near East and Far East'.

5. THE NEAR EAST AND THE FAR EAST

The mass of people are said to be worrying little about events in these areas, but the 'white-collared classes' and the more intellectual people are becoming increasingly perplexed. People want to know whether they may look forward to a successful issue in Egypt, or whether they must expect another Somaliland. Some people hope we shall soon bomb the Rumanian oil wells and take aggressive measures against Syria. The sale of oil by British, Dutch and American firms to the Japanese is also criticised.

6. BROADCASTING

Evening listening has certainly decreased, but the extent of this decrease is not yet known. The causes given by listeners are: poor reception; fear that the radio may hide the sirens, and the sounds of planes, bombs, and guns; the need for constant alertness; late arrival at home; earlier bedtime; and lack of radio in shelters. Many people misunderstand why the BBC fades or goes off the air during raids.

There are still complaints that fresh items of news do not get first place in news bulletins, and it is suggested that Sunday bulletins might be more comprehensive and not shorter than those on weekdays, as people have more leisure on Sundays.

NO 4: MONDAY 21 OCTOBER TO MONDAY 28 OCTOBER 1940

REPORTS RECEIVED ON GENERAL MORALE

1. GENERAL COMMENTS

On the whole people in London have been more cheerful this week. This appears to be due to the slackening off of air raids. The ups and downs in cheerfulness still seem to depend first on the amount of local bombing, and secondly on the amount of bombing in the whole country as shown by official bulletins.

A decline in bombing is usually associated with increased interest in general events (rather than local ones), but this has not been noticed during the past week. In casual conversation there has been hardly any mention of the Balkans, Egypt, or France. One Local Information Committee reports that in the first three weeks of October there were more grumbles than during the whole of August and September; this was attributed to diminished fears of invasion.

Anxiety about London's ability to stand up to the cumulative effects of raids throughout the winter is reported from Leeds and Bristol. Some London Information Committees express the same feeling.

A Southampton police report says: 'If large numbers of people, made homeless by raids, are herded together for too long, dissatisfaction and a defeatist spirit creeps in, whether grievances are fancied or real.'

Intensive raids at Coventry are said to have upset the newer and younger factory workers, though elsewhere in the Midland Region severe bombing is being taken with increasing calm.

Compulsory billeting has created strong feeling in certain areas among the middle and upper-middle classes. This infliction of the poor on the better off is epitomised by one of the latter as 'communism mixed with Hitlerism'.

Alarmist talk by refugees and evacuees has now almost ceased.

2. SPECULATION ABOUT THE FUTURE, INCLUDING PEACE AIMS

Expectation of a short war has now practically vanished. Though most people seem to be thinking little about *peace aims*, interest in this subject among the educated minority is once more increasing. One Postal Censorship unit records that reparations are mentioned for the first time.

Talk about *reprisals* is limited. Many still favour them, but there is little hysterical expression of this point of view, and even less criticism because they are not undertaken. At the same time, it is hoped by many people that we shall attack the Italians as vigorously as possible by sea and air and that we shall soon bomb the Rumanian oil wells.

3. RUMOURS

There have been fewer rumours this week, though the usual crop of Haw-Haws come from Ashchurch, Eastbourne, Hailsham, Lewes, Polegate and Rochester. In a good many places in North Wales, Haw-Haw is reported as saying: 'You may think you're safe in North Wales, but your turn is coming!' Rumours are not uncommon that the lull in raids is due to our use of a secret weapon. Some people believe that places which exhibit German planes 'receive special attention' from bombers; so strong was this feeling in Streatham that a Messerschmitt exhibited in aid of a Spitfire fund was removed 'in deference to public opinion'.

4. ANTI-SEMITISM

Anti-Semitism is still reported, but seems less strong than it was. Windsor is said to be 'packed with' Jews, and hundreds who arrived at Swindon were not very welcome. Llandudno has been referred to as 'Jerusalem by the sea'. The Southampton police report the distribution of printed and written anti-Jewish slogans, and some anti-Semitic remarks are still made about Tube shelterers.

5. EIRE AND NORTHERN IRELAND

The attitude to the war of people of Eire and Northern Ireland during September is the subject of a Special Postal Censorship study; its conclusions are summarised below.

EIRE: Invasion is widely anticipated; the majority of those who expect Germany to be the invader are pessimistic about Eire's chances. Manoeuvres by the Local Security Force were said to show up the country's unpreparedness. Many believe that England will be the invader, and 'a considerable number think they will be better off under Hitler'. Although the constant noise of planes at night makes many people nervous, most of them are 'listless and fatalistic' about the black-out and shelters. De Valera is the only Irish politician mentioned, and, though he is much criticised, the IRA is blamed even more. The bombing of London has produced 'a great if somewhat reluctant surge of admiration for the British people'. There is still a good deal of anti-British feeling. Churchill is praised by a minority; the majority recall his anti-Irish sympathies in the past. The only point on which all Eire writers agree is the demand for the return of Northern Ireland. The arrival of Irish refugees from England is frequently mentioned, but there is little sympathy for their plight. Many writers complain of a shortage of English news in the Irish broadcasts and newspapers.

NORTHERN IRELAND: In contrast with Eire the views expressed in Northern Ireland are absolutely clear-cut. There are four types of correspondents: Orangemen, loyal but tolerant Protestants, loyal Catholics, and IRA. With the first three groups Churchill is very popular; there is little or no praise for Lord Craigavon, who is widely criticised, and not only by Catholics. Many complain that Catholics are thrown out of their jobs, and that they are not allowed to join the Home Guard; even some Orangemen protest that Catholicism should not be regarded as evidence of disloyalty. Many young Catholics are said to be crossing the border to join the Eire Forces. Among patriotic sections there is as much anti-Italian feeling as anti-German. There is dissatisfaction because men who refuse to go and work in England lose their unemployment benefit.

REPORTED REACTIONS TO WAR EXPERIENCES

1. AIR RAIDS

(A) GENERAL REACTIONS

Despite the slackening of raids, particularly in the London area, air-raid victims still have many serious difficulties. The numerous separate authorities, with whom arrangements have to be made, cause much delay and consequent distress among the homeless, and reports again emphasize the need for centralised bureaux where everything can be dealt with at a single visit. In some areas, there has been criticism of Assistance Board officials for lack of sympathy in dealing with applications of air-raid victims and those claiming supplementary pensions.

(B) ATTITUDE TO AERIAL DEFENCE

In spite of the decrease in bombing, there is still some scepticism and dissatisfaction about the barrage, though this feeling has been partly offset 'by Joubert's hopeful references to night-fighters, and by the implications of the secret air defences debate'.

In the London area some people prefer mobile guns rather than those on fixed sites, as these are believed to attract raiders. It is also thought that certain landmarks, e.g. the Crystal Palace towers, are used by the enemy as guides.

Contradictory press references to the effects of bad weather on bombing have confused the public. For example, the *Daily Mail* (October 28) carries the headline: 'Winter will halt raiders'; this is followed by a sub-headline: 'The RAF cannot be held up.' Yet later in the week both the press and the BBC announced that 'owing to bad weather we did not conduct any raids on Germany'.

(C) SHELTERS

Improvement in public shelter arrangements continues slowly. There are fewer complaints about lack of amenities, but there is severe criticism in some bombed districts, mostly outside London, about shortage of shelters. Lack of school shelters is also complained of at Blythe, Watford and Kings

Lynn. There is, however, no new evidence about further demands for deep shelters.

From a study of those sheltering in the Tubes, 'it seems that about 1 Londoner in 25 shelters in the Tubes more or less regularly, though not necessarily going there every night. Much the largest single group is still that which uses home shelters'. One of the major difficulties in home shelters is dampness; this is also reported in many public shelters in the London area.

A growth is noticeable in corporate feeling in public shelters. 'An interesting feature is the apparently increasing habit of people going to the Tilbury shelter for a companionable evening and a cheap meal served by the Salvation Army canteen. Many people do this and then go back to their homes to sleep.'

(D) SIRENS

There has been a slight revival of the siren controversy because in several areas bombs have recently fallen without warning. 'This feeling is particularly strong in the South-Eastern, Eastern, and Midland Regions, and the South-East of Scotland.' In some places, the one-minute siren is criticised as too short; it is said also that there is often not enough time between warnings and bombs.

(E) CIVIL DEFENCE SERVICES

The fatigue of air-raid wardens is again mentioned, and there are even reports of their being asleep on duty. In several London districts untrained 'volunteers' have been taking on the wardens' duties so as to give the latter some relief. There are complaints in the Hull district about the reduction in the number of paid wardens in an area where the population has lately increased. Thus the duties of the already overworked wardens have been greatly added to.

(F) BLACK-OUT

The longer and darker nights are increasing conscientiousness about the black-out; and anxiety about infringements is growing. The lights of cars (both civilian and military), factories, pit mound fires and signals, and railway and tram 'flashes' are causing complaints in many districts.

2. EVACUATION

Evacuation continues, though it is slackening. The response to the Government's 'mother and children scheme' seems to vary directly with the severity of the raids, and this week it has been small. At the same time, in some places at present excluded from the full evacuation scheme, such as Cricklewood and Wembley, there are requests for their inclusion.

There is ill-feeling towards the upper and upper-middle classes in some reception areas because of their attempts to avoid taking in evacuees. Cambridge, Dereham, Penzance and Wisbech are mentioned in particular. In the North-Eastern Region, there are even protests by the landed classes about the possibility of compulsory billeting in large empty houses.

The old and infirm are still in serious difficulties about evacuation. Although those living in shelters or Rest Centres are being sent to hospitals or infirmaries in the country, this is only a small proportion of the numbers who want to be evacuated. The Government's private assisted evacuation scheme depends on the old people finding their own billets, which few of them are able to do; whole families are therefore restrained from going, because they are unwilling to leave dependent relatives behind. Another difficulty is that some old people are semi-cripples and cannot therefore go to shelters at night, so that relations feel compelled to stay with them during raids.

There is still much confusion both among landlords and evacuees about liabilities for rent, rates, etc.

3. HEALTH

As reported last week, there is still a demand for organised rest periods out of London for ARP workers; reports also urge strongly that similar arrangements should be made for heavy industrial workers 'on whom the effects of prolonged shifts are becoming noticeable'.

4. FOOD

There are 'persistent demands' for an extension of the categories of workers who are entitled to extra rations. This is said to apply particularly to miners, who want more bacon, and to many housewives who find the cooking fat ration inadequate.

5. TRADE AND COMMERCE

Apart from a recent 'rush on shops', particularly for articles of clothing, there is no sign of any public reaction to the Purchase Tax, though trade criticism of it continues, 'and is particularly strong in the Potteries'.

6. GPO & CENSORSHIP

Delay in postal services is much criticised. There are also many complaints about the comparative postal charges for letters to soldiers at home and abroad.

7. TRANSPORT

Travel facilities, particularly bus services, are the cause of widespread complaints, especially in districts where the population has been increased by evacuees; in some districts the inadequacy of the services is a serious inconvenience to industrial workers.

REPORTED REACTIONS TO NEWS

1. OFFICIAL COMMUNIQUES

The recent official announcement that 'on September 16th many German troops were embarked only to be taken off because invasion plans were stopped by the sustained offensive of the RAF' has been taken by many of the public to mean that the attempted invasion rumours had a basis in fact. As a result there have been difficulties for some MOI officials who had attempted to kill what was thought to be a false rumour, and the incident is said to have injured the 'standing of our official news service in general and the MOI in particular'. There is still some concern about the press publication of unconfirmed news, which is not afterwards either officially confirmed or denied (e.g. the alleged naval engagement off the Isle of Wight).

Criticism of the stereotyped announcements of bombing damage is once more becoming prominent.

In some places the public are sensitive to press mention of new buildings or new industrial undertakings, as it is feared that these may attract the enemy bombers.

2. POLITICAL AFFAIRS

The Prime Minister's broadcast to the French was very well received, but there were fewer comments than usual. There is still evidence of feeling against Lord Halifax, but it is less than last week.

3. EVENTS ABROAD

During the week events abroad have produced little effect on the public as a whole. People are said to be confused, and speculation is vague and uninformed. General de Gaulle has been hardly mentioned at all, and the same applies to the Far East. What interest there has been in the Near East has taken the form of anxiety. Some think that we are lagging behind in the diplomatic field, that we have been out-manoeuvred in Rumania, and that the same is likely to happen in Spain and Turkey. There is speculation as to whether we have the right men on the spot, and whether our secret service is as efficient as it might be.

4. BROADCASTING

A further detailed study by Listener Research has been made on the subject of radio listening during air raids. It was confirmed that even in London the great majority of people shelter in their own homes; the great majority therefore still have access to a radio set. Comparatively few people have radio sets in their private garden shelters and the number of sets in public shelters is negligible. In any place when severe raids begin, there is general reluctance to keep the radio on (the reasons for this were discussed in last week's report), but as raids become more frequent people once more start listening, particularly to the news and to light entertainments. The general deterioration of reception during air raids at night has caused both bewilderment and resentment.

Most people are quite unaware of why this happens. A typical comment comes from the Leicester Information Committee: 'The British command of the air does not extend to the ether.'

The disappearance of J. B. Priestley from the air has been regretted by the great majority, though a few accused him of being too partisan. In spite of his explanation that it was his own decision to cease broadcasting, many people have suggested that 'there is something behind it', and that he has been forced to stop.

There are requests that official announcements should be made a little earlier in the evenings 'to avoid clashing with warnings'.

NO 5: MONDAY 28 OCTOBER TO MONDAY 4 NOVEMBER 1940

REPORTS RECEIVED ON GENERAL MORALE

1. GENERAL COMMENTS

The cheerfulness of Londoners, noted last week, has continued.

Reports from many sources (RIOs, Postal Censorship, etc.) continue to point out that morale is steady and that people are determined to go on to ultimate victory; but a 'strain of war-weariness' in letters, and a feeling of stalemate in the war, are reported from four sources.

The heavy bombing of Coventry has produced a similar sequence of events to that which happened at the beginning of London's blitzkrieg. It seems that the reaction of an urban community to heavy bombing is fairly consistent:

1) A large group of jittery people of all classes evacuate, irrespective of any Government scheme. From Coventry they went to Stratford-on-Avon, Kidderminster, Budleigh, Warwick, Kenilworth, Alcester, etc.

2) The more nervous people who remain because they lack initiative or are unable to get away go at night to the safest possible place. In London, this is the Tube. At Coventry, it is the surrounding country; about 20,000 people are said to go to villages every night; many sleep in the fields or woods, and some in cars and charabancs which run special excursions for this purpose.

3) Complaints are made of inadequate aerial defence, and demands for deep shelters are fanned partly by the 'Communist' party. At the same time petty grumbling vanishes.

4) There are requests that soldiers should help to clear away debris and to relieve ARP workers.

5) In provincial areas there are complaints that local bombing is not given enough prominence in official communiques.

6) The morale of most people is affected very little by severe bombing, and improves quickly when raids slacken.

7) A symptom of this recovery seems to be an increase in minor grumbles, but major grumbles arising from the raids soon subside.

Billeting is one of the most serious causes of discontent this week. The enthusiasm of the hosts is dying down, and friction, where hosts and evacuees are of different social classes, is growing; it is discussed in detail later in this report.

2. SPECULATION ABOUT THE FUTURE, INCLUDING PEACE AIMS

People now seem prepared for a long war and a difficult winter; some think that the winter will weaken the enemy more than us, and make him an easy target for our officially predicted aerial superiority.

Interest in peace aims is still relatively slight except among the intellectual classes. Some anticipate without optimism peace-time conditions which will be 'nearly as bad' as the war. There is evidence of a growing ruthlessness in the public's attitude towards the Germans, though the desire for immediate reprisals remains limited. This ruthlessness is shown by the following extract from a letter: 'We must not be so lenient to the swines as we were in 1918 and must keep them well screwed down.' A police report records criticism of the 'excessive humanitarianism of the officer who ordered the broadcasting of the position of the survivors of the sunk Italian warship.' The enthusiasm of an Aberdeen audience at a MOI meeting when the speaker was excessively bellicose shows the same tendency. These reports suggest that in the absence of definite peace aims, there may be a growth of violent and indiscriminate anti-German feeling.

On the subject of immediate reprisals against Germany there are two main views. Some think the official policy of bombing only military objectives is the most effective one, while others believe that our airmen (especially the Canadians) are not too particular about their targets if there is difficulty in finding primary objectives. The demand for reprisals and the vigorous bombardment of Italy (particularly of her hydro-electric plants) is as strong as ever. We are accused of an excessively gentlemanly attitude towards Italy and this is attributed by some to Lord Halifax's supposedly Catholic sympathies.

3. RUMOURS

Rumours have not been very widespread. Stories of exaggerated bomb damage still circulate. There are several new Naval rumours; for example the new battleship *Beatty* is said to have been sunk during her trials as she was leaving the Clyde. This was apparently published as a Rome radio report in the *Western Mail* and *South Wales News*, and has not been denied.

Two other Service rumours allege that landings are being made by our forces in France and Holland, and that American planes are considered inferior by the RAF who hate flying them (this was heard from RAF men on two occasions).

German airmen who have bailed out are said to have been given a rough passage, East-Enders stringing them up to lampposts, and Canadians executing them.

4. ANTI-SEMITISM

There are still reports of anti-Semitism in reception areas.

5. EXTREMIST ACTIVITIES

Reports show that 'communists' are still trying to exploit the shelter situation and roof-spotter system at Letchworth, Southampton, Reading, Oxford and elsewhere. Accounts in the *Daily Worker* of riots outside the Tilbury shelter were greatly exaggerated.

Since intensive bombing began, conscientious objection is said to be losing ground steadily, even in Wales.

REPORTED REACTIONS TO WAR EXPERIENCES

1. AIR RAIDS

(A) GENERAL REACTIONS

In London anxiety about raids and fear of being made homeless seem to be decreasing, partly because the air offensive has slackened and also because shelter conditions are improving. In the Midlands, however, particularly in Birmingham and Coventry, 'people have been very disturbed by the severity of recent night raids'.

(B) SHELTERS

Complaints about lack of public and school shelters are still reported from a number of districts.

Improvements in London shelters continue to be made fairly quickly. But in the East End, a number of wholly unsuitable and insanitary places have been commandeered as shelters by the public, and, whatever was done structurally, it is doubtful if they could be made satisfactory.

There is still some anxiety about dampness in Anderson shelters.

(C) SIRENS

Certain districts continue to complain about timing and inaudibility of sirens.

(D) EVACUATION

On the basis of many reports the situation may be summarised as follows:

1. In spite of the complications produced by voluntary refugees, the Government evacuees were at first well received – far better than last year; hosts felt that the evacuees were this time in genuine need. In many areas, however, certain well-to-do people would not take in evacuees, and compulsory billeting had to be resorted to. The authorities were often reluctant to do this as the unco-operative people were usually of some influence locally. The extent of the voluntary refugee problem is shown by the figures for one Region (North Midland): official evacuees 108,762, voluntary refugees 82,297.

2. Friction between hosts and evacuees is now rapidly growing for several reasons:

   a. social incompatibilities.

   b. the use of one kitchen by two or more women.

   c. the unco-operative attitude of hosts, and the untidy and dirty habits of evacuees.

   d. overcrowding.

   e. the splitting up of families.

   f. lack of occupation for evacuee women.

All these factors, especially the last, helped to make the first evacuation a failure, and there is a great danger that the same thing may happen again. This is particularly stressed by experienced social workers.

3. Another difficulty is that Assistance Board offices are often a long way from the evacuees' new homes, and billeting allowances make no provision for travelling expenses.

4. Solutions which have proved satisfactory are as follows:

   a. billeting of one or more families in empty houses. This works well, provided the incapacity of most evacuees to pay anything like full rent and rates and to provide furniture is allowed for.

   b. communal mid-day meals in halls. These are of great value, especially if cooked by the evacuees themselves. They standardise treatment of evacuees, relieve hosts of kitchen pressure, and give occupation to the evacuee women.

   c. day nurseries have been organised in the same halls, so that evacuee women may go out to work, leaving their young children out of the way of the hosts. Sewing parties once or twice a week for evacuee women have also been successful.

5. An indirect reason why many women return home with their children is because they fear that their husbands are not being properly looked after. When they return, the husbands often give up night work or ARP duties to look after their families. The husbands are anxious that their wives and children should remain evacuated. Hostels for the men are the solution which has been most generally suggested.

6. The unevacuated adolescents are also a serious problem. Often their families are evacuated and they have no occupation in the evenings. The clubs which used to cater for them have in many cases closed down or been taken over for other purposes. As a result the adolescents are behaving badly and there is an increase in juvenile crime.

(E) ROOF SPOTTERS

According to the RIO, South-Western Region, the recent raid on Filton aerodrome has seriously affected confidence in the system, as it is now thought the spotter's warning does not allow enough time for workers to reach the shelters, which are some way from the factory buildings. The position is slightly better at night, though serious stoppages of work, more among the men than the women, now follow 'alerts' during the day.

In some places contradicting signals by spotters on different buildings cause confusion. Other spotters, especially those of the LPTB, are said to be insufficiently trained for the job.

2. TRADE AND COMMERCE

Many people are said to think that the Purchase Tax is likely to affect small incomes and small traders more seriously than large ones. There is much buying by the public of goods advertised as being pre-tax stock.

3. TRANSPORT

There are still many complaints about bus and train services. Dislocation of traffic in the Midlands is largely due to raids, and is causing much inconvenience to industrial workers; if delays get worse, it is feared production may suffer seriously.

4. AGRICULTURE

Reports from rural areas show an increasing amount of criticism by farmers of the Government's price fixing scheme, and of the decisions of local Agricultural Committees. The former complaint has been mentioned many times in the past few weeks.

5. RELATIONS BETWEEN CIVILIANS AND THE SERVICES

Many reports show that there is still a demand that the Army should be used in clearing away raid debris and assisting in ARP work generally.

In some areas farmers also would welcome military help in filling in bomb craters in their fields.

6. GPO AND CENSORSHIP

There are continued complaints about delay in postal, telegraph, and more particularly telephone services throughout the country.

REPORTED REACTIONS TO NEWS

1. OFFICIAL COMMUNIQUES

From many sources comes criticism of the fact that the sinking of the *Empress of Britain* was first announced by the Germans and then confirmed by our official news. People fear that this will encourage listening to the German radio and that belief in its accuracy will be increased. There is no evidence in fact to show an increase in such listening. The Ministry of Information is blamed for deficiencies in the news services of the War Departments.

Once more there are criticisms both that too little and too much news is released. There are complaints that heavy raids in Birmingham, Lancashire and Cheshire have been given little prominence in official communiques. On the other hand, it is feared that details of escapes from enemy occupied territory and accounts of builders collecting at Coventry for making munition works may help the enemy; if these are published, people fail to see why the name of a place at which the Queen inspected Girl Guides is suppressed.

2. AFFAIRS ABROAD

At first, the Italian attack aroused limited interest. Many people thought that Greece would be over-run in a few days but were not unduly alarmed. Another large group welcomed the invasion as a good chance for us to hit Mussolini hard, and to set up air-bases from which to bomb the Rumanian oil wells; it was even suggested rather naively that the invasion 'provided the opportunity for a victorious battle against a not overwhelmingly strong enemy'. Some people were anxious about our ability to give Greece the help which she needed without seriously weakening our forces in Africa. As the week went on without any overwhelming defeat for the Greeks, optimism has increased; this has been further encouraged by the statement (subsequently denied) that Russia was sending planes to Greece and Mr. Alexander's announcement that British aid had begun.

Otherwise there has been little interest in affairs abroad. People speak of the Vichy government with 'complete contempt', and in some areas the activities of Laval and Pétain are said to be causing 'anger and contempt for the French nation as a whole'.

3. BROADCASTING

From a great number of sources, there are reports of strong feeling because J. B. Priestley's broadcasts have stopped. It is said that 'sinister influences' and the 'old-school-tie brigade' have been at work. His views on social reform appear to be shared by the great majority. 'All he says and hopes for, is so exactly what we all feel and dread will not come true.'

There are a number of requests for more authoritative explanations of war events and factual statements on the lines of those of Joubert. It is also suggested that a specific time each week should be set aside for important speeches, as the notice given is often too short.

NO 6: MONDAY 4 NOVEMBER TO MONDAY 11 NOVEMBER 1940

REPORTS RECEIVED ON GENERAL MORALE

1. GENERAL COMMENTS

As usual, when morale is good, grumbles are on the increase. The main complaints are: rising prices; anomalies in rates of pay in the Services, and between skilled and unskilled workers; billeting difficulties of hosts and evacuees; problems of rent for evacuated and bombed property;

and compensation difficulties of raid victims, particularly among the middle classes.

Raids at Coventry have produced some depression. A Ministry speaker who has visited a number of factories and shelters says: 'there would be support for any plausible peace proposals'.

In the North Midland Region, some are said to be feeling 'a spirit of frustration; people are still saving, knitting and working for the war; they feel we shall win in the end, but when victory comes it won't matter very much to them'. This comment is similar in theme to a recent article by Priestley in the *News Chronicle*.

In academic circles in Scotland gloomy opinions are reported; the view is not that Hitler will win, but there is little prospect of his being beaten.

In spite of the weak spots, reports from RIOs, the Postal Censorship, and other sources show the determination of all classes to carry on to ultimate victory; nor is this determination associated with any over-optimism. The latest *News Chronicle* Gallup survey records 80% of the British people as being quite confident that Britain will win the war.

2. REPRISALS, PEACE AIMS, AND THE FUTURE

It seems that discussion about what is going to happen after the war is increasing; the majority, when they speak of it at all, are afraid 'things will be just as bad afterwards'. But among the more clear-cut comments from the Postal Censorship are forecasts that the younger generation will play a big part in altering things for the better, that 'the old-school tie will be burned at the stake', and that there will be 'a return to the land'.

The demand for bombing reprisals against Germany is still small, but against Italy it is continually growing greater. There are many complaints that our policy is lacking in 'guts', and that some influence in the Government is preventing vigorous measures. The Foreign Office is described as 'flabby' and 'sluggish'. Press stories of the Pope blessing Italian soldiers have roused some anger against the Papacy; many people are said to believe that Lord Halifax's religious sympathies prevent Rome from being attacked by the RAF, and diplomatic or strategic reasons appear not to have been thought of. There seems to be a possibility that anti-Catholic feeling may grow, particularly in view of Eire's attitude in connection with the naval bases.

There is more evidence of ruthless feelings towards the Germans; this is brought out particularly strongly in a Special Postal Censorship Report for October. 'Such phrases as "the foul filth that is Germany" and "the innate bestiality of all Germans" occur over and over again in letters, also expressions of the writers' bitter hate for all things German.' There is indignation at any suggestion of turning the other cheek, and there are many demands for full revenge.

3. RUMOURS

There is little change in the amount of rumour. In country districts Haw-Haw rumours are still fairly common, but are relatively rare in towns which have been heavily bombed. Tales of bomb damage also seem to be fewer and telephone censors say the introduction of the buzzer system (a buzzer being sounded when phone conversations are indiscreet) has led to a great reduction in the number of indiscreet conversations. The same report says that the worst offenders are shipping companies and serving soldiers and sailors.

The frustrated invasion rumour is still heard, and people remain convinced that large numbers of German bodies have been washed up on our shores.

4. ANTI-SEMITISM

There are still reports of anti-Semitism in some London shelters and in reception areas where there is special irritation each weekend when Jewish families are joined by their relatives working in London.

5. EXTREMIST ACTIVITIES

There are suggestions that the activities of the Communist Party, exerted through the ARP Co-ordinating Committees and the Shop Stewards' Movement, call for counter-measures. The *Daily Worker* is now printed in Glasgow and there are allegations that London communists who have moved up there are 'making trouble'.

6. EIRE AND NORTHERN IRELAND

There is some feeling about Eire's refusal to allow us to use her ports. The general feeling appears to be that Eire is another of the small countries which fail to realise that they must take sides or go under. No reports of opinion inside Eire have been received by us since the Prime Minister mentioned the question of the ports.

A special report by a careful observer in Dublin and County Cork confirms the growth of warm feeling towards England as a result of the air raids. In Dublin, however, a growing hostility to Germany is not always associated with increasing enthusiasm for England, and Churchill is unpopular, as 'being against Ireland' and 'standing for the old school tie'. In the rural parts of County Cork, friendship for England is widespread, particularly among the poor, and there is a rumour that De Valera has received a substantial loan from England for Irish defence. Churchill they regard as a 'grand wicked chap'. The country people would welcome English evacuee mothers and children, especially if they were of Irish descent. The LSF is reported to be increasingly well run, and to be bringing together all classes, except the extremists, on a democratic basis. Postal Censorship reports confirm most of these observations, and add the fact that there are many complaints of rising prices.

In Northern Ireland, the two main preoccupations have been Belfast's first air-raid alarm (which had a mixed reception, some treating it coolly and others being rather panicky), and unemployment. The linen and flax industries have been seriously hit and there are 70,000 registered unemployed. Many complaints are made that no steps are being taken to remedy the situation.

7. ADOLESCENTS IN LONDON

A special study of this subject has been made among probation officers, social workers, Ministry of Labour officials, Girl Guide officers, and wardens and secretaries of clubs for young people. The position of London's boys and girls between the ages of 14 and 18 is serious, since their earnings are considerably greater than before the war, the families of many of them have been evacuated, and they are bored and disgruntled at having to spend every evening and night in shelters. Many of the clubs which normally cater for them have shut down, either from lack of funds, or because they have been taken over for other purposes. Some have carried on, working during the daytime or at weekends, but these are of limited value only. As a result, juvenile delinquency and general bad behaviour have increased considerably; some of the boys have taken to looting. The solutions suggested are the establishment of special shelter clubs where they may also spend the night. Failing these, parts of large public shelters might be partitioned off to make places for quiet amusements. Social workers point out that these unoccupied adolescents are a fertile breeding ground for the more extreme political philosophies.

REPORTED REACTIONS TO WAR EXPERIENCES

1. AIR RAIDS

(A) GENERAL REACTIONS

The realisation that raids are just 'part of war-time conditions', and a determination to accept them as such, are increasingly evident. Those who have had little experience of them seem more prone to exaggeration and self-pity than others who have been badly bombed. The complaints of the real raid victims are rather of the 'appalling delays caused by red tape in the allocation of relief', and of the brusqueness of certain officials in dealing with their claims. Delays in removing furniture from damaged houses, and in the salvage and clearance of debris, are also much criticised.

(B) AERIAL DEFENCE

There is still some criticism of our defence. This seems to come mostly from places which have only lately had their first experience of severe bombing. Reports show widespread ignorance and misapprehension about the strategy of aerial defence, and it is frequently suggested that there is a need for continuous explanations on this subject. Lack of camouflage on certain conspicuous buildings is still the cause of much criticism.

(C) SHELTERS

Fewer complaints have been reported about conditions in shelters. In many districts, however, there is still said to be too few, particularly in schools. Demands for deep shelters are again reported from certain places.

Anxiety about dampness in Anderson and public shelters continues.

It is said that insufficient care is given to the fitting up of shelter bunks in the East End, and that the best use is not being made of the available space.

(D) BLACK-OUT

Anxiety about infringements of the black-out is reported from many places, and particularly about the lights of cars, trains, trams, etc. It is suggested that the BBC should continue to warn early risers in the Seven *and* Eight O'Clock News not to show lights.

(E) EVACUATION

Many evacuees, and landlords also, are uncertain of their legal position with regard to rents, rates, and other standing charges on evacuated property. Reports show the growing need for further official announcements about these matters, the special difficulties of which are dealt with in a detailed report on the subject. In certain badly bombed districts the position is a serious one for landlords who, in addition to losing most of their tenants, may also have lost much of their property.

There are more reports of anxiety among old people who wish to evacuate but cannot do so. Some who are not infirm, and do not come under the Government scheme, have nowhere to go. 'Many of them sit in tears at the offices of local authorities begging to be sent away.' Others, who might take advantage of the scheme, cannot afford to do so. 'Most of them live on a pension of 10/- a week, plus their "supplementary" of a few extra shillings. This is assessed for a limited period by the Assistance Board and may be withdrawn if the applicant is evacuated to an institution or hospital.' This summary of old people's difficulties is not exhaustive.

Unwillingness to accept evacuees is again reported from several districts. Profiteering in billets is alleged in a few areas. People with large houses and enough local 'pull' prefer refugees to evacuees, as they are a more paying proposition.

In certain districts, particularly Harrow, Enfield, and Wembley, there are still demands for an extension of the Government evacuation scheme. People who voluntarily evacuated from London at the beginning of the war now want to know if they are entitled to a billeting allowance. The suggestion has been made that resident families in the same district should join forces and live together in the same house, so as to leave one vacant for evacuees of a different social class.

2. FOOD

Complaints are reported from a few districts about a shortage of rationed foods, also of cheese, sultanas and raisins. Much of this trouble seems to be due to the presence of evacuees, and it is alleged that insufficient allowance has been made for them by those responsible for food distribution arrangements.

3. TRADE AND COMMERCE

There are signs that 'awareness of the Purchase Tax is increasing'. According to the Postal Censorship, the tax comes in for a good deal of criticism. 'There is a great deal of confusion about it and irritation among traders.' The commonest complaint still seems to be that 'it is unfair on the poorer classes'. The middle classes are said to be 'stocking up like mad' with goods of all kinds.

4. TRANSPORT

Reports show that there is still much dissatisfaction about the state of road and rail transport. In Birmingham and Coventry the problem 'threatens to become acute in industrial centres'. In the Home Counties, too, 'dissatisfaction is growing rather than dwindling'.

5. GPO AND POSTAL CENSORSHIP

Criticism is still made of delays in postal and telephone services, though complaints are rather fewer than last week.

6. COAL

Much dissatisfaction is reported about coal distribution. In some places the stocks are said to be extremely low, and 'demands are already far beyond the supplies available'.

REPORTED REACTIONS TO NEWS

1. THE WAR IN GENERAL

The two most talked of events this week have been the war in Greece and the re-election of Roosevelt. Except in those areas which are experiencing their first heavy bombing (such as Scotland), raids are no longer the main topic of conversation. People are once more thinking about the other theatres of war. The heavy shipping losses have been relatively little noticed.

2. OFFICIAL COMMUNIQUES

There are still complaints about the way in which the sinking of the *Empress of Britain* was announced. At first, it was said she had exploded as a result of bombing, while the Germans claimed that she was sunk by a torpedo. Our later official announcement that the U-boat which sunk her had been destroyed, once more confirms in the public mind the speed and accuracy of German news service. The Ministry of Information is criticised for this apparent muddle. There are still complaints because only London and Merseyside are named in Home Security communiques.

3. POLITICAL AFFAIRS

The Prime Minister's speech in Parliament roused less enthusiasm and interest than usual. His reference to 1943–4 was not generally taken too seriously. Two newspapers (the *Mail* and the *Sketch*) were openly critical of certain parts of the speech.

The Special Postal Censorship Report for October contains the following statement: 'The one desire of the British Public seems to be: Government of the people, for the people, by Mr. Churchill; but there is a distinct and growing uneasiness, amid all the admiration shown for him, at his becoming the leader of the Conservative Party.' This matter is not raised by reports from other sources.

An analysis of discussions at 62 newspaper bookstalls in the past fortnight on the popularity of broadcast speakers, shows that the Prime Minister is the most popular in 34 cases, Bevin second in 24, J. B. Priestley third in 10, and Morrison fourth in 9. Bevin's popularity is confirmed by the Special Postal Censorship Report.

4. AFFAIRS ABROAD

Reports show that, throughout the week, interest in, and optimism about, the war in Greece have steadily increased. However, after Norway and Dakar, people are taking the good news extremely cautiously, and will not be surprised, but only very disappointed, if Greece is over-run and we once more beat a strategic retreat.

5. BROADCASTING

Listening to German broadcasting is said to be increasing in certain parts of London, because of its recent priority with the news. A small statistical enquiry by the Lincolnshire Information Committee showed a surprisingly high number of listeners to the German radio. The reasons given for listening were the good quality of the musical programmes and of the reception.

6. FILMS

A recent news reel film which showed air-raid casualties being taken out from damaged houses was unpopular.

NO 7: MONDAY 11 NOVEMBER TO MONDAY 18 NOVEMBER 1940

REPORTS RECEIVED ON GENERAL MORALE

1. GENERAL COMMENTS

The successful naval action at Taranto provided the greatest tonic the public has had 'for a long time' and came just 'when people were growing more and more insistent in their demands for definite action against Italy'. Interest was deflected from raids at home to the war in the Mediterranean.

A special report on Coventry is attached.

2. REPRISALS, PEACE AIMS AND THE FUTURE

Postal Censorship reports indicate a growing number of people who 'speculate about the future of the war and the peace'. The majority think the war will be a long one. 'Mr. Churchill now thinks 1943–4; it will soon be 1950 we are fighting for', but a few are more complacent and are 'said to be talking about the war ending towards the end of next year'.

Desire for reprisals against Italy are widely expressed, often in the strongest terms, and the opinion is given that 'Italian morale is weak and the Italian government could be compelled to sue for a separate peace.'

3. RUMOURS

There has been no appreciable change in the number or significance of rumours reported this week, except for the special case of Coventry. A slight increase has been noticed in Scotland where raids have been somewhat heavier lately.

Haw-Haw rumours are reported to be increasing, especially among the middle classes.

REPORTED REACTIONS TO WAR EXPERIENCES

1. AIR RAIDS

(A) GENERAL REACTIONS

Reports again indicate that the general reactions to bombing, particularly where it has been heavy, is a stoical acceptance of its terrors and a determination to carry on as usual. Problems of relief, salvage, repairs and compensation still cause much anxiety.

Among the middle classes it is reported that hardship is caused by having to pay a valuation fee against compensation for house property destroyed by enemy action. There is also said to be 'impatience at the delay in the introduction of the Government's insurance scheme'.

Both the public and the press continue to be critical of delays in clearing away debris.

(B) AERIAL DEFENCE

There is still a belief that local defences are inadequate, particularly in the South-Western Region where apprehension seems to be growing. Complaints are reported from Bristol, Plymouth, Falmouth and Penzance. Anxiety persists also in certain parts of Scotland and in the Midlands. Even before the raid on Coventry many people were 'disturbed at the apparent lack of challenge to enemy planes which come over in daylight'. This feeling of insecurity, reported also from Birmingham and Leicester, is said to have been increased by 'the glowing accounts of London's barrage'.

(C) SHELTERS

Lack of school and public shelters is still reported from many places. On the other hand, the demand for deep shelters seems to have slackened.

It seems that 'the tendency to shelter at home is increasing'. This is often attributed to lack of heating in Anderson shelters or to their dampness; this is said to be becoming an extremely serious problem. Another cause seems to be distrust or dislike of surface shelters, of which, 'even in dangerous areas, less use is being made'.

(D) BLACK-OUT

There has apparently been a small increase in black-out offences. Yet at the same time impatience and anxiety about infringements are growing. In many areas there are even complaints that restrictions are not adequate. Unscreened lights at dusk, before the black-out has begun, are said to be a 'danger' and 'a source of growing apprehension'.

(E) SIRENS

Fewer complaints have been received about lack of warnings, but a special report from Penzance says that there is considerable anxiety there following a recent severe raid, of which no warning was given. Some apprehension has also been reported from parts of Scotland.

2. CIVIL DEFENCE

There are growing complaints from all parts of the country about the lack of winter clothing for Civil Defence workers, and to a lesser extent about their equipment. It is suggested that these defects account for the lack of volunteers from which some areas are suffering. So serious is the position in certain districts that wardens and rescue squads have refused to continue their duties until proper provision has been made for them in the way of clothing, and until their general conditions have been improved.

3. EVACUATION

Arrangements for relief of the homeless still seems to be entangled with red tape and are perhaps increased by the tactlessness and unsympathetic behaviour of certain officials which has again been reported. The need for Communal Feeding Centres is stressed in several reports.

Fewer complaints about billeting difficulties have been received, but allegations of profiteering show a slight increase. There are also more comments on 'the vulgar power of money', by which evacuees are said to be driven out to make room for those who can afford to pay more.

Unwillingness to accept evacuees is again reported from several districts. In certain places, however, the evacuees themselves are strongly criticised. The Postal Censorship (South-Western Region) reports that 'not a single letter has been noted this week in which they are well spoken of'.

Old people who wish to get away are still 'a big problem'; so are 'young sick people, who also find it difficult to make evacuation arrangements'.

An urgent need of clothes, particularly shoes and Wellington boots, for evacuee children in the country, is mentioned in reports from many parts of the London area.

An article in *The Times*, 19th November, criticised in detail the working and administration of the Government's evacuation schemes.

4. HEALTH

The possibility of epidemics during the winter seems to be causing increasing concern to the public. Comment is made upon 'the tardiness of putting the promised health measures into effect', and a reassurance of the steps being taken is suggested.

5. FOOD

There is a considerable increase in complaints about shortage of rationed as well as unrationed foods; in many districts price grumbles are secondary to those about supplies. Though it seems to be generally thought that evacuees are the main cause of shortages, there is a good deal of comment about distribution arrangements, which are said to have been made without due allowance for local increases in population.

In the S. Western Region it is said that 'the shortage of some foods is said to be due to the troops' preference for buying things in shops rather than at NAAFI canteens, where the prices are said to be higher'.

A shortage of cheese, which is reported from Wales, is said to be a serious matter for the miners 'as this is one of the staple foods for their "snacks"'.

6. TRANSPORT

There is more and stronger criticism about the transport situation in many districts, and particularly of bus services in the London area. The effect of increasing delays upon trade and industry is again emphasised.

7. TRADE AND COMMERCE

The method of applying the Purchase Tax still comes in for considerable criticism in the press. The tax itself seems to be 'slowly though increasingly felt by the public'. There is also criticism of a report that certain medical supplies needed by the Red Cross are not exempt from the tax.

8. COAL

There are more reports about lack of coal supplies. The tone of complaints on this subject is becoming more emphatic.

REPORTED REACTION TO NEWS

1. THE WAR IN GENERAL

The chief topics of discussion this week seem to have been the action of the Fleet Air Arm at Taranto, the bombing of Coventry, Molotov's visit to Berlin, and the fight put up by the *Jervis Bay*.

Comments about Taranto are enthusiastic but somewhat cautious. 'Whilst people do not express definite optimism about the results of this action, it is felt that at last we are taking the offensive in one theatre of the war.' 'Pleasure at the news from Taranto is tempered by suspicion.' Discussion on the situation in Greece itself shows a similar reserve; but admiration for the Greeks – and detestation of the Italians – increases.

The coincidence of Molotov's visit with the more dramatic events of the week seems to have overshadowed its significance; on the whole the event seems to have aroused only limited interest.

Great praise is given to the action of the *Jervis Bay*, though this is often coupled with surprise and some dismay 'that such an important convey should have been entrusted to a single armed merchant cruiser'.

2. POLITICAL AFFAIRS

The Postal Censorship reports some criticism of Mr. Churchill, though the bulk of opinion, except from Eire, is entirely approving. 'While there is absolute confidence in our power to win,' says one letter, 'there is no confidence in the direction of our affairs at present.' Another letter suggests that 'he is too timorous, too cautious in home affairs'. Letters from Eire are said to show 'growing pro-British feeling as to the outcome of the war', but there is an increased amount of anti-Churchill comment.

Feeling against Lord Halifax continues.

3. AFFAIRS ABROAD

The re-election of President Roosevelt has been greeted with overwhelming satisfaction. A few reports from Eire are rather lukewarm in their enthusiasm.

EIRE: Eire's refusal to grant the use of naval bases to Great Britain continues to rankle. 'Feeling against Eire and its attitude to neutrality is growing rapidly.' This comment is typical of many which have been received on the subject. Discussion of this problem, and arguments about the bombing of Rome, are said to have 'stirred up a religious controversy and considerable bitterness between Catholics'.

4. BROADCASTING

Reports indicate a slight but continuous increase in the number of people listening to Germany. The chief reason for this is said to be the poor reception of BBC programmes.

APPENDIX

SUMMARY OF SPECIAL REPORT ON COVENTRY

(Submitted Saturday 16 November 1940)

Observers sent to Coventry on Friday 15 November reported:

1) The shock effect was greater in Coventry than in the East End or any other bombed area previously studied. This was partly due to the concentrated nature of the damage and to extreme dislocation of services, partly to the small size of the town which meant that many people were directly or indirectly involved. The considerable proportion of imported labour and the fact that Coventry was economically flourishing contributed to this effect.

2) During Friday there was great depression, a widespread feeling of impotence and many open signs of hysteria. 'This is the end of Coventry' expressed the general feeling. Many people tried to leave the city before darkness fell. A quiet night followed by a fine morning changed the atmosphere for the better.

3) There was very little grumbling even about the inadequacies of shelters and in the town itself observers found no anti-war feeling. There was little recrimination or blame.

4) There was admiration for the Civil Defence services. AA defences were considered good, although inadequate, and there was a strong rumour of severe shortage of ammunition.

5) There were many strongly exaggerated rumours about casualties and damage which quickly spread to the surrounding countryside. They were increased by the lack of press and radio news. Many radio sets were put out of commission and there was inadequate distribution of newspapers.

6) The belief that this was a reprisal raid was general and as a result there was no demand for reprisals on our part, instead a fear of them was expressed. At the same time, after the first shock had worn off, there was evidence of a feeling which has been growing generally, of revenge and ruthlessness after the war.

Arising out of these observations certain action points emerged. They would seem of general application in countering shock and aiding recovery in heavily bombed towns. The rehabilitation of a bombed town is partly dependent upon the speed with which civilian morale can be restored. Whereas the methods for dealing with the immediate material consequences of the raid are efficient and speedy, the apparatus for dealing with the human problems raised is undeveloped, and there is an inadequate organisation for attending to the problem of 'civilian morale'.

1) MOBILE CANTEENS, ARMY KITCHENS AND COMMUNAL FEEDING: Arrangements should be made well beforehand for tackling the immediate necessities of food and hot drinks for the civilian population. The effect of well-stocked, well-placed canteens is spectacular.

2) TRANSPORT: Free transport for those who need it, either for work or evacuation, is essential.

3) NEWS: To counter rumour and release people from personal preoccupations, every effort should be made to supply news, either by assisting newspaper deliveries, setting up loudspeaker vans or by special bulletins.

4) INFORMATION: Loudspeaker vans providing information and advice about casualties, Rest Centres, canteens etc. should move through the town.

5) SOLIDARITY WITH THE GOVERNMENT AND LOCAL OFFICIALS: The appearance of the King, the Bishop, the Mayor, the Home Secretary etc. strengthens morale and counters the feeling of helplessness. In speeches and talks emphasis should be put on the future, on rebuilding, replanning etc.

6) CARE OF THE HOMELESS AND EVACUATION: Arrangements for the care of the homeless should be well publicised beforehand so that

there is a minimum of confusion and ignorance during the time of crisis. Peripheral Rest Centres are a great advantage. Stores of clothing, especially boots, and warm blankets are invaluable. Centralised offices for assistance reduce criticism. Social workers skilled in directing evacuation should speedily be brought into the town in order to control the movement of evacuees and refugees. Attempts should be made to persuade those whose evacuation is not desired to remain, and every encouragement given to them by means of transport and feeding facilities.

7) MINOR DAMAGE: Many people move away because of the discomfort of broken windows. The depression caused by minor damage could be mitigated by self help schemes prepared beforehand.

8) PERSPECTIVE: For the country as a whole an account as factual as security permits should be given. The publicising of over-estimations of morale cause suspicion and are contradicted by the reports of refugees.

Facts should be placed in perspective, but for the sake of morale in the bombed town damage and casualties should not be unduly minimised.

HOME INTELLIGENCE
19 November 1940

NO 8: MONDAY 18 NOVEMBER TO MONDAY 25 NOVEMBER 1940

Note: This report will in future be issued on Fridays and will next appear on 6 December.

REPORTS RECEIVED ON GENERAL MORALE

1. GENERAL COMMENTS

Determined endurance in the Midlands and a cheerful confidence elsewhere are the prevailing sentiments which appear this week.

'Italian failures' and the 'intensification of our offensive' are reasons given for the latter, but there are some expressions of disappointment that 'Taranto was not followed up by more offensive action.'

2. REPRISALS, PEACE AIMS AND THE FUTURE

Speculation about peace aims and the future has diminished this week, largely, it seems, because interest is focused on events abroad as well as at home.

Reprisals 'for Coventry' against Germany, and also against Italy, are mentioned by several newspapers, and are said to be 'demanded' by certain sections of the public. But there is little direct evidence of a strong public desire for the bombing of civilian objectives. The term 'reprisals' often seems to be confused with an intensified bombing of important targets. Some people believe the severe raid on Hamburg following the raid on Coventry was meant to be a 'reprisal'.

3. RUMOUR

Few significant rumours have been reported. The story that 'U-boat crews are using the Eire coast' persists. Some people attribute the slackening of raids on London to a belief that the raiders are Italians 'who can't take it'.

The beginning of an 'epidemic of spy stories' is reported from Scotland. Several of these are about fatal accidents to airmen due to 'sabotage'.

4. ALIENS

Some newspapers continue to ask for 'a more humane policy towards aliens', and that 'a better use should be made of them to further our war effort'.

REPORTED REACTIONS TO WAR EXPERIENCES

1. AIR RAIDS

(A) GENERAL REACTIONS

There have been fewer comments this week on the way people are standing up to raids. Their toughness of spirit and 'indifference' seem now to be taken for granted. Wales alone reports any sign of 'jitters'. 'Since the

Coventry raid many have reverted to sleeping in their shelters.' Of Coventry itself the Telephone Censorship reports that 'the morale, as disclosed by intercepted conversations, is of the highest order, notwithstanding the town's ordeal'. Elsewhere it is again stated that people in the more heavily bombed areas are standing up to it magnificently.

The difficulties of homeless people continue. Lack of information about their liabilities for rent and other standing charges 'is causing much confusion and hardship'. Attention has been drawn to special problems of this nature which affect 'people whose houses were being bought through building societies'.

There is still criticism of delay in repairing damaged property and in removing personal belongings from bombed houses. 'A tremendous outcry' is reported in one area where 'property damaged ten weeks ago is still covered with tarpaulins'.

More cases have been reported of people 'taking advantage at Rest Centres of facilities to which they are not entitled'.

(B) AERIAL DEFENCE

Criticism of defences which, apart from local complaints, had lately declined, has sprung up again this week. In the press and from other sources there have been comments on the 'harm done by premature and optimistic announcements' of our progress in methods to defeat the night bomber; Churchill and Joubert are both criticised for 'raising false hopes'. After the raid at Leicester on 21st November, there were 'strong comments on the insignificance of the anti-aircraft defences'.

The camouflage question, which has been dormant for some time, is revived in a complaint from people living near the MOI 'who are extremely nervous about its visibility as a target'. It is suggested that it should be made less conspicuous.

(C) SHELTERS

There are persistent complaints from many parts of the country about dampness in shelters, as well as about their shortage. More reports have been received of people sleeping at home as their shelters have been too wet to use. About shelter bunks, however, there is some satisfaction. 'Approval' and enthusiasm 'for them has been expressed in one London district', though this is qualified by a statement that 'the speed and efficiency with which they are fitted up differs greatly in the various boroughs'.

The reactions of the press to Lord Horder's report were wholly approving, though there has been much criticism about the way in which the Government handled the matter. There is not yet much evidence of the public's attitude to the subject. The criticisms of the press are on account of delay in issuing the report, and of the mutilations and addenda which have been made. These are said to 'suggest that the Government wanted to disarm as much criticism as it possibly could before issuing it'.

Several papers commented approvingly on the recommendation that local authorities should take swift and independent action to improve conditions in their own districts.

(D) CIVIL DEFENCE SERVICES

It is reported that in some parts of London rescue squads need more cranes and other gear. Comment has also been made on the need for better arrangements for feeding firemen while they are at work.

(E) SIRENS

Criticism of siren policy seems to be dying down. There are still a few complaints from places where there have been raids without warnings or where sirens have sounded after raids have begun.

(F) BLACK-OUT

There have also been fewer complaints about infringements of the blackout, though anxiety on the part of the public seems to persist in certain areas.

2. EVACUATION

Many of the problems referred to in the earlier reports have again been mentioned this week. In some areas hosts and evacuees continue a campaign of mutual back-biting. 'The evasion of billeting by wealthy householders' is again reported; and old people are still said to be 'a serious problem'.

Questions of rents, storage of furniture, and the cost of maintaining two homes are said to be leading 'to the return of some evacuees to heavily bombed areas'.

While certain difficulties seem to have lessened (e.g. complaints of over-crowding and of profiteering), new problems are coming to light. 'The social needs of evacuees are much more serious than the general public imagines,' says one report. 'The social centres and welfare committees arranged by the WVS have met some of the more urgent needs, but it is felt that a considerable extension of this type of work is necessary.'

A report from London Region says that 'foster parents and evacuated children are the cause of much anxiety when parents who are themselves evacuated leave no address, and thus lose touch with their families.'

There are still demands for re-classification of evacuation areas around London. Requests have been reported from Beckenham, Bromley, Carshalton, Cheam, Finchley, Wembley.

The press is beginning to show some anxiety about 'the linked problems of evacuation and education', though apart from a limited number of regional reports, there have so far been few references to this from other sources. According to one paper '92,000 juveniles are running wild in London.' Another says: 'In Ramsgate alone there are 600 children without education of any sort.'

3. HEALTH

There are still reports from many places of anxiety about health troubles during the winter.

The difficulty of finding doctors at night for civil emergencies is mentioned in several areas.

4. FOOD

Food shortages are still reported in several districts.

It is suggested that 'in view of the rapid increase in comments about rising prices there should be more official explanation about the related problems of supply, prices and wages'.

5. TRADE AND COMMERCE

Though little reaction has been reported this week to the effects of the Purchase Tax, Mass Observation reports that this, 'and the all-round' rise in the cost of living, are now beginning to be seriously felt, especially among the poorer sections of the community. Price grumbles are coming up again strongly.

REPORTED REACTIONS TO NEWS

1. THE WAR IN GENERAL

Though glad to hear of the success at Koritza, people are still 'chary of giving the Greeks unqualified praise', or of being too complacent about the position generally, for fear 'of a set back'. Germany is expected to 'take a hand there soon'.

There is some comment on the serious threat to our Atlantic shipping from submarines and bombers.

2. POLITICAL MATTERS

Press criticism of our foreign policy and of Lord Halifax has been intensified this week, and is reported also from other sources. 'Britain must adopt a more active diplomacy', and 'it is rather disturbing that German foreign policy seems to be more effective than our own'. The Glasgow press stresses that 'many want a Foreign Secretary in the House of Commons'. Sir Samuel Hoare also comes in for some censure: 'Why is he kept in Madrid when his pre-war policy is universally condemned?'

'Catholic influence' is again alleged to be the reason why we do not bomb Rome.

3. HOME AFFAIRS

Postal Censorship reveals obsession both in England and in Eire with the Irish ports.

There is some apprehension in Eire about the possibility of invasion by Britain or Germany. Many writers in Eire 'blame de Valera's short-sighted policy'. 'Approximately 70% of the comments show that both English and

Irish writers desire greater co-operation between the two countries. 30% show sympathy for de Valera's policy and difficulties.'

4. OFFICIAL SPEECHES AND ANNOUNCEMENTS

Mr. Greenwood's statement about damage done by the RAF was criticised as being 'over-optimistic' in many quarters.

Mr. Bevin's speech had a mixed reception.

5. BROADCASTING

There have been more complaints in the press, as well as from our own sources, about 'the jeering and sneering manner of some of our news broadcasts', especially those referring to Italy. 'The boasting tone of announcers is causing disgust.'

NO 9: MONDAY 25 NOVEMBER TO WEDNESDAY 4 DECEMBER 1940

Note: This report will in future be issued on Wednesdays and the next will appear on Wednesday 11 December.

REPORTS RECEIVED ON GENERAL MORALE

1. GENERAL COMMENTS

The main events of the ten days covered by this report have been the heavy raids on provincial towns. As in the past, their effect has been to produce a 'grim optimism', but there are some signs of strain. After Bristol's raid on 30th November, it was reported that 'there was no crying or whining and no talk of stopping the war'. Since the raid, some 3,000 people have been walking several miles each night to shelter in a tunnel scheduled for 200 only. Plymouth's raids were accepted by the people as inevitable, and they are said to be fully prepared for more to follow. The Southampton raid of 30th November was also faced bravely; but 'it would be a mistake to assume that there is now no undercurrent of despondency and anxiety, especially among women...a relatively small city seems more susceptible to shock than a widely flung community like London'. Here, as at Coventry, there has been a nightly exodus of people to the surrounding country. On 3rd December, it was reported that 'morale is shaken but unbroken; however, the more that can be done for it, the better'. There is no anti-war talk, but if constant raiding continues, some defeatism is anticipated, in particular among the women. The RIO stresses the need for an objective and authoritative radio talk on the extent of our bombing damage in Germany. The Leicester raid caused more surprise than shock, as the people imagined that their town was 'low on the list of places to be bombed'.

In Coventry, as the shock of the raid wore off, grumbling steadily increased. There is feeling that as soon as things are straightened out another raid will put them back where they were. Political activity and exploitation of the situation has been very slight, and anti-war sentiment inconspicuous; feeling in favour of reprisals has increased, but is still not marked. Optimism is less obvious than it was in the East End after the early days of the blitz.

There is still indignation in those provincial towns – Birmingham, Bristol, Southampton, Plymouth, Birkenhead, etc. – which, although severely raided, have been described anonymously in official communiques.

In London the quieter nights have made those who sleep in their homes or in private shelters more cheerful; but the chronic habituees of the deeper public shelters and Tubes have been more depressed, as their discomfort is no longer mitigated by thoughts of what they are escaping. Some 'war-weariness' is reported from Brixton, Woolwich and West Ham. Christmas is usually looked forward to as a pleasant break in the middle of the winter. This year these cheerful anticipations are largely absent; the emptiness of the shops and the lack of 'Christmas fare' is commented on.

The exaggerated hopes of an early conquest of the night bomber, produced by press articles (apparently officially inspired), have now led to severe disappointment, particularly in the heavily raided provincial towns.

In general, morale continues steady, and there is a general feeling that we shall win in the end, but only after a long struggle. In no less than 82 out of

88 returns from railway bookstalls, are the public described as being 'confident of final victory'. At the same time, the Special Postal Censorship Report for November, while emphasising the confidence and pride of the people as a whole, notes a larger number of writers than usual who show poor morale:

1. Many complain of the strain of raids. More of these complaints come from London and Liverpool than from the new centres of attack in the provinces.

2. A number of intelligent working-class writers adopt the attitude that 'England can never win, so why not end this useless slaughter?' This attitude is coupled with the suggestion that the war is 'an upper-class financial racket', run at the expense of the people. Such an attitude has been almost entirely absent from previous mails, and the uniformity of the opinions expressed lead the Censorship authorities to suggest that they are not spontaneous, but rather the result of political propaganda.

3. Some people are upset by loneliness due to the scattering of friends and relations.

2. REPRISALS, PEACE AIMS AND THE FUTURE

Reprisals are still demanded more by those who have not directly suffered from bombing than by raid victims; the women appear to be 'more blood thirsty than the men'. The word 'indiscriminate' as applied to bombing is widely misunderstood, some thinking that it means 'accidental'. A Mass Observation investigation showed about 45% each way, and the rest with no opinion; this agrees very closely with a British Institute of Public Opinion survey published recently in the *News Chronicle*.

Postal Censorship reports show a large number of people who feel that no peace can be considered which does not ensure that Germany will *never* again be able to declare war on the people of England. This is the commonest type of comment on post-war policy. Many writers want to exterminate, or at least ostracise, the whole German race.

On the whole, people are showing little interest in peace aims. 'Mention of constructive planning for a new Europe is completely absent from letters at present.' There seems to be a trace of war-weariness which dulls people's capacity for looking ahead in a constructive way, and the continued emphasis on negative sacrifice which has characterised speeches of Government spokesmen has added to this.

The Special Postal Censorship study shows that, among letter-writers, those who speculate about the future are of the following types:

1. Those who think it is too early to look ahead.

2. Those who think that some constructive planning should be undertaken, but have no idea along what lines.

3. Those who hope for violent levelling of class distinction and a redistribution of wealth.

4. Those who are pleased at the present levelling of class distinctions and believe that they will never reappear after the war.

5. A very large body of writers who assume that a socialist state is inevitable after the war, with the present Labour leaders as the right wing in a democratic parliament.

6. A large number who look forward to an Anglo-American Federation as the only basis for world reconstruction.

The press interest in the rebuilding of England and the criticism of the lack of scope of the new Ministry of Works and Buildings has found no reflection in reports on public opinion.

3. RUMOURS

Rumours have increased slightly. Stories that the damage and casualties at Coventry were much more severe than official announcements made out, have spread widely; and there is a popular belief that Polish airmen were very annoyed at not being allowed to take off to intercept the night raiders attacking both Coventry and Birmingham. The popularity of the Polish forces with the public is also stressed in Postal Censorship reports. A rumour of martial law in Southampton following its heavy raid is reported from Portsmouth.

A rumour that Liverpool dock-workers are deliberately 'going slow' in order to earn extra overtime pay is said to be causing high feeling among the public in that town.

Rumours attributed to Haw-Haw are reported from a number of places – Portsmouth, Newcastle, Leeds, Bristol, Weston-super-Mare, Exeter, Barnstaple and Northampton. They take the usual form of predictions of bombing, and of promised return visits after raids.

4. ANTI-SEMITISM

The Special Postal Censorship Report for November records a slight increase in anti-Semitic feeling. In Blackpool, Jews from London and Brighton are accused of buying houses, furnishing them with second-hand furniture, and selling and letting them at extortionate prices. Some of the Jews themselves confess to their fears in raids and envy the calm of the English.

REPORTED REACTIONS TO WAR EXPERIENCES

1. AIR RAIDS

(A) GENERAL

Within the last ten days a large number of sources – from which only the press conspicuously differs – have indicated a slight but distinct decline in cheerfulness. This is largely attributed to the persistence, and in some cases the intensification, of air raids. At the same time, there are still many reports of the public's fortitude and determination to carry on, especially in areas which have been severely bombed. 'The (Birmingham) public is determined not to allow even worse punishment to get them down.' Bristol and Plymouth were said to have 'taken the blow wonderfully'; Southampton's 'immediate reaction was admirable'.

In a detailed report on the Bristol raid of 24th November, the RIO, Southern Region, strongly emphasises the need for a future policy of 'instructing the public about the problems of sanitation and of emergency methods of dealing with it if the water supply should fail'.

(B) AERIAL DEFENCE

Criticism continues, mainly of the defences in the Midlands and Southern England. The popular idea of defence seems to centre round the use of fighter planes, irrespective of technical or strategical considerations, and it is again suggested that more explanation of these points is needed.

(C) SHELTERS

There are still a very large number of complaints about shelter conditions, among which dampness and inefficient sanitary arrangements predominate. The press and many other sources are still extremely critical of the delay in dealing with the whole problem.

Comments from the Postal Censorship show that 'as winter hardships increase, public feeling is growing stronger against the conditions in shelters, and the tendency is to use them as little as possible'. This seems to apply particularly to surface shelters, which are said to be neglected 'owing to their general discomfort and lack of warmth'. Reports show some increase in demands for deep shelters.

(D) BLACK-OUT

Police Duty Room reports show that 'complaints are still numerous' and 'early morning offenders' are said to cause some anxiety. References to the black-out from other sources have declined.

2. EVACUATION

Last week's remarks about evacuation still hold good. There are the same problems and complaints. The poor, the well-to-do, the old, the young, whether they be hosts or evacuees, each have their separate grievances, and seem to unite only in their disapproval of the billeting authorities.

Comment from the Telephone Censorship gives a fair summary of opinion on the subject as shown by our reports: 'The public is making the best of a bad job which they feel someone has muddled somewhere.'

Communal feeding seems to be one of the few matters of which there is no criticism. There are more reports of its success from London, Wales, the Midlands and Northern England.

Ebbw Vale District Council reports that there is a serious lack of clothing, and particularly of boots, for 'necessitous evacuees'; this complaint is borne out by other reports.

The RIO Southern Region says that more Information Bureaux are needed, and suggests that there should also be more provision for the recreation and entertainment of evacuees.

3. TRADE AND COMMERCE

As the public becomes increasingly aware of the way in which it is affected by the Purchase Tax more grievances are coming to light. People who have lost their homes through bombing complain of having to pay the tax on goods bought to replace those which have been lost. There are also complaints about the tax being imposed on Service uniforms. Some junior officers already find it impossible to buy their full equipment with the allowance made for this purpose, and the tax increases the amount by which they are out of pocket. It is also suggested that uniforms for voluntary organisations engaged on war work, such as the WVS, should not be taxed. The suggested solution of these problems is that 'the tax should be retained, but that higher grants should be made in individual cases'.

4. LABOUR

Serious trouble is reported in letters from contractors' camps in Scotland. Complaints are made about bad food, drunkenness, and accidents at work. The camps complained about are: Castle Dobie, Inchindown, Invergordon; Balfour Beatty, Orkney; W. J. R. Watson's, Virkie, Shetland.

A shortage of labour is reported from various parts of London. A Chelsea works manager complains that only old and infirm people are offered by the Exchange. Stepney and Bermondsey are also said to be affected by the shortage.

5. TRANSPORT

There are still many reports of delay in road and rail traffic particularly in the Midlands and the Home Counties. In Birmingham and Coventry motorists are criticised for not giving enough help.

6. COAL

Lack of supplies are still reported in several areas, among which Coventry is said to be feeling the shortage acutely. In London many merchants are said to be complaining of 'chaotic conditions'.

The South Staffordshire Information Committee reports that 'miners' leaders are viewing very seriously the increase in absenteeism. The Mines Department,' says this report, 'appear to take very little interest.' The main causes of this trouble seem to be lack of shelter accommodation for the miners' families, and transport difficulties, especially for night shifts after raids. Strong complaints have been made also about the men's food, which is said to be 'inadequate and of poor quality'. 'It is essential,' says the Committee, 'for the food question to be settled, as under present conditions the men cannot carry on for more than two or three days on end.'

7. AGRICULTURE

Throughout the Scottish press Mr. Ernest Brown's speech on 28th November, about Scotland's agricultural policy, is said to be 'satisfactory as far as it goes'; but the general comment is that 'it doesn't go very far'.

REPORTED REACTIONS TO NEWS

1. OFFICIAL COMMUNIQUES AND BROADCASTING

From all parts of the country there are reports of 'indignation and exasperation' at recent broadcasts and official communiques about the bombing of large provincial towns. For these the BBC is largely blamed, though the Ministry of Information is also criticised; the public does not differentiate at all clearly between the sources of official statements. People fail to understand why the names of some towns are announced, while others are suppressed, even when they have been mentioned on the German radio. They point out that descriptions of damage and behaviour of the public have often not coincided with the facts. In particular, the announcements implying that industry in Coventry was not badly affected, and that Birmingham was almost normal the day after its heavy raid, have created 'serious distrust of official news'. There are reports from many sources that this combination of official reticence with official inaccuracy and over-optimism has led to a considerable increase in listening to the German radio; its reception is still stated in many places to be better than that of the BBC. Only in the Eastern Region is Haw-Haw listening said not to have increased.

On the other hand, the BBC is also violently criticised for 'careless talk', which contrasts with the continued radio requests to the public to be discreet.

In a recent official announcement the full address of part of the Air Ministry in Worcester was given. The Worcester press is indignant and the public agitated at what is regarded as gratuitous help to the enemy. Similar complaints followed a broadcast in which a Welsh MP named the steel works at which Anderson shelters are made.

2. POLITICAL AFFAIRS

Several reports indicate that public feeling is in agreement with the widespread press comment that we are not mobilising our man-power and industry as fully as we should; in particular, it is said that the time for voluntary efforts is past and that we should now resort to compulsion, both in industry and labour. It is also suggested that apart from the Prime Minister there is not enough drive among members of the Cabinet.

There is still some criticism of Lord Halifax, coupled with suggestions that our foreign policy should be directed by younger men.

A summary of a special report from Scotland on communist activity in Scottish industry is attached as an appendix to this report.

3. FOREIGN AFFAIRS

The events in Albania continue to cause great satisfaction, but there is evidence from several sources that people are still not prepared to accept these successes on their face value. Events in Norway and the ultimate defeat of the Finns are still remembered, and it is expected that sooner or later Germany will take a hand in the situation. Only one report suggests that people feel we should be helping Greece more vigorously.

There has been very little interest among the public in the Indian situation. Well over fifty per cent of people questioned had no opinion about India. Mr. Gandhi was mentioned by about 1 in 12 only. Of those who held definite views, opinion was divided as to whether we or the Indians were to blame for the present situation. Interest in Spain was equally limited, and a majority of those who held definite views thought that she would not enter the war; some added that it would not matter greatly even if she did so.

There has been singularly little comment on our serious merchant shipping losses.

ADVERSE INFLUENCES ON MORALE

SUMMARY

The causes of the rather lower state of morale at present appear to be as follows (in order of importance):

1. The heavy provincial raids. The effect of these has been serious only in the areas acutely concerned. There is some evidence of anxiety in towns (e.g. Exeter) which anticipate raids in the near future and fear that their defences are inadequate.

2. The disappointment over the discovery that the semi-official press predictions of an early conquest of the night bomber were unfounded.

3. The inconsistencies in official accounts of bombing – sometimes naming towns, and sometimes not doing so, and often giving what the public regard as over-optimistic accounts of damage – have produced a distrust in official news generally.

4. The increasing scarcity of many goods and the rises in prices due to the Purchase Tax, etc.

5. Shelter difficulties. The delay in equipping public shelters, and the dampness and coldness of surface and Anderson shelters, are causing concern.

6. Evacuation and billeting difficulties.

7. 'War-weariness' – a feeling that Christmas is not going to provide the traditional break in the winter and a sense of frustration about the war generally. A feeling that there is nothing positive to look forward to in the future.

8. Some doubt about the 'totality' of our industrial war effort.

9. Shipping losses.

It seems extremely important to avoid 'heartening talk', unaccompanied by official explanation of the above points.

APPENDIX

COMMUNISTS AND SCOTTISH INDUSTRIAL WORKERS

1. After a long period of quiet, there are signs of unrest in Scottish industry.

2. A major factor in this is undoubtedly communist penetration.

3. Communist policy and influence have hitherto been negligible, as is shown by the record of its twists and turns in the last year.

4. There is, however, a continuous effort to find out what general pre-existing attitudes and grievances among the workers can be exploited. Once found, the communist method of exploitation is to create shadow organisations, e.g., ARP Co-ordinating Committees, People's Conventions.

5. The Shop Stewards' Movement is not a 'shadow' organisation. It is developed out of the existing system of shop stewards, which is part and parcel of trade union organisation, and which in war-time is in a position to expand its functions considerably.

6. The local and general industrial points of friction include
   (1) Rise in cost of living – effect of Purchase Tax.
   (2) Working after the siren.
   (3) Disputes over working conditions, appointments, dismissals, etc.

7. All these are linked up with the general denunciation of privilege. This again is based on a clear-cut exposition of history, economics, politics, etc. (Marxism) which is the subject of a continuous 'education of the workers' in small groups.

In practice the present trend of communist political policy seems to be the creating of disillusionment and defeatism on the French model. This is probably not sufficiently appreciated by the industrial workers.

8. Action in hand. A programme of public education, in supplement of measures now in operation, is in hand. It includes, among other things, the issue of special leaflets, the display of films, workshop and other meetings, and special action through the press. Help is being

obtained from the Ministry of Labour and National Service and leading trade unionists and co-operators.

9. Social policy. Propaganda will be relatively ineffective unless it expresses a constructive social policy, and it is suggested that a statement of social policy, developed on the lines of the recent statement of the Ministry of Labour and National Service, is highly desirable.

MINISTRY OF INFORMATION
EDINBURGH
2 December 1940

NO 10: WEDNESDAY 4 DECEMBER TO WEDNESDAY 11 DECEMBER 1940

REPORTS RECEIVED ON GENERAL MORALE

1. GENERAL COMMENTS

There are no marked changes in morale reported this week. Following the heavy provincial raids there have been the usual grumbles about the unpreparedness of the authorities. In Birmingham, the absence of heavy raids for 3 days 'has steadied public morale enormously and the nightly trek out from the city has considerably diminished'; but one report mentions people saying 'if only all the munitions factories had been hit, they would stop bombing us'. In Bristol, the RIO reports that in the poorer districts (particularly Knowle West, Bedminster, and South Mead) there is much talk of having been let down by the Government, and of the possibility of a negotiated peace. These reports come from such divergent sources as university lecturers, social workers, company directors and doctors. The feeling is said to be particularly marked among the women. The RIO showed these reports to the Regional Commissioner, who considers that 'now that the services are returning to normal, morale will be maintained at a high level'. He is perfectly happy about the present position and has no evidence of any exodus from the city.

Among more responsible upper- and middle-class people in Bristol, it is said that the BBC and official reports of the raids have produced a serious distrust of official news. People of the town are disappointed in the way the news was handled, that their raids have not been given the same publicity as Coventry, and that they have had no visit from the King. A public announcement that no such visit was to take place was booed.

In most places which have not yet been blitzed, the view is prevalent that their turn is coming soon. This is reported from Welsh industrial centres, Leeds, Bradford, Sheffield, York and Hull, Worcester, and also in large Scottish towns. Though there is naturally some trepidation, the attitude is usually 'we can take it as well as London and the Midlands'. In Glasgow the lack of raids is attributed to the inability of enemy bombers to reach the town. In the North-Eastern Region, a similar freedom from raids is thought to be due to the Germans not having enough planes to bomb more than one area at a time.

Many Londoners expressed mild chagrin at not being the centre of the stage last week. Sunday's heavy raid created no serious upset of morale but rather a sense of excitement.

In places which have not been bombed there are reports of some complacency and a tendency to relax concentration on the war effort. 'War-weariness' is also still noticed.

Many reports stress the need for emphasis on our damage to Germany. In particular photographs of damage would be extremely welcome. The Ministry's map of bombing in Germany is regarded as a first-rate piece of propaganda.

The seriousness of the shipping losses is beginning to penetrate to the public, but interest in the subject is still limited.

2. REPRISALS, PEACE AIMS AND THE FUTURE

Demands for reprisals come almost entirely from places which have not suffered severe bombing; in the Welsh area it is reported that the majority are content that we should continue to aim at military objectives as they feel this is the soundest war policy – also some of our bombs are bound to fall on houses. They much prefer, however, to hear of bombs on Germany rather than the Low Countries or occupied France. In London a decline in talk of reprisals is recorded. At Barking, when some Nazi airmen were buried, a woman put a wreath on a coffin inscribed 'To some mother's son'; the crowd showed no hostile feeling at this action and appeared rather to approve.

The feeling that Germany must not escape 'without scars' (as she is thought to have done after the last war) continues to be strong; a majority appear to think that we should impose much more severe peace terms on Germany than after the last war. A Gallup survey by the British Institute of Public Opinion found 68% of the public in favour of 'more severe peace terms', 17% favouring 'less severe', and 15% 'don't knows'.

The increasing press interest in peace aims and post-war reconstruction is beginning to produce some effect in London, though the provinces still report little interest, except among more thoughtful people. Working-class people in London think that the Labour members of the Government are 'in to stay' and look forward to a post-war socialist state.

3. RUMOURS

Haw-Haw rumours continue extremely prevalent, taking the usual form of bombing predictions. It must be emphasised that these rumours bear little or no relation to actual broadcasts from Germany, though reports continue to record a great increase in the amount of listening to the German radio. In the South-Western Region it has been noticed that Haw-Haw rumours tend to occur in towns which are having War-Weapons Weeks – e.g. Brighton. Places from which Haw-Haw rumours are reported are Oxford, Cambridge, Bristol, Exeter, Cheltenham, Leeds, Plymouth, East London, Nottingham, Southampton and Worcester. Many reports ask that some official action shall be taken to counteract these rumours, and that categorical denials shall be made; the reports also stress the point that the greatest counteracting force would be a more informative official news service.

4. EXTREMIST ACTIVITIES

After the raids in Bristol, the Daily Worker Defence League issued typewritten handouts giving instructions to the public about where to go and what to do if their homes had been damaged. In case of difficulties, the handouts suggested that people should go for help to the offices of the local ARP

Campaign Committee (a communist organisation). Advice bureaux for raid victims have also been set up in London by the Communist Party.

Fascist propaganda is reported to be going on in a quiet and underground way in Hoxton, Shoreditch and St. Pancras. 'It will be different when Hitler comes' is the usual argument, and poverty is used as a spearpoint of grievance. Reports suggest that 'Mosley's money is still circulating and if supplies dried up the propaganda would cease.'

5. NORTHERN IRELAND

Increasing unemployment in Northern Ireland from seasonal causes is leading to considerable criticism of the Government's failure to use the available man-power. The difficulties in establishing armament factories in this area are not realised by the public. Only about 600 refugees from the bombed cities of England have reached Northern Ireland, so that no reception problem has arisen. It is alleged that fake petrol coupons, price 2d each, are being imported to Northern Ireland from Eire.

6. EIRE

A special report on Eire from a competent observer makes the following points (confirmed by Postal Censorship reports):

1. On the Irish ports question, the great majority are adamant and it is believed that pressure would only increase their resistance. An approach via USA, provided there was no question of pressure, is considered the most hopeful line.

2. The bad effect of the Irish ports announcement on Eire opinion has now been largely offset by the relaxation in travel restrictions to Eire.

3. The heavy bombing of English towns has aroused great feelings of horror, but the reaction of the Irish is to say 'look what would happen to us if we handed over the ports'.

4. While British popularity has declined somewhat over the ports question, the belief that Britain is going to win in the end has steadily increased.

5. Italian stocks are on the down-grade and the successful resistance of Greece makes many people draw an analogy between Greece and Ireland. Russia is extremely unpopular.

6. The Local Security Force is proving a great success, and as a result of local efforts to raise funds for it, many rural activities analogous to the Women's Institutes and village dances are developing for the first time.

7. Culturally speaking, Eire at the moment is on the up-grade and there is an increasing interest in art and literature, particularly if 'home produced'. It is generally believed that England is indifferent to Eire's cultural activities, and it would help much if this idea could be dispelled.

7. ADOLESCENTS

The high wages which adolescents can now earn, and the absence of paternal control (with fathers in the forces and on night shifts), are said to be lowering both the conscientiousness and responsibility of the young people to parents and employers alike.

REPORTED REACTIONS TO WAR EXPERIENCES

1. AIR RAIDS

(A) GENERAL

Special reports from RIOs at Birmingham and Bristol (and vigorous comment in the *Daily Express*, 6th December) stress the urgent importance of local authorities of all large towns preparing at once to deal with blitz chaos. Among points specially mentioned are the need to provide:

(1) Facilities for distribution of news, posters, and official announcements.

(2) An official messenger service (cycle or motor-cycle).

(3) Information bureaux and registration centres for population movements.

(4) Emergency health measures (anti-typhoid inoculation, emergency sanitation, and water supply).

(5) Other emergency public utility services (stocks of fuel and candles, public transport).

(6) Emergency feeding arrangements, including mobile canteens and Communal Feeding Centres.

(7) Adequate Rest Centre accommodation outside the town, with stocks of clothes.

The press and other sources continue to emphasise the hardship and bitterness caused by delay in settling questions of rent, compensation, and pensions. The forms and regulations dealing with compensation and pensions are said to be so full of elegant verbiage that the ordinary public cannot understand them. Variations in the allowances granted to raid victims by different Assistance Boards are also causing a good deal of annoyance.

Delay in repairing damaged houses, and in the removal of furniture from them, is a recurrent sore, for which local authorities are held responsible. Sometimes there appears to be a genuine shortage of repair materials, but often householders complain that builders are ready to do the work but that local authorities will not pass their estimates.

The Telephone Censorship summary contains repeated complaints about the lack of a proper system of fire-watchers in Bristol raids. 'Far more should have been employed in warehouses and uninhabited shops' – 'Much material damage could have been avoided' etc., etc. It is also suggested that more help should have been given to the Civil Defence services by the Home Guard.

(B) SHELTERS

Complaints about shortage and dampness of shelters are still widely reported.

There seems to be some increase in the demand for deep shelters. It is believed, however, that these demands are largely fostered by Vigilance Committees, etc.

'People sleeping in shelters,' says a special London report, 'are more and more tending to form committees among themselves, often communist in character, to look after their own interests and to arrange entertainment.' In Birmingham also 'shelter policy is under examination, and unofficial committees of social workers have been formed to ascertain conditions at first hand'. It is suggested in the *Sunday Times* that 'it might be wise to concentrate responsibility for improvement and maintenance of shelters in the hands of one central authority since the Government is now bearing the whole cost'. The press (lay and medical) suggest also that a medical 'shelter chief' is needed.

2. EVACUATION

Evacuation problems continue to bulk large. Their nature has been indicated in previous reports. The size of the problem is shown by official figures quoted in *The Economist*. In reception areas there are about 1,500,000 official evacuees (excluding the enormous numbers of unofficial evacuees); on top of this, accommodation has to be found for about 1,000,000 soldiers.

On the good side of the picture, the following points are reported:

a. Evacuation succeeds best where large empty houses have been taken over as hostels and staffed by social workers of various kinds.

b. School children without parents have been dealt with most successfully in school camps. The proportion of children removed from these camps has been far smaller than from private billets.

c. In private billets, the greatest success has been achieved where the evacuees and hosts are of the same social class. Valuable palliatives for the difficulties of private evacuation have been communal feeding for evacuees, and arrangements whereby all the children (whether evacuees or hosts) go to school on the same days and not on alternate days (so as to give hosts at least 3 days a week free from all children).

d. Hostels for non-evacuated fathers and adolescents have proved most valuable, but many more are needed.

On the bad side, the following points are specially noted, though there are many others:

a. Those who refuse to evacuate themselves or their children represent a 'hard core' – apathetic and 'afraid of the unknown'.

b. The children remaining in London are becoming increasingly undisciplined; some parents are unenthusiastic about the reintroduction of compulsory education, and suggest that their children will have to travel long distances to unbombed schools.

c. Many old people still want to get away, but cannot find billets. Many of those who have been evacuated to country institutions are still untraced by their relatives.

d. Women and children are steadily trickling back to London. The reasons for this are: less intense raiding of London; unhappiness and boredom in the country – they feel unwelcome among strangers and often have nothing to do and nowhere to go; the cold of the country and winter conditions generally; desire of wives to live with their husbands, and look after them – as well as fear of 'other women'; financial straits of husbands, who cannot afford to pay rent at home and send maintenance.

e. In spite of this returning movement, in some London boroughs recently heavily bombed (e.g. Heston and Isleworth, Finchley, Wembley, etc.) there are requests that they should be made evacuation areas.

f. Many parents are deliberately using evacuation to get rid of their responsibilities. They refuse to buy the necessary clothes for their children, and often children and hosts have heard nothing from the parents since evacuation. In such cases, it is very difficult to find out if the parents are victims of raids or merely evading obligations.

g. Key-workers are joining their evacuated families and finding jobs in reception areas.

3. FOOD

There are an increasing number of serious grumbles about the price increases and shortages. Queues outside food shops are reported in the Northern Region. There is, too, some grumbling about the Milk Rationing Scheme, and about the ban on bananas, which are much eaten by the poorer classes. For the first time, Lord Woolton comes in for criticism, and he is accused of treating certain food shortages too light-heartedly.

REPORTED REACTIONS TO NEWS

1. THE WAR IN GENERAL

The Greek advance in Albania continues to give widespread satisfaction and no slowing down is expected, except in some intellectual circles. Coupled with the usual suggestions that we ought to hit the Italians harder, many people add that we should do more to help the Greeks, even at some risk to ourselves, both by harrying Italian supply routes and by aggressive action in Libya or East Africa. No reports have yet been received on the public's reaction to the British attack in Egypt.

2. OFFICIAL COMMUNIQUES AND BROADCASTING

Dissatisfaction over the reticence of official raid communiques, and the loss of faith in official news, continue to be reported.

A listener research study (the data collected between October 20th and 25th) aimed at discovering how many people listened to the radio during raids; the distribution of the civil population was as follows:

Civil defence duties	12%
Public shelters	17%
Private accommodation	71%

Of the people in private accommodation, 18% were in private shelters outside their houses and 25% in shelter rooms, while 28% ignored the raid. A detailed study of listening showed that where there was an alert without a raid, there was little or no decline in the volume of listening, whereas in areas with a raid about two-thirds of the normal number listened.

The *War Commentary* broadcasts are stated to be increasingly popular.

3. POLITICAL AFFAIRS

There is the usual crop of criticism about Lord Halifax, and some even suggest that the Foreign Office views the retreat of the Italians as a 'cruel disappointment'.

From one Region it is stated that there is some demand for the re-establishment of local government elections. A more critical interest is now said to be taken in local government than in peace-time and people feel that elections would do something to increase efficiency and to prevent local councillors regarding themselves as 'little dictators'.

APPENDIX

NORTHAMPTON BY-ELECTION

Polling Day:	6th December, 1940	
Result:	G. Spencer Summers (Nat. Con.)	16,587
	W. Stanley Seamark (Christian Pacifist)	1,167
	Majority	15,420

29.9% voted (out of date electoral roll)

Peace Candidate's vote 6½% of total vote.

1. This is the first by-election since the collapse of France. It coincided with the ILP debate in the House when 4 votes (plus 2 tellers) were for peace against 345 votes opposing the motion.

2. Organised anti-war feeling was very slight in Northampton. The PPU did not vote en bloc for the Peace candidate.

3. The Communist Party advised their members and sympathisers not to vote for the Peace candidate. Labour was neutral; Liberals voted for the Government candidate.

4. The vote for the Peace candidate was higher than was expected. (Conservative local association estimated 600–700 votes.) The Peace candidate had feeble local status, and beyond issuing an election address conducted no campaign (even on polling day he remained in his shop).

5. The Peace vote represented unorganised, vaguely religious peace sentiment. It was not related to any constructive or political attitude.

6. An observer's study of the campaign showed that Northampton had been barely touched by the war, and the amount of local war grievances was very low. Food distribution, billeting and local services were well arranged. Northampton has a tradition of sturdy nonconformity (Bradlaugh). Studied against its background the election

result is considered to show a state of relaxed interest in the outcome of the war, a slightly declining confidence in the future, and the growth of unorganised, irrational peace sentiment.

There was, however, no striking decline in the general determination to carry on with the war.

HOME INTELLIGENCE
11 December 1940

NO 11: WEDNESDAY 11 DECEMBER TO WEDNESDAY 18 DECEMBER 1940

GENERAL COMMENTS

1. GENERAL MORALE AND REACTIONS TO NEWS

Reports stress that people in all walks of life are both more cheerful and more confident following the continuous good news from Egypt and Albania. Whereas people enjoyed the Greek successes by proxy, in Egypt they feel *our* Army has justified itself, and they can genuinely share the glory. No set-backs are anticipated in Libya; some people think that Italy will be rapidly and completely knocked out of the war, and a few that the end of the war is in sight. The thought that we are at last 'hitting Italy hard' is said to be all the more pleasing because it had been hoped for, for so long. Interest in news has greatly increased, and it is reported that, in many public houses, there is now complete silence when the news is being broadcast; this has not happened for some months.

In the provincial towns which have been blitzed, determination continues, though there are some weak spots. The general tenor of telephone conversations from Bristol is less cheerful than a week ago. While anti-war sentiments are rare or absent, reports say that there is a negative attitude of resignation. The Local Information Committee suggests that more propaganda is needed among the women 'to offset the effects of raids'. It seems that, immediately after a severe raid, one pats oneself on the back for one's courage and endurance. There is, too, so much to be done that there is little time for contemplation. After a few days, the most acute problems have been settled, and the haloes have worn somewhat thin; realities have to be faced by those who have lost their homes, their jobs, or their businesses. Telephone censors say that the morale of Southampton, as they hear it, is excellent; complaints have been remarkably rare, and there is a tone of defiance. In Portsmouth, on the other hand, there is expectation and resignation. 'People seem to feel that they are getting no public credit for their continued fortitude.' Sheffield is said to be 'in good heart, with the people tired but not glum'. While the great majority welcome the publication of the names of the blitzed towns, a few fear that if this is combined with the information that the town is carrying on, it is an invitation to the enemy to return.

High prices and scarcity of goods are the main causes of widespread grumbling. More people are attributing these to the shipping losses, and some are anticipating a serious food shortage next year. At the same time, the shortages are generally regarded as a price worth paying for victory. Concern about shipping losses was also increased by Mr. Churchill's references to the Coastal Command. While the reasons for not regularly announcing enemy submarine sinkings are appreciated, there are requests for some general statement about what the Navy is doing to protect merchant shipping.

People are looking forward a little more to Christmas, though there is confusion about travelling facilities. In Somerset, for instance, there is a persistent rumour that people will not be allowed to travel by rail after December 20th.

War-weariness is reported here and there, but is less in evidence than in the last few weeks.

There is very little interest in India.

The possibility of invasion appears to have vanished from the public mind, but no reports have been received since Lord Beaverbrook's speech.

2. REPRISALS

The demand for reprisals is increasing, especially in places where there has not been much bombing. In Bristol, a growing number of people are said to favour mass raids on the centres of large German towns, both as an 'act of self-defence', and as a sound military move. Business men in particular point out that the destruction of offices and public services produces a number of bottle-necks in industries far removed from the scene of the raid. In the Southern Region, people are reported to be getting a little tired of the slogan 'Britain can take it', and they are stirred more by reports such as that of '400 Krupps workmen killed'. They believe, moreover, that when bad weather prevents our carrying out bombing raids, the bad weather is over the target areas. On these occasions, they think that German towns should be indiscriminately bombed. Reports suggest that, if this is a misapprehension, it should be corrected. People are also growing more sceptical about our damage to Germany; an authoritative denial should, they think, have followed Hitler's speech when he said that none of his war factories had been seriously damaged. It is said, too, that 'something more convincing than Joubert is required on the subject of our bombing of Germany'. In passing, it may be said that people are mildly sorry to be hearing no more from Joubert; they attribute the discontinuance of his broadcasts to the fact that 'he gave away too much, and was too optimistic about beating the night bomber'.

3. PEACE AIMS

The increasing press interest in peace aims is associated with an increasing public interest. This is by no means confined only to the more intelligent people. The working classes are concerned particularly with the problems of unemployment and social reconstruction. In the international sphere, an army of occupation in Germany, and a European or Anglo-American Federation are mentioned. No reports have been received on reactions to Mr. Morrison's suggestion of an international air police force.

In a recent British Institute of Public Opinion Survey, 43% of people favoured publication of our war aims, 35% were against this, and the rest held no opinion.

4. RUMOURS

Reports come from many sources on the growth of Haw-Haw rumours and of his predicting a blitz of Peterborough, Bristol, Guildford, Nottingham, Cambridge, Reading, Aldershot, Hazlemere, Andover, Bournemouth, etc. It is said that these rumours are causing widespread and genuine anxiety; absenteeism at one engineering works is said to have followed one Haw-Haw rumour. These rumours are often spread by people who are normally responsible and sensible.

Gross exaggerations of bombing damage are also circulating, though less than formerly.

5. EXTREMIST ACTIVITY

Communist propaganda is increasing. The coming 'Peoples' Convention' is being widely advertised by circulars and other means, and ARP Co-ordinating Committees, the Shop Stewards' Movement, and unofficial committees in public shelters are active in the exploitation of grievances.

The Shop Stewards' Movement is becoming more active on Clydeside, and many workers are unaware that, in addition to their usual trade union subscription, they are paying an unofficial levy of 3d or 6d per week to the Shop Stewards' Consultative Conference.

National press publicity has been given to communist interrupters at public speeches. In a press conference at Edinburgh, Mr. Bevin stressed the point that a few communist interrupters wanted all the publicity they could get, and that nine-tenths of his meeting went off in an orderly manner. Yet the press devoted almost all of their reports to the 5 minutes of sensational interruptions.

It is reported that the *Daily Worker* is the only newspaper on sale in many public shelters. As a result, it is bought by many who might prefer other papers. In shelters, also, it has been found that the provision of counter-attractions – films, lectures, etc. – has caused the activities of communist shelter committees to be neglected. In the North-Eastern Region, communist house-to-house canvassing on the subject of inadequate shelter provision is going on.

In factories, film displays have proved to be a successful way of combating subversive anti-war propaganda.

SPECIAL COMMENTS

6. AIR RAIDS

(A) GENERAL

With the slackening of the blitz there has been a decline in criticism of arrangements for air-raid after-care. Complaints have mostly come from Birmingham and Southampton, where it is said there are not enough Rest Centres. The Regions Adviser reports that in certain bombed districts instructions to 'Boil all water' have been issued to people who have lost both gas and electricity. This point has apparently been used by communists 'to show that the authorities have made no serious effort to understand the problems of the people'. It is suggested that the phrase: 'Drink only boiled water or milk' would be more suitable.

The press is emphatic about the need for authorities in unbombed areas to plan 'the co-ordination of public services' to deal with the possible effects of severe raiding.

On the whole, the Government's Compensation Bill has been very well received by the press, though there is so far little evidence of what the public thinks about it. Some criticism has been made in the papers of 'the disparity between payment for damage and total loss of property', and also of the fact that 'insurance of moveable business property is compulsory, while that of private goods and chattels is voluntary'.

(B) SIRENS

In spite of the decrease in raids, there has been some revival, particularly in the South-Western Region, of complaints about the inaudibility of sirens.

(C) BLACK-OUT

Anxiety about the black-out is still fairly common. Early morning offenders and motorists are given most of the blame.

7. SHELTERS

Dampness continues to be one of the biggest shelter grievances; there are complaints about it from many districts.

8. EVACUATION

There is still a small but steady trickle of evacuees returning from reception areas to their homes. The slackening of raids on London, and the increased severity of those on the provinces, are among the reasons given for this. Others are said to be the return of school children for Christmas holidays, and postal delays, which cause wives to return home as they are not able to hear regularly from their husbands.

Complaints from reception areas seem to be dying down, particularly where communal feeding and welfare centres have been started. It is said, however, that in some places billeting officers have threatened to resign when asked to enforce compulsory billeting.

Difficulties are still reported about the removal of furniture from evacuees' homes.

9. HEALTH

There have been few comments about health matters this week. The RIO Scotland suggests that as the word 'inoculation' is associated with 'painful after effects' an alternative should be used. It is suggested also that the appeal to be inoculated should be made 'not to parents but to children themselves' – e.g. badges should be given to all children who have been treated, and children's comic papers, strip cartoons, etc. should publicise the chance of winning these badges.

It is reported that not more than 7% of the staff in a large Tilbury factory have accepted free inoculation against diphtheria and colds.

10. LABOUR

The press is still critical of unemployment figures and of delay in turning over non-essential industries to war-time production. 'Progress of the Government's training schemes are disappointing' – 'We are still fumbling and delaying on the industrial side of our war effort' – 'The process must be quicker if next year's Army and industrial needs are to be met.' These are typical of many references to the industrial situation.

The Advisory Committee of the London Region have asked that in view of many enquiries from both employers and workers there should be an official announcement about hours and conditions of work on Christmas and Boxing days.

11. TRANSPORT

There is still a large number of complaints about transport difficulties, particularly of passenger traffic during rush hours. The London, Southern and Midland Regions seem to be among the worst sufferers, the position in Birmingham being reported as 'still acute'. Troubles are also reported in the Northern, North-Eastern, North Midland, Eastern, Southern & North-Western Regions, and there is still much criticism in the press.

12. COAL

The press also continues to be strongly critical of the coal shortage, of which there are reports from many sources.

13. TRADE AND COMMERCE

The RIO Belfast reports that firms in Northern Ireland are complaining of the effects of the Excess Profits Tax and of 'the difficulties in which Ulster traders find themselves (as a result of it) compared with traders in Eire'.

14. FOOD

The food situation is giving rise to rapidly increasing grumbles. Though prices are causing a good many complaints, shortages of both rationed and unrationed foods are the cause of even more. The foods, apart from dairy produce, which seem to be mostly affected, are vegetables, particularly onions, lemons, bananas and other fruit, biscuits and confectionery. In some places milk also is said to be scarce, and in certain areas the free milk scheme for schools is no longer in operation. 'Inequalities of distribution' are blamed for many of these shortages, though there are also complaints that price control seems immediately to diminish supplies.

NO 12: WEDNESDAY 18 DECEMBER TO TUESDAY 24 DECEMBER 1940

GENERAL COMMENTS

1. GENERAL MORALE AND REACTION TO NEWS

The continuing good news from Africa and Greece has made people feel justified in forgetting the war for a little and thinking instead of Christmas and their families. There are suggestions that some are over-optimistic about the recent successes, forgetting that it is the Italians and not the Germans who are being beaten. The most conservative of these expect that Tunis and Syria will join de Gaulle, while others think that the war will now be much shorter. The Prime Minister's and Lord Beaverbrook's references to invasion aroused a passing interest; people were glad to hear that the Army would remain keyed up over Christmas; but the prospect of invasion is for the most part shadowy and there is no alarm. The lull in the raids on the South of England has led to speculations of unpleasant surprises in store, but there is no agitation at the prospect.

There are requests that the names of the regiments taking part in the Egyptian campaign should be announced as soon as possible.

Raid communiques are still criticised. Statements that industrial damage in blitzed towns is small, is resented, both as an inaccuracy and as an invitation to the enemy to return and complete the job. Grimsby is upset because the *Daily Mirror* described it as a second Devonport; people are afraid this may attract the attention of the Germans.

2. REPRISALS

Increasing bitterness towards the whole German race is still reported. Liberal-minded people fear this 'may make the peace more difficult to win'. In a special study made by Local Information Committees in the North-Eastern Region, it was found that about 58% of people favoured reprisals. The percentage favouring reprisals was smaller among the more intelligent. The number who thought reprisals would break German morale was roughly equal to the number who thought these would strengthen it.

It is again suggested that the time has come to stop the slogan 'Britain can take it.' The public is now more concerned about 'giving it'.

3. RUMOURS

Haw-Haw rumours continue. A broadcast by W. A. Sinclair is suggested as an antidote.

The only other common rumour is that large numbers of corpses in bombed public shelters are to remain there, the shelters being bricked up to form communal catafalques.

4. EXTREMIST ACTIVITIES

The communists continue to proselytise for the People's Convention. It is suggested that the vagueness of its aims gains the support of left-wing psychopaths. Such people attend protest meetings, trades union meetings, left book club discussions, etc., en masse, outnumbering the more moderate and more apathetic majorities. The Communist Party is active among unemployed Durham miners who are discontented with the Government's solution of putting the younger miners into the Army and the older ones to coalfields in other parts of the country, as this impoverishes the district. Wherever the physical condition of public shelters is improved, and entertainments, films and talks instituted, it is noticed that subversive propaganda fails. This has been specially marked in Bermondsey, where there is now not a single communist shelter committee.

5. EIRE

A special monthly Postal Censorship report on opinion in Eire makes, among others, the following points:

a. Fear of invasion is less, but fear of trouble over the ports is great. The majority want to keep out of the war (though a majority of Irish in England are indignant at their country's attitude).

b. Anti-British feeling is less in evidence, but the blitz in England has increased the fear that any deviation from neutrality will land the towns of Ireland in a worse plight, since they are thought to have no AA defences.

c. On the need for abolishing partition, the South is unanimous.

d. It is useless to expect rational or logical thought or sentiment in Eire. The historical, the religious, the mythical, and the frankly ridiculous continually obtrude themselves. Hopes that a Hitler victory will settle partition are expressed in the same town in which a Spitfire fund is organised; the wife of a German embassy official wins a fur coat in a raffle in aid of another Spitfire fund; and the Local Security Force refuse to patrol a certain beach in Donegal after 12 at night 'because they are afraid of the fairies'.

6. NORTHERN IRELAND

The same report makes the following points about the North:

a. On the subject of the ports, Northern Ireland echoes with mournful voice 'We told you so.'

b. The death of Lord Craigavon will make no difference to the feelings of the North about partition. 'Always remember that Ulster is yours – British.' King-Hall's broadcast was widely resented.

c. There are many complaints of unemployment, and of the sending of men to work in England, instead of finding them work at home.

d. The religious controversy 'still rages fiercely'.

SPECIAL COMMENTS

During the past few weeks acclimatisation to the dangers and difficulties of the blitz has steadily continued. As conditions have improved or been remedied, there has been a progressive decline in the old grumbles about aerial defence, shelters, evacuation, property troubles, and so forth. The outstanding grumbles at the moment are about different matters.

7. FOOD

Scarcity of food seems to be causing the most concern, though in view of the extent to which shortages have been reported, there are surprisingly few complaints. There is 'an increased realisation that shortage of food and luxuries must be faced'.

It seems to be commonly supposed that distribution arrangements (particularly in reception areas) and control of prices are the main causes of shortages. The importance of the shipping losses is still not fully realised.

8. COAL

In view of an official announcement early in the year that there would be adequate coal supplies this winter, comments on the present shortage are, to put it mildly, ironical. There have been many complaints, mostly from Southern England. Shortages have been reported this week in: Oxfordshire, Buckinghamshire, Berkshire, Surrey, Hampshire, Isle of Wight, Somerset, Devon and Cornwall, as well as in many parts of London.

9. TRANSPORT

Complaints about the inadequacy of local bus services in the provinces are as numerous as ever. There are still, too, complaints that the services drive recklessly.

NO 13: TUESDAY 24 DECEMBER 1940 TO WEDNESDAY 1 JANUARY 1941

GENERAL COMMENTS

1. GENERAL MORALE AND REACTION TO NEWS

A few weeks ago, people were looking forward to Christmas without enthusiasm. But the realisation turned out to be better than anticipation. Even in blitzed Manchester, 'there were Boxing Day crowds in pantomimes and cinemas', while everywhere, bomb-free nights and the generally more hopeful news of the war combined to make people feel Christmas should be enjoyed. Now they are facing the New Year optimistically; peace next Christmas is spoken of; and some are saying 'the worst of the war is over'.

There was not much speculation about the Christmas 'truce'. Most people seemed to take it for granted, and many anticipated it. Such comment as there was either compared Mussolini's Christmas bombing of Corfu with Hitler's abstention – and thought Hitler came out of it best, or speculated on what fresh devilment the Fuhrer was plotting (a new secret weapon was even hinted at). No one seemed to notice the inconsistency of the Boxing Day evening papers, the early editions of which spoke of a 'truce in perfect bombing weather', while later editions said 'bad weather stopped all bombing'. One effect the Christmas 'truce' certainly did *not* have, and that was to produce any weakening of the people's determination to see the war through.

In Sheffield, Bristol, Liverpool, Birmingham, and Manchester, people, for the most part, remain undaunted by the blitz. In Manchester, there were some doubts about 'the women being able to stick it' after the second intensive raid. Many people of all classes left the city; but after two nights, the majority returned 'more or less re-conditioned, but still wondering if they could stand a repetition of the raid'. Portsmouth, too, was described as 'a little jittery' following a terrific explosion on December 23rd, thought by the public to be due to a plane full of mines crashing in a slum district. Anxiety about our failure to check the night bomber continues, and there is some criticism of Civil Defence organisation, though not of personnel.

There appear to be two schools of thought about the war in the Mediterranean. The one holds that Italy is now finished and will soon be completely knocked out. The other is more cautious and is anticipating some 'dirty work' there by Germany before long.

Discussion of the shipping losses has diminished a little, except in sea-port towns where the dangers of their men are ever present in the minds of the townsfolk. Anxiety continues, and some people are afraid that the German's blockade is more effective than ours. There is some criticism of the way in which the news of the shipping losses is presented; the authorities are accused of 'trying to minimise their extent and importance'.

The return of Mr. Eden to the Foreign Office is popular; and it is felt that Lord Halifax is well suited to his new post. 'The square peg has found its appropriate hole at last.'

The Prime Minister's address to Italy caused delight all round. 'It was a general surprise and he timed it perfectly' people said – and added that there was more in it than met the eye. The King's Christmas message 'struck just the right note' for the majority, though informed opinion thought it too long and uninspired.

2. REPRISALS

On this subject there is little new to add. There is no diminution in the feelings of ruthlessness towards Germany as a whole (the growth of which has been recorded in these reports), and in the main people's feelings about reprisals are governed by expediency rather than humanity. They appear willing to fall in with whatever the experts think will be the most profitable line of bombing attack, but would be more than pleased if this line included the 'wholesale blitzing of German towns'. In the West of Scotland, there are indications that the reprisals question is becoming a sectarian matter in the mixed Clydeside population, and this, it is thought, may lead to trouble.

3. PEACE AIMS

The press and public continue to ask for a definition of our peace aims. For the first time there are signs that the ordinary people are beginning to take an interest in the question of town-planning. As the acute effects of being blitzed have worn off, many Bristolians are looking forward to a new Bristol, as beautiful as the old – and without its bottle-necks.

4. RUMOURS

Haw-Haw rumours are still common, though not as common as they have been in the last few weeks. Barnstaple was to be bombed on Christmas Day; Hitler was saving both Hull and Manchester – Hull for the invasion, Manchester for his capital. Now that the Luftwaffe has quashed the second of these, Haw-Haw is said to have announced the dates of Manchester's blitz in advance.

The commonest rumours now appear to be stories of greatly exaggerated casualties in the blitzed towns. In the Northern Region, the transference of Civil Defence workers to help Manchester under the 'mutual aid scheme' helped to cause exaggerated rumours, and it is suggested that the scheme should be given publicity to prevent people thinking that this transference necessarily indicates desperate damage.

In the West of Scotland, there are rumours that hit-and-run landing parties are invading the French, Belgian and Dutch coasts in motor-torpedo boats, and killing any Germans they may find. In one place in Holland, no Germans are said to have been found, and the Dutch gave the visitors a rousing welcome. The landing parties are said to be formed of two battalions chosen for their physical fitness, and are said to be in training in Ayrshire and Dunbartonshire.

Troops, lorry-drivers, and railwaymen are still talking very carelessly.

5. EXTREMIST ACTIVITIES

The communists continue to be active, but are reported to be largely ineffective. The campaign for the People's Convention appears to be languishing a little, in spite of attempts to obtain support from trades unions, professional organisations, co-operative societies, churches, and young people's clubs. Damage to the Free Trade Hall, Manchester, has compelled the Convention to find a new home in London.

Interest in pacifist activity is still almost negligible.

SPECIAL COMMENTS

6. AIR RAIDS

The entire press has been concerned with the problems of fire-watching and, on the whole, has favoured an extension of civilian aid as a permanent measure. First reactions to the Home Secretary's broadcast show that people are not unwilling to face conscription, although it is hoped that voluntary response will be sufficient to meet the need; it is added that conscripted labour should be paid.

7. FOOD

Reports on the food situation exceed in number those on almost every other subject. There are still surprisingly few grumbles, but people seem to be more preoccupied by food problems than with others which, a little while ago, were thought to be of far greater importance. Though there is a good deal of discussion about prices, shortages seem to cause even more comment. Police reports state that there have been food queues at Ashton-under-Lyne and Walsall.

The following foods are those of which shortages are most often reported:

Milk.	Vegetables, particularly onions and leeks.
Eggs.	Fruit, particularly apples, oranges and bananas.
Cheese.	Dried fruits.
Meat.	Tinned foods, particularly milk.
Bacon.	Marmalade and jam.
Fish.	Confectionery.

The shortage of tinned milk is specially mentioned as a cause of 'considerable hardship among the poorer sections of the community'.

Shortages of milk, eggs and fish are said to be accentuating the difficulties of people who are placed on a diet.

NAAFI canteens are criticised for 'the profusion of their supplies which compares unfavourably with the lack of food in many retail shops'.

8. EVACUATION

Complaints about evacuation are slowly declining, and some reports mention 'improved relations between hosts and evacuees'. But many evacuees who have been unable to face the discomforts of their situation and have returned to their homes were probably the loudest complainers. There is no evidence that the basic problems of evacuation are yet solved.

Overcrowding is causing some concern, not only in reception areas, but in blitzed towns also where homeless families have gone to live with relatives or friends.

9. SHELTERS

The insanitary and generally unsatisfactory condition of certain large public shelters, which have often been referred to in these reports, has been the subject of two special articles by the Labour Correspondent of *The Times* (27th, 28th December 1940). These articles fully confirm the matters to which we have previously drawn attention.

There are still some reports, though fewer than in recent weeks, about shortage and dampness of shelters. The demand for deep shelters has also slackened considerably, having been reported this week from only a few places in the Southern Region. In Manchester, where there have recently been several demands, it has been decided by the authorities that no more surface shelters shall be built, and that instead basement premises will be adapted for use as shelters.

Chesterfield Information Committee reports that employees in small businesses and factories are asking for a scheme of official shelter inspection, as some of them are said to distrust the protection provided in the places where they work.

10. LABOUR

There has been a decided lessening of press criticism of the Government's handling of employment arrangements; comments from other sources have also declined.

Complaints have again been made about the shortage of skilled and juvenile labour in London. One of the reasons given for this is that 'Evacuated children who have now reached school leaving age are trying to find employment in reception areas.'

11. TRANSPORT

There is still a good deal of concern about the unsatisfactory state of transport and particularly of passenger traffic. It is said that the free lift scheme 'is not working as well as it might' in London, Birmingham and Manchester.

The RIO Southern Region reports that 'Southampton wants better transport arrangements for those who work in the town but continue to sleep outside it.' It is estimated that this applies to about a quarter of the workers in this area.

APPENDIX

PSYCHOLOGICAL REACTIONS TO AIR RAIDS

A special report on this subject by Dr. P. E. Vernon, Director of Psychology at Glasgow University, has been submitted by the RIO Scotland. This report is based on studies made in all parts of Britain since September last. From it, and from other evidence in the hands of Home Intelligence, the following points emerge:

1. There is a section of the population, at a maximum 10%, in whom the mental make-up is weaker than the rest. These people when faced with difficulties or dangers, instead of facing them, develop 'nervous illnesses' (termed 'neuroses' – or 'shell-shock'); their consequent incapacity gives them an honourable escape from their difficulties.

2. In combatant armies and navies (particularly if conscript), these cases have proved a most serious problem, in this war, as in other wars. Soldiers and sailors who 'cannot go on facing' the assaults of the enemy develop nervous symptoms which make them useless as fighters and compel the authorities to send them to base hospitals. Few of such patients are ever suitable for active service again.

3. Before the war it was anticipated that there would be many civilian casualties of this type as a result of bombing, and big preparations were made. Two special 'psychiatric' hospitals were set up at Mill Hill and Sutton for London's 'shell-shocked' patients.

4. In practice there has been an astoundingly small number of such casualties. At Liverpool, less than 1% of air-raid casualties were psychological cases, and experience has been the same elsewhere. Patients who were previously suffering from illnesses have, on the whole, been made no worse by air raids. The suicide rate has fallen, as it did in the Great War.

5. The number of patients admitted to mental hospitals has increased but this is not due to more mental disease. Many homes have been broken up, and as a result chronically insane people who were looked after satisfactorily at home have now been transferred to mental hospitals.

6. In practice it has been found that evacuation, with the consequent break up of family life, has been a much more serious psychological problem than bombing. Undoubtedly many of the potential psychiatric cases have evacuated themselves or been evacuated, so that they are now in reception areas; and in reception areas the number of such patients has increased.

7. The problem of psychological illness in the civilian population has then apparently solved itself. Whereas in the battlefield a psychological illness enables the sufferer to escape from danger, in the bombed cities it does not do so. The refuges from bombing (the country and the deep shelter) are reached, not by having a breakdown, but by having sufficient determination to get there.

HOME INTELLIGENCE

II

JANUARY TO MARCH 1941

---

2 JANUARY The Blitz continues with a raid on Cardiff, followed by attacks on Bristol (3 January), Avonmouth (4, 16 January), Manchester (9 January), Portsmouth (10 January), Plymouth-Devonport (13 January), Derby (15 January), Swansea (17 January), Southampton (19 January).

5 JANUARY In the Western Desert Australian forces capture the Libyan town of Bardia and take 40,000 Italian prisoners.

6–9 JANUARY The Ministry of Food introduces two successive reductions in the meat ration.

12 JANUARY The communist-led 'People's Convention' meets in London.

19 JANUARY British and imperial forces begin an offensive against Italian East Africa.

21 JANUARY The government bans publication of the *Daily Worker*. The ban remains in force until August 1942.

22 JANUARY Australian forces take Tobruk capturing 30,000 Italian prisoners.

26 JANUARY Defeated United States presidential candidate Wendell Willkie arrives in Britain for a tour of bombed cities.

5–7 FEBRUARY Remnants of the Italian 10th Army in Libya surrender after the Battle of Beda Fomm.

14 FEBRUARY First detachments of General Erwin Rommel's Afrika Korps arrive in Tripoli.

19 AND 20 FEBRUARY Swansea is raided, followed by attacks on Cardiff (3, 4 March), Portsmouth (10 March), Birmingham (11 March), Liverpool-Birkenhead (12, 13 March), Hull (13, 18 March), Glasgow-Clydeside (13, 14 March), Sheffield (14 March), Bristol-Avonmouth (16 March), Plymouth-Devonport (20, 21 March).

4 MARCH British commandos launch a successful raid on the German-occupied Lofoten Islands in northern Norway.

5 MARCH The Essential Work Order empowers the Ministry of Labour to forbid essential workers in 'scheduled undertakings' from leaving their jobs, and employers from sacking them.

11 MARCH President Roosevelt signs the Lend-Lease Act.

15 MARCH Women aged 20 and 21 are compelled to register for war work to which they might then be directed by order of the Ministry of Labour.

16 MARCH British and imperial forces launch a successful amphibious operation to recapture British Somaliland from the Italians.

17 MARCH Jam rationing is introduced.

24 MARCH Rommel launches a German-Italian offensive in Libya.

27 MARCH Air force officers in Yugoslavia mount a coup overthrowing the pro-Axis government of Prince Paul.

28–29 MARCH The Royal Navy inflicts a major defeat on Italian warships at Cape Matapan.

NO 14: WEDNESDAY 1 JANUARY TO WEDNESDAY 8 JANUARY 1941

Note: The figures in brackets refer to sources of information, a list of which is given at the end of the report

GENERAL COMMENTS

1. GENERAL MORALE AND REACTION TO NEWS

In the general satisfaction at the news from Africa troubles and difficulties at home have assumed much smaller proportions. It is widely anticipated that the fall of Mussolini, and with him Italy, is now only a matter of time – and not a long time at that (12, 22 Inverness P.C., 6, 8, 5x, 39). There is no evidence of anxiety – even among women whose relatives are serving in the East – at the news of German aerial reinforcements for the Italians; it is suggested that the news got lost in the recent spate of Axis rumours and in the rejoicing at the advance in Africa (4, 5x, 6, 26, 39). *The Times* report that we were sending Italian prisoners to a 'concentration camp' (sic) at Ramgarh, India, has aroused some comment (39).

Many now expect the war to be over within a year (5x, 22 Reading P.C., 39).

As usual, the greatest evidence of confidence and determination comes from London and other blitzed cities (3, 23 Manchester T.C., 5x, 22 Leeds P.C., 7, 8). In blitz-free areas, there is both greater anxiety and greater apathy. In the North Midland Region, for example, 'apart from periodic bursts of interest and activity (at the moment "fire-crowing" is the subject of such a burst) there is some evidence of war-weariness, and lack of effort; personal expenditure is still very irresponsible, and young people are unwilling to form Savings Groups; farmers regard it as a "damn good" war' (3). It is suggested, too, in Scotland, that there is some over-confidence, and that people would work harder if they were a little more afraid (22 Edinburgh P.C.). Similar reports come from rural Wales (39).

The blitzed provincial towns are more and more falling into line with London. Sheffield has taken it 'extremely well' (22 Leeds P.C.). Bristol anticipated further raids with its 'thumbs up!' (7), and took its latest blitz with little of the dismay which followed earlier raids. 'People are now reach-ing the stage where they get up each morning, sweep up the debris, and carry on' (14 Bristol). The recent raid on Weston-super-Mare was taken sur-prisingly well, for the town was full of evacuees. A few of these considered returning home, and there was a little talk of deep shelters, but no jitteri-ness. The general belief was that the town had been bombed by mistake for Avonmouth. Some 'mischievous glee' was reported from Bristol, when those who had sought safety at Weston found that fate had overtaken them (14 Bristol).

Reports from Birmingham show that, for the first time, people are learn-ing from blitz conditions how much they owe to those who maintain ser-vices, like water, gas, electricity and transport, which previously they had taken for granted (22 Birmingham P.C.).

In Cardiff's blitz everyone was 'calm, cool and collected, and there was no panic or hysteria'. There was great admiration for the fire services (8). As usual, a statement that the essential services were not affected was strenuously objected to, as an invitation to the Germans to return (similar indignation at reports of 'little industrial damage' is noted elsewhere (14 N. Western, 23 Bristol T.C.)). In spite of the Weston-super-Mare incident, there is a widespread belief in the Cardiff area that the Germans' short-wave directional service enables them to pick out towns with complete accuracy, while we have nothing of this kind and are forced to rely on the personal factor in navigation (14 Cardiff).

On the meagreness of blitz news, there are still complaints. The release of pictures of damaged Manchester buildings has added to the resentment in Salford and Stretford. Liverpool, too, thinks that its damage has been minimised (10). In Manchester, in spite of appeals to the public, sightseers have added to transport difficulties (23 Manchester T.C.).

In telephone conversations, the blitz seems to have assumed much the same level as the weather (23 Liverpool T.C.).

Discussion of invasion seems to be declining, though, in the South-Eastern Region, the Home Guard are expecting to hear the bells within 2 months, and even suggest that 'they can repel the invaders without help from the regular Army' (12, 39).

One regional report states that Weygand is much discussed, and that he is 'looked upon as a potential ally' (1).

2. REPRISALS

Other people's blitzes are still a more potent factor in causing a demand for reprisals than one's own. London's fire-raid made Portsmouth, Cardiff, and the south-east speak strongly for reprisals (8, 12, 23 Portsmouth T.C.). The raids on Mannheim and Bremen caused lively satisfaction, and Birmingham and Cardiff feel they need 'bucking-up' by similar raids on Berlin (4, 8, 14 N. Ireland, 22 Birmingham P.C.). In the commentaries of news reels of London's fire-raid, revenge on Berlin was mentioned, and these remarks have been received with a fair amount of applause (39, Granada Cinemas Report). More thoughtful people deplored the tone of the remarks, which they regarded as contrary to Government policy (5x, 39).

3. PEACE AIMS

With sensational war-news, discussion of peace aims tends to recede, and this week has been no exception. The weekly press continues to discuss the problem with vigour and enterprise; *Picture Post* devotes an entire number to the subject (18).

4. RUMOURS

Rumours are declining, though careless talk continues (3, 4, 7). The publication of the approximate total casualties in the Manchester area has allayed the wilder exaggerations, but has been succeeded by a story that women bailed out of German planes brought down in the Manchester blitz (10, 26). The instructions to Civil Defence workers about the exploding incendiaries have led to some rumours in the South-Eastern Region that all incendiaries are now too dangerous to handle and are best left alone (12).

A rumour originating apparently in Ireland is that Frank Phillips the announcer has got 10 years' imprisonment for conveying information to the enemy through his intonation (22 Reading P.C., 23 Special T.C.).

Rumours of invasion rehearsals come from Ross-shire, and fears are expressed that we may lose many men by drowning, as the authorities are said to be putting 11 men into collapsible boats made for 8 only (22 Inverness P.C.).

5. NORTHERN IRELAND

Anticipation of a blitz on Belfast is growing, and civil defence preparations are greatly increasing. The news of England's blitz is making people wonder how long the great cities can stand this treatment. Invasion in the spring is widely expected, and Eire is considered a likely site for attack. It is suggested that the bombing of Eire was a test of its reactions, or alternatively, an attempt to intimidate de Valera. The suggestion that the bombing was accidental is ridiculed (12, 14 N. Ireland).

6. EIRE

No reports have yet been received on Eire's reaction to her bombs. It has been suggested that the IRA will exploit the bombs to strengthen the case for union, and consequent neutrality of the six counties (39). There are complaints of large numbers of able-bodied young Englishmen happily evading conscription by living in Dublin; Trinity College is said to be 'swarming with them' (22 Leeds P.C.). An increasing number of Irish people living in England say they are ashamed to admit their nationality, because people are so contemptuous of their country's neutrality (22 Edinburgh P.C., Special P.C.).

7. AIR RAIDS

The response to the Home Secretary's appeal for fire-watchers seems, on the whole, to have been very satisfactory (2, 4, 5x, 7, 9, 18, 23 Manchester T.C.). There has been comment, however, on the 'vagueness' of Mr. Morrison's announcement, which does not specify 'whether a man's office should take precedence over his home', or vice versa (4, 6). Publicity for the scheme seems to have been ahead of administrative arrangements, and in some cases wardens knew nothing of it until they received applications for enrolment (39).

Criticism of arrangements for the homeless is still being reported (5x, 18, 26). In Manchester 'a number of people complained bitterly of the treatment meted out to them at Rest Centres, from which they are often bundled off in a highly nervous state, and dumped into empty rooms, where they have to spend the night, cold and overcrowded, and where little preparation has been made to receive them' (35). Efforts to cope with the problem have been denounced in the press by Manchester's ex-Lord Mayor, and local papers have also commented on the situation (10, 19 N. Western).

Though complaints about the black-out seem to be slowly declining, the RIO Belfast says: 'In the opinion of the Air Force authorities and of the Ministry of Public Security, the black-out in Northern Ireland is at present very unsatisfactory' (13).

8. CIVIL DEFENCE

It has again been suggested that Civil Defence workers should be entitled to the same free travelling facilities as the Services (5x). There have been many grumbles about this matter, particularly among the AFS. Cheap vouchers for visiting evacuated families are often said to be of little use as they are valid only for three days, of which two may be spent in travelling.

The need for proper rest and refreshment facilities for AFS and ARP workers has been emphasised in the press (18, 26). The lack of these facilities has also given rise to some complaints among personnel, particularly firemen, for whom more mobile canteens are said to be needed (5x, 39).

9. SHELTERS

There have been the usual complaints about shelters this week, as well as reports of communist-sponsored agitations for deep shelters. 'They haven't been into their shelter because they can't swim,' says a typical letter mentioned by the Postal Censorship (22 Glasgow P.C.). Most people would prefer 'to risk a night at home rather than spend it in a surface shelter'. The weather, as much as the safety factor, seems to affect opinion about this type, of which there are, as usual, numerous complaints (5x, 26).

A census of shelters made on December 2nd by the Ministry of Health showed the shelter population to be distributed as follows:

London Region (as a whole)   5% in public shelters
                               19% in domestic and communal
                                  shelters, including Andersons
The LCC area   8% in public shelters
                               21% in domestic and communal
                                  shelters, including Andersons

Press criticism of shelter conditions continues. Lord Cranley, a member of the LCC, has described in the *Sunday Times*, 5th January, a tour of shelters in the London area. 'I was implored,' he states, 'to do anything that was possible to alleviate their appalling conditions' (18).

10. EVACUATION

Although the superficial problems of evacuation are being gradually, if extremely slowly, settled, the fundamental difficulties still need to be solved. While there are more reports this week of evacuees 'settling down' (7, 18, 23 Plymouth T.C.), there are others about them 'returning to their homes' (3, 5x, 7, 22 Cardiff P.C.).

The Gilbertian situation in a heavily blitzed city which is not an evacuation area is described in a report from the RIO Bristol. In the absence of planned evacuation the enterprise of local authorities and voluntary organisations in providing occupation and amusement has merely been palliative.

The situation in Bristol is that there are roughly three classes of evacuees, all of whom are, of course, unassisted. The first are those who can afford to pay to get away. The second are those who can only afford to stay away until their money is exhausted, and must then return to their homes, if these are still standing. The third are the nocturnal evacuees, many of whom leave the city every night in cars, lorries or vans, to sleep in circumstances of great discomfort in the surrounding countryside (14 Bristol, 23 Portsmouth T.C.).

11. FOOD

It seems a fair summary of the food situation to say that in spite of shortages, high prices, queues, and other difficulties, 'the position is being accepted with good grace'. The only stipulation the public makes is that distribution must be on an equitable basis (3, 4, 5x, 7). Grumbles are still at a low ebb, and there seems to have been only a mild reaction to the announcement of a cut in the meat ration (1, 3, 6, 7).

The press is becoming increasingly critical of rationing arrangements which permit places classified as catering establishments to serve large quantities of rationed foods to customers without coupons (18).

Distribution arrangements are again mentioned as a cause of shortages (9, 22 Cambridge P.C.), and unofficial rationing by retailers is said 'to result in unfair distribution' (5x).

There are reports from the Southern and South-Western Regions of people who live in blitzed areas travelling from their home towns to do their shopping elsewhere. In Bath and Winchester, whence shoppers come from Bristol and Southampton, this manoeuvre is said to have increased local food problems (6, 7).

There are complaints of an imposition which wholesalers are said to be forcing on retailers, 'who can only buy onions by arranging to take supplies of other goods which he cannot sell' (5x).

REFERENCES

1   RIO Northern Region (Newcastle)
2   RIO North-Eastern Region (Leeds)
3   RIO North Midland Region
     (Nottingham)
4   RIO Eastern Region (Cambridge)
5   RIO London Region (London)
5x   Special London reports
6   RIO Southern Region (Reading)
7   RIO South-Western Region (Bristol)
8   RIO Wales (Cardiff)
9   RIO Midland Region (Birmingham)
10   RIO North-Western Region
     (Manchester)
11   RIO Scotland (Edinburgh)
12   RIO South-Eastern Region
     (Tunbridge Wells)

13   RIO Northern Ireland (Belfast)
14   Special reports from RIOs
15   Fortnightly Intelligence reports
     from RIO Scotland
16   MOI speakers' reports
17   Local Information Committees'
     reports
18   Home Press summaries (MOI)
19   Regional Press summaries (MOI)
20   Grievances in Hansard (MOI)
21   Anti-Lie Bureau reports (MOI)
22   Postal Censorship reports
23   Telephone Censorship summaries
24   Police duty-room reports from Chief
     Constables
25   Special Branch Security summaries

26 Mass Observation reports

27 War-time Social Survey reports

28 BBC monitoring service reports

29 BBC listener research reports

30 BBC special reports

31 Citizens' Advice Bureaux reports

32 Association of Welfare Supervisors reports

33 WVS reports

34 Scottish Unionist Whip's Intelligence reports

35 Liberal Party Intelligence reports

36 Economic League's monthly reports

37 WH Smith's reports

38 War Office Postbag reports

39 Reports from primary sources

APPENDIX I

MOVEMENTS OF POPULATION

The Statistics and Intelligence Division of the Ministry of Food has recently completed a detailed study of the changes in civilian population since the outbreak of war. A brief summary of the main conclusions is given below. (The detailed report may be seen on application to the Home Intelligence Division.) For several reasons, it was decided that registrations with retailers for sugar provided the best index of population movements, and these were used.

Region	Percentage of mid-1939 resident population, resident on November 30, 1940
1. Northern	94.1%
2. North-Eastern	96.8%
3. North Midland	98.5%
4. Eastern	101.6%
5. London	74.5%
6. Southern	106.9%
7. South-Western	115.0%
9. Midland	100.7%
10. North-Western	98.5%
12. South-Eastern	82.9%
ENGLAND	94.3%
WALES	106.5%
SCOTLAND	95.5%

NORTHERN IRELAND 99.6%

UNITED KINGDOM 95.2%

Changes in some important towns or areas over the same period

Tyneside	91.6%
Durham, Sunderland	93.6%
East Riding	92.2%
Leeds, Harrogate, Wakefield	97.5%
Grimsby	93.1%
Peterboro', Spalding	108.5%
Leicester, Loughboro'	105.5%
Northampton, Kettering	114.4%
Suffolk	94.2%
Cambs, Hunts, & Beds	112.6%
Colchester	78.1%
Southend & Maldon	57.1%
Hertford	134.6%
St. Albans	126.1%
Watford	115.1%
Central London	78.5%
Inner NW	64.1%
Inner NE	58.9%
Inner SE	65.4%
Inner SW	67.8%
Outer NW	86.3%
Outer NE	93.9%
Outer SE	82.1%
Outer SW	80.9%
Oxford, Aylesbury	128.9%
Reading, Newbury, Slough	129.7%
Surrey	110.5%
Bournemouth, New Forest, Isle of Wight	96.6%

Cornwall	122.0%
Devon	114.2%
South Somerset	128.8%
Bristol Region	108.7%
Gloucester, Cheltenham	124.4%
North Wilts	119.9%
South Wilts	105.8%
Dorset	98.8%
Birmingham	95.6%
Coventry, Nuneaton, Warwick	101.6%
Wolverhampton	103.1%
Shrewsbury	112.0%
Worcester	112.5%
Hereford	111.9%
Cumberland, Westmorland, Barrow	111.9%
Preston & N. Lancs	113.1%
Liverpool & W. Lancs	95.0%
Manchester, Bolton and Stockport	93.9%
East Kent	63.8%
West Kent	89.1%
East Sussex	83.3%
West Sussex	99.1%
Caernarvon	122.6%
Merioneth	114.8%
West Denbighshire	121.8%
Pembroke & Cardigan	114.1%
Carmarthen & Swansea	102.2%

Scotland:

S.E.	91.7%	W.	96.7%
E.	95.8%	N.E.	94.6%
N.	95.3%		

APPENDIX II

WAR-TIME SOCIAL SURVEY

INFLUENCE OF THE NATIONAL MILK SCHEME AND THE CONDENSED MILK SHORTAGE ON MILK CONSUMPTION

1. The following is a brief summary of a full report by the War-time Social Survey. The investigation was undertaken at the request of the Ministry of Food. It had two objects:

   a) To discover if fresh milk had replaced condensed milk – which people were unable to buy because of the shortage.

   b) To discover to what extent milk supplied free or at reduced rates, under the National Milk Scheme, represented new milk consumption (rather than the same consumption as before, at a reduced rate).

2. The areas studied were London (Borough of St. Pancras), Reading, Leeds and Cardiff. The investigation was required to be done quickly, so was of smaller scope than desirable. 910 informants were interviewed. Random samples were taken:

   a) From all households receiving milk under the National Milk Scheme (Group A).

   b) From all households of the population, excluding those in Group A (Group B).

   The interviews were conducted between December 2nd and December 17th 1940.

3. Housewives were asked to compare the weekly consumption of their households during a typical week in June, before the condensed milk shortage and the introduction of the National Milk Scheme, with a typical week in November. Memory factors were found to be a less serious difficulty than was anticipated.

4. Of the general population (Group B), 57% of households had failed to compensate for their reduction in condensed milk consumption by fresh milk consumption.

5. Of those coming under the National Milk Scheme (Group A), 33% had failed to compensate thus.

6. Of those coming under the National Milk Scheme (Group A), 52% of households had *increased* their *total* milk consumption (but nearly half of these had increased it by *less* than the amount they were receiving through the scheme).

7. Of the same group, 23% of households had *decreased* their total milk consumption, in spite of the milk they were receiving through the scheme.

8. If households receiving milk under the scheme (Group A) are compared with those not receiving it (Group B), it is found that:

	Group A*	Group B
Increased household consumption since June	51.3%	11.5%
Decreased household consumption since June	19.8%	31.5%

*These figures differ slightly from those in paras. 6 & 7, since they exclude dried milk and fresh milk obtained at school.

9. The National Milk Scheme has therefore succeeded in producing a *real* increase of consumption in those to whom it applies.

10. The reception of the interviewers was excellent. Only 5 informants (0.54%) did not wish to be interviewed.

HOME INTELLIGENCE

NO 15: WEDNESDAY 8 JANUARY TO WEDNESDAY 15 JANUARY 1941

NOTE: The figures in brackets refer to sources of information, a list of which is given at the end of the report.

GENERAL COMMENTS

1. GENERAL STATE OF CONFIDENCE AND ATTITUDE TO INVASION POSSIBILITIES

Satisfaction at our African successes and confidence in the outcome of the war continue, but people are once more thinking more of their own personal problems, such as shortages (1, 3, 4, 5x, 7, 22 Reading P.C.). There is a general realisation that we have not yet come to grips with our real enemy, Germany, but, in spite of this, there seems to be little anxiety (or even thought) about the impending struggle; reports continue to stress that, associated with the New Year and helped on by Cabinet speeches, there is a widespread belief that victory will be achieved this year (5x, 22 Birmingham P.C., Glasgow P.C., Edinburgh P.C.).

This general confidence is reflected in the attitude of the public to the possibilities of invasion. Regional reports point out that invasion is little discussed, except in some middle-class districts. 'The subject seems to have been swamped by the blitz.' People are puzzled by the repeated official warnings, as they cannot understand how invasion could be successful so long as the Navy commands the sea and the RAF the air over Britain during daylight. An invasion attempt would be welcomed as 'Hitler's greatest blunder'. Many appear to have forgotten the instructions they were given in 1940, while others are asking if these still hold good (1, 4, 6, 7, 9, 11, 13, 22 Leeds P.C., 39).

A special study has been made during the past week on the attitude of Londoners to invasion possibilities (26). No spontaneous comments were recorded, but the subject was discussed with a large number of people. Just over half the people interviewed thought there would not be an attempted invasion; a quarter thought there would be, but many of these expressed some doubt; the rest held no opinion. More men than women expected it, and middle-class people expected it more than the working classes.

There was an overwhelming confidence that if invasion came, it would be easily defeated. When asked how far they thought the invaders would get, many thought it unlikely that they would be able to land; of those who thought landing possible, nearly all agreed that the invaders would not get beyond the coast; only about one person in a hundred anticipated any greater penetration than this. At the same time, plane and parachute landings were mentioned but no one regarded these as major dangers.

Those expecting invasion expected it soon. No one put it later than May, and some expected it within a week or so. Four times as many people said they would be glad of invasion as said they would be sorry; but the people who said they would be glad were largely those who did not expect it. Invasion would be welcomed as an opportunity to 'get at' the Germans, as a chance to speed up the war, as something to be 'got over', or as a relief from boredom. The danger of a German invasion of Ireland was often spontaneously mentioned.

A little under half the people thought that poison gas would be used; many of these thought it would be the last resort, when Germany became desperate. Exceedingly few expected it as a part of invasion, and many pointed out that its use was unlikely as it was a two-edged weapon, and we would not be slow to follow Germany's example. There seems little serious anticipation of gas warfare, and less preparation.

In another special study (26), it has been found that the blitz has been faced best in those cities which have either seriously expected raids or have experienced many minor raids as a preliminary. By analogy, it is reasonable to suppose that if invasion is a serious possibility in the near future, it would be wise if the public faced the situation rather more realistically.

2. REACTIONS TO THE BLITZ

Reports continue to point out that heavy raids increase rather than diminish the determination of the people in the blitzed towns (10, 22 Bristol, Cambridge P.C., 23 Manchester T.C., Bristol T.C.). In the unblitzed Northern Region, it is anticipated that 'it will be their turn before long', and the absence of raids so far, together with the apparently easy victory over the

Italians (and, it is added, the depressing effect of the Limitation of Supplies Order on ordinary trade and commerce) are thought to have led to some slackening of effort (1).

The Portsmouth blitz was very well faced (6, 14 Reading, 23 Portsmouth T.C.). In spite of the failure of the electric lighting supply early in the raid, behaviour was orderly and there was no panic. The release of the name of Portsmouth to the press was unfortunately accompanied by accounts which, in the opinion of the local public, greatly minimised the damage. In particular, the statement that fires were extinguished by dawn after the attack caused 'distrust and indignation', since public buildings were still blazing in the afternoon (6, 23 Portsmouth T.C.). It is rumoured that the local authorities knew of the impending attack before it was delivered, and there are complaints that they did not profit by this knowledge, nor by the experience of other blitzed towns (23 Portsmouth T.C.). There was considerable unorganised evacuation, but not on the same scale as at Southampton (6). The majority of the evacuees (apart from the homeless) were women and children, and many spent the night in the shelters on Portsdown Hill, in villages, and even in the open (23 Portsmouth T.C.).

In Bristol's last raid, a large number of bombs fell in the open country, and it is widely believed that an efficient decoy system is in operation. The general opinion is said to be that morale was better after this raid than any previous one; this is attributed to the success of civilians in dealing with incendiaries, to the evacuation of the more jittery people, and to the vigorous efforts which have been made in the past few weeks in providing entertainments and parties for shelterers and others (14 Bristol).

In the Birmingham area, the continued freedom from heavy raids has enabled the local authorities to make good much damage, and has also helped to restore the spirit of the public. People are still not risking being in the centre of big towns at night, but rush evacuation to the countryside has stopped (9).

A special report (26) stresses the extremely good morale of Liverpool in all groups of the population, except the dock-workers. This is attributed to the long acclimatization to raids which the town has had, to the toughness of the population bred from poverty, to a surprising solidarity of the Catholic Irish, and to the presence in the town of large numbers of Naval

ratings who do not allow raids to interfere with their amusement. By contrast, Manchester was found to resemble much more closely the other
blitzed towns, and there were many complaints of municipal inefficiency.

The early hour at which London's recent night raids have stopped has
given rise to much speculation as to whether we are not at last finding
something which will drive away the night bomber (5x).

3. REPRISALS

There is no doubt that the publicity given to the London fire-blitz has
stimulated everywhere – even to some extent in London – a demand for
reprisals, particularly on Berlin (3, 5x, 7, 8, 13, 22 Leeds, Glasgow, Edinburgh,
Belfast, Reading, Inverness P.C.) The exact form which reprisals should
take is apparently undefined in the public mind. Since its fourth major
blitz, the demand for reprisals in Bristol has grown (7). There are requests
for more pictures of RAF damage to Germany, and also, if possible, for more
details of our raids on Germany, particularly the number and size of the
bombs dropped (7, 24).

4. RUMOURS

Rumours this week are not numerous. There are still exaggerated stories in
circulation about raid damage and casualties in Manchester, Liverpool and
Sheffield (1, 3, 8), and careless talk in buses by women armament factory
workers is noted (14 Edinburgh). In Bristol, there is a widespread rumour
(apparently based on fact) that the Civil Defence services were forewarned
some hours before the raid of January 3/4. The information is said to have
come from wardens' posts, though one rumour stated that the Ministry of
Information informed the Air Ministry of the impending raid at 3.00 p.m.
Prominent tradesmen and factory owners asked if, in future, they could
receive these advance warnings, so as to prepare their fire-watchers, but
their requests were 'firmly turned down' (14 Bristol, 23 Bristol T.C.). The
only other new rumours are that the Germans are bombing the churches to
prevent their bells ringing when invasion comes (23 Bristol T.C.), and that
Germany is so short of metals that incendiary bombs are now encased in
cardboard or other substitutes (5x).

5. PEACE AIMS

A special report on this subject has been made by Postal Censorship (22 Special P.C.). The views of the great majority of lower-middle- and working-class writers are summarised thus:

1. They are quite certain of victory and no other possibility is even remotely considered.

2. While they are well pleased to receive help from America, they are satisfied that we can win on our own – and would prefer to do so.

3. Their main 'peace aim' is that Germany should be wiped off the map, or alternatively that all Germans should be exterminated. Many writers think that since they are now in the front line, their wishes in this respect (and in the others which follow) must be treated as a right which they have earned. More moderate demands are for a protectorate and occupation of Germany for 25 years (22 Inverness P.C.).

4. They are looking forward confidently to a post-war levelling of class distinction and a redistribution of wealth. There are many writers who are convinced that the rich are still making money out of the war.

5. They anticipate a post-war Government which is either 'national' (with a strong socialist complexion) or labour, with either Mr. Churchill or Mr. Bevin as Prime Minister.

More educated writers (a much smaller section) are considerably disquieted about our non-declaration of peace aims. Many who were previously anti-socialist are now prepared for socialism as 'the only possibility' (22 Bristol P.C.). There is a widely expressed hope that party politics and party squabbles will not revive and that some form of federalism will come, particularly between the British Empire and the United States.

Social workers and other responsible people in London hope that post-war reconstruction will not be entrusted to the present local authorities, as they consider that the blitz has shown that they are not fitted for the task (5x, 39).

6. EXTREMIST ACTIVITIES

A full report on the well-attended People's Convention will be found in Appendix II. At the same time, reports from Chief Constables and others continue to stress the ineffectiveness of communist activities. Meetings are very poorly attended, and the great majority of the public show no interest in them (3, 24, 39). Press reports of the Shop Stewards' Conference in Scotland stated that 2,000 people were present; in fact, there were only 400 (11).

Some feeling is reported because conscientious objectors can earn £5 a week doing forestry at piece-work rates (14 Edinburgh).

An increase in anti-Semitism in middle-class and business circles is reported from the Northern Region (1).

SPECIAL COMMENTS

7. AIR RAIDS

In connection with fire-watching it is stated by businessmen in the City that there is a widespread feeling that some of the big property companies have an unfair advantage because their tenants have to shoulder full responsibility for fire spotting. The question is asked 'Why should I have to engage and pay spotters to protect my landlord's property?' Volunteer spotters are also beginning to wonder why they should risk their lives to save other people's property (5x).

Reports suggest that in some places efficient operation of the scheme is hampered by lack of sufficient 'guidance and instructions' (2, 39). It is also said that in certain areas it is difficult to get the necessary number of paid watchers from Labour Exchanges (2), and some employers are said to be 'enrolling men already engaged in other forms of civil defence'.

The RIO Edinburgh says that the response to the appeal in Scotland has been 'very poor', though a statement by the Regional Commissioner on Scotland's reaction to the appeal was given an excellent press and was supported by correspondents who agreed that 'a measure of compulsion is necessary'.

The question of wages is much disputed. In some cases these are said to be 'totally inadequate'; on the other hand, AFS personnel are said to be discontented because they are getting only £3 a week, whereas some fire spotters are being offered £5 (2, 5x, 39).

In spite of the damage done to churches and other buildings of historical interest in the City fire of 5th January, it is reported that several days later many of the surviving churches were locked up, and that entrance in case of fire would have been impossible (18).

The Telephone Censorship from Portsmouth says, with regard to the raid there on 10th January, 'there have been signs of discontent at the lack of foresight shown by the local authorities'. In particular, there are complaints of lack of food and accommodation for the homeless.

The attitude of the authorities towards the homeless in other areas again comes in for unfavourable comment, particularly in the North Country press (18, 19 Leeds, 22 Belfast Special P.C.).

8. SHELTERS

Replying to Lord Cranley's indictment of London shelter conditions, reported last week, Mr. Key, Civil Defence Commissioner, said that certain of the charges made were 'grossly inaccurate' and that in other cases 'remedies were already being applied'. This is confirmed by our own reports (5x, 18).

Though shelters in Manchester were 'severely criticised' by Lord Horder during his recent visit to the city, there have, on the whole, been fewer shelter complaints this week (18).

9. FOOD

The public's attitude, according to our evidence, is best described in the words of the RIO Eastern Region. 'There is still considerable discussion, though little grumbling about the food situation in general' (4). The meat shortage, to which there are many references (1, 2, 3, 4, 6, 8, 9, 12, 22 Cambridge P.C.), has been accepted with resignation, and although reports of other shortages are increasing, these, too, seem to be accepted more or less philosophically. The Postal Censorship report says: 'There is no single instance in which the writer appears to have any idea of the cause of shortage, nor of the reasons for food restrictions' (22 Special P.C.).

Interest in communal feeding seems to be growing, particularly in Northern England, and it is suggested that there should be 'a publicity campaign outlining the official policy of this matter' (1, 5x,18).

General satisfaction is expressed, particularly among the lower-middle classes, of the principle of the Maximum Prices Order which came into operation on 13th January (5x, 13, 18). Distribution arrangements, however, are increasingly criticised, as are the allowances made to hotels and other catering establishments (1, 2, 3, 18). Reports of food queues are also increasing (1, 5x, 7, 9, 22 Special P.C., 27). A special study of them in Shoreditch showed that 50% of those interviewed complained of queuing, especially on Saturdays. 27% complained with considerable bitterness about the meat shortage and the reduction of the ration. The rest took these difficulties in good part.

There are more complaints of the alleged unfairness in the rations allowed to the soldiers compared with those allowed to farm workers and those engaged on certain heavy jobs (2, 3, 8, 18).

10. INDUSTRY

The announcement about the new War Production Executive Committees aroused very little public interest. It was severely criticised, however, by many sections of the press.

REFERENCES

1	RIO Northern Region (Newcastle)
2	RIO North-Eastern Region (Leeds)
3	RIO North Midland Region (Nottingham)
4	RIO Eastern Region (Cambridge)
5	RIO London Region (London)
5x	Special London reports
6	RIO Southern Region (Reading)
7	RIO South-Western Region (Bristol)
8	RIO Wales (Cardiff)
9	RIO Midland Region (Birmingham)
10	RIO North-Western Region (Manchester)
11	RIO Scotland (Edinburgh)
12	RIO South-Eastern Region (Tunbridge Wells)
13	RIO Northern Ireland (Belfast)
14	Special reports from RIOs
15	Fortnightly Intelligence reports from RIO Scotland
16	MOI speakers' reports
17	Local Information Committees' reports
18	Home Press summaries (MOI)
19	Regional Press summaries (MOI)
20	Grievances in Hansard (MOI)

21 Anti-Lie Bureau reports (MOI)

22 Postal Censorship reports

23 Telephone Censorship summaries

24 Police duty-room reports from Chief
Constables

25 Special Branch Security summaries

26 Mass Observation reports

27 War-time Social Survey reports

28 BBC monitoring service reports

29 BBC listener research reports

30 BBC special reports

31 Citizens' Advice Bureaux reports

32 Association of Welfare Supervisors
reports

33 WVS reports

34 Scottish Unionist Whip's Intelligence
reports

35 Liberal Party Intelligence reports

36 Economic League's monthly reports

37 WH Smith's reports

38 War Office Postbag reports

39 Reports from primary sources

APPENDIX I

POPULAR ATTITUDES TOWARDS SOME
BELLIGERENTS AND NON-BELLIGERENTS

During the last few weeks a special study has been made in which the views of rather over a thousand persons were collected and analysed. The study was intended as a preliminary to any publicity which might be undertaken by this Ministry.

A statistical cross-section of the population was not sought and the conclusions represent the opinions of the more informed and articulate sections of the community. In the sample, skilled artisans and middle classes predominated.

The percentages given below are significant mainly for the general attitudes they reveal rather than for their exact statistical value. The results are closely supported by a qualitative study of Postal Censorship and other reports available to this department.

Many people expressed neutral and vague opinions: for simplicity these figures are omitted from the percentage results.

ATTENTION IS DIRECTED TO THE FOLLOWING POINTS:

a. The high percentage of hostility towards the Vichy government. Recent reports, however, show that this hostility is very slowly declining. The results should be compared with the high degree of unfavourable reaction to the Free French Forces.

b. The very low degree of unfavourable reaction to the Czechs appears to depend, in part, on a feeling of responsibility for Munich.

c. The high degree of favourable reaction towards the Italians.

d. The comparatively high degree of unfavourable reaction towards America combined with the high proportion of people who found themselves unable to express a definite opinion.

1. THE VICHY GOVERNMENT

71%   definitely hostile

7%   favourable

Condemned as being 'a tool and puppet', 'in the hands of Hitler', 'reactionary', 'Fascist', 'unrepresentative of the French people', and 'contemptible'.

Those who viewed it favourably did so mainly on pacifist grounds. Some consider that Pétain's action saved many lives, the loss of which would have benefited none.

Few appeared to regard friendship with France as a goal or as a likely or desirable characteristic of future European relationships.

2. THE FREE FRENCH FORCES

42%   favourable

32%   unfavourable

They were praised for their bravery to continue their struggle, particularly when separated from their homes and families, and admired for their courage, loyalty, idealism and patriotism.

They were condemned for being ineffectual and inefficient (Dakar frequently mentioned) or alternatively for being reactionary and undemocratic (particularly their leaders) or untrustworthy.

3. THE POLES

33%   favourable

22%   unfavourable

They were twice as popular with women as with men.

They were praised for their bravery and given sympathy or pity for the oppression they had suffered.

They were criticised for their reactionary and undemocratic leaders, for their predatory behaviour towards Czechoslovakia, and for the backward condition of their people. They were compared with the Franco regime in Spain.

Poles in England (mainly soldiers) were well thought of, especially by women, who mainly praised their appearance and virility.

4. THE CZECHS

55%   favourable
9%   unfavourable

They were the most popular group studied and were admired as champions of freedom and genuine democracy. They were pitied for the wrongs they had suffered and for our betrayal of them at Munich. They were considered brave and their freedom from 'Fifth Columnists' was commented on.

Their critics regarded them as personally dull, unattractive and uninteresting.

5. THE ITALIANS

36%   unfavourable
20%   favourable (apart from their leaders)

Women and working-class people regarded them much more unfavourably than men and middle-class people.

They were praised for being a likeable peace-loving people whose heart is neither in war nor in Fascism.

They were condemned for being lazy, lacking in guts, cowardly and easily misled.

Mussolini tended to be regarded as a semi-comic figure (not unlike the character created in *The Great Dictator*). He roused little violent hatred.

6. THE USA

27%   favourable

26%   unfavourable

Note the high proportion of people unable to express an opinion. Women were far more favourable than men, young people than older people.

Americans are praised for being a pleasant mixed race, anti-Nazi and pro-British, generous and frank, dynamic and go-ahead.

They are criticised for being mercenary, stupid and ostrich-like, conceited and smug, wordy and self-interested.

This result indicates a clear need for further background information and interpretation of Anglo-American relationships.

7. THE DUTCH

37%   favourable

11%   unfavourable

They are liked for their solid homely virtues, cleanliness, and bravery under threat.

Unfavourable comment stresses their important Fifth Column, their 'mercenary and greedy' outlook and the dullness of their national characteristics.

8. THE GREEKS

35%   favourable

19%   unfavourable

Women favour them more than men.

There was a high proportion of indefinite replies. Many people express complete ignorance about Greece and the Greeks, and have a fragmentary idea of Greek history and geography.

Greeks are praised for their unexpected bravery, for their historic traditions.

Criticised as being unimportant and for dirty and slovenly habits. They are thought to be cruel and have a low standard of living and popular culture.

HOME INTELLIGENCE
13 January 1941

APPENDIX II

THE PEOPLE'S CONVENTION

Held in London, 12 January 1941

The following notes on the Convention are taken from a detailed study which is available if required.

1. In spite of initial difficulties, the Convention was well organised and extremely well attended. There were 2,300 delegates (see end of this note for distribution) and over 1,000 people attended most of the meetings. Numbers of people were unable to get in.

2. The dominant age group of the delegates was 25–35. Very few people of 50+ were observed. There were more men than women. Only a very small percentage of middle and upper classes attended. CP members did not dominate the Convention numerically and obviously efforts had been made to bring 'sympathisers' and 'fellow travellers' to the meeting.

3. The speeches of Pritt and Palme Dutt were greeted with the greatest enthusiasm and our observations indicate that Pritt's 'leadership' position has considerably improved. There were a number of well-known non-party people among the audience, including popular Jewish band leaders and others with reputations in the cultural field.

   Important speaking time, however, was given to W. J. R. Squance, former General Secretary of the Associated Society of Locomotive Engineers and Firemen, and Harry Adams, an official of a building trade union.

4. The Convention accepted the eight-point programme, the centrepiece of which is the achievement of a People's Peace by a People's Government.

5. Domestic grievances, around which *Daily Worker* policy has centred for some time, were vigorously ventilated, but food, shelters, wages, compensation, etc. were of secondary interest both in the programme of the Convention and in the response aroused.

6. 'The achievement of peace' was the dominating issue of the Convention. Pritt denied pro-Hitler accusations and put forward the Convention's 'peace offer'.

'Our policy is to offer to the peoples of the enemy a peace of no annexations and no reparations or indemnities, with liberty to all peoples to determine their own destiny. We know that the German people, freed from the fears based on the declarations of British propagandists, will no longer be willing to fight and suffer for Hitler's aims but will accept such an offer if it be made by a people's Government in whom they have confidence.'

7. Interest and discussion centred on world affairs, and the atmosphere of the Convention must have demonstrated to CP leaders the fact that the interest of the extreme left wing is still concerned primarily with world organisation and international affairs.

8. The rareness of common meeting places nowadays brought to this occasion a special sense of 'left-wing solidarity' and the similarity of regional interests. The means whereby contacts between provincial delegates could be maintained and developed was eagerly discussed in the lobbies and raised on the platform.

9. Plans for securing a People's Government and a People's Peace amounted to little more than the getting together of like-minded persons in ever-increasing numbers, particularly by regional conventions, plans for which were stated to be well in hand.

10. Accounts of the Convention appearing in the press showed that most of the provincial press gave objective descriptions of the meeting with little critical interpretation. The national press devoted considerable space to the Convention and some of the headlines devised were curiously misleading to those unaware of the political issues involved, e.g. 'Offer of Peace to the Enemy Proposed' (*Times*); 'Peace Meeting in London; 2,000 Delegates' (*Telegraph*); 'Mr. Pritt holds Peace Jamboree' (*Daily Express*); '2,000 at People's Convention; Its Policy for Peace' (*East Anglian Daily Times*). The *Herald* and the *Worker* carry on a slanging match: 'The People's Convention is an incendiary bomb which has failed to explode...It will not impair the fighting faith of British workers in their trade unions and in the Labour Party.' 'They have now worked out the latest major "party tactic and line" which can be described as "revolutionary

defeatism".' 'Mr. Pritt, a political innocent' (*Daily Herald*). The *Daily Worker* singles out comment from the *Herald* as being the only attack worth noticing: 'Bile overcomes consistency.' 'Napier's 3,000 workers repudiate the *Herald*'s venomous attack.' 'Having failed to prevent the Convention, it now complains that insufficient discussion took place.'

An interestingly analytical leader appeared in the *Birmingham Post*, January 13th: 'Appeasement: New Style'.

HOME INTELLIGENCE
15 January 1941

DISTRIBUTION OF DELEGATES

ANALYSIS OF DELEGATES
(OCCUPATIONAL)

Trades Union groups	500
Factory groups	430
Political parties	230
Local convention groups	213
Youth organisations	108
Co-op	81
Discussion groups	63
Cultural societies	26
Women's organisations	19
Colonial representatives	14
Miscellaneous	87

ANALYSIS OF DELEGATES
(GEOGRAPHICAL)

London	905
Scotland	117
S. Wales	100
N.E. England	97
Sheffield	95

Birmingham	87
Eastern Counties	71
Leeds	68
S. Midlands	67
Home Counties	55
Lancashire	45
Hants and Dorset	42
Bristol	34
S.W. England	8

APPENDIX III

FURTHER DETAILS OF POPULATION MOVEMENTS

A further report by the Statistics and Intelligence Division of the Ministry of Food summarises the population changes between mid-1939 and November 30th, 1940, in evacuation, neutral and reception areas. It is based on the same criteria as the report summarised last week. It is pointed out that in reception areas, the figures tend to be too low, and in evacuation areas, the figures tend to be too high; this is because many people who live in the country shop regularly and are therefore registered with retailers in towns. To indicate the direction of the allowance to be made, a + or – sign has been added to each percentage.

	Percentage of mid-1939 population resident on November 30th 1940		
	Evacuation areas (%)	Neutral areas (%)	Reception areas (%)
1. Northern	92 –	99 –	93 +
2. North-Eastern	95 –	101 –	95 +
3. North Midland	99 –	107 –	102 +
4. Eastern	86 –	92 –	108 +
Eastern II	67 –	107 –	117 +
5. London	69 –	92 –	

6. Southern	79 –	135 –	112 +
7. South-Western		101 –	120 +
9. Midland	95 –	103 –	106 +
10. North-Western	92 –	98 –	107 +
12. South-Eastern	64 –	87 –	102 +
ENGLAND	81 –	98 –	108 +
WALES		104 –	107 +
SCOTLAND	94 –	104 –	94 +
GREAT BRITAIN	82 –	99 –	106 +

HOME INTELLIGENCE

NO 16: WEDNESDAY 15 JANUARY TO WEDNESDAY 22 JANUARY 1941

GENERAL COMMENTS

1. GENERAL STATE OF CONFIDENCE AND REACTION TO NEWS

While there is no evidence of any change in the high level of optimism and confidence noted last week, people seem to be a little more alive to the struggles which have yet to be faced. This is due to several factors:

a. The Prime Minister's Glasgow speech.

b. The new evidence of German air activity in the Mediterranean. This is 'taken seriously but not anxiously', and 'many are surprised that such help has not been given before'.

c. The rather slower tempo of events in Africa.

d. The large amount of space which the national press has devoted to invasion dangers.

But in many parts, the general public are still not taking 'invasion warnings' seriously. It taxes the public imagination to see how invasion could possibly be successful; though a number think a successful German invasion of Eire a much more practical proposition.

From the blitzed towns there is little new to report. The Plymouth blitz of 13th January was taken with courage and cheerfulness. The local papers could not be published because of lack of power but were able to improvise arrangements at Exeter. Here both a morning and an evening paper were printed and despatched to Plymouth and throughout Devon and Cornwall by road. After the Portsmouth blitz of 10th January, it is reported that morale was on the whole excellent (due to the admixture of civilian and Service population), but, particularly among women, there were 'small patches of defeatism'. The attitude of such people is summed up thus: 'We hit the other fellow and he hits us, and neither of us gets anywhere.'

The increasing amount of news about American aid to Britain has not been altogether favourably received. On the one hand, people are glad of the promises and pledges for the future; on the other, they feel that achievement has not kept pace with the promises. This has tended to make a number 'curiously uninterested in American developments', while others draw cynical comparisons with the last war.

As usual, when the news tends to be good, criticism of news presentation is small, and 'there is no longer the cynical hostility to official news which there was 3 months ago'. The timing of the release of the news of the bombing of the *Illustrious* and the *Southampton* was criticised on two mutually incompatible scores. Some people complained of our being 3 days behind the Axis with the news, while others were 'disgusted' because the announcement was made too soon for all the relatives of casualties to be informed. It would seem that an explanation to the public of the official policy on the timing of announcements about naval and shipping losses would be helpful.

There are suggestions that more should be done to publicise the civil defence regions, and the regional commissioners, as most people are said to have only the haziest ideas on the subject.

2. REPRISALS

The London fire-blitz is certainly the most potent stimulus for 'reprisal' demands which has yet occurred. Reports on this subject are still numerous.

Many seem to have been more angry at the destruction of historic and artistic London buildings than over raids when loss of life was much more severe. In a special report from the RIO Scotland, it is pointed out that, after every blitz, the question of reprisals is always raised at 'War Commentary' meetings. With equal regularity, the audience is satisfied by the explanations of an official bombing policy which the lecturers give.

3. RUMOURS

Few rumours have been reported. The story of the shelter full of corpses converted into a communal tomb is still cropping up after each blitz. Following the rumour of official fore-knowledge of Bristol's blitz, another rumour alleges that the authorities were warned to expect a gas attack the following night. It is rumoured in Aberdeen that barges for invasion of France and Holland are being built on the Clyde. Eire's petrol shortage is rumoured to be due to deliberate British policy, so that the Irish petrol pumps may not be full in the event of invasion. Only one Haw-Haw rumour has been reported – from Colwyn Bay.

4. BROADCASTING

A special Listener Research study on the subject of the public attitude to radio talks has been made through 1,250 honorary listener correspondents. It was found that:

a. During the past year, there has been a definite increase in interest in talks about the progress of the war, provided that these are *really informative*, and are not merely 'pep' talks.

b. The public appetite for practical talks – hints on dealing with war problems, gardening, cooking, war-time health matters, civil defence, etc. – has increased slightly in the same period.

c. A similar slight increase in interest is noted in talks which have nothing whatever to do with the war.

There is no evidence to show that more people are actually listening, but the maintenance of past figures is very satisfactory, in view of the numbers who are separated from their sets by Home Guard duties, blitz conditions, etc.

SPECIAL COMMENTS

5. AIR RAIDS

The announcement of plans for fire-watching has been generally welcomed as evidence of the Government's use of its compulsory powers. Some women are said to be aggrieved because they are not at present included in the scheme. Other people feel that it lets them out of taking the initiative but are willing to co-operate when told what to do. In Scotland, where the response for volunteer watchers was reported last week to be 'very poor', the situation is said now to have improved.

There have been more objections to 'the unfairness of the scheme', which puts all responsibility on the occupier of premises and none on the owner. The difficulty of getting watchers from Labour Exchanges is again reported, as are complaints about 'demands for exorbitant wages'. The disproportionately high pay which some watchers are getting is the cause of serious dissatisfaction among firemen, particularly in the London area.

There is evidence of a slight but perceptible increase in public apprehension about the possible use of poison gas.

6. SHELTERS

There has been very little comment on shelters this week, though recent bad weather has revived complaints in some Regions.

7. EVACUATION

Unofficial evacuees from blitzed towns, who are not subjected to medical inspection, are alleged in some cases to be 'dirty and verminous'.

In certain areas Citizens' Advice Bureaux report that they are 'overburdened with problems of unofficial evacuees'.

8. FOOD

The food situation remains more or less unchanged. The scarcity of meat is still much the biggest problem in most areas, and though the majority accept the shortage philosophically, there is a minority which is loud in its complaints. There has lately been a revival of unspecified complaints about wastage of food in military camps. The centralisation of food stocks in large towns is also still criticised, as this is thought to increase the risk of their destruction by bombing. Reports from various sources continue to show the success of communal feeding arrangements.

9. AGRICULTURE

The press, particularly in agricultural regions, is protesting vigorously against the calling-up of skilled farm workers. Local branches of the National Farmers Union are also critical of this policy, and it is suggested that 'it would be wiser to release more men from the Services to work on the land, rather than to take them away from it'.

Objections are reported to the employment of the Women's Land Army because its members lack sufficient farming experience; many of them are also said to be physically unequal to the work they are expected to do. There are some complaints about them from farmers' wives who prefer looking after men, as they are thought to fit in better with domestic arrangements.

10. PENSIONS AND ALLOWANCES

Citizens' Advice Bureaux report that 'complaints are frequently made of delays in settlement of claims of both civil and military pensions'. Great hardship is said to be caused in many of these cases, and 'weeks are said to elapse before some claims are even acknowledged'. There is also much criticism about the allocation of dependants' allowances, and it is said that investigators 'do not take sufficiently into account the heavy financial commitments of many households'.

11. PRISONERS OF WAR

Citizens' Advice Bureaux and other sources report a large number of complaints about the non-delivery of parcels to prisoners of war. The British Red Cross is largely held to blame for this.

APPENDIX

PUBLIC OPINION IN EIRE

In a special report by a skilled observer the present position of public opinion in rural Eire and Dublin is outlined. In reading this summary, it is important to realise that in Eire emotions are often more important than logic; the chain of causality can only be worked out if allowance is made for historical and emotional factors, together with a certain racial perversity. The following points are made:

RURAL IRELAND

Here the main subjects of public concern are as follows:

1. The *bombing* of Eire. For a few days after the raids, panic predominated over indignation. Even the sound of a motor-engine made people look up or move to cover. The attitude towards planes seemed 'almost superstitious'. Since the only fatalities were in a remote country area, people felt that 'you were safe nowhere'. The German origin of the bombs was announced in the papers in a very brief paragraph only. The public feel that 'the Germans are very wicked', but at the same time 'if one side doesn't bomb us the other will'.

2. The acute *petrol shortage* has brought the war home sharply. Rumour stated that five petrol tankers had been sunk inside Irish territorial waters. The ration is now half-a-gallon a week, and for taxi drivers a gallon a day. The fact that the Government encouraged people to re-licence their cars has led to general indignation. The present situation may well mean ruin to thousands of people connected with the motor trade. It also affects large numbers of country people who regularly hire cars for outings and pack in incredible numbers. No shortage, except that of tea, could bring home clearer to Eire the precariousness of her position.

3. The taking over of the *A-Section* of the *LSF* (men of military age) by the Army. This is regarded as a precaution against possible IRA activities. The oath taken by the LSF is 'loyalty to Eire' – not to any specific Government – and, in a crisis, it is felt that some of these armed young

men might interpret this as loyalty to the IRA. The Army will now assume responsibility for the safety of the LSF arms, so that, on the whole, the change over is popular, as it appears to make for greater security.

4. Roosevelt's speeches and *US help* for Britain. First, this confirms the idea that the war will spread; secondly, it is thought to heighten the chances of British victory; thirdly, it has created a certain glumness among quite a large number of people who would have preferred an indecisive American attitude. Among these people (sufferers from the Irish persecution mania) there is a growing and uneasy realisation of another America besides Irish America. There is considerable dread of loss of American sympathy for Eire, and a great desire to bid for American support for Irish neutrality and for their help in obtaining supplies.

5. The *fire of London*. This gave a great horrific thrill. Photographs of the ruins were largely featured in the papers. The usual reaction is 'Will it happen to us?' There is little compassionate reaction and no aesthetic reaction. The general feeling is that 'London was too rich', though the destruction of the churches (even Protestant churches) is condemned.

6. Irish *agricultural* problems. The threatened wheat shortage gives an opening for the Cosgraveite party to condemn the Government's encouragement of industry at the expense of agriculture. The demands of the farmers are steadily growing. Meetings, demonstrations and marches of farmers to demand better terms for compulsory tillage are reported all over the country. Dairy farming is on the decline this year, partly due to the tilling up of grazing land, partly to the prolonged drought last summer, and partly due to a shortage of imported cattle food.

DUBLIN

Here pessimism is general; it is due to the time of year, the severe weather, flu and colds, petrol shortage, and a feeling in all classes of instability and danger. People appear to realise that, in England, Eire is either disliked or regarded as negligible; they resent this and at the same time take it to heart. It is suggested that if America enters the war, Eire will feel completely left out of the picture; the taunt of insignificance may have a helpful effect on their attitude. Special points are:

1. *Dublin's reactions* to its *bombing*. The attitude is essentially evasive; people don't want to take up any definite attitude. Three theories are offered: that the bombings were accidental (this is the most popular); that they were a threat by Germany on account of secret concessions by de Valera to England and America; and that they were a provocative act by British planes disguised as Germans, with German bombs used. This theory is very prevalent in the West of Ireland, which has always been anti-British. 'Absurd as it may seem, there is no doubt that the bomb-ings have temporarily increased anti-British feeling in Dublin amongst the lower classes and the more ignorant people. There seems to be an underlying suspicion that Britain may be pleased by the incidents.' On the whole, Dublin took its bombs better than was expected; now the city feels, as it were, grown-up. The national love of excitement and unusual happenings have acted as a hopeful counter-poise to the Irish dread of war. The fact that one bomb fell on the South Circular road (a Jewish quarter) is frequently commented on and it is said that *if* the bombs were German, and *if* it was intentional, they were aiming at the Jews.

2. *Invasion fears* are still very general in Dublin. It is now expected the Germans will be the invaders, but it is feared that this will mean the re-entry of Britain into Eire; there is still a neurotic fear of British reoccupation, which after so many centuries will take a lot of getting rid of. If the Irish could be convinced that Britain would regard per-manent reoccupation of Eire as neither desirable nor expedient, it would do much good. Apart from the reoccupation question, stories of a British invasion are now generally treated as German propaganda.

3. The *ports question*. People are still unwilling publicly to connect the petrol shortage with their attitude to the ports question, but under-neath they are beginning to make this connection. The Irish are frightened of each other and are always closely watching each other, and this mutual fear is inhibiting. The degree of British protection which Eire's shipping enjoys is not generally known, and if a brief, clear and explicit statement of the Irish position were to be made in

the British Parliament it would almost certainly be reprinted in the Irish papers. In so far as the Irish acknowledge British protection they regard it as a debt. 'Britain gave us a bad deal for centuries; she owes this to us now.'

From other sources, the salient points of this special report are confirmed. English, Scotch, Welsh and Northern Irish letter-writers all agree in thinking the bombing of Dublin a good thing; 'that will teach them to co-operate with us' is the typical attitude.

HOME INTELLIGENCE
22 January 1941

NO 17: WEDNESDAY 22 JANUARY TO WEDNESDAY 29 JANUARY 1941

GENERAL COMMENTS

1. GENERAL STATE OF CONFIDENCE AND REACTION TO NEWS

Though the realization is growing that 'we are in for a critical period in the near future', a feeling of confidence still prevails. Anticipations that 'the end of the war is drawing near' are fairly frequent. 'The tide of battle is fast changing, and this year will see old England on top of the lot' is a remark quoted by Postal Censorship which characterizes the trend of many letters. Delighted with 'the crumbling of Italian forces', many people are inclined to believe that 'Italy is on the verge of capitulation.' The absence of air raids has caused a certain amount of speculation about Hitler having 'something up his sleeve', but the possibility of this seems to arouse no serious anxiety. The suspicion is gaining ground that what his sleeve conceals are plans for invasion, probably through Eire. There is, however, complete confidence in our ability to deal successfully with such an adventure. At the same time, many people appear to have forgotten the instructions issued about 'staying put', etc., and it is suggested that some of the earlier publicity about what to do should be revived.

Interest in America's attitude shows some signs of stimulation. This is attributed partly to Roosevelt's extremely cordial welcome to Halifax, and partly to Willkie's visit to this country, which are described as 'alleviating the unimaginative and critical apathy' of the public's attitude towards American assistance.

2. REPRISALS

There is still a chorus of opinion favouring reprisals.

3. EXTREMIST ACTIVITIES

Except for a leader in the *Daily Mirror*, press reaction to the suppression of the *Daily Worker* was favourable. Subsequent articles by Cummings in the *News Chronicle*, by Frank Owen in the *Evening Standard*, and an article by Cameronian in *Reynold's* expressed doubt about the means invoked to impose the ban. *The Tribune* says that the ban 'will enormously strengthen the communists' propaganda'.

German propaganda stations make use of the news, as might have been expected. Haw-Haw gives the news with little comment; Workers' Challenge and NBBS, while dissociating themselves from communism, make much of the fear and tyranny which caused this 'suppression of workers' liberties'.

Indirect methods of studying public reactions showed that as many people opposed the ban as supported it. Many, however, were disinterested. Those who were against suppression gave as their main reason the importance of having a safety valve for airing grievances. There was little evidence that people thought that the *Daily Worker* and/or the Communist Party were engaged in sabotage or subversive activities.

The main communist periodicals now circulating in this country are:

Challenge	weekly
World News and Views	weekly
Labour Monthly	monthly
Russia Today	monthly
Inside the Empire	monthly
Labour Research	monthly
New Propellor	monthly

There are in addition a number of specialist publications addressed to workers in various industries.

4. POLITICAL MATTERS

The debate on production and man-power aroused only a confused reaction: many people welcomed the sign of Government activity, but Bevin's statement was given a critical press, and the Prime Minister's assurance that 'the Government was getting into its stride' was received with some scepticism. The omission to set up a national wages policy was also criticised in several papers.

5. BROADCASTING

Interest in enemy broadcasts is the subject of a BBC listener research report, 20th January. From this it appears 'there has been no increase in listening over the last few months, and though there may be a tendency to under-estimate the amount of listening, there is every reason to accept the evidence as broadly indicative'. Listening to Italian and other foreign stations is said to be negligible. The report indicates a decline in 'the audience, as well as the influence, of Haw-Haw, and probably of Workers' Challenge too'. This is corroborated by evidence from other sources, which confirm also that the chief inducements to listen to foreign stations are bad reception of BBC programmes, and the hope of hearing news which might be delayed or suppressed by British censorship.

Listener research has also made recently a special summary of the public's radio habits which shows that 'about 15 million of the total adult population of 35 million listen nightly'. On weekdays the audience rarely exceeds an average of 3½ million in the morning, 'or reaches as much as 3 million in the afternoon'. Other averages are:

WEEKDAYS		SUNDAYS (morning and afternoon) 4½ million
6.30 p.m.	3½ million	
8.30 p.m.	6 million (Sat. 11 million)	nearly 8 million
9.30 p.m.	5 million (Sat. 6 million)	over 6½ million
11.00 p.m.	1½ million	

The audience average is highest at one o'clock on Sundays, when there are about 17½ million listeners.

Priestley's return to the microphone has not aroused much comment, but what has been said has been, on the whole, favourable.

6. RUMOURS

A decline in Haw-Haw rumours is indicated by the direct evidence of Police Duty Room reports, and indirectly by the very small number quoted by other sources.

Among tales of mystery and imagination reported this week are accounts of 50,000 parachutists descending on Newcastle – a story afterwards attributed to the escape of a barrage balloon; the machine-gunning of the King and Queen (after they had watched a mock raid at a Suffolk aerodrome); and a 'gas scare' at Southampton, resulting apparently from the destruction of a cold storage plant.

7. AIR TRAINING CORPS

'Great enthusiasm' is reported for the Air Training Corps. The only criticism is that the scheme was said to have been 'prematurely announced on the wireless, so that the authorities were overwhelmed with enquiries to which they could give no reply'.

8. JUVENILE CRIME

Growing alarm is recorded at the growth of juvenile crime.

SPECIAL COMMENTS

9. AIR RAIDS

Slackening of nightly air raids has led to a reduction of the Tube shelter population from its peak – 177,500 on 27th September 1940 – to 65,000 on 28th January 1941.

The compulsory nature of the Fire-Fighters' Order still receives favourable comments. Progress in organisation for protection of residential property is reported from Manchester, with accompanying 'slowness of organising business and commercial schemes'. Good response to appeal is reported from several Regions, and movement to provide both voluntary and paid fire-fighters has been 'much accelerated' in Scotland. Some perplexity is voiced by volunteers with regard to 'payment for hours put in at night', and/or whether they will be given a food allowance, and of details of compensation for injuries incurred while on duty. Misgivings are stated to exist among women who anticipate 'that their menfolk will be taken away at night leaving them to look after children and cope with incendiary bombs single-handed'.

This week there has been considerable press criticism of the Government's Raid Compensation scheme, chiefly on the grounds that 'owners have to pay a fixed contribution, though no clause is made for the compensation to be paid at any fixed time'.

Although there is still occasional expression of apprehension of a possible sudden use of gas, the proportion of people carrying gas-masks has dropped to 'less than half' in 10 out of 16 towns studied, and to 'less than 2% in Yorkshire, apart from school children and some factory workers'. A recent survey taken in Barnsley, Halifax and Cleckheaton reveals 'a general belief that the chances of a gas attack are extremely remote'.

It is said in Manchester that 'as a result of the blitz 50,000 people are without masks'.

10. SHELTERS

Improvement in many communal London shelters is reported to be 'moving at a good round pace', but many complaints are voiced at persistent flooding and dampness in large numbers of Anderson shelters, in spite of recent concreting. Bad effects on the health of pregnant and nursing mothers who travel long distances to spend nights in communal shelters with little food are deplored. Requests for facilities for drying clothes and for lock-ups of valuables are requested in the East End of London where pilfering is reported, and workmen cannot dry their clothes.

11. EVACUATION

The publication of the Government White Paper on Evacuation has roused considerable press comment, but raises no new issue of importance.

Little change in the actual situation is reported, but appreciation of the value of Communal Feeding Centres is reported to be growing in some reception areas.

The 'trickle back to the South Coast' is shown by Postal Censorship to have grown into a 'steady flow'.

The nocturnal and weekend evacuation from Bristol is stated to be causing much local controversy and irritation and also a serious crowding of all roads leading out to the country. 'Disorganised voluntary evacuation is helping to strengthen class bitterness and to prepare the ground for defeatism and subversive propaganda.' (Note: Bristol has now been declared an official evacuation area, so this situation should gradually be eased.)

Main reason for mothers and young children returning to London is still stated to be the impossibility of 'managing on present rate of allowances for working man and wife who maintain two homes'.

12. FOOD

The food situation still occupies the forefront of the public mind and complaints are increasing in number and variety.

Shortage of meat and difficulties of obtaining substitutes are main reasons for grumbling, especially among the working classes who cannot easily think of new dishes to take the place of those made from unobtainable commodities.

Lack of meat and other proteins is reported to be a serious grievance in factory canteens and Government training centres. The supply of meat to restaurants and people able to eat there without coupons arouses protest.

The difference between Service and civilian rations is shown when soldiers are on leave, and causes difficulties to retailers and much adverse comment – e.g. that they are allowed 7/6d for meat per week as compared with 1/2d. Complaints of waste in Army camps are received from many sources, and that NAAFI canteens are 'heavily stocked' in districts where there are serious shortages.

Criticism of distribution is growing and Postal Censorship begins to show criticism of Lord Woolton, largely for tardy price control which 'tends to make foods disappear from the markets' and restrictions on unrationed food.

Queues for and inequalities in supplies of eggs to local retailers come in for many unfavourable comments. Local authorities and retailers are often blamed for shortages by the general public and there is much resentment when 'full rations are not obtainable'.

A recent BIPO survey reveals that 42% of housewives have 'difficulty in getting unrationed foods'; 29% stated 'no difficulty; 16% said, 'price too high'; 13%, 'don't know'.

13. TRADE AND INDUSTRY

'Tremendous need for more day nurseries and more day centres for children of women workers. Lack of these facilities is said to be one of the greatest drawbacks to women entering essential industries.'

Women workers, especially married ones, are seriously concerned about the shopping situation. 'For working women the dinner hour, their only shopping time, does not enable them to buy the food they need, as much of it is sold out early in the morning and many shops close during the middle of the day.' Some factories stagger hours for women workers to meet this need, but this practice is not universal and some women workers are reported to have left industry because of these difficulties.

NO 18: WEDNESDAY 29 JANUARY TO WEDNESDAY 5 FEBRUARY 1941

GENERAL COMMENTS

1. GENERAL STATE OF CONFIDENCE AND REACTION TO NEWS

There is little change to report since last week.

The successes in Libya continue to give satisfaction, but 'people are inclined to take them for granted'.

The lull in raids still causes relatively little speculation.

Owing to the vigorous press campaign there is more awareness of the possibilities of invasion, but most people have not considered seriously what they will do when it comes; many have forgotten the previous Government instructions; some wonder if these still hold good; and a few speculate about whether the Government is as unprepared for gas attack as it appeared to be for the blitz.

Boredom with the war is reported. Local and domestic problems are bulking larger in people's minds than national ones.

Confidence, even over-confidence, and complacency about the issue of the war are marked.

2. RUMOUR

Few rumours are reported, and Haw-Haw's alleged sayings are also rare. Tales of costly invasion failures are once more starting to crop up.

SPECIAL COMMENTS

3. AIR RAIDS

The press continue to give warning of the probable use of gas. Though there is no evidence that the public is seriously alarmed, gas-mask carrying has appreciably increased. There is, however, considerable ignorance about the whole subject of gas.

Fire-watching arrangements are much discussed. In most areas these seem to be progressing satisfactorily, though the smooth working of the scheme is said to be hampered in some places by the unco-operative attitude of business and office staffs.

4. SHELTERS

Shelter conditions in London continue to improve.

There are still complaints from the provinces, though criticism in most cases is less severe than it was.

5. EVACUATION

Though the situation remains fundamentally unchanged, discussion of evacuation problems has declined. Small numbers of evacuees are still returning to their homes.

6. FOOD

Comments on this subject are much the same as in recent weeks.

Shortages are 'accepted philosophically'; distribution arrangements are still the subject of complaint, particularly the way in which these operate in favour of restaurant habituees; wastage of food in the Army is again reported from various sources.

Ministry of Food advertisements and BBC 'Kitchen Front' talks are criticised for suggesting the use of foods which, in some areas, are unobtainable, e.g. frying fats, oats, and oatmeal.

7. INDUSTRY

Comment on industrial matters is confined almost entirely to the press. There is general approval of the Government's man-power plans, though it is anticipated that there will be some delays in putting them into full or immediate operation.

8. AGRICULTURE

The provincial and also the London press reflects the serious apprehension of farmers about the calling up of 'key men'. The 'disastrous effects' which their absence may have on the food situation is repeatedly emphasised.

NO 19: WEDNESDAY 5 FEBRUARY TO WEDNESDAY 12 FEBRUARY 1941

GENERAL COMMENTS

1. GENERAL STATE OF CONFIDENCE AND REACTION TO NEWS

There has been no fluctuation in public feeling, which the news from Libya, East Africa and Greece sustains at a fairly high level of complacency. Though a good deal of superficial speculation is reported about developments in France, reference to affairs in the Balkans is confined to a very few sources.

The probability of invasion is being discussed more widely – and with greater confidence – than ever; anticipation that it may occur in Britain and

Eire simultaneously seems to be growing. There are many who think that if it comes it will be 'the turning point in the war'; there is not so much as a hint of the possibility of its success, nor is there any evidence of serious apprehension about what might be expected to happen. But partly owing to alarms and excursions in the press and partly, it is said, because of the Prime Minister's and Sir John Dill's recent speeches, there has been a wider awakening to the fact that very few people know what they should be prepared to do. There have been many requests for 'more specific and up-to-date instructions about the duties of civilians'. In particular, the order to 'stay put' needs to be made clearer. Individual interpretations of the phrase show that in one district 'people plan to return home if they are away'; in another 'to move to a safer area'; and that elsewhere they are 'building up reserves of petrol to bolt if the enemy lands'.

'The need for more education about gas' is also emphasised in several reports, some of which indicate a developing undercurrent of anxiety on this subject. The confidential warning against encouraging its discussion is said to be a deterrent to giving advice to those who want it.

The diminution of night bombing still induces an uneasy relief and also a good deal of speculation. Among hypotheses to account for its present decline are that preparations are in hand for:

Intensified air war in the Mediterranean.
Seizure of the French Navy and Mediterranean ports.
Occupation of Bizerta.
Assault on Bulgaria.

2. BROADCASTING

The Prime Minister's speech was extremely well received. His confidence in the future was particularly appreciated, and his reference to 1942 is said to have 'placed the situation in the right perspective'. Though parts of the speech were said 'to have made some peoples' flesh creep', listeners were also 'relieved to feel that they were really hearing the truth'. The reference to America was considered extremely opportune, but the warning to Bulgaria 'aroused little comment'. There were many references to the cheerfulness of his delivery which 'increased the feeling of intimacy with his audience'.

Priestley's *Postscripts* continue to cause a good deal of inconclusive argument. BBC listener research shows that 80% of those who listen to the Sunday news at nine o'clock listen also to his *Postscript*; whereas there is usually an audience of only 65% for those of other speakers.

Four out of five Chief Constables' reports mentioning his talks say they are 'much appreciated'; the fifth 'fears his comments may lead to disunity'.

3. REPRISALS

There has been a slight decrease in the demand for reprisals. Postal Censorship is, as usual, the chief source of this vindictiveness, which seems to find a free if more premeditated expression in letters than in conversation.

4. RUMOURS

Fewer rumours have been reported this week. Haw-Haw's stock remains low. Stories of attempted invasion have come from various parts of the country. Some specifically mention Cornwall as the place where it is supposed to have occurred.

Other rumours are of foot-and-mouth disease having been spread by enemy aeroplanes, and of Ribbentrop's death. Stories of foul play have lately been circulating in connection with the deaths of several well-known people.

5. EIRE

The British public's interest in Eire is confined mostly to expressions of contempt for, and impatience with, the policy of Mr. de Valera's government. Though people in Eire are complaining strongly about their difficulties, in England there is very little sympathy for their afflictions, nor any understanding of what causes them.

Southern Irish living in this country are becoming more and more favourably disposed towards our cause. Though not indifferent to Eire's situation, many of its subjects when writing home are loud in their praises of England, and urge their friends to join us in the war.

In Eire itself there is little change. The possibility of invasion is dreaded, and there is no such boldness or confidence as is felt in this country. Yet 'despite the feverish uncertainty about their own future', there is said to be 'a profound faith in the victory of Britain'.

SPECIAL COMMENTS

6. AIR RAIDS

Reports show that some recently blitzed cities are returning to a more normal way of life, and that the public is beginning to patronise cinemas and other places of entertainment again.

Fire-watching organisation and arrangements continue to be an important preoccupation and are stated to be progressing satisfactorily on the whole, although there are still requests for more specific directions. Unwillingness of employees to guard employers' premises is one of the chief difficulties. There are reports also of the growing tiredness of workers who are forced by circumstances to undertake more than one night's watching a week.

The nightly trek out of recently bombed cities is causing confusion and dislocation of local services. A statement of policy on the part of the authorities is asked for.

Moving furniture from bombed and vulnerable areas is reported to be a problem which seriously affects people's morale.

7. SHELTERS

A steady improvement continues.

For the whole population of the London Region there is provision now for	80%
as compared with the December figure of	75%
In the Metropolitan area there is provision now for	91%
of the whole population, as compared with the December figure of	81%
Of these, Regional figures for public shelters are	19%
and for domestic shelters	61%
In the Metropolitan area the figures for public shelters are	25%
and domestic shelters	66%

Progress is also reported in sanitation, ventilation, medical provision and comfort.

In the other Regions the position is reported to be far less satisfactory. 'Strong feeling' is stated to exist in certain heavily bombed areas on the question of surface shelters. 'Though few of them have been badly damaged these have affected people adversely.'

The condition of school shelters is reported to be a constantly recurring point of controversy outside London.

8. FOOD

Food problems are a growing responsibility for housewives and a major source of comment. The situation is still not unhealthy and people are prepared to accept shortages philosophically on the whole, but it is stated that 'morale is seriously menaced by discrepancies between Government statements about the food situation and actual facts'.

There is a growing feeling that the protein content is insufficient for heavy workers and for children, and that the prices of controlled foods are too high.

Food queues are reported from several places: e.g. St. Helens, Peterborough, Southampton and Coventry.

Complaints of specific shortages come chiefly from reception areas and are still stated to be increasing the hostility of residents towards evacuees.

Lord Woolton is reported to be losing some of his popularity, and he is especially criticised for bad distribution. 'When people cannot get their promised 1/2d worth of meat they are either angry or start wondering what is going wrong.'

Complaints of restaurant meals which contain meat, and other protein, obtainable without coupons are still reported.

Foods which arouse most controversy when they are short, apart from meat, are shown to be cheese, rabbits, eggs, marmalade, biscuits, cereals, cooking fats, tinned meat, fresh fruit and sweets. Rabbits are reported to be a major food topic of speculation. People are asking why have they disappeared from the market as soon as their price was controlled? Why are they being gassed in country districts when we cannot get enough substitutes for meat?

9. INDUSTRY

Billeting workers drafted to new districts has proved difficult and is stated to be one reason why there is not sufficient mobility in labour. Food difficulties are another reason. It is often impossible for workers drafted to industrial districts to get even enough of rationed foods, if these are wanted in a hurry.

10. AGRICULTURE

Farming prices are reported to be the subject of discussion in agricultural circles and the Ministry of Food is criticised for not seeing that the Prices Order is carried out. Farmers are alarmed at the recent Ploughing Orders, which are stated to upset the natural economy of some districts, and fear the loss of skilled workers and the threatened extension of daylight saving in the summer. Rationing of chicken food is also arousing complaints. It is suggested that more publicity is needed to explain the background of these misunderstandings and complaints.

11. CIVILIANS AND THE ARMY

Many complaints of bad driving, especially of lorries, on the part of the Army are reported.

Complaints are still received about the lavishness of Army rations and waste in camps.

Some resentment is reported at the penalisation of soldiers' dependents when [the soldiers] have committed breaches of military discipline. Non-payment of ration allowances to men on sick leave until return to duty causes inconvenience and distress in their homes.

12. PENSIONS AND ALLOWANCES

Serious complaints are reported at the administration of supplementary old age pensions. There is often a delay of as much as two months in getting them through.

NO 20: WEDNESDAY 12 FEBRUARY TO WEDNESDAY 19 FEBRUARY 1941

GENERAL COMMENTS

1. GENERAL STATE OF CONFIDENCE AND REACTION TO NEWS

Almost everywhere people are paying greater lip-service to the prospect of invasion. In London, for instance, at the end of January 35% of people expected it; on February 10, the figure had risen to 53%. Two-thirds of people questioned thought it would be a good thing for us, a quarter thought it would be a bad thing, while the rest hold no opinion. 'Expectation of invasion with confidence in the outcome' is the keynote of the great majority of reports. In mid-Wales, and the Northern and the North-Eastern Regions, however, invasion is regarded as a dim and rather unlikely prospect. But behind this 'nominal expectation', few people seem to have visualised invasion as a really serious affair. It is still treated rather as an exciting and thrilling kind of game in which we may soon be involved. People are impatient at the delay, they talk of fighting with any weapon which comes to hand (kettles of hot water, shot-guns etc.), and they boast that every German will be cut to pieces. Only on the subject of gas is there slight perturbation, showing itself in rumours that gas has already been used (see 'Rumours') and in letters and phone calls urging friends and relations to be prepared. But the great majority are still not carrying their gas-masks. Although more people are asking for instructions about what to do when invasion comes, there is still a great mass who have not faced the situation in a sufficiently realistic way to make them think about the practical difficulties which will arise. When people were asked how they thought *others* would behave when invasion came, nearly a quarter expected some panic. 'Stay put' has ceased to be an automatic answer. The brief MOI announcement about what 'staying put' means seems to have made little impression. Women, it is said, may move either to join their evacuated children, or because they fear violation by the invaders. In reception areas, it is feared that the richer type of evacuee, 'having no roots in the place', will be only too ready to move on once more, and in the New Forest area, many are stated to have cars ready and suitcases packed following talk that large-scale evacuation of the district would follow German landing.

After invasion, food shortages and difficulties are the main topic of public discussion (see 'Food').

On the news in general, the trend of comment is as follows. There is still a paean of praise for the Prime Minister's recent broadcast. African news continues to give satisfaction, though there is no doubt in the public mind that it is only the weak end of the Axis that we are hammering. The landing of our paratroops in Italy causes much discussion and a desire for fuller details; also the suggestion that should the Italians treat them dishonourably, we ought to retaliate on Italian prisoners. The news from the Balkans creates no great anxiety nor interest; there is evidence of feeling of remoteness, ignorance, and complacency; those who express opinions regard Yugoslavia and Bulgaria as Hitler's as soon as he likes to take them, and it is not expected that Greece would long be able to withstand a German onslaught; of Turkey, it is hoped she will be able to resist, but her failure to do so would cause no great surprise; some think that Axis preoccupations in the Near East diminish the chances of invasion at home. The activities of Japan are watched without alarm. Unoccupied France is observed with some slight sympathy, but with little expectation that she will ever stand firm or be of much value to us. The lull in raids is spoken of as 'calm before the storm', and few believe that the weather is really the cause.

The amount of neurotic illness as a result of raids has been disclosed by the Ministry of Health. Only 5% of all people incapacitated by air raids were suffering from 'nervous shock'. Some of these cases were probably physical in origin, the result of blast. The great majority had recovered within a week or two. In December 1940, the number of civilian neuroses due to air raids requiring admission to special psychiatric hospitals was: London 25; rest of England 3. In January there were still fewer cases. The total percentage of shock cases needing first-aid treatment in September was twice that in December. At out-patient psychiatric clinics, the number of new cases seen in 1940 was below that of 1939. Following the Coventry raid, the number of neurotic out-patients was the same as usual, and no patients needed admission to special centres. In Home Intelligence Weekly Report No. 13, an appendix on 'Psychological Reactions to Air Raids' pointed out that the reason for the small number of neurotic casualties was probably the escape of the potentially neurotic to the country or the deep shelter – an escape which was hindered rather than aided by a neurotic reaction. It has further been suggested that another factor which limits civilian as compared with Service psychiatric casualties is that the civilian is called upon to face the risk of death, whereas the soldier is in addition called upon to inflict death.

On the subjects of reprisals, peace aims, and extremist activities there is nothing new to report.

2. RUMOURS

This week rumours have increased both in number and distribution. Invasion and gas have been the main subjects. Stories of invasion attempts in Truro and in Lincolnshire are mentioned. 300 paratroops were said to have been rounded up near Lowestoft. Paratroops dressed as women are believed to have fallen in Leicestershire and at Skegness. It is also rumoured that we are moving conveys of barges towards the coast and that frequent sorties test the defences of Belgium and France.

On the subject of gas, it is believed, even by responsible people in official positions, that gas raids have already occurred in Liverpool and in Kent. Another rumour reported from London, Southampton and Bristol which is treated seriously is that incendiary bombs omit an arsenical smoke, and that people should always stand with their backs to the wind when tackling them. In the Edinburgh Region where a continuous inshore east wind is usual at this time of year, it is feared that this may be used by the enemy to carry gas.

Rumours that germs of foot-and-mouth disease have been dropped by German planes are reported from Northern Ireland.

Haw-Haw is said to have mentioned the Orkneys, Inverness, and Yarmouth.

3. BROADCASTING

A Listener Research survey on a random sample of 2,200 listeners showed that 58% of people were satisfied with the care of the BBC in controlling the vulgarity of its comedians; 13% would like greater care; 10% would like less care; while the rest held no opinion.

4. BRITISH OPINION ON AMERICA

A special study of this subject up to February 17th has been made by the Postal Censorship. Its main conclusions are given below. The study is, of course, subject to the limitation that much of what is censored is intended to be read by Americans, but it is substantially confirmed from other sources.

1. A comparatively small number of correspondents mention the subject, and almost all belong to the educated classes. This does not mean that the public as a whole is not interested, but working-class writers seldom mention political matters unless they affect them directly.

2. There is an increasing feeling that we are fighting America's battles as well as our own, and for this reason the tools should be given and not sold. Pro-British American slogans cause irritation to many people, as it is felt that words are cheaper to give than destroyers. Some suggest that America wants to pose as the saviours of Britain after the war.

3. The great majority are satisfied that aid should be in material and not in men.

4. Many appreciate the aid so far received, but are increasingly anxious at the slowness with which help is reaching us, and the 'apparently interminable discussions' about the Lease-and-Lend bill.

5. Others openly criticise the apparent apathy and self-interest of the Americas, and accuse them of being 'Dollar Mad'.

6. There is unanimous admiration and respect for President Roosevelt. He is felt to be a genuine friend.

7. Mr. Wendell Willkie has become very popular with the general public, thanks both to his genial and easy-going manner, and to the sportsmanlike way in which he took his electoral defeat.

8. Many writers believe that a closer co-operation and understanding with America is essential both now and after the war to ensure a per-

manent peace, and a number hope for a reunion between the Commonwealth and the States.

9. Americans in England are even more critical than Englishmen of their country's attitude to the war.

SPECIAL COMMENTS

5. FOOD

Food continues to be one of the main preoccupations of the public.

There are signs of some unreasoned resentment against shop-keepers – wholesalers, and retailers – among people who do not look beyond the shop in front of them to find the real reasons for shortages. They complain also of shops being closed at lunch time, at food being sold out early and at non-rationed food being sold only to favoured customers.

Queues for non-rationed goods are much resented. In some districts shop-keepers are telling housewives to come at 9 a.m. and this results in queues and much ill-feeling. Queues for meat and other foods are reported from Enfield, Chesterfield, Nottingham, Bewdley, Stourport, Stafford, West Bromwich and Dudley. The mayors of the last five places express the opinion that 'food queues are a bigger menace to public morale than several serious German air raids'.

Restaurant meals are still criticised and there are complaints in many districts that soldiers are buying food freely in cafes in spite of their extra meat ration.

Complaints of profiteering are reported. Lord Woolton is urged to 'take a firm hand and allow no profiteering in this grave phase of the nation's history'. He is accused of being 'too optimistic' in his broadcast talks and of 'not explaining the real reason why there are shortages, with the result that unfair blame tends to attach itself to butchers and retailers causing much unnecessary ill-feeling'. There has not been time to analyse public reactions to Lord Woolton's statement in the House of Lords yesterday.

Vigorous protests continue to be reported from mine-workers' associations and miners' wives of the inadequacy of the meat ration and the shortage of cheese for miners. There are indications that housewives are beginning to get together to watch their local food situation and report on price and other irregularities.

Lack of fruit worries many people, especially those with children, and the suggestion is put forward that 'a ration of orange juice would be more suitable for them than tea'.

There is evidence, however, that people are beginning to adjust themselves to the new food situation (old people are reported to be finding it more difficult to do this than young) and housewives to show more ingenuity in catering and cooking than before.

Preliminary results of a sample investigation in Harrow between February 3rd and 8th conducted by War-time Social Survey: 32% of those interviewed did not complain about food difficulties, of the rest all said they had difficulty. The *price* of fish figured most prominently and afterwards the *shortage* of meat, cheese and eggs in that order. This result shows the existence and nature of the particular food difficulties but gives no information on the trend of public feeling about them.

6. AIR RAIDS

The nightly trek out of Southampton, Portsmouth and Bristol continues on a reduced scale. The organisation of fire-watching is still proving a difficulty in areas with business premises. Some resentment is expressed that employers should call on volunteers, who consider that their own homes and families should come first. Confusion of mind over precise directions still exists and the distribution of the fire-watching leaflet has been shown by investigation in London to have been erratic. The use of compulsory powers is demanded in many districts as large numbers of streets are said still to have no organisation for watching. Promised equipment of tin hats etc. is reported to be urgently demanded, especially in working-class districts. Fire-fighting is stated to be having 'a good effect on the morale of people' in blitzed towns, e.g. in Plymouth and Bristol.

Delay in salvaging furniture in bombed houses is still a major source of grievance and its obvious connection with looting is widely commented on.

The insurance of furniture and other private belongings is rousing some controversy as to whether it should be compulsory or not.

7. SHELTERS

Portsmouth people are stated to be leaving the city in large numbers each evening to spend the night in shelters on a hill overlooking the city. The men are said to sleep on benches while the women stand all night and sleep only in the morning when the men have gone to work.

A decline in the general vitality among regular shelter-users in London is remarked on by Social and Civil Defence workers. Medical opinion in Bristol attributes the widespread bronchial trouble following flu to nights 'spent in cold damp shelters'.

Amid general improvement in London, unofficial shelters – in church crypts etc. – continue to be bad spots of unhygienic conditions.

The collapse of surface shelters in Bristol, unaffected by bomb or blast, is stated to be 'having a very bad psychological effect on people expected to use similar structures during raids'. These shelters are now being rebuilt.

8. EVACUATION

The situation remains very much the same. A trickle back to London and other vulnerable areas continues on a small scale.

Complaints are reported that the Bristol evacuation scheme is not 'all-embracing'. Arrangements for 'temporary rest' evacuation are now functioning successfully.

Merseyside teachers complain of 'unfair billeting and overcrowding of evacuees'.

9. TRADE AND INDUSTRY

Retailers are reported to be 'seriously worried' by the rapidly altering situation and are asking for a lead from the Government as to what they should do. Small shop-keepers everywhere are stated to be going out of business as they cannot get their supplies.

The thought of compulsory service is reported to be 'frightening some women'. A sense of insecurity is apparently being engendered by the lack of a definition of Government policy. On the other hand, 'married women are considering giving up war work because they find everything sold out when they go to buy their food at night'.

Unemployment in Northern Ireland is rousing bitter comment in correspondence, and there is a wide demand that war industry should be established there.

Shortage of labour in the West Highlands is reported to be due to lack of entertainment.

Public confidence is said to be disturbed in Glasgow because iron and steel industries do not appear to be working at full speed.

The national and regional press continue to criticize the Government handling of the industrial situation, and to prophesy that the restriction on the textile trade will lead to general dislocation and the closing down of a large percentage of mills before the workers can be properly absorbed into the war industries.

10. TRANSPORT

Complaints are reported that poor transport wastes 'hundreds of thousands of working hours by dockyard workers in Portsmouth'. Further complaints of workers' difficulties and delays are reported from London and other Regions.

NO 21: WEDNESDAY 19 FEBRUARY TO WEDNESDAY 26 FEBRUARY 1941

GENERAL COMMENTS

1. GENERAL STATE OF CONFIDENCE AND REACTION TO NEWS

Public interest still centres around the subject of invasion. Anticipation of its probability seems to be increasing slightly; and confidence in our ability to repel the attempt continues. There is still, however, much uncertainty about the part the public will have to play, and private plans are being made to meet the situation. Evacuees, having no special loyalties to their temporary homes, are regarded as unlikely to 'stay put'. Some mothers are bringing their children back from reception areas 'because of the invasion threat'; others are making arrangements to try and join their evacuated children 'if it comes'.

The apathy about events in the Balkans, mentioned in last week's report, has to some extent been dissipated by the recent developments in that area. But there is still a good deal of ignorance and confusion about what the latest moves mean. The Turko-Bulgarian agreement has, if anything, increased this bewildered feeling; nor has it been diminished by the conflicting political and press interpretations of the pact. Feelings about Turkey, though on the whole friendly, are rather uncertain. There is some fear that 'the Turks may rat on us'; also that they have a secret treaty with Russia 'and will not fight when it comes to the point'. These expressions belong to the minority.

People are beginning to realise that before long we may be at grips in the Middle East with Germany, who is regarded as being 'our real enemy'; consequently, interest in the campaigns against Italy has slightly decreased.

The situation developing between Japan, America and this country has so far aroused comparatively little interest, in spite of the continuous references made to it in the press.

More details have been asked for about the First Lord's statement on the sinking and capture of enemy ships. Discussion about the landing of our paratroops in Italy also continues. The absence of further official comment on these matters is regarded with some misgiving, and a good many people are sceptical of the results which may have been achieved.

Generally speaking, the public's attitude to the war as a whole is still one of complacency. This applies particularly to areas which have had little or no experience of the blitz, and also to rural districts; one of these is described as being 'a County unconscious of the tiger at the door'. The main preoccupations at home are still of a domestic sort; food is much the most important of these.

The heavy bombing of Swansea, and incidents at Bermondsey and Hendon, show that after the recent lull in raids, people who had become 'conditioned to the blitz' have now lost some of their toughness and indifference. This was seen particularly in Bermondsey and Southwark, following the disaster at London Bridge arches on 17th February. Though there was little sign of defeatism, much bitterness and ill-feeling was shown towards 'the authorities' for allowing the arches to be used as shelters. In Hendon the damage was fairly extensive, and there was a good deal of 'jitteriness' during the raid on the next night; rumours were prevalent that 'a new and terrible bomb had been used'. The fact that no siren had been sounded was severely criticised, and was assumed by some people to mean that no warning is given if there is only a single raider.

2. RUMOURS

There are still some stories about attempts at invasion, one of which is supposed to have been 'frustrated by HMS *Renown* at Holyhead'. The Postal Censorship mentions a story current in Eire, of 'an approaching air armistice'. A report from Pembroke says that 'large quantities of British arms and material, together with a nucleus of British troops, have been deposited in Eire'. Fishguard and Holyhead are mentioned as 'open ports' by which refugees are expected to enter this country in the near future.

There are still rumours that British forces intend to invade Holland in the next few weeks.

A 'gas practice' at Brighton gave rise to a story, reported from as far away as Halifax, that there had, in fact, been a gas attack on Brighton.

Various stories are in circulation about the landing of German aeroplanes in this country. They are said to have arrived during darkness at Mildenhall aerodrome, among other places, and afterwards to have taken off again.

SPECIAL COMMENTS

3. FOOD

Food remains one of the chief items of public interest, and shortages and increased prices continue to form the main complaints. Queues are reported from many districts, and are causing much inconvenience and hardship. Chief Constables remark on the time involved by the police in controlling some of them. It is also stated that in some areas people are travelling from one district to another to join the queues. The position indicates that all-round rationing would be welcome, also extra rations for miners and heavy industrial workers, for whom cheese and pork are said to be important foods. Suggestions continue that Civil Defence workers should be treated on the same scale as the Services.

The reappearance of non-rationed foods after temporary shortages is stated in some areas to have been accompanied by unfair increases in prices.

Egg producers in various districts have protested about the uneconomic fixing of egg prices.

Complaints are reported of alleged overcharging in hotels and restaurants, and people have submitted menus to the Ministry of Food asking for prices to be checked.

4. LABOUR

A SPECIAL REPORT FROM SCOTLAND: The proposed 'Guaranteed Week' for dockers appears to have met with a certain amount of disapproval and hostility on Clydeside. It is considered that when they have become familiar with the scheme objections to it will be lessened. It is thought by some of the men that the scheme will do away with casual workers, of whom there are many; this objection is based on the argument that 'the first Guaranteed Week will be paid for in arrears'. It appears that dockers who have been engaged on casual labour for the previous week will begin the first week of the new scheme with less than a week's money in hand.

The fact that the Glasgow Dockers' Union and the Scottish Transport and General Workers' Union have broken away from the Transport and General Workers' Union is something of a hindrance to launching the scheme satisfactorily. On the whole, the trades union element does not appear to be in favour of the scheme.

Reports from Lancashire show that cotton operatives are absenting themselves from work in order to do their shopping and also to collect Army allowances from Post Offices.

5. CIVIL DEFENCE

FIRE-WATCHING: Reports generally show that in many areas there is a shortage of personnel and in some places of equipment also. Some employers are demanding a levy from their work people for the employment of paid fire-watchers.

6. ALLOWANCES AND GRANTS

Reports are still being received showing delay in dealing with special allowances for dependents. Apprehension is caused that revised payments to soldiers may leave dependents financially worse off. Reductions of supplementary war service grants made when soldiers gain promotion is said to deter them from trying to get it.

Concerning the payment of funeral grants to the relatives of air-raid victims, there appears to be some confusion about the regulations. The situation needs clarification.

APPENDIX

RELATIONS BETWEEN WORKERS AND MANAGEMENTS IN SCOTLAND

(Based on a special report from RIO Scotland)

1. COMPLAINTS

Tales of slackness in war production, of defects of supply, and of faults of management are common in the Scottish industrial areas. These tales have their effect on output, and they have an undesirable effect also on public opinion outside the workshops. Complaints, whether justified or not, are seized on and exploited by the disruptive and militant elements.

In one area there is recurring complaint among the workers in four big factories and shipyards and among people outside that 'so far as production was concerned, everybody from workers to employers is only "kidding" – despite the fact that in some of the places concerned the workers are working three nights late and doing a seven-day week'. In the railway shops in another place, there were highly coloured tales a week or two ago about the men playing cards all night. In yet another neighbourhood there is much talk about slack conditions in the Admiralty shipyard.

Information suggests that difficulties as to supply are much exaggerated by local propaganda and gossip. There have been no major hold-ups in supply of material. In some shipyards, improvement is reported in the last four months.

Prolonged overtime and lack of canteens have, however, worn down many of the workers. In railway workshops, workers who a few months ago had to stand about doing nothing are now switched to different departments. There are, however, complaints that workers are still asked to stay on for night work when there is not enough to do, and that inspectors and foremen in several departments are slack. In some cases the nature of the work demands that a large supply of labour should be on hand for rush jobs; this involves periodical slackness, with large groups doing practically nothing.

2. MANAGEMENT FAULTS

It is strongly emphasized by people with first-hand experience of conditions in many shops and yards that delays in production can often be explained by bad management, and that output is good where management is good.

There are numerous scattered examples of faults of management. Some arise where skilled workers object to having their time wasted doing a routine job when they could be doing their own highly skilled work elsewhere. Thus, a worker in an aircraft factory who objected to routine work was given a week's notice, and instructed to come in every morning and afternoon to sign on until his notice expired. He offered to work the week but was refused. He also offered the information that all round the factory was a notice saying 'Every minute counts'.

There are complaints of a certain disinclination on the part of some managers to use shop steward machinery for negotiation with the workers on minor points such as a proposed change in working hours. The result in one such instance was a two days' strike.

Trade union leaders and organisers complain of lack of co-operation on the part of foremen and under-managers.

3. SHOP STEWARDS

As has previously been noted, some shop stewards are out to make trouble. The natural resentment of foremen and under-managers then tends to play into the hands of the militants. It also leads to hasty and seemingly arrogant action towards shop stewards who are not out to make trouble but are pursuing their proper function. This bad feeling tends also to create resentment among employers against trade unions as such, since the employers concerned naturally confuse the trade unions themselves with the militant shop stewards.

Trade unions are taking action against the disruptive elements. For example, the Amalgamated Engineering Union has debarred its shop stewards from attending in their official capacity any unauthorised meeting such as the Shop Stewards' Consultative Conference.

4. OVERTIME AND TRANSPORT DIFFICULTIES

Other factors which tend to decrease output and which favour absenteeism and disruptive propaganda are prolonged overtime, and transport difficulties. A particular case is cited where men have lost all interest in their work after a long period of working twelve hours a day. There are great transport difficulties in certain areas, but negotiations are continuing with corporations and other transport authorities. There are complaints that men arriving late, owing to transport difficulties, are shut out for an hour or even a morning.

5. A GOOD EXAMPLE

Good results from one engineering firm are quoted and some of their principles are set out as follows:

(1) Each job is planned from the start.

(2) There is regular consultation with shop stewards about the general nature of jobs and about workers' grievances. Shop stewards have weekly meetings in firm's time, and on important occasions, the directors join the meeting at a later stage.

(3) Special attention is paid to the welfare of workers by maintenance of good canteens and by helping arrangements with transport.

6. SUGGESTIONS

(1) There is need for a better spirit in the workshops in accordance with 'the comradeship of the trenches' of the last war, and for more factories modelled on lines of the engineering shop referred to above.

(2) Co-operation between workers' representatives and firms should be extended.

(3) There is need for more special conferences, on lines of Mr. Bevin's Glasgow Conference in December, to explain the meaning of war-time industrial co-operation, and to deal also with discipline, use of shop steward machinery, and canteen and general welfare.

(4) Trade unions should be asked to intensify their disciplinary action against shop stewards who are acting disruptively.

HOME INTELLIGENCE

NO 22: WEDNESDAY 26 FEBRUARY TO WEDNESDAY 5 MARCH 1941

GENERAL COMMENTS

1. GENERAL STATE OF CONFIDENCE AND REACTION TO NEWS

This week the main feature has been a considerable rise in the volume of public comment on foreign affairs, and this follows closely the lines of press comment. At the same time, interest in the prospect of invasion has declined slightly. An increasing number of people now think invasion unlikely to occur this year. This view has arisen largely because of events in the Balkans. It is thought that a major German offensive against Greece, Yugoslavia and Turkey is likely at any moment, and that Hitler will not risk war on two fronts at the same time. Further, it is suspected that the collapse of Italy in Africa has upset Hitler's plans, and that he will now concentrate on intensifying his blockade of Britain by air and submarine attack on our shipping, and by air attack on our ports. Invasion is beginning to be regarded as only likely after a successful blockade, or as a desperate fling when the blockade has failed. If it comes (and people are now less inclined to say 'when it comes'), there is still general confidence that it will fail. Enquiries about what to do if it does come have also declined.

As far as enemy activities are concerned, interest in the Balkans is steadily increasing. Mr. Eden's visit to Turkey has done much to remove the doubts, noted last week, about her determination to resist. On the other hand, the chances of Greece and Yugoslavia against the Luftwaffe and the Reichswehr are thought to be small – some giving them only a few days. These possibilities are discussed without anxiety.

The relative freedom of London from raids is attributed by some people to improved defences on the outskirts. The ripples of the Hendon bomb and the London Bridge railway arches disaster continue to spread. There are tales of phenomenal numbers killed by the Hendon bomb; it was 'a new and horrible type'; it was incandescent; it took a very long time to fall; and it made a noise 'like a motor-car gone wrong'. The arches disaster has produced a decline in the popularity of railway arch shelters generally, and questions about why the Government allows them to be used. In other regions, where blitzes are regarded as routine, their absence in weather which is apparently good for flying is causing surprise, speculation, and even a trace of anxiety. Further reports on the Swansea blitzes echo the experiences of the other blitzed towns. 'An ounce of practical help is worth a pound of comforting words,' says an observer. Mr. Malcolm Smith's broad-cast describing the cheerful feelings of Cardiff – and even of the relatives of the dead – created serious indignation throughout the city. The appearance of Swansea refugees in the more remote parts of West Wales brought the real nature of the war home to the country people for the first time. Elsewhere in Wales it was rumoured that it had been necessary to call out the military 'to keep order' in Swansea.

2. BROADCASTING

Mr. Priestley's latest *Postscript* on 'New Men' has restored his popularity. His talks on 'Communal Feeding' and 'Musings in a Railway Train' were less liked. 'New Men' was particularly welcomed by those who remembered the toll of the best of the younger generation in the last war.

3. PEACE AIMS

Once more, interest in peace aims appears to be increasing, both among the general public and among men in the Services. The following generalisa-tions emerge:

  1. There is an absence of thought along conventional party lines. Political slogans, whether right or left, are little spoken of.

2. The main cleavage is not between class and class, but between the young and the old. Older people remember the unemployment and chaos after the last war, and fear a repetition. Younger people are, however, determined that the post-war economic upset 'must not, and will not, happen again'.

3. On the home front, it is hoped that the extremes of wealth and poverty will be swept away, that there will be a greater degree of social security for all, and that what is loosely termed 'privilege' will also be got rid of; though many expect that 'privilege' will put up a stern fight.

4. In the international sphere, the only clearly defined attitude is that there must be no repetition of German aggression. A majority favour a severe peace, some think in terms of international confederation, and there is only unanimity on the point that half measures either way are useless.

4. RUMOURS

The only fresh rumour worth noting is that the Germans have a new gas in the form of flakes; respirators are said not to protect against this, unless a wet sock is tied over the filter. This rumour appears to have arisen from a misunderstanding of certain fire-fighting instructions.

Other old rumours which are once more in circulation are:

1. The blitzing of towns where the Chaplin film *The Great Dictator* is shown.

2. Foot-and-mouth disease is spread by hooves of infected animals dropped from planes.

3. Eire is about to be, or has been, invaded.

4. We are about to invade Italy 'via its toe'.

SPECIAL COMMENTS

5. FIRE-WATCHING

There is still some confusion and uncertainty about the liabilities of those who have to organise fire-watchers. Doubts are expressed also about the efficiency of the voluntary system, and in some places the scheme is held up by lack of man-power; Civil Defence workers in other branches of ARP are therefore being asked to do this work in addition to their other duties. It appears that under Section 30 of the Fire Watchers' Order no one is exempt from watching unless they have already undertaken to do at least 48 hours' Civil Defence duty a month. Many people are doing much more without having signed this undertaking; and so in Dundee, for instance, part-time special constables are being asked to become fire-watchers at their places of employment.

Some people, though willing to watch if asked by local authorities, are reluctant to do so for their employers because so little attention is paid to their conditions. In certain cases a lack of feeding arrangements is said to hamper the scheme, and it is suggested that 'a mobile canteen system would be useful for covering business premises where there are no canteen facilities'. Fire-watchers feel, too, that they should be entitled to the same extra rations as the Home Guard, with whom they often work.

6. GAS

Although the expectation of gas appears from our reports to be increasing, the number of people carrying respirators has not risen. There are more suggestions that the practice should be made compulsory for everyone; alternatively, it is said that compulsion should at least be applied to factory and office workers, and to cinema goers.

In the South-Eastern Region it is rumoured that at certain places 'local authorities will release tear-gas in the main streets without warning, so as to teach the people always to carry their masks'.

7. SHELTERS

Criticism of shelters is still declining. On the whole, complaints are now few, and conditions continue to improve. Local authorities in the South-Western and North-Western Regions are said to be alarmed by the dangerous conditions of some public shelters, and there is still much distrust of the brick surface type. There are also protests in the North-Western Region about the improper use of certain public shelters. Apart from this, however, there has been very little comment on the subject.

8. FOOD

The chief complaints continue to be:

1. *Maldistribution*, which is still given as the cause for many shortages. The distribution of unrationed foods in reception areas is said to bring hardship to residents and evacuees. There are many suggestions that food should be diverted from evacuation to reception areas. The free movement of self-evacuees is blamed for difficult conditions.

2. *Inadequate rations* for workers in heavy industries and on the land. The difficulty in getting unrationed foods like cheese and eggs aggravates the situation where these workers are in the habit of eating 'packed' meals. It is suggested that cheese should be reserved for these workers.

3. *The use of ordinary shops by Service personnel*, as well as NAAFI canteens. It is suggested that restrictions should be placed on purchases from shops.

4. *Shopping habits*. The various methods for obtaining extra supplies of unrationed foods continue to be criticised. Shopping hours still present grave difficulties for women workers. (An enterprising firm in the Midlands, recognising this problem, has begun 'a shopping time rota' by means of which every housewife employed has a shopping morning every seventh day.)

9. EVACUATION

Conditions in reception areas (except for the food situation) continue to improve.

Suggestions are made that 'evacuees should be conscripted for war work'.

Evacuation from Bristol has had a poor response. From a total of 27,000 children whom it was hoped to evacuate, only 7,000 have been arranged for as a first consignment.

10. LABOUR

There is some concern expressed among women about the 'conscription of labour' and reports state that 'a clear Government policy' would be appreciated.

There is little sign that women of the middle classes without previous experience of paid work are considering taking steps to become employed.

11. TRANSPORT

There are still many complaints about transport by rail and bus.

In the Northern Region the unpopularity of the Railway Companies is stated to be growing steadily, first because the companies are accused of making little effort to overcome dislocations in passenger services, and secondly, because of the increased dividends recently announced. It is interesting that a BIPO survey conducted in January shows that 34% attributed the rise in fares to the railways taking advantage of the situation.

APPENDIX

DUNBARTONSHIRE BY-ELECTION

(1) Polling on February 27th resulted:

McKinlay (Labour)...21,900
MacEwen (Communist)...3,862

(2) 25,700 of an electorate of about 67,000 (nominal, perhaps 45,000 effective) polled. This was a higher poll than the last by-election, in Northampton, when approximately 30% voted.

(3) The poll was the highest yet scored by a Communist since the war, and the first time a Communist candidate did not forfeit his deposit.

(4) Labour fought on a Labour Party platform and Conservative co-operation was not apparent either in meetings or in election literature. It is estimated, however, that the votes cast for McKinlay contain some thousands from Unionists, Liberals and Nationalists.

(5) The constituency has few natural unities, either of geography or of social class. It contains the Vale of Leven, 'the reddest strip of Britain'; a large new housing estate (Knightswood) for which the Labour candidate has been largely responsible; and considerable middle- and upper-class residential areas (Helensburgh). The area has been virtually untouched by evacuation, but much influenced by difficulties in industrial relations on Clydeside. Politically the electorate has been

described as 'unreliable', 'a see-saw', 'the stepping-stone'. Four County Council representatives are Communist.

(6) Although the constituency has suffered little from direct impacts of the war (no raids), there are a number of real grievances widely felt. In the industrial field economic class distinctions are strongly felt, the provision of welfare facilities is noticeably poor, transport for workers is extremely bad, and common talk contains persistent allegations about inefficient management, supply muddles and lack of supervision in key places. There is a strong local grievance that the Minister of Aircraft Production has not thought it worth while to visit the area. On the day before polling there was a lockout of shipyard workers which aroused violent feelings over the whole industrial area. This feeling increased with the strike which took place on polling day.

(7) Neither McKinlay nor MacEwen were very strong candidates. There was general tolerance about the election, and meetings produced no strong scenes.

(8) McKinlay's policy was very simple: 'behind Churchill' and 'against the Reds'.

(9) MacEwen's policy (put forward with much more energy in the conduct of meetings and a much wider distribution of literature) was mainly the exploitation of grievances: profiteering, rationing, ARP and shelters, growing Fascism in Britain, self-determination for India. Several of these points failed to arouse interest and were soon dropped, e.g. India, ARP. There was some theoretical argument about the People's Government securing peace, but at no time did a Communist speaker state that he was 'for peace'.

(10) An observers' study of the campaign showed that the size of the Communist vote was felt by those on the spot to be an advance for the CP. It would also appear that the Communists succeeded in mobilising more goodwill than was reflected in the actual vote. In election discussions people heard expressing sympathy for the point of view put forward by the Communist candidate remained unconvinced that the Communists in any way represented an alternative Government. The vagueness of their general arguments

was commented upon and it was frequently remarked that they were ill-adjusted to local Scottish conditions. Lack of Conservative support for the Labour candidate caused some surprise and promoted discussions about 'the unreality of Government unity'.

(11) The general conclusion of our report is that a situation of some danger is revealed and that a close watch ought to be kept on developments in this area.

HOME INTELLIGENCE
5 March 1941

NO 23: WEDNESDAY 5 MARCH TO WEDNESDAY 12 MARCH 1941

GENERAL COMMENTS

1. GENERAL STATE OF CONFIDENCE AND REACTION TO NEWS

If one reviews the general feelings of the public as a whole over the past month, the following points stand out:

1. While the great majority are certain we shall win in the end, there is less excitement and enthusiasm about the war – and also less interest in it – than there has been for some time.

2. The reasons for this lack of enthusiasm are various: First, people are directly affected, perhaps more than they realise, by colds, influenza, overtime work, lack of opportunity to get away, the winter, the shortages of food and other commodities, and evacuation difficulties. Secondly, there have been no sensational developments in the war at home. The blitzing of individual towns no longer affects the feelings of the country as a whole; the 'horrific thrill' of Coventry is, as it were, played out. Our successes in Libya and our dangers in the Balkans are too remote to mean much to the bulk of the public; at the most they are regarded as sideshows unlikely to affect the main issue of the war, and few people consider the possible effects in neutral countries,

if we fail in the Balkans. Thirdly, there is a growing conviction that invasion is becoming increasingly unlikely this year, and that attrition, by blitz and blockade, is rather to be anticipated.

3. At the same time, there are suggestions that we are not adopting a sufficiently aggressive policy. The Lofoten Islands Raid was welcomed, but many people are asking why we are not bombing the Germans in Rumania and Bulgaria, and why we are not blitzing Berlin and Rome. In the blitzed towns, in particular, where in the past talk of reprisals was limited, it is now steadily growing, concurrently with recovery from the acute shocks.

4. While the popularity of Mr. Churchill remains as great as ever, there has been a falling off in the popularity of other Cabinet Ministers. In particular, it is being suggested that the Labour leaders are now less representative of the working people than they were when in opposition.

5. In the absence of any definite announcements about peace aims, an increasing number of people are recalling events after the last war, and are expecting a repetition of the miscarriages and misadventures, and there is rather less evidence of a positive and constructive attitude towards the future.

Thus, public feeling at the present time suggests a combination of complacency and boredom, with a philosophical or tired acceptance of present difficulties. There is little defeatism, but positive interest in the war is declining, especially among women, who are less well informed about the background of the war.

Although it may be neither possible nor desirable to keep enthusiasm at concert pitch, this analysis reveals certain ill-defined weaknesses in the public temper.

2. THE RECENT RAIDS

The public reaction to provincial raids has followed the well-recognised pattern of nightly evacuation, ripples of rumour, natural anxiety over furniture deteriorating in damaged houses etc. But a new feature has been a decline in Haw-Haw rumours, their place being taken by a new type of rumour which attributes any blitz to a speech or a newspaper article saying how well the town was carrying on. In Swansea, a speech by the Lord Privy Seal was blamed; at Bristol, an article in the *Daily Express* comparing Bristol with a town bombed by the RAF in Germany led to blame being attached to Lord Beaverbrook. Fire-watching and fire-fighting, giving an active occupation during raids to a greater number of civilians, is also a new feature with a stimulating effect. At the same time, the nightly trek from the towns is depleting fire-watching ranks, and leading to other difficulties by leaving many houses empty.

The return of the heavy raiding to London, although in theory expected, was in practice an unpleasant surprise, particularly to women. Many appear to have hoped that really heavy raids on London would not again be possible. The majority took them well. Younger people who had the opportunity for civilian fire-fighting welcomed it, and even in heavily bombed areas there was no rush to evacuate. But old age pensioners were very upset. Many had returned from evacuation areas because in the country they lost their supplementary pensions, and without them they could not afford to keep two homes going. Their reaction to the return of the blitz is 'a justifiable hopelessness'. One other group was also adversely affected – the middle- and upper-middle-class hotel-dwelling ladies. A feeling that 'they can carry on no longer' is however not a new thing in this group.

3. RUMOURS

Rumours have not been numerous. The usual tales of excessive casualties have followed each raid, and stories of foot-and-mouth disease, this time from infected hay dropped by the enemy, are still occurring. There are rumours that certain East Coast towns are to be compulsorily evacuated forthwith. A parachutist caught near Huntingdon is said to have had over £500 on him.

4. EXTREMIST ACTIVITIES

A Special Postal Censorship Report shows that 'communist influences' are appearing in certain Scottish contractors' camps. A contractor's agent is afraid that the type of workman being sent to the camps from Glasgow is likely to try to stir up trouble. Although conditions in most of the camps have been greatly improved, attempts to create dissatisfaction among the workmen continue.

Postal Censorship also reports the recent establishment of a neo-Fascist organisation called the League of Roland. Evidence suggests that this may be linked with Lord Lymington's League of Husbandry.

5. SUMMER TIME

The decision to increase Summer Time by an hour has aroused very little discussion. Even from agricultural areas there have been fewer protests than might have been expected.

SPECIAL COMMENTS

6. AIR RAIDS

FIRE-WATCHING: A shortage of volunteers is still holding up arrangements in certain areas. 'The requirements of the Order are thought to be rather exacting' in some cases; at Berwick, for instance, 40% of the town's population will be needed to fulfil the demands. The need for a compulsory system is being considered in Manchester, as an appeal for volunteers to form a pool for watching business premises has been a failure.

There are complaints from many districts about difficulties in getting helmets, ladders, stirrup pumps, buckets, and other necessary equipment.

GAS: Comments on this subject are declining. There is still some apprehension about it being used, though apparently the carrying of respirators has not increased. One RIO reports that there is 'dissatisfaction with the Government's lack of clear directions'. Another says: 'The belief is that if there were a real danger the Government would issue an Order to make the carrying of masks compulsory.' It appears that the issue of such an Order would make the public believe that the danger was *imminent*. If it failed to materialise, the public might quickly become doubtful about its reality (as has happened over invasion).

AA DEFENCES: There has been a revival of criticism of these defences in the South-Western Region. Following recent air raids at Falmouth, and on an aircraft factory at Yate, there were protests about the apparent immunity of the raiders. At Falmouth sirens, balloons, and guns were said to have gone into action only after bombs had been dropped.

7. FOOD

The public's interest in communal feeding is increasing. It is realised that it helps to overcome difficulties of shortages and distribution. In places where communal kitchens have been successful there have been demands for more of them, and also for more works canteens and school kitchens.

Queues are again reported in various parts of the country. A good many of these are for food used in 'packed meals', such as pork pies, cheese etc.

The main food complaints (some old, some new) this week are that:

1. Restaurants are able to include rationed food in their menus.
2. By registering at different shops members of one family can get extra unrationed supplies.
3. Evacuees with time on their hands are able to buy more unrationed food than local residents.
4. No extra rations have yet been granted for Civil Defence or heavy workers; in addition, they ask for preferential treatment in regard to cheese, eggs, marmalade.
5. Services' personnel are getting more than their share, sometimes by 'living out' with their wives and having meals also at camp or aerodrome.
6. Shortages following price control. People are asking the Ministry of Food not to control vegetables.
7. Back-door sales from food shops to 'special customers' are occurring.
8. Large food shops have greater relative supplies than small ones.

Women have stated they would not mind shortages provided they knew that distribution was fair. There are complaints that country dwellers who can afford to do so are getting extra supplies from the big London stores.

It has been reported that trade rings exist which buy up food stocks from damaged shops, at salvage prices, and then sell them in other districts at retail or 'monopoly' prices.

8. TRADE

SHORTAGES AND LIMOSO (LIMITATION OF SUPPLIES ORDER)

Special investigators of the Board of Trade are studying shortages throughout the country, particularly to find out the effects of LIMOSO on supplies. The results of this investigation show, among other important points, that:

1. The degree of shortage varies considerably from one reception area to another; there are also shortages, of course, in neutral and evacuation areas.

2. The commonest shortages are underwear, and pots and pans.

3. There seems to be some abuse of the powers under which a Town Clerk may certify a retailer's requirements. This is said to be the result of pressure brought to bear by retail traders, who are to some extent encouraged in this by commercial travellers.

4. There are wide differences in retailers' plans for helping each other by replacing blitz-damaged stocks. This co-operation is affected by several factors; these include the amount of local expectancy or complaisance about air raids, whether competition has been fierce or friendly, and the presence or absence of a 'local strong personality'.

CONCENTRATION OF FACTORIES

The proposals by the President of the Board of Trade and the Ministry of Labour are 'recognised as being inevitable and sound', but there is some anxiety among the smaller manufacturers about 'questions of goodwill' and it is felt that their position at the end of the war will be very difficult.

SALVAGE

In some districts householders are discouraged from collecting their scrap because local salvage arrangements seem to be ineffective. There are sometimes not enough compartments in the dust-carts to take all the varied scrap, and piles are left beside the dustbins.

The idea that salvage is really not of much importance is also helped by the sight of uncollected metal in bombed houses and elsewhere. There is also severe criticism of the bonfires made by men clearing up raid damage.

9. LABOUR

WOMEN AND INDUSTRY

A study has been made of the reasons why more women are not working in factories. Interviews were made for five large firms (Hoover, Gillette, Kodak, Glacier Metal and Arrow Switches) with 601 housewives in their own homes. These were the results:

1. 46.5% were unwilling to work in a factory (279).
    42.7% were willing to do so, provided their problems were solved (257).
    10.8% were willing to start at once if acceptable (65).

2. Of the 257 who were willing to do so if their problems were solved, the main difficulties were:

    163 – children to look after (108 had very young children or babies, 48 had children attending school, 7 had children working).
    24 – family meals and housework.
    19 – husband would object.
    16– would be unable to do shopping.
    11 – ARP work.
    24 – other difficulties.

3. Of the 108 women with very young children,

    54 – were interested in Day Nurseries.
    25– were not.
    29– were undecided.

4. Thus, out of 601 women, 65 would be willing to start work at once, while 54 might be persuaded to do so if there were day nurseries for their children.

It is suggested that the employment of soldiers' wives would solve the difficulty which working women experience in finding someone to look after their children.

The unwillingness of many women to leave their home towns to work elsewhere is pointed out, and it is felt that some plan should be adopted to persuade them to do so.

10. EVACUATION

There are still suggestions that idle evacuees should be put to some form of work.

The trickle back to evacuation areas continues. Again, the reasons given are the possibilities of invasion, and financial difficulties. An attempt to solve one of these troubles is being made by Fulham Council, which allows an evacuated family to store its furniture in one room of their vacated flat at a cost of 4/- per week. The rest of the accommodation is then let by the Council to other tenants.

APPENDIX

'HOW TO TACKLE A FIRE-BOMB'

Report from Home Intelligence on the pictorial press advertisement inserted in the Sunday papers of March 2nd.

1. There is general agreement that the advertisement was seen and read by the majority of the public. RIOs consider it was 'seen by the majority', 'Sunday papers are read more carefully than others', 'reached industrial areas but not villages' (Scotland). Evidence from Mass Observation shows that in a small sample of interviews, approximately 60% had seen and read the advertisement. In a village in Worcestershire where a detailed study was made, rather over half of those questioned had seen the advertisement but many of these had not been sufficiently interested to study it in detail. More men than women had read it and interviewers encountered some evidence of resistance on the part of women to its subject matter.

2. The broadcast announcements of the forthcoming advertisement were very little heard, or, if they were heard, they were not remembered. Mass Observation records that 20% of those interviewed said they remembered an announcement, but there was considerable vagueness in their replies.

3. Not one report records any opposition to the use of Sunday papers. (Even Northern Ireland states 'no opposition', but Sunday papers have a smaller coverage there). Some people expressed doubt that the Sunday papers would reach everyone.

4. Most RIOs stress the need for additional publicity by poster, broadcast, leaflet, etc. Several suggested the desirability of reprinting the advertisement and giving it a special circulation.

5. RIOs consider that the advertisement was not generally cut out and pinned up. Reports from special contacts, however, show that a limited number of people seemed to have cut it out; few pinned it up. Mass Observation records that nearly 15% of the London sample said they had cut it out, but there was no evidence that they had pinned it up.

6. On the whole the public appeared to think the instructions adequate. 10% of MO's interviews showed the need for some clarification.

The principal difficulty, mentioned by women, was that sandbags were too heavy to handle, particularly to raise to face level. Many mention the filthy condition of sandbags at the foot of lamp posts.

There was some discussion of explosive fire bombs and some people (particularly women) expressed apprehension. One RIO thought that on this particular aspect of the problem 'the campaign deceives the public and is extremely bad propaganda'.

A common difficulty mentioned was shortage of stirrup pumps and buckets, and a small number of extremely strong criticisms of Government policy are recorded. Some people said that they could not possibly collect all the implements suggested.

7. The pictorial method of presentation was everywhere praised but there were important criticisms of special aspects. Detailed interviews

showed that the pictures had been studied with care. The commonest criticism was of the inaccuracy of certain positions taken up by the fire-fighter. 'He held his head far too high,' 'He's changed his hand.' William Hickey's criticisms in the *Daily Express* were noted and, undoubtedly, had caused the pictures to be scrutinised again. The advertisement was generally recognised as authoritative but there was criticism that the make-up was 'too much like a commercial advertisement', that it did not stand out sufficiently well from the rest of the page, and that arrangements for cutting out were not sufficiently emphasised.

Some people wished that a woman had been represented, others that more difficult situations had been shown, e.g. incendiary in a roof cranny.

CONCLUSION

The advertisement appears to have registered well and its pictorial form was generally appreciated. Detailed interviews showed a freedom from anxiety about the various problems involved. Although few people have had experience of dealing with fire bombs, the majority appear to have confidence that they can tackle them successfully.

HOME INTELLIGENCE
10 March 1941

NO 24: WEDNESDAY 12 MARCH TO WEDNESDAY 19 MARCH 1941

GENERAL COMMENTS

1. GENERAL STATE OF CONFIDENCE AND REACTION TO NEWS

This week the main factor affecting public confidence has been the renewed heavy raids on provincial cities. They are, however, localised in their effects. Each presents special aspects and these are described under 'Air Raids' later in this report. Of the public morale during and after these raids, it can be said that it followed familiar lines. Those who saw both Clydeside's blitz and the first blitz in the East End noted a striking similarity, with Glasgow coming out, if anything, slightly better. There was no panic, and private and public evacuation went forward in an orderly manner. The inevitable delays in official assistance were accepted cheerfully and patiently, and there was remarkably little grumbling. The extreme cold was much remarked on in the shelters. The engineering apprentices, who were on strike, offered their services in any post-raid work.

The almost continuous raiding of Portsmouth and Southampton during the past fortnight have proved a severe strain. A special note from the RIO points out that if this bombardment continues, the maintenance of civilian morale will depend very largely on the material care of the citizens by the authorities. In these towns, the young and vigorous troops are on the whole better cared for than the civilians of all ages – yet both are in the front line. The nightly trek from Portsmouth has reached considerable dimensions. Battleships in the harbour are said by some people to be attracting the heavy raids. The casualty figures for Merseyside and Clydeside came as an unpleasant surprise to the public.

Following the unpleasant surprise of the high shipping losses, the reaction to the news has been more cheerful. Our success against the night bombers, the passage of the 'Lease-and-Lend' bill, and Mr. Roosevelt's speech have combined to make more intelligent people think that an important corner has been turned. The night-fighter successes have produced a new attitude to the barrage; a fierce barrage is no longer greeted with universal satisfaction, as some now think it a sign that night-fighters are not up. Interest in the Balkans has declined a little; such interest as exists follows the lines indicated in the last two weeks' reports. It is, however, widely rumoured that we now have military forces in Greece.

Few reports on public reaction to the press details of the invasion pamphlet have as yet been received. It is, however, stated that it has aroused the flagging interest. The fact that the Government feel such a pamphlet necessary at the moment has once more brought the possibility of invasion home to people. The precise instructions are 'cordially welcomed'. In many areas, doubts about the reality of the invasion danger are, however, still reported.

A few special grumbles worth noting are as follows:

1. Certain groups among the working classes are upset at having to pay income tax for the first time. Reports suggest that education and explanation about this alleged 'exploitation' is required.

2. The Channel Island refugees complain of official indifference on the part of the Home Office, and are blaming it, rather than the Germans, for the lack of news from the islands.

2. RAF BOMBING

A special report on public reaction to RAF bombing of Germany from the RIO Southern Region makes the following points (largely confirmed by reports from other sources):

1. It is generally appreciated that it is harder for us to bomb Germany than for the Germans to bomb us; and that we have fewer bombers than they have.

2. Many, however – particularly inhabitants of the blitzed cities – doubt whether our bombing is as effective as it might be.

3. Personal experience of severe blitzes makes people feel that, instead of sporadic raids over a wide area, the soundest line is concentrated attack on a single town, night after night, until its inhabitants are demoralised and the towns' civic buildings, shops, houses and industries are destroyed. Are we, it is suggested, still too strict in our definition of military objectives? If our civil population are front-line workers, so too are the Germans. Many Southampton people who suffered two nights of blitz feel that had the process gone on for another three or four nights, the whole town would have had to have been evacuated. This is what they think should happen to the German towns. It is suggested that the knowledge that the Germans were getting a taste of their own medicine would be a great stimulus to the morale of the blitzed cities.

4. The fact that we are not now mentioning the bombing of Hamm and other railway centres leads to suggestions that we have found this type of attack valueless; many have now seen with their own eyes the speed with which railway communications can be restored.

5. It is further suggested that, by now, the quays of the invasion ports should be little better than rubble. Why, it is asked, do we continue to attack them, and why do we not allow invasion forces to accumulate and then wipe them out of existence?

3. RUMOURS

A fairly widespread rumour that the Princesses Elizabeth and Margaret Rose have been evacuated to America in the battleship *King George V* apparently originated in enemy broadcast material. Apart from this, there is little new to record. Exaggerated stories of damage on Merseyside and Clydeside followed the usual lines; in addition, in one recent blitz it is said that a German plane wrote the figure 10 in the sky, indicating the time of the next night's raid. The enemy are accused of dropping metal darts. It is also said that we are to give the United States battleships in exchange for numbers of escort vessels, that there is still a secret U-boat base on the west coast of Ireland, and that the Government expects the war to be over this year. In support of this view, recent optimistic hints by our politicians are quoted. The official references to 'other devices' used in bringing down night bombers have led to rumours of spools of wire shot into the air.

There are still complaints of careless talk by munition workers, particularly in public conveyances. At Shoeburyness, a secret television apparatus is openly discussed by the population.

SPECIAL COMMENTS

4. AIR RAIDS

The Leeds raid on March 14th–15th was the most intense the city has yet been through, though compared with earlier blitzes on other towns, it was not so severe. Morale is said to have been 'excellent', and the emergency arrangements worked well. The only publicity given out by the local authorities (through the Secretary of the Local Information Committee) was a warning about the penalties for looting.

In the Clydeside raid on March 13th very extensive damage was done. A great deal of this was caused by fire, particularly in the Parkhall Housing Estate. It is reported that here the shortage, and in some cases the 'gross neglect', of fire-watchers was an extremely serious matter; as a result, very few of the houses are in a habitable state. Though there seems, on the whole, to have been very little panic during the raid, there was a considerable amount of both organised and private evacuation afterwards. Dislocation of transport made this a slow process, though otherwise it was carried out efficiently. Emergency services and food supplies were also affected severely, though only temporarily, by the dislocation of traffic, and some of the Rest Centres were unusable because of time bombs. In these and other matters the Ministry's loudspeaker vans were reported to be particularly helpful.

5. FIRE-WATCHING

There are still reports of a shortage of watchers. In some cases, however, employers are apparently dismissing their paid watchers and are asking their own workers to take on the job of watching. Cases have also been reported of employers 'bringing pressure to bear on their work people to leave Civil Defence duties and take up fire-watching'. The relative importance of one's home and one's employer's property is still much disputed. 'There is a great need,' says one report, 'for the Government to give a strong lead in this matter.'

6. FOOD

Though food is still a major problem in most homes, housewives are coping with it more philosophically. They are prepared to put up with their difficulties, provided there is equality of sacrifices; at present many of them are still not satisfied that equality has been achieved.

The rationing of preserves has been welcomed as an indication that the authorities aim at equality in distribution, but the small quantity to be received caused surprise and concern. Complaints have, however, been made that people who could afford to do so were able to buy up all available

stocks in the day allowed them between the announcement and the introduction of rationing.

The main food difficulties reported this week are:

1. Replacing emergency stocks after consumption following an air raid,
   or when normal supplies have been held up by transport difficulties.

2. Shortages of food for heavy workers, especially of cheese.

3. The high price of fish, as a substitute for meat. (It is alleged that some
   fishermen are limiting their efforts, because of high prices).

4. Shopping difficulties of women war-workers, whose problems are
   increasing as shortages become more acute.

5. The provision of something sweet for children, now that preserves
   are rationed.

Potato bars have been much discussed, and hopeful traders are considering their prospects.

7. LABOUR

The Glasgow dockers, whose suspicions of the guaranteed week have previously been rather vague, have now voiced more concrete reasons for their
distrust of the scheme:

1. As they will not be guaranteed a working week *at the docks*, the
   assumption is that they will be forced, when work is slow at the boats,
   to do railway unloading etc., to which they are not accustomed. In
   stressing the importance of being allowed to follow their own class of
   work, they instance occasions when men, unused to a certain job,
   have taken many times as long to do that job. As they work at piece-
   rates, this has naturally proved an uneconomic proposition for them.

2. The new scheme will limit their freedom. Under the old scheme, if
   they worked on Sundays (for which they were paid double time) they
   felt entitled to take Monday off.

3. The new scheme will prevent dockers working and collecting
   unemployment insurance money at the same time. Further, their
   wages will now be able to be checked for income tax purposes.

Local press articles appear to have confused the dockers, and the minimum wage (£4.2s.6d) is mistaken by the men for a total possible wage.

A 'Snappers Union' has been formed, and it is expected to grow rapidly. (A Snapper is a man outside the Dockers' Union who is only employed after the regular Badge men have all been engaged.) The new union has said it is prepared to accept the Government scheme.

APPRENTICES' STRIKES: It has proved difficult to find the real leaders of the apprentices' strikes in Scotland; their precise reasons for striking are also obscure. Out of the vagueness and confusion, however, the fact that Government trainees receive higher rates of wages emerges as the primary cause. The apprentices say that, in many cases, the trainees are so unskilful that they have to depend on the apprentices to do their work for them. Also it is thought that the trainees are dodging military service.

Incitement to strike is coming from an unofficial body, the Apprentices' Committee, which is a communist 'shadow' organisation. This Committee is outside trade union control, and the majority of apprentices are not in any union. These facts make trade union and Ministry of Labour co-operation particularly difficult, and machinery for dealing with unofficial strikes by negotiation must inevitably be hard to set up and operate.

Two strikes are reported from the Belfast shipyard of Messrs. Harland and Wolff; one of these is also an apprentices' strike and the same grievances occur as in Scotland.

WOMEN IN INDUSTRY: Mr. Bevin's broadcast and press publicity made a considerable impression and a special report from a group of factories shows that the subject is a major topic of conversation among women employees.

There is much speculation about the conditions under which compulsion will be applied. The main objection so far reported is that women may be expected to work and live away from home. There are inquiries about the care of husbands and children in such circumstances, but it is hoped that married women will be given special consideration.

Social workers foresee certain difficulties about the feeding of babies, and point out that ante-natal and post-natal clinics urge mothers to breast-feed their babies, while at the same time young mothers on war work are informed that they can leave their babies at nursery centres from the age of four weeks. It is suggested that some guidance on this question may soon become necessary.

8. TRADE

SHORTAGES: Noticeable shortages of cigarettes and tobacco are reported and people are suggesting that retailers are holding stocks in expectation of a tax increase.

Shortages of cigarettes and tobacco after heavy raids is said to have a depressing effect on morale.

9. EVACUATION

There has been some further evacuation of children from London areas since recent raids, but the trickle of returning evacuees continues. Financial difficulties and billeting problems are blamed and in some places billeting officers are said not to be trying to smooth out difficulties but are telling evacuees that if they are not pleased, they had better go back to London. A new complaint from country hostesses is that parents, eager to visit their children, descend on their guardians at the weekends and do not bring rations, thus adding considerably to existing food difficulties. Parents are also accused of sending money to evacuees for sweets and cinemas, but not for clothes.

From a total of 8,708 children evacuated from Belfast, 4,952 have returned home.

APPENDIX

1. POPULATION CHANGES

The latest figures of population changes given by the Ministry of Food are based on the ration book issue up to March 1 (plus a due allowance for persons not holding ration books).

Region	% of mid-1939 population on March 1, 1941
1. Northern	95
2. North-Eastern	96
3. North Midland	103

4.	Eastern	105
	Eastern II	101
5.	London	71
6.	Southern	109
7.	South-Western	116
9.	Midland	101
10.	North-Western	97
13.	South-Eastern	92
	ENGLAND	94
	North Wales	114
	South Wales	105
	WALES	107
	SCOTLAND	96
	NORTHERN IRELAND	100
	ISLE OF MAN (Feb 1, including internees)	113
	UNITED KINGDOM	95

2. LONDON'S SHELTERS

The following details about public shelters in the London Region have been issued by the Ministry of Health:

The total capacity of public shelters in the Region is now:

> 1,307,250 for night use.
>
> 1,280,750 for day use.

A decline in the number of shelterers occurred during January and February. In public shelters (excluding Tubes) the numbers were:

> 6th January – 270,317
>
> 3rd February – 202,776

In Tubes, the numbers were:

> 1st January – 80,500
>
> 30th January – 62,000
>
> 27th February – 54,000

During February, bunks were installed for 66,000 people, bringing the number of bunks in the Region up to 528,000. In the same month 7,980 heating stoves were delivered to local authorities; nearly 21,000 have been delivered up to date, and of these 7,431 have already been installed.

Feeding facilities are now available in:

199 out of 274	shelters holding 500 or more
444 out of 830	shelters holding 200–500
1,390 out of 5,701	shelters holding under 200

155 shelters are normally occupied at night by 500 people or more. All these have Medical Aid Posts. In addition, shelters can be grouped together to provide a population of 500 or more for the purpose of establishing a Medical Aid Post. 54 such groups have been established, and nearly 84% of them now have Aid Posts. 260 trained nurses are at work in these posts.

HOME INTELLIGENCE

NO 25: WEDNESDAY 19 MARCH TO WEDNESDAY 26 MARCH 1941

GENERAL COMMENTS

1. GENERAL STATE OF CONFIDENCE AND REACTION TO NEWS

THE BLITZES: The two heavy blitzes of March 20th and 21st on Plymouth are described by the Regional Information Officer as comparable with the raids on Bristol and Coventry. In his preliminary report, he makes the following points:

1. There is considerable feeling among civilians about the alleged deficiencies of the AA defences, compared with earlier and less destructive raids.

2. The large provincial towns of the South-West are accepting the fact that if they are 'due for a blitz' they must expect the destruction of the

centre of their towns, and that nothing can prevent it. In Plymouth the people stood up to the blitz 'exceptionally well'. For the first few nights afterwards, many went out to the country in cars and slept in them.

3. There is some criticism of the civic organisation at Plymouth on the ground that it has not stood up to the blitz too well; this is attributed to the concentration of local power in 'a few elderly hands'.

4. The first raid opened within half an hour of the departure of the King and Queen who had been touring the city. During the day, the rediffusion relay system (which serves about 10,000 homes) broadcast details of the royal tour. The public linked the raid and the royal visit together, attributing the one to the other, and suggesting that the local rediffusion of the details of the tour was unwise. The rumour that the blitz was due to the royal visit has been reported from other Regions, and is similar to the recent rumours that other blitzes followed visits from prominent people.

It is reported that as an aftermath of the Portsmouth raids, there is an undercurrent of uneasiness among civilians as it is believed that certain naval and military establishments in the neighbourhood are being evacuated. Civilian workers, both in the dockyards and the Civil Defence services, claim that they should not be treated with less consideration than the fighting services. The facts are that one Naval unit only has been evacuated; this was because its accommodation had been destroyed.

In the Bristol raid of March 16th–17th, the RIO reports that there is some feeling about the large number of casualties sustained by fire-fighting parties. People are also concerned because, although the casualties of Clydeside and Merseyside were officially announced, those of Bristol were not.

The general atmosphere after the Clydeside raid is described as one of 'carrying on, with a sense of relief at having been able to stand up to the ordeal'. The public are expecting further raids, though the tension is said to be slackening a little. The fact that some public houses are voluntarily closing at 9.30 instead of 10 in an effort to get people off the streets early is strengthening the belief that another blitz is imminent. There have been many strong expressions of disbelief in the official casualty figures. Popular estimates range from 2,000 to 5,000 killed, and some people are suggesting that the Government could not possibly have known the true figures at the time the announcements were made. An extension of this is a growing disbelief in official raid casualty figures in general. 'The Ministry of Information bears the brunt of the criticism.' The coupling of the Merseyside and Clydeside figures has, however, had a good effect, by showing that others had trouble as serious as Clydeside. There has been considerable private evacuation from Clydeside of women and children, particularly from the dock area. As after the Coventry raid of last November, 'Irish are making plans to cross to Eire – and safety.' On the whole, evacuees have been well received, though some middle-class hosts are making the usual type of complaints: the children are 'dirty and verminous', the adults 'ungrateful', and some of them are said to be 'just stopping (in Milngavie) for a free holiday'.

There is also criticism of some of the arrangements for dealing with the situation after the raid. The RIO quotes a Clydeside contact as saying: 'Everyone feels the repair question is unplanned.' In one district people whose homes had been damaged were indignant because wood for boarding up windows etc. was reserved for shops and public buildings, so that none was available for private houses. Demolition squads were criticised for being too slow at their work. They, on the other hand, complained that they were not properly equipped, and that more mobile cranes should have been available. Workers in certain districts have been inconvenienced by the transport situation. 'Those living at a considerable distance from Clydebank and other industrial areas are still finding it difficult to get to their work.' Some of them who were delayed on Saturday were annoyed because they arrived too late to collect their pay.

The East End blitz was regarded by the people in the affected districts as the worst they have yet suffered. Many were physically tired at the end of a winter often spent in damaged houses or shelters, with long hours at work. They faced the bombing with resignation, and even in places a listless indifference. On the whole, the homeless showed great patience, though they are less willing than they were to wait in queues for assistance. There was no rush evacuation following the raid.

AMERICA: From most Regions there is reported to be a rapid growth of pro-American feeling. The Lease-and-Lend bill, Mr. Roosevelt's speech, and the news of further help have combined to produce this. America's self-interest is now seldom mentioned, and instead, many people are predicting that she will soon be in the war with us.

INVASION PROSPECTS: Further reports stress that the new instructions are regarded as clear and helpful, and sound common-sense. Of a sample of Londoners, 70% had seen them, and 65% had read them or had heard them on the wireless. Criticism was very rare; a few thought the repetition unnecessary, and a few middle-class people described the instructions as 'patronising'. In country parts civilians are said to be still rather doubtful about how to deal with armed parachutists.

Only in Wales is there reported to be any wide belief that invasion is likely. Elsewhere the probability is regarded as remote.

EASTER HOLIDAY: There are many requests that the Government should announce its decision about Easter holidays as soon as possible, to avoid the necessity for last-minute changes of plan by the general public.

THE BALKANS: Interest in the Balkans continues to be slight. In spite of press optimism, Yugoslavia has for some time been regarded as being lost; while it is not expected that Greece will be able to stand up to a German onslaught, it is hoped that we will give her all the help we can, even at some sacrifice of our own interests.

2. REPRISALS

Public feeling is steadily growing stronger in favour of reprisals. In the past, the blitzed cities and towns have been less inclined than the safe areas to urge heavy attacks on German cities. Now the situation appears to be changing. In Glasgow, for example, the 'demand for reprisals is now becoming stronger among civilians; Service men, home on compassionate leave, are blazing angry and all out for the heaviest possible reprisals.' Since the raids on Leeds and Hull, in the North-Eastern Region there are increasing demands for reprisals 'on the heaviest scale'. Similar feeling is reported from London, the South-Eastern, Southern, North Midland and Midland Regions. Our bombing policy is described as 'flabby'. More and more it is being suggested that we should 'lay off' military objectives for a few nights and instead annihilate one or more German towns – preferably Berlin. In view of press reports of pessimism among the German Army and public, it is felt that now is the time to strike them hard. Further, it is generally believed that the German civilians 'would not be able to stand up to the kind of pounding which our blitzed cities have had'.

3. RUMOURS

Rumours have been rather more numerous this week.

In the Clydeside area, the following are reported:

1. That Mr. Churchill visited Glasgow after the blitz, and severely criticised the state of the air defences. 'He was especially wild because all our fighters are in the South, and the Clyde had no real protection.' This rumour represents a new type.

2. That Haw-Haw has promised Glasgow five days of peace to bury their dead.

Exaggerations of damage, either in Glasgow or elsewhere, were not common, reality having apparently kept place with rumour. In other parts of Scotland, rumour alleged that Dundee and Perth had been heavily attacked.

Elsewhere, Haw-Haw rumours are once more occurring, with Sheffield, Bognor, Chichester, Scarborough and a Free French battleship outside Portsmouth as their subjects.

Two other rumours, apparently based on fact, are:

1. That enemy planes are guided by beam radio, and that our night-fighters' successes were due to our planes flying along the beam.

2. That decoy beacons and fires in the Mendips are attracting German bombers, and that one of these decoys is within 200 yards of a hospital.

4. EIRE

A special report by Postal Censorship suggests that opinion in Eire is gradually becoming more favourable towards this country. This change seems to be caused less by a dawning affection or respect for England than by force of circumstance. There is very little modification of feeling, however, over the question of 'the Ports'.

The government of Eire is being increasingly criticised; even Mr. de Valera himself is not immune from censure. Among the chief causes of discontent are:

The rise in the cost of living.
Increasing unemployment.
Shortage of food and other supplies.
The government's agricultural policy.
The strictness of the press and film censorship.

There are also complaints that the government is taking no steps to check profiteering.

SPECIAL COMMENTS

5. AIR RAIDS

FIRE-WATCHING: There is still a good deal of confusion among fire-watchers about the way their job should be done. One of the reasons given for this is 'that no-one seems to be charged with the job of seeing that they carry out their duties'; nor are there any precise instructions about where they should be during alert periods (as distinct from 'alarms'). In some cases this uncertainty is said to be leading to 'deliberate evasion of fire-watching duties'.

FUNERAL ARRANGEMENTS: Reports from the London Region state that 'many poor people are more or less in the hands of undertakers' when making arrangements for burying air-raid victims. 'The usual procedure is for the undertaker to ask the amount of their insurance, and to base his charge on this.' It is suggested that some form of Government price control should be introduced to stop this practice.

Criticism has been made of the inefficiency of mortuary arrangements at Bristol, which is attributed 'to the low mentality of those engaged in this grim work'. Medical authorities say that identification of bodies is sometimes made difficult because their identity cards are removed by the police – 'presumably for security reasons'.

6. FOOD

Fewer minor grumbles have been reported this week, but the main difficulties are becoming gradually more serious, and there is deepening anxiety about the food situation.

There are complaints from certain industrial areas about the difficulty of getting proper meals at factory canteens; employers state emphatically that this is causing serious concern. In the Midlands, a campaign to recruit industrial labour is being seriously hampered by this problem. The allowance of food is described as quite inadequate; consequently the workers, particularly the women, are leaving their jobs. If this situation is not quickly improved, it is thought that repercussions in industry may be very serious.

The distribution of eggs is still causing many complaints. In Nottingham, for instance, though some shops are short of them, a direct supply company in the city receives thousands of eggs a day, and customers who queue up for them can get as many as four dozen at a time.

Though there have been fewer reports of queues this week, they still come from many parts of the country. In Coventry there are strong complaints that it is difficult to obtain enough food to maintain health.

The need is also stressed for teaching housewives to make better use of available foods. It is said that more tinned food than ever is being used, and many people are wondering what is to happen when it is less easy to get.

Complaints of wastage in NAAFI canteens have again been received. Explanations which have been given are that if surplus food is returned, subsequent rations are based on the smaller consumption, and that no credit notes are given for returns.

7. LABOUR

WOMEN IN INDUSTRY: Registration of women has been more discussed than any other subject on the home front this week. Although the scheme is generally approved, it is causing much confusion and anxiety; at the same time most of the criticisms have been constructive.

From the Services comes great anxiety. 'A man does his best because he has a wife or sweetheart waiting for him at home' is an expression which covers many of the men's feelings.

The opinion is generally expressed that mothers with young children should not be recruited for industry until all other woman-power has been exhausted. This feeling is so strong that it is suggested that older women, whose children are able to look after themselves, should be conscripted before them. While there are still so many 'idle women and particularly young childless wives living in billets, and unmarried girls, not in employment', mothers are reluctant to go into industry. Many of them are willing to work if they can be sure of good day-nurseries; but it is realised that even this will mean a great strain on them, and it is wondered what the effect will be upon the future generation.

A survey in the North-Eastern Region of 20-year-old girls shows some of them to be reluctant to leave home; those who do not mind doing so would prefer to join the Services rather than go into industry.

It seems that publicity may be needed to save an influx of women into the wrong jobs and the chances of panic-changing. Few women seem to know whether the jobs they are now engaged on will be regarded as reserved occupations.

It is also pointed out that many who are already engaged in full-time voluntary war work will be unable to continue this if their domestic servants are called up.

8. TRADE

The working woman's chief difficulty of finding no time to do her shopping is still a very real hardship, and is now more noticeable than ever, as the number of women in industry increases. It is again suggested that shops should make rearrangements in their hours to meet new needs.

The main complaint from shoppers this week is the increase in the prices of children's clothes, though in general these are not affected by the Purchase Tax.

There is evidence that neither the Purchase Tax nor the Limitation of Supplies Order seem to be properly understood either by the public or by many retailers.

9. EVACUATION

Evacuee grumbles are fewer.

There would appear to be less discrepancy between registrations and departures of evacuees than is often thought. From a total of 53,957 unaccompanied children registered in London from the 15th September 1940 to 8th March 1941, 46,750 actually departed.

APPENDIX

CLYDEBANK RAID – PUBLIC BEHAVIOUR

1. GENERAL

It is agreed by all observers that the bearing of the people in Clydebank was beyond praise. They are of a high moral and intellectual calibre. A large proportion are skilled workers. On neither day was there any sign of panic or of a blind rush away from the devastated area in spite of the great intensity and long duration of the attacks. There was, of course, a considerable private evacuation, but the people moving out knew what they were doing. On the Saturday morning in the Parkhall area men were active in and about their ruined houses. Women and children were cheerful. There were one or two faint grumbles about local government leaders, but in the main the people concerned themselves most about the whereabouts of relatives and friends. Little or no mention was made to outsiders of family losses. For example, two well-dressed men asked us quietly about arrangements for private burial, but gave no details; and there were many expressions of relief at having escaped death or injury.

The remarkable immunity of Anderson and surface shelters, both of which types survived very near hits by heavy bombs and mines, was talked about with great surprise and relief. The advocates of 'deep shelters', by concentrating on the aspect of protection and safety (as against that of quiet), had persuaded many that the existing shelters were comparatively unsafe. The effectiveness of the shelters, and of the strutted closes, was an important influence in restoring and maintaining confidence.

On Friday and on Saturday morning there was much expressed anxiety about furniture but this gave place later on the Saturday, after the people had moved about and mixed with others, to a disregard for material possessions. 'I thought I was badly off,' women would say, 'until I saw what had happened to poor Mrs. So-and-so.' But they were still naturally preoccupied with the practical problem of the safe-keeping or removal of furniture. Later, in the centre of the town, the same cheerfulness and patience was even more in evidence. People standing in the queues showed an amazing desire not to give trouble to helpers coming in from outside. By this time it seemed to be taken for granted that the officials were facing many great difficulties and were doing their best. There was no sign of recriminations for alleged deficiencies in the past; the faint grumbles mentioned above were not typical. The people were naturally reluctant to ask for relief. 'I've come to report war damage' was a phrase often heard.

There was a striking absence of references to the 'capitalist bosses' who had been formerly charged as responsible for the war by the articulate and political-minded Clydebank workers. Only two drunk men could be found who were repeating the once familiar ritual.

Many visitors from the south, including some skilled observers of public behaviour and opinion, were most apprehensive of the possible effects of heavy raids on the Clyde. The people, they said, were mainly unprepared for bombing; many were indifferent to the war; many were taken up with disputes and hostilities to employers, to local or national government. All this was to a certain extent true and it therefore renders all the more striking the actual behaviour and demeanour of the Clydebank people in the most intensive and damaging raid on any single town in the course of the war. Mr. W. A. Sinclair, who spent the first days of the London raids in East End shelters, writes of the Saturday:

> Morale appeared to me to be very high indeed, and distinguishably higher than in the East End of London under comparable conditions last September. This is of course a dubious comparison, as the Cockney's active cheerfulness and the Clydesider's quiet composure are not readily commensurable, but in so far as the comparison can be made, the Clydebank morale did appear to me to be higher. This may indicate a quality of character, or it may merely indicate that my estimate of the psychological unpreparedness had been grossly exaggerated. I have as yet no opinion on this.

2. FIRE-FIGHTING UNPREPAREDNESS

A considerable part of the devastation caused by fire in Radnor Park and Parkhall might have been prevented had the people adequately equipped and prepared themselves. The man who said (before the raid) 'The workers have nothing at stake in this war; they should have nothing to do with it' was providing some sort of justification for an apathy shown by many beside himself. Another incident reveals this exceptional unpreparedness. An inquiry conducted by us into the public response to the pictorial advertisements on fire-bomb fighting (in the Sunday paper of March 2) shows that roughly 60% to 70% of the Scottish public saw and paid attention to this advertisement. But in Clydebank (where very few do not read Sunday papers) it was hardly ever mentioned. At a War Commentary meeting in Clydebank on March 9 (a week after, to be true), out of a group of over 300 only 12 could remember seeing this advertisement.

It is true that the fault was not entirely on the side of the private individual. Some people who had ordered stirrup pumps had difficulty in getting them. The two bags of sand to a house or tenement landing were insufficient to cope with the recurring showers of fire-bombs. There were no ladders from the top tenement landings to the high ceilings of Radnor Park tenements. The breakdown of water supply compelled the Fire Brigade and the Auxiliary Fire Service (as other reports show) to confine their attention to the lower parts of the town. But with all this it remains the fact that the people themselves by taking adequate preparations could have saved a half or more of destroyed Clydebank. This is now almost universally admitted by the victims themselves. The lesson will be driven home in Ministry of Information meetings and by other means.

This evidence of mental unpreparedness for bombing would seem to show that Clydebank morale is rooted, in Mr. Sinclair's words quoted above, in a 'quality of character', the quality of courage.

3. RECEPTION AREAS

There are reports of some bitterness in isolated cases where private householders have refused admission to raid victims. On Wednesday, for example, Glasgow Postal Censorship reports a demand that 'all churches and halls should be opened to refugees who have been badly received in Alyth, Perthshire'. But these reports are exceptional and the behaviour of the bombed-out people in the Vale of Leven and elsewhere in the face of very trying circumstances has again been marked by quiet patience. 'Local and national government officials,' says an observer who has travelled in all the blitzed areas, 'have a great deal to live up to to be worthy of these people.'

From Milngavie comes the report that half of the bombed-out people 'instead of coming to be washed went to listen to the band in the public park – this sounded to me an excellent sign'. Agreed.

4. REPRISALS

There was little evidence of a strong demand for reprisals at first among the mass of the raid victims. Little enmity was expressed towards Germans, though Hitler ('that man') was frequently mentioned in tones of loathing. But the quiet thinking type of folk who had hitherto been against the bombing of the German people had changed their minds. 'It's not a nice thing to bomb civilians,' they said, '*but* we've got to. The Germans are laughing at us.' 'It's obvious he's out to destroy our morale by destroying our houses. It's high time we set out to break their morale.' This opinion is growing stronger every day. It is helped by the universal conviction in Clydebank that the attack on the houses of Parkhall and Radnor Park, carried out in brilliant moonlight, was quite deliberate. (In this connection a German 'Broadcast from the Front' on Monday by a Clyde raider is significant – 'The multitude of ships in the river,' he said, 'was tempting. But our orders were different.')

5. THE RETURN TO WORK

The most vital sign of the underlying toughness and determination of Clydebank has been shown by the return of the workers. On Monday of this week the Apprentices' Committee decided to recommend the striking apprentices to get back to work, but the bombed-out apprentices had already made up their minds. They had been to the gates of Yarrow's that morning trying to get in. The great bulk of the workers had made their way back to Clydebank from wherever they were, anxious to start. We made some enquiries as to where the workers normally resident in Clydebank intended to spend the night. Those who were preparing to stay in Clydebank had no anxieties as to where they would go. They were going up to such and such a shelter; they were sleeping in the works shelter. No, they weren't worrying about special billets in Clydebank. All they wanted was their grub, and when was the Town Hall going to open for tea? At this point the Town Hall opened and the men swarmed in to enjoy a remarkably large and appetising meal.

6. FACTORS AFFECTING MORALE

The main topics of conversation among the bombed-out people just now indicate the factors most likely to maintain or weaken the splendid spirit and toughness of the workers. Chief of these without a doubt is that of compensation for war damage. If the workers and their families feel that they are being treated fairly by the Government in this respect, they will overlook other and relatively minor inconveniences. Workers given generous immediate relief 'come out and along the road as though they had pulled off a double'. A recurrent question is 'When will we be paid for war damage? Soon or after the war?' They are keen to get back to as near normal as possible; this means for them a new outfit of clothes, a new house or comfortable quarters or the guarantee of such in the not too remote future; in short, the chance of a new start. As one worker put it, 'If the Government does fairly by us it'll be a terrific spoke in the wheel of the Communist Party. The Communist Party say the State is the organ of suppression of the workers but if we are treated fairly it will take all the sting out of that kind of criticism.'

A present sore spot is that some people who removed and stored their furniture, assuming that they would be compensated, are now becoming aware that so far they are unlikely to be refunded their expenses of removal and storage (the latter may be considerable – some are paying 10/- a week for storage). They have misunderstood the instruction (often heard at second or third hand) that the Government would remove and store furniture. This instruction applies, we understand, to furniture left for official removal and storage – furniture left in the street has been removed and the category now being removed is that of furniture in houses scheduled for demolition. The people who removed their own furniture thought that they were acting in the spirit of the Government's intention.

A related problem, little mentioned just now, is 'Will we be expected to pay rent for our uninhabitable Clydebank house?'

An exceptionally important point (in that it will still influence morale tremendously the more workers are convinced that on the big question of war damage they are getting a fair deal) is that raised in our previous report on 'Workers and Managements'.

The anger and determination of the men to get even with Hitler for what he has done to Clydebank, and may do to other places, should without doubt make them even more keenly critical of any apparent delays on the management side. Their previous reaction to any such appearance of slackness tended to be a cynical one and as such was exploited by the 'revolutionary defeatists'. We are watching to see how the communists will attempt to meet the new mood of the workers. Meanwhile it is all the more important that the management should take the leading shop stewards into their confidence in the case of any hold-up which cannot be explained in terms of the difficulties caused by the bombing.

Other secondary factors are the comfort and safety of families in reception areas, the adequacy or otherwise of transport to the yards and workshops (for those removed from Clydebank), the provision of temporary sleeping accommodation (for workers remaining in Clydebank) – the dry weather in the last few days has eased many problems here – and the provision of adequate meals in Clydebank. This last service is being carried out very well indeed. The others are less advanced.

With regard to housing and sleeping accommodation for the workers, is consideration being given to the building for the workers of a hut town on the moors? Clydebank, with its shipyards, is a tempting target which the Luftwaffe is likely to visit again. If this is the official view it would seem unwise to do much more in the town than first-aid repairs to houses, and to provide near the town war-time huts on the Army model for the men now without a doubt in the front line.

7. PRESENTATION OF NEWS

There is considerable irritation in Clydebank at the treatment of the raids in the official communiques before Tuesday 18th inst. The announcement on Wednesday morning, 19th inst., of the casualties over the whole area as being 500 dead and 800 injured is regarded with some scepticism. There are however few wild rumours in Clydebank itself.

PUBLIC RELATIONS BRANCH
ST. ANDREW'S HOUSE
EDINBURGH
20 March 1941

NO 26: WEDNESDAY 26 MARCH TO WEDNESDAY 2 APRIL 1941

GENERAL COMMENTS

1. GENERAL STATE OF CONFIDENCE AND REACTION TO NEWS

This week, the decline in heavy raids and the news from the Mediterranean, Yugoslavia, and Africa have combined to produce an atmosphere of optimism and cheerfulness about the war. The revolution in Yugoslavia was welcomed with surprise as a 'sign that we have regained the diplomatic initiative', and as an indication that the 'neutral countries are at last realising which is going to be the winning side'. The news has produced all the more effect because the great majority of people had previously regarded Yugoslavia as being as good as German. There are still a few who are anxious about the ability of Greece (and, indeed, Yugoslavia) to stand up to German attack without military assistance, and if we do assist her, they fear another Dunkirk; but for the most part, people are well content to contemplate the present without speculating about the future.

The advances in Africa and the Naval victory in the Mediterranean have led many people to expect that one or two more heavy blows will see Italy definitely out of the war. Indeed, what is described as 'the turn of the tide in our favour' is felt to be so obvious that optimists are predicting that the war will be over before the end of the year. The Naval successes were a particularly welcome tonic at Plymouth.

It is reported that a considerable number of people trace a causal connection between the week's successes and the National Day of Prayer.

In Glasgow, as an apparent result of the raids, there was much greater interest in, and enthusiasm about, the news than is usual. Another post-blitz change of sentiment in Glasgow is a new feeling of partnership with the English blitzed cities: 'The people are now satisfied that they are bearing their full share of Britain's difficulties, and bearing it just as well.' Disbelief in the official casualty figures has continued to be widespread, but no reports have been received since Mr. Morrison announced the revised figures. Mr. Morrison said that since the communique was issued on March 18 giving the figures of casualties in the two night raids on Clydeside on March 13 and 14, the numbers had risen and now amounted for the two nights combined to about 1,100 killed and 1,000 seriously injured.

He explained that it was impossible in the early stages to obtain definite figures.

He felt it important to correct any impression that the original announcements were deliberately designed to minimise the seriousness of the damage sustained.

A similar disbelief in the official figures is reported from Liverpool, Birkenhead, and Wallasey. In Wales, too, there are said to be doubts about the total figures for February, in view of the extent of the Cardiff and Swansea raids.

In London, it is reported that, in the badly bombed boroughs, people seem to be taking longer to recover from the raids than they did last year; they are, however, very appreciative of the greatly improved social services for dealing with post-raid conditions (Administrative Centres, Rest Centres etc.); the only adverse comments reported are about insufficiency of staff to deal quickly with the applicants, and about delay in salvaging furniture.

The Government invasion instructions continue to be welcomed as 'a sensible precaution'. The main invasion problem now seems to be the method of distinguishing our own troops from Germans dressed in our uniforms, and special identification marks are being suggested by the public. But belief in the likelihood of invasion is now very low. The same attitude is reported towards the official advice about gas. 'There is no undue perturbation,' but several reports state that many people would welcome compulsory gas-mask carrying.

The seriousness of the Battle of the Atlantic is fully realised, and as an apparent consequence, grumbles about food are few.

The popularity of America is steadily rising. The mention of American aid at meetings and in cinemas is now often greeted with applause. One report suggests that a broadcast by 'the ordinary American man in the street', on the lines of 'In Town Tonight', would be much appreciated.

The unpopularity of France (and there now appears to be less discrimination between the French people and the Vichy government) has also grown rapidly. From several Regions, it is reported that there is strong feeling and 'grave concern' about the passage of American food ships to France (to feed, it is suspected, Germany). Mr. Dalton's firm words about Admiral Darlan are welcomed, and it is hoped that these will be followed by equally firm action.

2. REPRISALS

Public feeling in favour of reprisals continues to be very strong, both in the blitzed towns and in the rest of the country. It follows much the same lines as those indicated last week. The moral aspects of the problem are now almost entirely discounted. Personal experience has made the inhabitants of the blitzed towns believe that attack on the centres of population is 'a paying military proposition', and they demand that we should apply the lesson to Hamburg and Berlin. Our apparent reluctance to bomb the Rumanian oil wells is also once more being commented on. Air Ministry announcements that a town has been bombed 50 times (and is apparently still in existence) makes them consider that our raids must be 'child's play' or 'woefully inaccurate'. The recent official statements in the press and on the radio about our bombing 'have made little impression, and people will want a lot of convincing that really heavy raids on civilian centres in Germany are not our most efficacious weapon'. Further, every official statement about our increasing bombing and reserve strength leads to fresh questions as to whether we are yet exerting our power to the full, and the phrase 'a small force of our bombers' in communiques is a particular cause of dubious comment.

3. RUMOURS

This week, rumours have again been fairly numerous, but localised.

1. Tales of exaggerated raid casualties, and a revival of the stories of funeral services over entombed shelterers, are reported from several Regions.

2. Rumours of a connection between raids and events in this country are also prevalent:

   Bristol's last raid was attributed to a reference to that town in a recent speech by Mr. Bevin.

Weston-super-Mare is expecting a raid because of its War Weapons Week.

The Filton aeroplane works is said not yet to have suffered severe attack because it is still supplying planes for foreign governments – etc. etc.

3. From two Regions, there are reports of a fairly widespread rumour of incendiary bombs which release gas, thus preventing the efforts of fire-fighters. The more circumstantial story adds that the gas is colourless and odourless; that it rapidly produces depression and suicidal attempts; and that there have already been many victims, though this has been hushed up. The Manchester and Glasgow raids are named, and another version suggests that the gas is merely tear-gas.

4. In Nottingham, on March 30, the rumour was widely circulated that Mussolini was superseded or dead; at one cinema the performance was stopped, so that his assassination could be announced. This rumour apparently arose from press speculations.

5. It is said that the Germans are landing raiding parties on our shores, as we are said to be doing on the coasts of France and Holland.

4. SUNDAY THEATRES AND MUSIC HALLS

A report from the RIO Scotland states that comparatively little interest has been aroused there by the proposal to open these entertainments on Sundays. On the whole, there has been less opposition to the idea than might have been expected. Both the press and the public are tolerant without being particularly enthusiastic. But it is felt that 'any pressure from Sabbatarian groups to bring the matter to a head' may arouse a strong reaction against them.

A preliminary enquiry made in London last week showed that the great majority of those interviewed were in favour of Sunday opening. There are no reports yet on the reaction to the Parliamentary veto.

5. EXTREMIST ACTIVITIES

PACIFISM: The RIO Northern Region reports that 'A women's branch of the North Pacifists Advisory Bureau has just been formed to cover the Tyneside area.' Its objects are: 'To give advice and, if necessary, financial assistance to women who have conscientious objections to the registration and conscription of women to help in the war effort.'

SPECIAL COMMENTS

6. FOOD

The tone of this week's reports suggests that women are beginning to realise that primarily their food problems are unavoidable. Though fewer complaints have been reported, shortages are causing some depression and anxiety, and in one town in the Midlands it is said that lack of food is 'definitely weakening morale'.

Nevertheless, there is still a belief that many shortages are avoidable as they are caused by the failure to adjust distribution to cover local increases in population; it is also believed that there is still too much waste of food, and that this is caused partly by the way it is allocated. Suggestions continue to be made that meals in NAAFI canteens should be restricted. It is also said that some people are using tins of food for their cats and dogs.

There has been a good deal of comment about the size of the cheese ration. Miners, on the other hand, are pleased with the increase in their allowance, and other categories of workers hope they will be similarly favoured.

Most of this week's reports of queues, many of which are for eggs, are from the Midlands. The demand for 'all-round rationing' is encouraged by the reported 'abuse of the queuing system' (this is particularly a subject of comment in Postal Censorship).

It is reported from a reception area in Scotland that after a recent blitz the local inhabitants distributed their stocks of tinned food and 'ready dinners' among evacuees sent into the district, and although the inhabitants were praised for their public-spirited generosity, the Ministry of Food regretted that it was unable to replace the stocks which had been given away. This affair has been the cause of bitter complaints, and the local people are said to feel uncertain whether their humanitarianism would again get the better of their discretion if there were another blitz.

There is conflicting evidence about the success of Communal Feeding Centres. Though many places have reported a growing demand for them, and that those already established are very popular, in some London districts they are not being used to their full capacity; it is felt that in these cases their popularity would be improved if they were given better publicity.

7. LABOUR

The registration of women is undoubtedly the most discussed labour topic of the week. In collaboration with the Ministry of Labour certain big stores have set up information bureaux to deal with enquiries on the subject. For further details see Appendix to this report.

8. TRADE

TOBACCO: Scarcity of tobacco and cigarettes is being reported with increasing frequency. In the North-Eastern Region the shortage is said to be reaching 'famine proportions'. The popular idea that NAAFI canteens are better supplied than retail tobacconists is 'exasperating to war-workers' who have to go short. Supplies in London seem generally better than elsewhere.

Shopping difficulties continue to be acute for working women.

9. AGRICULTURE

The Monkstown Branch of the Ulster Farmers' Union have called upon their Executive Committee 'to take all steps possible to obtain from the Ministry of Food a promise that none of the 1941 harvest shall find its way to the brewers or distillers until the food supply of the people and the live-stock has been made secure'. They have also demanded 'that at least one-half of the brewers' and distillers' present stock of grain shall be made available for the feeding of live-stock'.

10. EVACUATION

A special report on the Gibraltar refugees living in hostels in London shows that they are homesick, and because they get little reliable news are apt to be victims of doubt and rumour. They have not got used to English food, nor do they appreciate special war-time difficulties. Although some services provide certain recreational and other facilities, education is only supplied for some of the children, and the women have little to do. It is suggested that their morale could be improved by some sort of news service.

There are 11,000 of these refugees (of whom 4,000 are children), and they are housed in 20 hostels in various London districts.

APPENDIX

THE REGISTRATION OF WOMEN

The following subjects have been brought to the attention of Home Intelligence and the questions listed below have been extracted from our files.

1. THE POSITION OF MARRIED WOMEN WITH YOUNG CHILDREN

There is evidence of considerable apprehension both among young married women and their husbands about the possibility of 'conscription' being applied to mothers with young children. Many feel that these mothers should be exempted, and concern is expressed that the future generation will suffer unless this is done. At the same time many young mothers are quite ready to do war work if they can feel sure that in their absence their children will be properly cared for. The idea of nursery centres is welcomed although the hope is expressed that they will be well run but 'not too official'. Mothers would like to be allowed to visit their children during their own lunch hour for example. The fact that little proper nursery accommodation has yet been provided is well known among working-class mothers and there is some scepticism that local authorities will, in fact, provide these facilities.

2. THE POSITION OF WOMEN WITH HUSBANDS ON ACTIVE SERVICE

There are reports that men in the Services are expressing anxiety and even indignation at the prospect of their wives being called up. Publicity addressed to Service men is suggested. Many wives are willing to work but would like to be given an assurance that they will be given time off when their husbands are home on leave.

3. WAGES AND HOURS

WAGES: Are wages to be standardised? Alternatively, will a schedule of industrial wages be available to women when they sign on? There appears to be a general impression that wages for women are low in all factories except those engaged on munitions. There is some apprehension about 'conscription' into non-union shops. There is also confusion about the weekly allowance paid to trainees: some women think that the 36/- will be the amount the trainee receives when she gets a job.

HOURS: Will women be expected to work on night shifts (the fear of this possibility is often given as a reason for women preferring to join the Services)? Will women be expected to do much overtime? Will arrangements be made for part-time work?

4. MOBILITY

This subject has caused a good deal of apprehension. Married women as well as fathers and mothers of young daughters are worried about the possibility of compulsory mobility. Young women signing on at Labour Exchanges near factories in their own neighbourhood are doing so in order to secure work near their home.

5. SHOPPING DIFFICULTIES

This is a serious and widespread consideration. Women envisage shortages and shopping difficulties becoming much more acute. There is a widespread demand that these domestic difficulties should be taken fully into account both by employers, shop-keepers and the Government.

6. VOLUNTEERS AND CONSCRIPTS

There is general confusion about the meaning of registration. Many women think that by volunteering now they would secure some advantage. Many are asking whether they should leave their present occupations at once and there are many enquiries about which occupations will be reserved. The publication of a list of reserved occupations is urgently asked for.

Those who are volunteering now complain that jobs are not available at the Labour Exchanges and there is some criticism of the conduct of

Labour Exchanges in being unable to advise on jobs in other nearby neighbourhoods.

7. WOMEN IN DOMESTIC SERVICE

Many women doing full-time voluntary war work leave the conduct of their homes to the charge of maids. They want to know whether, in these circumstances, maids will be exempt. Mothers of young families with other responsibilities as well are also gravely concerned that necessary domestic help will be filched from them. Here it is frequently mentioned that alien women employed in domestic service should not be encouraged to leave useful jobs for more remunerative work in a munitions factory.

8. SOCIAL CLASS AND REGISTRATION

Some statement on the universality of the call-up and its egalitarian application would be welcomed. There is a good deal of suspicion that 'influence' will be used to get exemption and that part-time voluntary war work will be used as a loophole to avoid compulsory service.

9. TRADES UNIONS

Some women recognise the value of trades union protection and are anxious to know whether trades union conditions will apply to them after 'conscription'.

10. WOMEN IN UNIVERSITY TRAINING

Women at present in training and those contemplating a university career want to know what their position will be.

NOTE: Our reports show that women are eager to play their part in the war effort but have been confused by the publicity which has accompanied the recent Order. The fact that on previous occasions Government publicity has been ahead of planning has to some extent dampened enthusiasm.

HOME INTELLIGENCE
31 March 1941

III
APRIL TO JUNE 1941

1 APRIL British and imperial forces capture Asmara in Italian Eritrea.

3 APRIL A coup by army officers brings a pro-Axis government to power in Iraq under Rashid Ali; Bristol-Avonmouth is raided followed by attacks on Avonmouth (4 April), Glasgow-Clydeside (7 April), Liverpool-Birkenhead (7 April), Coventry (8 April), Tyneside (9 April), Birmingham (9, 10 April), Bristol-Avonmouth (11 April), Belfast (15 April).

6 APRIL German forces invade Greece and Yugoslavia; British and imperial forces take Addis Ababa in Italian Ethiopia.

7 APRIL The Chancellor of the Exchequer, Kingsley Wood, introduces a landmark budget which extends the scope of income tax to include millions of wage earners.

10 APRIL Rommel begins the siege of Tobruk.

16 APRIL London suffers its heaviest raid to date. More than sixty public buildings are damaged, including St Paul's Cathedral. This is followed by attacks on Portsmouth (17, 27 April), Plymouth-Devonport (21, 22, 23, 28, 29 April), Sunderland (25 April), Liverpool-Birkenhead (26 April).

17 APRIL Yugoslavia surrenders to the Axis powers.

24 APRIL–1 MAY British and Commonwealth forces are evacuated from Greece.

1–7 MAY Merseyside is bombed for seven consecutive nights, the longest unbroken sequence of serious attacks on any provincial area during the war. Attacks are also made on Belfast (4 May), Barrow-in-Furness (4 May), Glasgow-Clydeside (5, 6 May), Hull (7, 8 May), Nottingham (8 May), Sheffield (8 May), Birmingham (16 May).

2 MAY British military intervention in Iraq. The revolt collapses on 30 May and Rashid Ali flees the country.

9 MAY German aircraft begin to arrive at air bases in Vichy-controlled Syria.

10 MAY Hitler's deputy, Rudolf Hess, lands in Scotland; in the last major attack on London during the Blitz, the chamber of the House of Commons is destroyed.

20 MAY German airborne forces land in Crete and begin to secure the island.

24 MAY HMS *Hood* is sunk in the Denmark Strait by the German battleship *Bismarck* and cruiser *Prinz Eugen*; on 27 May the *Bismarck* is sunk after a pursuit by the Royal Navy.

1 JUNE British and Commonwealth forces complete their evacuation of Crete; the rationing of clothes and footwear is announced by Oliver Lyttelton, the President of the Board of Trade.

8 JUNE British, Commonwealth, imperial and Free French forces invade Syria-Lebanon. Damascus is captured on 21 June.

22 JUNE Hitler launches Operation Barbarossa, the German invasion of the Soviet Union. Churchill broadcasts the same day offering all possible aid to the USSR.

NO 27: WEDNESDAY 2 APRIL TO WEDNESDAY 9 APRIL 1941

GENERAL COMMENTS

1. GENERAL STATE OF CONFIDENCE AND REACTION TO NEWS

THE WAR IN AFRICA

Our successes in Eritrea and Abyssinia have not entirely counter-balanced the fall of Benghazi in the public mind. Though many people attributed its fall to inevitable withdrawals necessary if we were to help Greece and Yugoslavia, there are a considerable number who do not accept this explanation. They are unable to understand how the Germans were able to ship so much equipment to Libya, and some are saying that whenever we meet the Italians we advance, but whenever we meet the Germans we retreat. Confidence in General Wavell continues, and it is even rumoured that he wanted to go on to Tripoli but was not allowed to by the higher authorities. It is hoped that we shall soon be able to release troops from East Africa to 'put matters right' in Libya.

Once again, the authorities, and in particular the Ministry of Information, are criticised for trying to minimise the unpleasant news. It is said that we proclaimed the importance of Benghazi when we captured it, but when we lost it, we treated it as of much less importance. This is described as 'not quite frank', an 'attempt to wrap up our failures' etc. The BBC is also criticised for saying that the German forces in Libya were small. Many people are inclined to regard anything but an unvarnished statement of bad news as a reflection on their ability to stand up to it.

GREECE AND YUGOSLAVIA

The German attack in the Balkans was at first regarded as a relief from the prolonged tension. While the resistance of Yugoslavia is thought to have been an unpleasant surprise for Hitler, it is anticipated that the Germans will rapidly over-run a large part of that country and also some part of

Greece. Many people are reported to regard this 'as a welcome opportunity for us to get to grips with the Nazis'. Some are asking whether our Army in Greece is adequately equipped, but anticipation of 'another Dunkirk' (mentioned in last week's report) seems to have declined. There are, as yet, no reports of reactions to the latest news; but it can be said that if a major disaster in Greece and Yugoslavia is to be anticipated, the majority of the public are quite unprepared for it.

INVASION FEARS

Those have declined still further, as it is thought that the Balkan campaign will 'keep Hitler busy for a while'. The publicity campaign for voluntary coastal evacuation is regarded by the public 'with scepticism'; it is said that if the Government was serious it would order compulsory evacuation and provide billets for evacuees. There is rather more discussion on the subject of gas, but little expectation that gas attack is imminent, or that it will be used other than as a desperate measure. Many people are reported to be getting their gas-masks inspected at ARP centres.

NIGHT RAIDS

The announcement of the full casualties of the Clydeside raid has done much to dispel rumour and exaggeration. The main topics exercising Clydebank opinion appear to be billeting and travelling difficulties.

The night raids of Thursday and Friday on Bristol were met by a barrage which provoked much favourable comment and 'a great increase in confidence'. It is believed that the new barrage caused many of the bombers to release their bombs over non-vulnerable areas. But there was 'great resentment' at an article in the *Daily Mail* of April 7th, which described how Bristol had beaten the night bombers. This is regarded as a plain invitation to the enemy to return to the attack. An earlier raid was widely attributed to a similar newspaper article.

Belfast's first raid was relatively small. Civil Defence services, Rest Centres etc. worked efficiently, and the public are reported to be 'in good heart'.

The nightly trek out of Birkenhead, Wallasey and other places is reported to be continuing.

BBC NEWS BULLETINS

This week there has been a renewal of the criticism of BBC bulletins on the ground of 'dreary repetition' and 'staleness'. It is noticeable that this criticism occurs whenever there is tension over war events. It seems likely, therefore, that it is an indication of increasing listening to *several* bulletins daily, rather than anything in the actual bulletins themselves. At all events, reports stress that the repetition leads to irritation and resentment, and by some illogical process to a disbelief in news, and it is suggested that a clearer line should be drawn in the bulletins between 'new' news and news contained in the previous bulletin.

2. REPRISALS

There is no change of feeling on this subject.

3. RUMOURS

Rumours have been rather more numerous this week, including a number of Haw-Haw rumours – but no unusual types have been reported.

4. SUNDAY THEATRES

The ban on Sunday theatres has aroused comparatively little interest. It is generally regarded as a well-organized victory for the Sabbatarians, and possibly the brewing interests. Many people are disappointed and regard it as 'unfair' in view of the fact that Sunday opening of cinemas is permitted. There is, however, no inclination to dispute the decision. Only in the rural area of South Wales is opinion 'overwhelmingly in favour of the ban'.

There are some disapproving comments that so many MPs failed to vote; they are being accused of apathy and even of being 'lily-livered' over a vocal minority of their constituents.

SPECIAL COMMENTS

5. FOOD

There is little change in the food situation. The usual complaints are repeated. Hardships still appear to be more severe in the Midlands than elsewhere.

6. TRADE

The shortage of cigarettes and tobacco is becoming a serious problem, particularly in the North, and in the Midlands. Supplies in the South are also said to be meagre compared with those available in London.

POINTS OF PUBLIC CONCERN NO. 1

The tone and frequency of reports on the following subjects indicate that they are possible 'tension points'. Though not of equal or, in some cases, individual importance, their total effect may well have a good deal of influence on public feeling.

POLICY POINTS

1. CASUALTIES: There is a decided tendency to scepticism about our official air-raid casualty figures; delay in announcing these also provokes unfavourable comment. There appears to be very little appreciation of the security factor affecting such announcements.

2. BOMBING POLICY: Concern is expressed about what is thought to be the apparent ineffectiveness of our raids on Germany, compared with German raids on this country, e.g. 'What would be left of Glasgow if it were bombed, as Cologne is said to have been bombed, 68 times?'

3. REPRISALS: Approval for a policy of reprisals appears to be steadily growing. This is generally taken to mean the bombing of civilian centres as legitimate military targets. The Government's disinclination to follow this course is often strongly criticised.

FOOD

1. SHORTAGES: Providing they are satisfied that shortages are unavoidable, the public is prepared to put up with them philosophically.

2. DISTRIBUTION: Criticism about the allocation of food stocks comes mostly from reception areas, and from those to which there has been a big movement of industrial workers; the Midlands are particularly affected.

Complaints are made that stocks are allocated without population changes being taken into account. Transport authorities are also blamed for the dislocation of supplies.

3. QUEUES: These are reported from all over the country. In those formed for unrationed food, trouble is sometimes caused by the working of a 'family racket'.

4. RATIONS: Certain types of industrial workers, in addition to those already receiving extra rations, are asking for increased allowances of meat, bacon or cheese.

5. JAM: Many housewives claim that the lack of sugar for home-made jam is going to prove a serious hardship.

6. FAVOURITISM: When supplies of unrationed food are scarce, some retailers will only sell these to their registered customers; this is the cause of much ill-feeling, though others regard it as a protection against abuse.

7. NAAFI: There is a common belief that NAAFI canteens are well supplied with food which is often not available to the public. This is said also about tobacco and cigarettes.

AIR RAIDS

1. PROPERTY: Unsalvaged furniture in bombed houses is the cause of much anxiety to its owners.

2. COMPENSATION: Difficulties in connection with this subject are continually being reported.

3. FIRE-WATCHING: Workers already engaged in other forms of civil defence object to having to act as fire-watchers for their employers. Some watchers also criticise the conditions under which they have to carry out their jobs; e.g., lack of feeding or cooking arrangements.

4. CIVIL DEFENCE: Shortages of gear and equipment for fire-watchers and rescue squads is reported from several districts; these defects sometimes lead to unjustified criticism of the local Civil Defence services.

5. TRAVEL FACILITIES: Railway vouchers which are valid only for three days are of little use to Civil Defence workers whose families are evacuated, as it is sometimes necessary to spend 24 hours of that period in travelling to see them.

EVACUATION

1. EXPENSE: The cost of keeping up two establishments has been causing evacuees to return to their homes. It also deters old age pensioners from allowing themselves to be evacuated.

2. DOMESTIC RESPONSIBILITIES: A suspicion among evacuated women that their husbands and elder children may not be properly looked after – or that the former may be too well cared for – is another reason why some of them return home.

3. EVACUEES: Many women resent the idleness of evacuees which gives them more time for buying food than the ordinary housewife can afford.

CONSCRIPTION OF WOMEN

1. SHOPPING: The shopping difficulties with which working women are faced is causing serious and widespread anxiety. As shortages become more acute these difficulties are likely to increase, and there are demands that problems such as this shall be fully taken into account by employers, shop-keepers and the Government.

2. NIGHT SHIFTS: A good many women are apprehensive of having to work on night shifts, and also of doing overtime; for this reason some of them prefer to join the Services.

3. HUSBANDS ON ACTIVE SERVICE: Men in the Services are anxious, and in some cases indignant, at the prospect of their wives being called up. Married women who are quite willing to work would like an assurance that they would be given time off when their husbands are at home on leave.

4. CLASS DISTINCTION: There is a good deal of suspicion that 'influence' will be used by some women to get exemption from the call-up, and that

part-time voluntary war work will be used as a loophole to avoid compulsory service.

WAGES

1. The wide differences between the scale of industrial wages, and rates of pay in the fighting and Civil Defence services, in agriculture and in essential trades, is a serious grievance; so, too, is the pay of the AFS compared with that of regular firemen. There is also a good deal of resentment about the high wages which are earned by some adolescents.

TRADE

1. There is some anxiety among small shop-keepers about the possibility of their businesses being 'telescoped'. It is feared that if this is done they may not be able to resume individual trading after the war, and will be 'sacrificed to multiple firms'.

2. PRICE CONTROL: Much annoyance is caused by shortages which invariably occur as soon as it is announced that the price of an article is to be controlled.

3. TOBACCO: Shortages of tobacco and cigarettes are reported from all parts of the country, and are said to be becoming more serious.

SALVAGE

There are frequent complaints from housewives about careless or inadequate salvage arrangements.

TRANSPORT

Road transport, particularly in industrial areas, is often said to be insufficient to deal with rush hour traffic. The railway authorities are also blamed for inadequate passenger services.

JUVENILE CRIME

The increase in looting and other forms of juvenile crime is the cause of serious anxiety to many parents.

APPENDIX

EFFECTS OF ENEMY AIR-RAID ACTION UPON HULL, ON THE NIGHTS OF THURSDAY 13 MARCH, FRIDAY 14 MARCH, AND TUESDAY 18 MARCH 1941

Report by Hull and East Riding Information Committee (No. 2)

Sub-committee: Rev. Canon A. Berry
                        Councillor Mrs. Hanger
                        Mr. James M. Peddie

The immediate post-raid effects of each of these raids are dealt with separately, but value has been derived from our ability to take a retrospective view of the reaction resulting from these raids and to make estimates of the cumulative psychological effects.

THE RAID OF THURSDAY 13 MARCH

On the night of Thursday the 13th March, Hull suffered a severe raid. There were over 150 incidents in various parts of the city. 26 reception centres were thrown open, and a total of 1,773 admissions were made to such reception centres. At the District Offices up to the evening of the 16th March, a total of 3,294 persons were dealt with and of these 2,216 reported for billeting. These figures give some indication of the extent of the social dislocation created by the raid. It was a heavy raid but not a 'blitz'.

A general evacuation took place in one working-class area, due to unexploded bombs.

In the course of our investigations we visited the St. Paul's area, Bean Street, Fountain Road Centres and the North Hull Estate, as well as making investigations in numerous other districts where bomb damage was experienced. In all of these districts we had the opportunity of having conversations with people both immediately following the raid and some days later. This to our minds adds to the value of the report, as it gave us the opportunity of forming an estimate of the cumulative psychological effects.

THE ST. PAUL'S AREA

In the St. Paul's area, the effect of the raid upon public morale was serious. We arrived at the considered opinion that this area did not stand up to the raid shock as well as did other districts. The morale of the people was lower than that observed elsewhere. This in our opinion has a physical basis.

The St. Paul's area is poverty stricken with intolerably bad housing conditions. The general social and cultural standards of the people are low and have been for years. Migration to the suburbs from this district to the more congenial Corporation Housing Estates has apparently robbed the locality of its more vigorous elements, and left a residue of population that appears to have very little energy and with their 'morale strength' definitely sapped.

It is not the purpose of this report to engage upon any sociological study, but merely to report faithfully upon the facts as we find them, yet in explanation, we must express our belief that what we saw can be considered a legacy of enervating pre-war social conditions that prevailed in this area.

POST-RAID REACTION

The immediate post-raid reaction in the St. Paul's area was one of *complete helplessness and resignation*. It was this attitude of resignation that provided the most disquieting feature. It was not a healthy willingness to accept misfortune without grumbling, but hopeless and indeed helpless incapacity to appreciate the significance of their plight, and the reasons for the disaster.

Naturally we did observe some exceptions to this general condition, but they were in the minority, and do not affect the general impressions we formed concerning the condition of the whole district.

In the centres dealing with these unfortunate people, we found that the officials experienced far more irksome difficulties than was the case in other parts of the city, and this can perhaps be considered due to the conditions described above.

SPECIAL TREATMENT NEEDED

We feel that the existence of such 'black spots' of morale should be recognised, for surely they are not completely unique. War-time social changes are perhaps having the effect of improving the relative material position of these people. Yet we believe that the Ministry of Information, so far as its work in stimulating and maintaining morale is concerned, should, *either directly or through its local committees, deal with the particular problems that such districts demand.*

There is a feeling of apathy settling upon the district which can and should be dispelled. As pointed out, the basic cause is perhaps physical, but in our view these 'black spots' present special problems which need individual attention and specialised campaigning. The general flow of Ministry of Information material leaves these people untouched.

NORTH HULL ESTATE

By contrast the people of the district of the North Hull Estate gave a remarkable demonstration of high morale. We were able to move throughout the whole of the affected area and had many conversations. We can frankly state that in not one single case did we see any undue fear or weakening of morale. Obviously in the first post-raid hours, shock was felt, but the recovery was really remarkable.

Our further visits to this district some days after the raid demonstrated how this rapid recovery had been maintained. So far as damage to morale was concerned, we have no hesitation in saying that the bombing raid was completely valueless.

COMMENTS UPON RECEPTION CENTRE ORGANISATION

In the King's Hall Reception Centre we had the opportunity of interviewing a number of people on the evening following the night of the raid. There appeared to be several who had not been allocated to any particular billets.

We saw one young woman, an expectant mother in her 20s with four children, who had apparently lost contact with the authorities and was not aware of any place to where she could be taken. The woman appeared incapable of making any effort for herself, and it appeared to us rather easy for the authorities to lose contact with such people. The woman herself was not very intelligent, and appeared to have no interest at all in her condition or surroundings. She was an unfortunate case. At the College of Commerce, they had no knowledge of this person nor of her family, and this we thought was regrettable, as she obviously needed some attention.

There was another young woman anxiously enquiring for her father. He was not in the King's Hall Centre. The person in charge said that she had left him in bed in the Methodist Chapel opposite. We went across. The Chapel was empty, and the old man had apparently gone or had been removed without the person in charge being aware of the fact. The College of Commerce were unable to give any particulars.

STRAIN UPON THE SERVICES

The strain upon the services was certainly much greater than that of previous raids. The scattered nature of the incidents and the number of centres that had to be opened meant a greatly increased burden. There did not appear in our opinion to be the ease of movement in the organisation that was apparent on the occasion of the East Hull Raid, previously reported.

This is not intended as a criticism but merely, as are the incidents quoted above, given to demonstrate the considerable strength of organisation that is needed to stand up to any heavy raid, or a raid with numerous scattered incidents. It must be realised that the *actual burden upon the organisation grows in increasing ratio with any increase in the range and extent of the damage*.

BEAN STREET RAID: FRIDAY NIGHT 14 MARCH

A parachute mine was dropped in the Bean Street District, West Hull, on the night of the 14th March. Considerable damage was done. In view of the damage and the resultant shock the people of this district stood up amazingly well to the disaster.

A large number of people were affected. We had the opportunity of discussing with many persons and judging the immediate effect and later observing their reaction some days later. The first reaction was one of considerable shock, but their recovery was rapid. It is to this rapidity of recovery that we can pay tribute, indicating as it does the high morale of the people.

The following incident is quoted as being typical of the spirit shown by the people of Bean Street. It is interesting to mention that Bean Street is almost as poor a district as the St. Paul's area and the actual shock effect of the raid should perhaps have been even greater in view of the damage done.

HOW THE BARBER TOOK IT!

At noon on the Saturday following the Friday night raid, one of the signatories to this report was in a barber's shop in the city. Conversation veered round to the raid of the previous night, and the dropping of the parachute mine in the Bean Street Area. 'I got a packet,' said the barber. 'The Mrs., myself and the two kids were in the cupboard under the stairs, then I popped out to put the kettle on and the lad joined me.

We were both just sat round the fire – and then we got it. Never heard a damn thing – it must have come down in carpet slippers. But I knew what was up when the house fell in – soot poured down upon us. If it had not have been such tough luck, I should have laughed – the kid and myself looked like a couple of nigger minstrels.'

The man's wife and family were unharmed, but it required a big heart for a man to talk like he did, when his home had been smashed only a few hours before.

COMMENTS UPON THE BARRAGE

The anti-aircraft barrage of the night of the raid was intense. The following day, people appeared to have been impressed by the strength of our defences, and many expressed the opinion that the damage would have been much greater had it not been for the barrage. It is interesting to compare this reaction with that following the Thursday 'blitz'.

PUBLICITY FOR SOCIAL WELFARE FACILITIES

In several districts following both raids, we found a number of people who had actually been affected by the raid, but were unaware of the facilities available. Some minor criticisms were expressed by one or two persons because they were not easily and quickly informed as to where they could go. We ourselves realised the tremendous difficulties involved and found that many who complained did not make the effort to find and use the facilities to an extent that was possible. It would appear, however, in many cases that it is necessary for extraordinary measures to be taken in order to ensure that *everyone needing help receives it*.

We mention this fact largely as a suggestion that the Local Information Committee itself might be able to give some assistance towards the end of securing more publicity for existing post-raid welfare facilities.

RAID OF TUESDAY 18 MARCH 1941

The aerial attack on the night of Tuesday the 18th March was the heaviest that Hull has ever experienced. The period of the alarm lasted for almost 9 hours, and between 9.15 p.m. and 4 a.m. there was incessant noise of aerial bombardment, gunfire and the intermittent dropping of bombs. The noise was intense, and the constant droning of the planes throughout the night, with hardly a moment's respite, was for many people a nerve-shattering ordeal.

BARRAGE

There were many who hoped that night, judging by the extent of the gun-fire, that substantial damage was being inflicted upon the enemy, and the following morning there were many expressions of disappointment at the efficiency of the barrage, when the bomb damage was seen and it was learned that no planes had been brought down. A large proportion of the general public appeared to be somewhat critical.

We personally feel that there is need for public education of the real pur-pose of a barrage. Up to now the public have been taught that noise during a raid is reassuring, because it would spring from the guns inflicting dam-age upon the raiders. On the morning following the 'blitz' many awoke to the fact that the noise that was thought to be deadly to the enemy, was actu-ally that of bombs destroying our own city.

PSYCHOLOGICAL REACTION

We had the opportunity of completing a most detailed study extending over a wide area of the city, and covering many individual investigations, so far as psychological reaction of the raid is concerned.

We are in a position now to take a retrospective view, and estimate the psychological effects in their true perspective. There is no doubt that the morale of those who were actually affected by the raid, or who were in the immediate vicinity of the bombing, was low on the morning following the raid. The people were greatly shocked and affrighted, and a feeling of horror was uppermost.

When the disorder and the destruction of the 'blitz' was seen at its worst in the early morning following the night of the raid, there were many expressions of 'Is it worth it?'; 'This simply cannot go on.' Sentiments such as these demonstrated the dominant feeling of the affected public that morning.

They were not isolated expressions. This feeling of despondency persisted throughout the whole of the day following the raid, but the ultimate dispersal was extraordinarily visible. It is this fact that is deserving of particular mention. Spirits were low after the raid, but the recovery was phenomenal.

Towards the evening of Wednesday, the 19th March, there was a feeling that a repeat bombing might be made, but it was not. By Friday in a general sense psychological normality had been about reached.

The raid was an extremely serious one, and the scattered nature of the bombing caused almost all of the town to be affected. Shock was certainly more apparent than after any previous raid. This can of course be attributed to the fact that the raid was more serious and far longer than any experienced before.

REHOUSING AND PSYCHOLOGICAL EFFECT

The extent of the raid was such as to make the greatest call that has been made so far upon the services of the post-raid welfare. On previous occasions we have had cause to comment upon the enthusiasm and keenness that has characterised the work of the officials of the Corporation and the voluntary workers concerned with post-raid social welfare.

As a result of our investigations following Tuesday night's 'blitz' we feel fully justified in expressing appreciation of the selflessness, good spirit and enthusiasm that the workers displayed. In the course of our investigations, we observed a few incidents some of which we will mention. These and others were passed on to the officials concerned, and the manner of their acceptance of this information to our mind demonstrated the willingness to do all they could to make the organisation as efficient as possible.

Without a doubt the work of speedy rehousing and post-raid social welfare is one of the greatest factors in maintaining morale. It deals with the people immediately following the destruction of their homes, and the ultimate influence of the impression that is created in the minds of the affected public is considerable. If the work of this post-raid social welfare had to break down, the psychological reaction would be disastrous.

Every effort put forward in this direction is a great contribution towards the maintenance of public morale and, from this angle, deserves special mention.

FIRE-WATCHING – MORALE BY-PRODUCT

An extremely interesting psychological study was observed, relating to the effect of fire-watching. In one working-class district, a rather large fire seriously endangered almost the whole street of small houses. Fire-watchers in the vicinity, supplemented by a great number of residents, rendered very useful work.

This is mentioned not merely to draw attention to the work of fire-watchers, but to illustrate a rather interesting and perhaps important fact that despite the terrifying experience to which the residents had been subject during the raid, the following morning we found that the topic of conversation was not 'the terror' but 'the job' they had done. Because they had the opportunity of doing something during the raid, was perhaps responsible for keeping their mind off the more terrifying aspects of the bombing.

This is perhaps a 'morale maintenance' by-product of Mr. Herbert Morrison's Fire-Watching Scheme.

EFFECT ON SERVICES

Over a rather large area the gas was cut off for some days, causing rather considerable inconvenience. In several places road communications were interfered with, but certainly not seriously. Telephones were naturally down in many quarters, but there was by no means a cessation or abnormal dislocation of transport and communications. The people accepted the inconvenience of the absence of gas with extreme good humour. This certainly had no adverse influence at all upon people's morale or temper.

The Communal Feeding Organisation certainly responded to the need created by the loss of individual means of cooking.

POST-RAID SERVICES

These services operated under difficult conditions, and on the whole the manner in which they responded is deserving of commendation. We did however receive one or two complaints of minor breakdowns, which we pass on with a view to constructive criticism.

In one case, it was learned there appeared to be no contact between one centre and another; apparently there was no telephone communication, and no messenger services operated. There were rather a large number of persons who visited the St. Mary's centre because of an unexploded bomb. When they arrived the officials apparently did not know where to send the evacuees. They were then directed to Park Road, from there to Middleton Street, and then on to All Saints. As the people were walking it was obviously creative of some dissatisfaction.

It is realised that alternative accommodation during any raid might suddenly be called into use, but we would suggest that rapid and alternative means of communication be made available, so that those in charge of centres will be fully alive as to the position elsewhere.

From our investigations we find that temporary district offices are certainly not successful. It appears to be difficult for people to learn quickly the place to which they should report. This presents special difficulties for people who are desirous of making their own arrangements. Such persons are expected to inform the authorities, yet the difficulty of knowing where to report presents something of a problem.

We found that on more than one occasion, responsible persons such as wardens did not appear to be as fully alive to information concerning facilities available for post-raid welfare.

We appreciate that many persons who did not make immediate contact with the authorities were themselves to blame, yet we do feel that something more could be done to make it possible for these services to be brought more quickly to the notice of affected persons, when an emergency arises.

In the King's Hall during the morning following the raid, there was a large number of persons making application for Emergency Food Cards. According to information received, the staff were unable to deal with these people that morning, and this resulted in some dissatisfaction.

At the YPI Centre for some reason or other, no breakfast was available until very late in the morning, approaching lunch time. This was apparently due to the fact that those responsible for the feeding services had not been kept fully informed. This is rather difficult to understand and it is even more inexplicable that emergency food was not drawn from the cafe premises, for such could without a doubt have been replaced.

These are some of the difficulties that were brought to our notice. They must be regarded as isolated incidents and are not intended to be taken as a general reflection upon the efficiency of the organisation, but as an indication of the need for constant revision and examination of the organisation, in the light of practical application.

GENERAL OBSERVATIONS ON MORALE

This report covers three severe raids, one of which was on such a scale as to merit the description of a 'blitz'. Shock was certainly felt in the hours immediately following these raids and some districts stood up to the attacks better than others, but there can be no doubt at all that public morale following these three severe attacks remains high and unimpaired.

NO 28: WEDNESDAY 9 APRIL TO WEDNESDAY 16 APRIL 1941

GENERAL COMMENTS

1. CONDITIONS IN THE HEAVILY RAIDED CITIES

COVENTRY: On April 11, the day following the second serious raid, the main features were extreme tiredness of the population, and 'a definite lowering of morale'. People were seen going to sleep in Feeding Centres and in the streets. There was much grumbling that the new raids were the result of optimistic press statements after Coventry's first blitz, indicating that the industries of the town were carrying on. There were many requests that nothing of the kind should be said on this occasion. One incident is described by the Deputy Regional Information Officer as 'significant and symptomatic'. An anonymous note was left in a Ministry of Information loudspeaker ear which read: 'It's time the so-called Ministry of Misinformation was closed down. Any more blah about Coventry factories not being affected, and you ought to be hounded out of the city.' This feeling of sensitiveness has continued, and an article in the *Daily Sketch* of April 12, headed 'COVENTRY CARRIED ON – AS BEFORE', was regarded by the public as likely to provoke further raids. On the whole, however, the press has said little this time which could cause upset.

Other points which are commented on specifically are as follows:

1. The spectacle of the 'dreadful scene of desolation' had an upsetting effect, but there were no sightseers. This was partly due to strict traffic control, and partly to the fact that 'most people having been blitzed themselves, were not very interested in other people's blitzing'.

2. On the morning of April 11, many people were unable to find the whereabouts of Rest Centres and other restorative services. This was attributed to their extreme fatigue and to an influx of police from other areas, unfamiliar with the emergency arrangements. Five loudspeaker vans were later in operation, but it was suggested that with a tired-out public, posters were more valuable than the spoken word.

3. Transport was a great difficulty. Very few buses were running, and 'an organized system of lifts would have been a great help'.

4. Friendless factory girls who had come in from other places to do munitions work were in need of special care.

5. The depressing effect of mass funerals was noted, but there was no resentment about them. There was some feeling that they should be conducted with 'greater pomp'. The identification of bodies was stated to be proving difficult and causing much distress.

6. The lowering of morale was not so noticeable in the suburban fringe of the town.

During the weekend the position both as to morale, and as to post-blitz organisation, improved considerably. The prompt announcement of the name of Coventry as the raided town helped to limit rumours in the Midland Region.

BIRMINGHAM: After Birmingham's raid, there were no complaints about the press treatment of the situation. 'People in the areas seriously bombed gave evidence of strain for a day or two, but a quiet weekend proved a healing influence. The main trouble in Birmingham arose from sightseers.' The absence of strict traffic control led to considerable congestion.

PORTSMOUTH AND SOUTHAMPTON: The Regional Information Officer reports that the continued raiding is proving a severe strain. 'The view is expressed quite freely in Portsmouth that before the war is over, the whole town will have been destroyed.' It is stated that there is great need for arrangements whereby essential war-workers and others could get away for an occasional few nights free from bombing.

PLYMOUTH: The post-blitz morale of Plymouth is described as 'extraordinarily good'. This is attributed to the strong naval traditions of the town (there are few families without some connection with the Navy), and to the fact that heavy raiding has always been expected, though not as heavy as in fact it was. An unsatisfactory feature is that people are now 'feeling rather pleased with themselves, and are *not* expecting a repetition. ("We've *had* our packet.")' The presence of the Services was most helpful, and the opening of the Naval Barracks as a temporary Rest Centre was enormously appreciated. The public rapidly adjusted itself to the upset of public utility services, but there is still some indignation at the failure of the water supplies for fire-fighting. People do not understand why sea-water could not have been used; and, at the time, the fact that buildings were left to burn caused some feelings of hopelessness. It is rumoured that firemen's hoses were left lying in the streets and were destroyed by fire. The most depressing sight in the town is the burnt-out city centre. Most people have to pass it to get to what remains of the main shopping area 'and it always brings the blitz back to people and they start talking about it again'. The slowness of repairs to houses, and the consequent enforced absence from home, is another adverse factor, but the huge task facing the local authorities is generally realised. There is much local praise for the post-blitz activities of Lady Astor.

POSTSCRIPT

CONDITIONS IN THE HEAVILY RAIDED CITIES (CONTINUED)

BRISTOL: The raid of April 11/12 was described by the Regional Information Officer as 'savage and prolonged'. He makes the following points in a special report:

1. It is widely believed that the enemy planes attacked at a very low level, thus avoiding the searchlights. It is claimed that in the bright moonlight the swastikas on the planes were visible.

2. Before the raid, there was considerable feeling in the city because press reports, particularly that of the *Daily Mail*, had suggested that Bristol had successfully countered its last heavy raid. The disillusionment of the false hopes of a conquest of the night bomber produced a serious effect.

3. Loudspeaker vans proved most valuable.

LATE POSTSCRIPT

NORTHERN IRELAND: The Regional Information Officer sends the following preliminary report on the Northern Ireland raid of April 15/16:

The heaviest attack was on Belfast, but there were also incidents at Londonderry, Bangor, and Newtownards. Great damage was done to business premises and private houses, and there was some industrial damage.

The editorial and advertising offices of the *Belfast Telegraph* were badly damaged, but the paper will be published this afternoon (April 16th). The *Irish News* had its morning issue printed by the *Belfast News Letter*.

The biggest fires are not yet under control (12 noon, April 16); fire-fighting and Civil Defence services are being taxed to capacity, the former having to call for outside help.

The first official communique had to be rushed to the newspaper offices by the RIO by car, owing to telephone dislocation.

Before breakfast, 5,000 copies of each of two emergency posters (one dealing with the boiling of drinking water and the other with the evacuation of school children and mothers) were ordered from the RIO's emergency printers. These posters were issued in batches as they came from the presses.

By 9.10 a.m. four loudspeakers were out, followed by 2 more at 10.30 a.m.

The Central Information Bureau is working smoothly.

2. REACTION TO WAR NEWS

GREECE AND YUGOSLAVIA: German successes in Yugoslavia have been anticipated, but the speed of their advance to Salonika (combined with the news from Libya) has 'given the impression of invincibility wherever the Germans operate'. There is some fear that the British forces in Greece may not be adequate, and that there is danger of their being caught in a trap.

LIBYA: Suggestions that we are minimising the seriousness of the situation in Libya continue to be reported. 'A Cairo spokesman' in particular comes in for severe censure and even ridicule. Comparisons are drawn between the present German advance, and the advance of last spring, and the more gloomy are asking: 'When will they get to Suez?' The failure of the Navy to prevent the German landing in Libya is also still commented on. There is, however, continued faith in General Wavell.

In spite of these reverses and gloomy forebodings, there is less anxiety about the war as a whole than might be expected. There is very little thought or discussion of invasion, and except in places where there has been intensive anti-gas publicity, interest in the subject of gas is again dying down.

THE BUDGET was well received. The main points raised by the public were as follows:

1. The principle of compulsory saving is popular, but there is some doubt about whether the money will really be paid back after the war.

2. There is considerable relief that there are no new taxes on beer and tobacco. From a number of areas it is reported that the cigarette and tobacco shortage in the provinces was widely attributed to a deliberate hold-up of supplies in case of fresh taxation.

3. The middle classes are glad that direct taxation is at last to affect the labouring classes, whose incomes in munitions factories and on Government contracts the middle classes regard as excessive. Little

comment is reported from the working classes themselves, and it seems likely that many have failed to realise how they will be affected.

4. It is feared that men who have previously been working hard and making good money in munition factories will tend to reduce their hours of work simply to avoid the tax.

5. It is suggested that the severity of the taxation on high incomes will still further encourage employers to pay high wages rather than see all added profits going in taxation.

6. It is pointed out that the new taxation bears hardest on those with fixed or diminishing incomes, and on 'family men'.

3. REPRISALS

There are no reports from the towns concerned of any strong feeling for immediate reprisals following the recent heavy raids. In other parts of the country, it is still suggested that sporadic raiding by small forces of our bombers is of very little value. The attack on Kiel gave much satisfaction, and personal experience leads many people to think that 'repeat performances' on the same town would be 'the soundest way of getting at Germany'. Repeated blitzing of a medium-sized town (including, if possible, its civic centre) is generally thought to be the most effective form of aerial attack.

4. RUMOURS

Apart from exaggerated casualty stories, this week has been singularly free from rumours.

5. BROADCASTING

There has been little comment on broadcasting. A. P. Herbert's rhymed *Postscript* was regarded as 'rather childish'. The Pope's Easter broadcast aroused very slight interest and was considered 'useless at a time like this'.

6. FOREIGN SEAMEN AT PLYMOUTH AND FALMOUTH

A special report on this subject makes the following points (the sailors referred to are mostly mercantile seamen, but no clear line is drawn by the public between these and foreign naval ratings):

1. The Dutch are extremely popular. Their virility is stated to be causing serious trouble in Falmouth, where there has been an influx of the less desirable type of women.

2. The Poles are equally popular – 'natural gentlemen' – 'as good as Englishmen'.

3. The French are extremely unpopular. It is widely suspected in Plymouth that spies have been detected among the Free French in that port.

SPECIAL COMMENTS

7. FOOD

The food situation is generally considered to be slightly easier. Queues are still numerous in Birmingham and other Midland towns (particularly for eggs, cakes and sausages). In Plymouth, though there are queues for chocolate, sweets and biscuits, the cause is rather a shortage of shops than of supplies.

In rural areas, the village institute jam-making plan is still criticised, but no satisfactory alternatives have been suggested.

The requests by heavy workers for an extra cheese ration continue.

Guidance is asked for as to whether it is 'unpatriotic' for housewives to pickle eggs at the present time.

The multiplicity of methods adopted by distributors in milk-rationing is criticised.

8. CIGARETTES

The cigarette shortage in the provinces is leading to criticism of the fact that there is no general shortage in London. Cigarette queues are reported in Oxford and in the Midland Region. The pre-budget shortage in Manchester caused bitter feeling against shop-keepers, who complained that the real trouble was lack of transport and shipping. The fact that comparatively large quantities of cigarettes appeared in Manchester immediately after the budget confirmed the public in their resentment.

9. THE COTTON INDUSTRY IN LANCASHIRE

Confusion has been caused in the minds of cotton workers by what appears to be a sudden reversal of Government policy. Until a short time ago, the Cotton Board was trying to convince the workers of their importance in the war effort. Now, however, supplies of raw material are restricted and mills are closing down. It is officially explained that shipping space is too valuable to be filled with bulky cargoes, that only certain export markets continue to be important, and that although mills close, the Government is anxious to keep their machinery in condition so that they can open up again at short notice. The suggestion is put forward that general propaganda to the Lancashire cotton workers along these lines would be useful.

NO 29: WEDNESDAY 16 APRIL TO WEDNESDAY 23 APRIL 1941

GENERAL COMMENTS

1. GENERAL STATE OF CONFIDENCE AND REACTION TO NEWS

Once again, a clear line must be drawn between public feeling in the heavily-raided towns and in the rest of the country. In the former, war news has taken second place to the raids themselves, though even there, the news has been studied seriously. In the latter, the public reactions vary from 'vague depression' to 'deep anxiety', with a big decline in complacency, which was previously noticeable in places which had so far been little touched by the war.

The London raid on Wednesday night found the public mentally unprepared. It was generally believed that heavy raids on the capital were unlikely, for the following reasons:

(a) The enemy bombing tactics were thought to be directed for the present primarily against our ports.

(b) It was suggested that bombers could not be spared from the Balkans.

(c) Our night-fighters' recent successes were beginning to produce a half-hearted hope that the conquest of the night bomber was in sight.

(d) There had been no really heavy raids on London for some time, and as a result, the public had become 'unconditioned'.

Nevertheless, the effect on the public was not as severe as after the first blitz in September last year. The morning after the raid most people were tired and depressed, and it was not unusual to hear such remarks as: 'A few more nights like this and it would be all up with us'; 'If the Germans have any sense they'll be back again tonight.' Transport difficulties added to the general fatigue, and the strain and lack of sleep showed themselves in 'edginess'. About 10% of people who were questioned got no sleep at all, and another 58% said they had slept less than 4 hours. In the two raid-free nights before the next attack, there was a marked recovery and a restoration of confidence; feeling was a good deal less upset by Saturday's raid. Arrangements for the care of raid victims worked as well as could be expected under very difficult conditions, and there were few complaints. Since the raids, the number of shelter users has greatly increased, and shelters which were practically empty are now full. There was little or no rush evacuation, though increased applications, particularly among elderly people, are reported from some districts.

The main features of the Belfast raid of April 15/16 (briefly reported last week) were the fire-fighting difficulties and the evacuee situation. Belfast has no large neighbouring towns on which to call for fire-fighting help, and in spite of assistance from the surrounding districts, help had to be asked for from Dublin and some English cities. The evacuee situation was extremely difficult. People left the town by train, bus, car, cycle, and even on foot. Many who asked for travelling vouchers had, in fact, not lost their homes, and there was much private evacuation. Several thousand people are said to have spent Wednesday night in the neighbourhood of Castlereagh hills, a few miles from Belfast; estimates of the total number of evacuees vary between 20,000 and 30,000 (though the figure of 70,000 is stated by the Regional Information Officer to have been given in later reports). Many of those who left the city on Wednesday night returned the following morning. On Thursday night there was a smaller exodus, but 'it seems likely that the evening trek and the morning return will continue for some little time'. Large numbers of women and children are remaining in the country 'until things settle down again'. Of the general state of morale, the RIO says: 'The people were not excited, but calm and grim – not least those who trudged along the roads with their families, carrying young children and pushing perambulators containing bedding, food, and other necessities. There was no attitudinising, no artificial jauntiness, no false boasting that "we can take this and a lot more". If the bombed-out people were temporarily stunned, the general state of morale was as good as could be expected after so ferocious an attack…One immediate result of the blitz was a rush of young men and women to the recruiting offices to join the forces.'

Other raids present few new features. At Bristol the Lord Mayor is arranging with the YMCA and YWCA to open summer holiday camps outside the city to give workers short raid-free holidays. At Plymouth there is considerable criticism of fire-fighting arrangements which are unfavourably compared with Bristol's. It is alleged that many of the brigades which travelled to Plymouth from distant places were unable to operate because of non-standardisation of equipment.

The combination of the raids, and the news from Greece and Libya, has produced an air of unpleasant apprehension. This crystallises out in two questions which a large number of people are asking:

1. 'Are the Germans *always* going to beat us whenever we meet them on land?'
2. 'How is it all going to end?'

Though these questions are rhetorical rather than despairing, an occasional suggestion is made that compromise may ultimately be the only solution. In a few working-class areas (for example, the Bedminster district of Bristol), some defeatist talk is reported, particularly among women.

On the subject of the news itself, there is rather more anxiety over Libya than over Greece. 'Another Dunkirk' in Greece would not be entirely unexpected; but the speed of the German advance in Libya has come as a most unpleasant surprise. Two criticisms are commonly being made: first, that we should not have halted in our advance but should have pressed on to

Tripoli; and secondly, that we should not have used men to attack Italian East Africa, when Libya was more important. There is some mild speculation about what Turkey is going to do, and some criticism of 'our continued appeasement policy in Spain'.

There is growing criticism of the way official news is presented to the public. The Ministry of Information, the BBC and the press are indiscriminately blamed for various misdemeanours. There is, however, a definite feeling, which seems to be one of the chief causes of annoyance, that 'the Government does not trust the public'. Had the news been given, for example, of German troops congregating in Libya, 'this would have lessened the shock and surprise of their advance'. It is widely complained that our failures are still being minimised, and that trivial successes against 'a single Messerschmitt' are given undue importance. In this connection radio news bulletins are regarded as the worst offenders. The delay in official news, and the publication of communiques from Axis sources, which subsequently turn out to be true, are said to be causing more and more people to listen to Haw-Haw's broadcasts 'in order to learn what is really happening'. While there is little trust in German air and naval communiques, it is generally believed that their military communiques are accurate.

The proposal to publish shipping losses only once a month is also criticised on the ground that between the announcements 'enemy lies, aided by rumour and exaggeration, will hold the field uncontradicted or corrected'.

2. REPRISALS

The German announcement that the London blitz was a reprisal for our raid on Berlin has led to suggestions that Hitler is concerned about Berlin's capacity to 'stand up to heavy bombing'. It also made a number of people think that an equally heavy raid the following night was unlikely. As usual, in the badly bombed areas, there has been little immediate outcry for reprisals. Religious scruples about bombing enemy civilians continue to decline. The Government's announcement on the subject of bombing Rome was welcomed.

Press references to Bremen as 'the Bristol of Germany' have made Bristol people rather sensitive on the subject of our raids on Bremen, and immediate reprisals were anticipated after our last raid on that city. These failed to happen, and the RIO suggests that this may have had something to do with the killing of the story.

3. RUMOURS

Except for exaggerated casualty stories, there have been no new rumours of importance this week. Queues are said to act as a forcing-bed for rumours, and it is suggested that a special appeal should be made to those who habitually wait in them.

4. FOOD

There seems to have been less discussion about food than at any time during the past few weeks. The old grumbles persist, but apart from milk rationing difficulties, no new ones of importance have been reported. Some milkmen have adopted the system of cutting off supplies for one day a week. This presents housewives with the difficulty of keeping milk fresh for two days – a difficulty which will be increased as the weather grows hotter. It is reported that in some districts 'free milk' and 'cheap milk' is being sold privately by the people to whom it is issued. It does not seem to be generally realised that this is an illegal practice.

There are still reports of dissatisfaction with the jam-making scheme. Some owners of small orchards are still under the impression that they may have to sell their fruit at a loss.

The price of salad vegetables is causing many complaints, particularly among working-class families, who can no longer afford salads.

5. REGISTRATION OF WOMEN

Reports on the first registration of women show that it went off smoothly and efficiently. The girls were cheerful, and there were no signs of reluctance or depression. They appeared to be proud of the fact that they were being called on to play their part in the war effort.

It has been suggested that it would have been a good idea to have had uniformed members of the various Women's Services in attendance at the Exchanges. At the entrances to some Exchanges communist leaflets are being distributed.

6. LABOUR

It is reported by the RIO, Midland Region, that local factory workers are absenting themselves 'two or three days a week rather than pay income tax on their earnings at 10/- in the £'.

7. TRADE

The scarcity of cigarettes is reported again from several parts of the country; the provinces are comparing their poor supplies with those of London, where visitors report that there are plenty to be got.

8. BROADCASTING

A. P. Herbert's *Postscripts* have aroused none of the enthusiasm, and little of the controversy, which followed those given by J. B. Priestley. Though reports show no strong feeling either for or against Mr. Herbert, he is described in some of them as 'superficial', 'fatuous', and 'boring'; there is also some disapproval of his 'levity'.

NO 30: WEDNESDAY 23 APRIL TO WEDNESDAY 30 APRIL 1941

GENERAL COMMENTS

1. GENERAL STATE OF CONFIDENCE AND REACTION TO NEWS

Perhaps the best indices of long-term change in the public's attitude to the war at the present time are results recently obtained by the British Institute of Public Opinion. These surveys were done by Gallup methods on samples of 2,250 people. On 9th November 1940, and again on 7th March 1941, the public was asked 'What do you think is the most important war problem the British Government must solve this Spring?' The results were as follows:

	9.11.40	7.3.41
Night bombing	12%	7.7%
Maintaining sufficient food supplies	12%	16%

Safer shelters	11.5%	1%
Submarine warfare and shipping losses	8.2%	28%
Preparing for the coming offensive	3.6%	5.2%
Near East situation and the Balkans	2.7%	3%
Production of armaments and aircraft	Nil	3.6%
Threat of invasion	Nil	7.1%

The remaining 30% on each occasion was composed of multiple unclassifiable suggestions.

The latest of these surveys was made before the recent heavy raids started, and before the Near Eastern situation appeared to deteriorate. In spite of this, it shows a widespread public realisation that the Battle of the Atlantic and the problem of food supplies are of outstanding importance. This is confirmed by the results of two further questions asked on 7th March this year:

1. 'Do you think Germany could win the war by defeating Great Britain in the Mediterranean and the Near East?'

Yes	No	Don't know
12%	66%	22%

2. 'From what you have experienced or read about, or heard during the past few weeks, do you think it is possible or impossible for Germany to win the war by air attack alone on this country?'

Yes, possible	No, impossible	Don't know
10%	78%	12%

This result shows little change, when compared with the results of the same question on 12th November last year (6% yes; 80% no; 14% don't know). A regional 'breakdown' of the latest survey gave the following result:

	Yes, possible	No, impossible	Don't know
Bombed S.E. areas (excluding Kent)	10%	73%	17%
Bombed provincial areas	9%	81%	10%
All other areas	9%	79%	12%

It will be seen that the highest level of doubt is in London, and the lowest in the bombed provincial areas. It is possible that, following the recent heavy raids, the provincial figure would now be nearest the London figure.

On the attitude of the public to America and Japan, the following results are of interest:

1. Question: 'How do you feel towards the United States?' (March 7th, 1941)

Result:

Very friendly	Friendly	Unfriendly	Not interested	Don't know
39%	49%	2%	6%	4%

2. Question: 'If the Japanese attempt to seize either our colonies or any of the colonies of our Allies, in the Ear East, should we go to war with them?'

Result:

Yes	No	Don't know
64%	12%	24%

The important figures here are the 12% of 'Nos' and the 24% of 'Don't knows'. The commonest reasons given for holding these views were:

'We've too much on our hands already' – 50%
'Only if the Americans declare war too' – 22%
'An economic embargo would be enough' – 22%

It is usual to find that, the further away the events, the less acute is the public feeling about them; these results bear out this generalisation.

We come now to public reactions in the course of the past week. There is rather less tension, but still much anxiety about the course of the war. The evacuation of Greece has caused sorrow rather than surprise. There is much sympathy for the Greeks, and considerable concern about our apparent inferiority in the air and in armoured fighting vehicles. Speculation about where the Germans will strike next follows press comment closely. There is no longer much faith in Turkey's ability to stand up to Germany, and it is suggested that she may either surrender (or actually join the Axis) or be by-passed, so that the Germans will reach Iraq and Iran via the Ukraine. Attacks on Spain and Egypt are also expected, and the fate of the

French fleet is once more discussed. The slowing down of the German advance in Libya has given rise to hopes, mixed with fears that these hopes may be false.

In general, the Prime Minister's speech is described as having had a 'sobering and stimulating' effect. It has increased the realisation of the importance of the Battle of the Atlantic, but has added to the thirst for details of the progress of this battle. In particular, there are fears that the monthly figures for shipping losses may turn out to be very large indeed; and people are asking why we cannot be told how many U-boats have so far been sunk. The Prime Minister's speech has not received, it would appear, as much approval as usual, and this is a new feature. On the one hand, it is said that 'he told us nothing new'. On the other, it is thought that he minimised the public anxiety in the blitzed towns, and it is suggested that 'his presence was enough to make people hide their anxiety – but it's there all the same'. In all parts, too, there is anxiety on the major issue of how, even assuming we do win the battle of the Atlantic, we are going to win the final battle with a Germany occupying almost the whole of Europe. People, from their own experience, do not believe that bombing is a decisive weapon – and they hope that their own experience will show the same for blockade. So far, our activities on land do not make them over-optimistic in that direction. While there is, characteristically, little tendency to press for a logical solution to this apparent impasse, there is a growing belief that such an impasse does exist.

The criticism of official news presentation, which we reported last week, has increased, and its tone is unchanged. It appears that the familiar process of pushing the blame for military disappointments on to the news services is once more taking place. There are requests for more interpretation of the news. The Director-General's broadcast aroused only a limited amount of spontaneous comment; such comment was almost entirely favourable, but 'many intelligent people are still asking what exactly the Ministry of Information is aiming at in its home front propaganda?'

2. THE RECENT RAIDS

The outstanding feature of the recent heavy provincial raids has been the nightly exodus from the bombed towns. From Portsmouth and Southampton, the trek still goes on, and transport facilities are seriously congested. From Plymouth, there is an estimate that 7,000 to 8,000 people trek out at night to sleep in halls and other buildings at Plympton, St. Mary Rural and Ivybridge. These trekkers cause a double problem. First, accommodation has to be found for them. Secondly, they leave their homes without any form of fire protection. The nightly trek has been a regular feature of provincial blitzes, but if raids do not recur, the number of trekkers rapidly declines.

It is known that there is a section of the population, estimated at a maximum of 1 in 10, who are of weaker constitutional mental make-up than the rest. These people react to difficult situations in two ways – either by a cowardly retreat, or by a neurotic mental breakdown. Among the fighting Services there is no possibility of the former escape, and the amount of neurotic breakdown has been correspondingly large. Among civilians, on the other hand, there has been almost no neurotic breakdown. Such a breakdown involves admission to hospital, and the widespread publicity given to the bombing of hospitals has apparently convinced the public that the neurotic escape to hospital is the surest way of becoming a military target. So instead, the potentially neurotic section of the population take to the roads each evening and seek safety in dispersal. In London, however, they have what they believe to be an equally safe escape in the Tube stations. So the problem of the nightly trek is in London only the problem of the trek to the Tubes.

Turning now to the individual cities, in Plymouth an outstanding feature of the people was their physical fatigue. As at Coventry, loudspeaker announcements seem to have made little impression, and the deputy RIO organised a team of women social workers to visit the public in their homes, to give individual help and encouragement. After the third night of raiding, there was much feeling against the official communique describing the raid, which was thought to be 'callous'. It is difficult to see how this can be overcome, as a short objective description must inevitably seem to minimise the situation when heard by those who are worn out by three nights of heavy and concentrated raids. Similar complaints (that the town's sufferings were being minimised) come from Portsmouth. Around Belfast, the problems of unorganised evacuation (exactly parallel to those which followed the first heavy raids on London) are having to be dealt with. In London, the main post-raid problems are rent difficulties over damaged premises, and the evacuation of the 'under fives'. For domestic or financial reasons the mothers of these children cannot take them to the country, and there are many requests for residential country day-nurseries.

3. RUMOUR

There has been a slight increase in the amount of rumour circulating this week. Haw-Haw rumours are once more reported, and a new variation on an old theme is that we are refraining from bombing the Rumanian oil wells because of the large amount of British capital which is said to be locked up there.

SPECIAL COMMENTS

4. LABOUR

Among labour problems which come to light this week, that of immigrant labour is a serious one. A special report from Birmingham states that men and women sent to work and live away from their homes have often proved 'unemployable' for various and obvious reasons. Employers find it difficult to control bad time-keeping and bad work, especially as threats of dismissal no longer carry any weight. There are also more complaints this week of absenteeism, which is again attributed to attempts to avoid having to pay income tax by earning higher wages. From industrial areas there are reports of a severe shortage of welfare officers and social workers.

REGISTRATION OF WOMEN: Women who have registered, and who are doubtful about the national importance of their present jobs, are anxious that their positions should be made clear as soon as possible. Cases have been reported of women leaving their jobs without waiting for official guidance, and taking up other work which they believe to be more essential. Some industrial welfare officers are anxious because their staffs have already been depleted by this process.

Women who will not have to register for some time appear to be dismayed because girls who are now about to be conscripted will get 'the pick of the jobs'. It is also pointed out that by the time older women are called up, those who were conscripted earlier will have had considerable experience, and therefore stand better chances of promotion. There is some anxiety in case the younger women should be sent to work in vulnerable areas.

Complaints have also been made in country districts that middle- and upper-class women are using 'moral suasion' to induce their servants not to undertake war work.

5. FOOD

In areas where food supplies have been interrupted by raids, the demand for communal feeding has increased. It seems, however, that men are more conservative than women in their feeding habits; many men still prefer to take packed mid-day meals with them to work rather than eat in their works canteen or at Feeding Centres. Those who expect a hot meal in the evening add greatly to the shopping and catering problems of their wives, particularly where wives are also going out to work. Suggestions are, therefore, being made that special communal feeding propaganda should be directed to the men.

The jam-making scheme still displeases both the housewife and the small fruit grower. Some of the growers are threatening to let their fruit rot unless they receive what they consider to be adequate prices for it.

There are more reports of people waiting in queues without knowing what is to be had at the other end of them.

Criticism of the milk rationing scheme continues. In spite of the Ministry of Food's disapproval of 'the one day out', it is said that milkmen are still doing this in certain districts.

There is a fairly wide belief that horse-flesh is being incorporated in 'chicken and ham' rolls, and it is stated that this fact is mentioned on the invoices sent from the wholesalers to the retailers. One report suggests that if horse-flesh is, in fact, being used, it would be best for the authorities 'to make a clean breast of it and publicize Lord Woolton eating it at a public luncheon'.

6. TRADE

The cigarette shortage is still causing serious dissatisfaction. In certain areas it is said to have 'an adverse effect on workers'; some people consider it a greater hardship than any other shortage.

7. NURSERIES AND CHILD-MINDERS

Though there is much opinion in favour of day nurseries, it is thought that these are only a partial solution of a widespread and complicated problem. One of the main objections to them is the difficulty of bringing children to and from them, when the nursery, the home, and the mother's work are a long way apart. This difficulty is much increased when the mother has also to do her own shopping, cooking and household duties. Transport delays, and the black-out, particularly in winter, also make things harder for her. There is a suggestion that residential nurseries would be an alternative scheme.

The idea of a child-minder still seems to be that she is a kind of Dickensian crone. Even if they were subject to some form of official supervision, it seems likely that child-minders would still be distrusted.

8. FUNERALS FOR RAID VICTIMS

The question of the cost of funerals for raid victims is again being raised. From one London district, it is reported that whole families have been wiped out and insurance policies lost, with the result that relatives are running into debt 'to bury them properly'. Suggestions are made that 'something in the nature of a simple military funeral, at the public expense' should be made a routine for raid victims, so as to cut down the lavish expenditure which the poor feel is their duty towards the dead.

APPENDIX I

INDUSTRIAL AREAS CAMPAIGN IN SCOTLAND

SMALLER MEETINGS, INFORMAL DISCUSSION GROUPS, AND OTHER ACTIVITIES

In our reports on communists and Scottish industrial workers (See Appendix, Home Intelligence weekly report No. 9) it was pointed out that the main effect of disruptive elements in industry was not a direct one – the slowing up of production by strikes etc. – but rather indirect – the fostering of cynicism and disillusionment about the war. This cynicism is the natural response of many of the younger men who have been unemployed during most of the twenty years between the two wars, and it is rapidly acquired by others. It has been made fashionable, not only by the native tendency of the Scot (particularly in West Scotland) to grumble and 'girn', but also by the assiduous encouragement of communist 'educators'. The result is that the majority of the politically minded workers on Clydeside use the language and slogans of communism, although in practice they show that they have no use for the Communist Party. The Clyde has never been quieter and more determined about anything than it is just now about finishing with Hitler.

The plan to promote small meetings and informal discussion groups among the workers has, for its main purpose, to produce a number who will speak up in the workshops and elsewhere, and make articulate the real feelings of the workers about the war, feelings demonstrated adequately in their behaviour. The organiser, Mr. William Roberts, is a Clydebank man who has worked many years in Singers as a skilled mechanic, and previously in shipyards. He studied politics, economics and philosophy at Newbattle Abbey, the Scottish residential college for workers' education. Before his appointment Mr. Roberts was running informal discussion groups in his spare time.

The organiser has not only got going several effective formal and informal discussion groups; he has also been invaluable as an advance outpost against communist infiltration through 'shadow' organisations; and gave valuable service throughout and since the very heavy air raids on Clydebank last month.

This report accordingly falls into two parts.

(1) Organisation of meetings and discussion groups.

(2) Special action against communist 'shadow' organisations.

(1) ORGANISATION OF MEETINGS AND GROUPS

After a fortnight's training in preparation and delivery of talks designed to promote friendly and informal discussion, the organiser went on to organise two formal and two informal discussion group meetings every week.

The formal groups were attached to War Commentary meetings in Bridgeton and Clydebank respectively; the informal groups, or 'Kitchen meetings', were held in private houses in the Clydebank district.

The three Clydebank groups have been dispersed by the raids. The two houses in which the 'kitchen meetings' were held have been destroyed. In place of these meetings the organiser has developed new types of meeting, described below, partly in Clydebank and partly in the reception areas, not only among former group members but among new people. Meantime, two new formal groups have been formed, one attached to the Springburn War Commentary and the other to the Govan War Commentary.

Throughout the whole period, addresses followed by discussions have been given to established groups such as ARP groups, church debating societies etc. and, as noted below, the organiser has acted as guest speaker in various War Commentary meetings, describing his experiences as a voluntary fire-fighter in the Clydebank raids.

METHODS OF WORK

(A) FORMAL MEETINGS (ATTACHED TO WAR COMMENTARIES)

The attendance at these groups generally begins at about a dozen and becomes stabilised at between 15 and 20. Attendances are occasionally affected by air raids but only when there have been local incidents on immediately preceding evenings. The groups are mixed; industrial workers and housewives with the former predominating.

The topics for discussion usually arise out of the big War Commentary meeting on the Sunday. As the groups develop, however, interest is shown in such topics as 'The Origin of the War', 'The Background of the Battle of the Atlantic', 'Democracy at War' and other topics. For example, the first Clydebank discussion arose out of Chaplin's film, *The Great Dictator*. In following weeks the main topic was the 'Freedom of the Press' (*Daily Worker* suppression).

(B) INFORMAL DISCUSSION GROUPS – 'KITCHEN MEETINGS'

The following account of a series of 'kitchen meetings' gives a good example of this informal method of work.

One woman of my acquaintance came to me one day and asked me to come up to her house and attempt to discredit the communist family who lived next door. She explained that she herself knew practically nothing about politics or the war, an ignorance which she also attributed to her neighbours, but claimed that both the man and his wife were most voluble, having 'a string of fancy words' about the war before which she, her husband, and the other neighbours were dumb. Things were made most uncomfortable for her by the never-ending insistence that we couldn't possibly win the war, that the Government weren't giving us the real figures of air-raid victims, that this was a war between the capitalists of Britain and Germany, and that we, the workers, had nothing to do with it, and should therefore see to it that it was stopped.

The first time I called on her I found that about twelve other women were also present. I just listened to the woman CP member and occasionally interjected until she had had her say. She really had no more consciousness of what she was saying than a gramophone record has. After criticising her, she, by implication, admitted this, but maintained that 'her husband would be a match for me'.

Well, on the second occasion there was a larger audience, in fact, about 16 of us. The husband was as hopeless as his wife; in fact, even more so, because he used such terms as dialectics, materialistic conception of history etc., which I asked him to define, but he couldn't; this, of course, went a long way in lowering his prestige among the others.

We met a third and a fourth time, but on the fourth occasion the CP enthusiasts didn't turn up as they had gone to the pictures.

On the next occasion the communists returned to the fray to find their hitherto inarticulate neighbours had now found words to express themselves, thanks to the group and to the big War Commentary meeting.

(C) NEW TYPES OF MEETING

The raids which shattered Clydebank social life might well have put a stop to the discussion groups experiment in that area. But the informal technique has proved flexible enough to adapt itself even to a blitz. For example, the organiser is a great deal in and around Clydebank and the Vale of Leven where he meets members of his groups. These then become the nucleus of a discussion there and then.

The organiser also visits Rest Centres in the evening when the workers are there, and starts discussions. Here a new method has been invented. One of his acquaintances, living in the centre, is deaf. What could be more natural than to shout into his ear facts and figures in the course of an argument about the raids or the Battle of the Atlantic? Others soon gather round and take part. This discussion, begun among a crowd of dockers on the day of the adoption of the new Ministry of Transport scheme, soon developed on vigorous lines. On one or two occasions it looked as though a fight would develop, but one docker took the part of the organiser, and in the upshot he was invited to return as soon as he was free.

(2) SPECIAL ACTION AGAINST COMMUNIST 'SHADOW' ORGANISATIONS

(A) ATTENDANCE AT COMMUNIST MEETINGS

It is a definite part of the organiser's work to attend communist meetings wherever possible. Meetings are usually a surer guide to policy than are publications. It is much easier – and safer – to speak frankly in a meeting. Hence the importance of this continuous contact. As the organiser says: '*I cannot help feeling that if the MOI, or the Labour Party or any other such group, seize this moment the CP will be practically knocked out*. If, however, they are given time to collect their units and rally their forces, they may again be as big a nuisance as formerly. I would suggest MOI meetings regularly on Sundays with a first class speaker. This would have to be done *at once*, though it may be uphill work for a time both as to numbers and hostile criticism.'

(B) INTELLIGENCE WORK ON INDUSTRIAL GRIEVANCES

Workers who know the organiser frequently report industrial grievances to him. Since one of the chief communist activities is the exploitation of existing grievances, an essential job in counteracting these people is to have a quick and ready way of discovering concrete grievances, and this is done effectively by the organiser.

(C) APPRENTICES' COMMITTEE

The Apprentices' Committee, that mysterious self-appointed body which claimed to lead the wave of apprentice strikes in Scotland early in March, was composed of nine young communists and one non-communist. The latter, upset by the apparent disinclination of his colleagues to come to any settlement (they kept in the background in a most perplexing way for a week), consulted our organiser. The organiser advised him strongly to remain on the Committee. He was also advised to consult those who were trying to get a settlement, and did so.

(D) OTHER SHADOW ORGANISATIONS

A valuable activity is that of explaining to Catholic and other non-communist workers the fairly successful manoeuvres of the communists in creating 'shadow' movements which are so tempting to political inno-cents, who are thereby helped to avoid being involved in any of these movements.

FUTURE DEVELOPMENTS

The period under review may be regarded as one of experiment which has established the value of these informal methods of work in starting fruitful discussions among industrial workers and housewives who would nor-mally find it uncongenial or difficult to attend meetings. A speaker who speaks their own language, and who is prepared to go among them, can do good service not only in counteracting communist misrepresentations, but also in meeting the much more difficult problem of general apathy and con-fusion about the war. The well-established groups also show a healthy ten-dency to go on to discuss positive issues. In the next three months, as these develop, small groups of industrial workers will be better armed with facts and ideas enabling them to put into words the real issues of the war and the determination of the workers that it should finish in the right way. The whole summer period in its turn should be regarded as a preparation for the problems and stresses of next winter.

PUBLIC RELATIONS BRANCH
ST. ANDREW'S HOUSE
EDINBURGH
24 April 1941

APPENDIX II

REPORT ON CONDITIONS IN BARROW-IN-FURNESS
FOLLOWING THE NIGHT RAIDS OF 13, 14, 15, 16 APRIL

A slightly abbreviated report from the offices of the Ministry of Information, North-Western Region, Manchester.

Barrow-in-Furness is in an isolated position on the Lancashire coast and difficult of access from other towns in the North-Western Region, and in consequence some anxiety has been felt about provision of adequate services there following any heavy raid. It is a town depending on one industry – the shipbuilding yards, which suffered severe depression between the end of the last war and re-armament. There are strong left-wing tendencies in the borough and there have been several communist meetings recently. From time to time communist literature is distributed in the town.

Because of its position and the nature of its occupation, the town has little in sympathy with the countryside round about it and tends towards an 'isolationist' policy. For example, on the occasion of a recent royal visit to the North, Barrow refused to recognise the police passes which were accepted generally in the rest of the Lancashire county and insisted on having its own passes.

In January this year enemy aircraft were reported over Barrow but no bombs were dropped. Again in March machines were over the town. On the night of April 13th–14th a stick of bombs was dropped in a thickly populated area in the centre of the town and there were casualties. The following night the town had another stick of bombs. Altogether there were some thirty-eight killed and probably about three hundred people were homeless. One Rest Centre was opened, and reports show that it was considerably overcrowded. On the 16th a second Rest Centre was opened and conditions improved.

A Manchester press man who was on holiday and visited relatives in Barrow 'just in time for the bombing' made it his business to tell us that conditions in the town were 'chaotic'. Nobody know where to go for anything and there was nobody to tell them where to go. He added that he did not like to think what would happen if the town had a real blitz.

The Chief Labour Agent for the Region, Mr. Wallis, visited the town and said that the Rest Centre first opened was overcrowded. He visited the bombed area with Labour representatives who are a strong faction on the local council. The morale of the people seemed to be splendid, although the damage to their homes was very severe. The houses were of a small cottage type, easily demolished or damaged by blast. He said he thought that members of the council were doing all they could.

The pastor of a popular mission church in the centre of Barrow, who has a high reputation for social work, went out of his way to tell us that conditions in the town had been very bad and he was worried about it. He is a member of our Local Information Committee and one of the two Observers. He said that he felt that if he had to write a report it would be very critical.

The Secretary of our Local Information Committee, Mrs. M. G. Tanner, writes to us 'in the interests of the country it would appear to be an undesirable moment for communist propaganda. Whilst very shaken and frightened, the spirit of the people was one of making the best of their difficulties and troubles.'

Another informant visited Barrow several days after the attack and was obliged to spend some time waiting in the Town Hall. He said that the building seemed to be old-fashioned and inconvenient, and there did not seem to be anything in the nature of a central information bureau. There was a uniformed commissionaire who dealt with callers on the principle that they could not expect to walk into the Town Hall and do as they liked.

The general impression seems to be that there is urgent need for planning of centralization of services for the public after heavy raids in Barrow and for letting the public know now exactly where these services can be obtained.

It should be pointed out that after the first night's bombing the Town Clerk was rung up from this Regional Office of the Ministry of Information and reminded that if there was any way in which we could be helpful in distributing information to the public we were at his service. He replied that the raid was not very serious and that everything was going quite well. Following the second night's raid the Secretary of our Information Committee was rung up with a similar message and again the reply was that everything seemed to be going quite well.

Since the bombing, enemy machines have been over Barrow again, although there was practically no activity over the whole of the rest of the Region. It seems fairly clear that the Luftwaffe is taking a special interest in the district.

The tendency in Barrow is to assume that the bombing of the town was a mistake and need never have happened. Among the explanations given are – that machines were on their way to Northern Ireland (the attention of the pilots being attracted by anti-aircraft guns opening fire), or that the purple warning was not received and so lights were left on in the shipyard thus attracting the attention of the enemy machines.

Approach on the subject of local services is difficult because of the 'isolationism' already mentioned, because of complacency and because of the war-time prosperity of the town which is being enjoyed to the full. People are working long hours and making money and are reluctant to interrupt these activities to attend committee meetings and talk about local administration in any form. In view of the town's past ordeal of depression it is not difficult to understand the outlook.

NO 31: WEDNESDAY 30 APRIL TO WEDNESDAY 7 MAY 1941

GENERAL COMMENTS

1. GENERAL STATE OF CONFIDENCE AND REACTION TO NEWS

The feelings of despondency and suspense, which were apparent during the evacuation from Greece, have now had time to run their course. In their place a sense of irritation is growing up and a desire to find someone or something to blame. This is not necessarily in connection with the Balkan campaign, though there is some sharp criticism of our military intelligence, but applies, at the moment, to any unfavourable war conditions. Even Mr. Churchill has not been free from criticism, perhaps as the personification of the Government. We have discovered no comment, so far, on his speech to the Poles. Towards the end of the week an improvement in spirits was noticeable, when the first reaction from anxiety had worked itself out. Typical of this was the change in the public's attitude to the news from Iraq. In the first half of the week the expectation was of another disaster, and the usual comment was that we are always too late with our preparations. Later comments reflect the growing idea that our action had precipitated the military coup and thrown out Germany's time-table.

A gradual changing of the public's idea of the probable length of the war has been accelerated by the Greek and Libyan reverses. Coming after a period of good news from Africa and the Mediterranean, the effect of these has been particularly deflating. It has reduced to 13% (according to the poll of the British Institute of Public Opinion) those who still expect the war to be over in a year's time. At the outbreak, 27% expected it to end within a few months; only 11% then thought it would last three years or more. Now 23% expect this, not as the total length of the war, but in addition to the past 20 months. While expectation of a quick war has diminished considerably of late, the number (38%) who have never had any opinion on its probable length remains unchanged from the beginning.

Complaints about the presentation of news are as strong as ever. They fall roughly into three categories.

(a) The slightness and triviality of the items quoted: e.g. one Messerschmitt reported shot down in the Channel, but in the midst of the evacuation no mention of Greece. This gave rise to a rumour that the worst was being kept from the public.

(b) The minimising of air-raid damage in our worst-hit towns, which many thousands of people can check for themselves. This led to a belief that our losses in Greece had also been 'edited', and there was a demand for Hitler's 'fantastic' figures to be denied by the Government, and for official figures to be disclosed.

(c) 'Pep' talks which do not 'pep'. These are summarised by the comment: 'To listen to this sort of blah, you'd think all we had to do was wait for Jerry to see sense and give up.' In another report the view is expressed that 'at the moment, the way in which news is given out is doing far more to depress the people, and even to discredit the Government, than any other factor. Something should be done, even for the Ministry's own reputation, which is low enough in all conscience.'

One result of the Greek evacuation, coupled with the reticence of the BBC and the Service communiques (to which there are again ferocious references), has been the increase in the number of listeners to Haw-Haw. This has been reported from many sources. The German broadcasts are not regarded as more reliable than ours, but as being almost as reliable, and so much fuller that this outweighs their untruthfulness. It is thought not to be enough to discredit them on the grounds of lying while they continue to give more up-to-date news than we do.

Among people who listen habitually – notably those with relations in the Navy and Merchant Service – Haw-Haw's prestige has gone up through the intensification of the Battle of the Atlantic. On several occasions lately he is said to have given the first news that a ship, mentioned by name, has been torpedoed, and this has later proved correct.

Changes in the Cabinet seem to have aroused practically no interest. Though there was very little criticism of the new appointments, the fact that it was thought necessary at this time to make any changes at all was regarded with slight misgiving in some quarters. Those who showed any interest in the subject were puzzled by the significance of Lord Beaverbrook's metamorphosis.

SPECIAL COMMENTS

2. AIR RAIDS

Owing to the serious dislocation of telephone and teleprinter services, very little information is yet available about the Belfast and Merseyside raids during the early part of this week. A brief report from the RIO on the Belfast raid of Sunday night states that damage in the central business areas has been considerable. The evacuation position is less acute than in the previous raid of April 15/16. Owing to the failure of the electric current, many thousands of wireless sets are out of action, and it is, therefore, impossible for people to hear the news bulletins.

3. GAS LEAFLETS

The following results are those of an enquiry by Mass Observation into the effects of the leaflet: 'What to do about gas'. These results are, of course, subject to the limitations of this method of investigation.

285 people were questioned, the majority of whom were in London. Within the distribution areas 'there were considerable numbers who had not read or seen it', but among those who had done so, it apparently had a good effect, and was remembered in some detail. Though it has increased their knowledge of what to do, no very large number of people seem to have been sufficiently impressed to take action. Gas-mask carrying has not gone up, and only about one-third of those who now know what to do about food protection have taken the necessary precautions. There still seems to be extensive ignorance of what to do when gas rattles are heard, and there is confusion about antidotes to splashing. The conclusion reached in the report is that 'there is still a definite need for more education on the subject of gas'.

4. RUMOURS

Apart from an increase in stories attributed to Haw-Haw, the rumour situation is unchanged. From two separate sources it has been reported that Mr. Churchill's health is failing, and that Lord Beaverbrook is being 'nursed for Premier'. This note has been much sounded on the German radio.

Again there are reports of the amount of gossip which goes on in queues, and of the way 'rumours are bandied about in them'.

5. LABOUR

Reports from almost all industrial areas indicate that absenteeism, which is already a serious problem for war production factories, is on the increase; among young workers it is particularly prevalent. Wages are so high, compared with what they would be earning in peace-time, that they can well afford to lose a few days' pay when they feel like it, knowing this to be their only risk, since they can no longer be dismissed.

Income tax (another cause of absenteeism) is an innovation for which the necessity, as part of the war effort, has not yet been brought home to the majority of workers. Rather than pay the tax, many of them prefer to keep their earnings below the taxable level, and enjoy extra leisure instead. The Lease-and-Lend bill is also said to provide an excuse for staying away from work, on the assumption that 'America will now make the stuff for us.'

At Bridgend, in an industrial community of 40,000, conditions are reported to be particularly bad, it being a matter for boasting among the girls that they can absent themselves whenever they like, and a number of employees have been fined for false clocking-in. In another district men have been taking a day off for a journey to fetch cigarettes. (The cigarette shortage, in which London is believed to be unfairly favoured, is becoming an important trouble in factories.)

Criticism of inefficiency in industrial management is said to be made by the more responsible element among the workers in certain areas. In Stoke and Birmingham there are complaints that the people in charge of factories are often appointed for their technical ability alone, and are no good as administrators. It is said that work people arriving at the factory are kept idle, on day and night shifts, either from lack of direction or lack of material, until their keenness evaporates and they settle down to a routine of getting through time as easily as possible.

6. FOOD

Complaints this week are mostly about prices. The cost of fish is serious for many working people, for whom it is often an important item in the evening meal. Although there are frequent accusations of 'profiteering' and 'racketeering', people are apparently unwilling to come forward with evidence against shop-keepers of whom they complain.

There are still many reports of queues throughout the country. Working women who cannot find time to do their essential shopping are exasperated by those who have plenty of time to stand in queues and who are, therefore, said to obtain 'more than their fair share'.

There are many reports of shortages; eggs seem to be particularly scarce, especially in London. There is also said to be a scarcity of beer and alcohol in some districts.

The 'milkless day' continues in many places and still causes much criticism.

POINTS OF PUBLIC CONCERN NO. 2, 7 MAY 1941

1. NEWS PRESENTATION

Dissatisfaction with the presentation of news is rapidly growing. The Government is accused of 'not trusting the public'; the Service departments and the Ministry of Information are severely criticised; there are also many complaints about the tone and triviality of BBC news broadcasts. The press is, however, fairly free from blame.

2. REPRISALS

Though the demand for reprisals (i.e. the bombing of civilian centres as legitimate military targets) has recently been less in evidence, a large number of people still approve the idea, and a 'Bomb Berlin' candidate is standing at the Kings Norton by-election.

3. AIR RAIDS

FIRE-FIGHTING: There has lately been some anxiety about fire-fighting arrangements. The public, sometimes unaware of the technical difficulties, is apt to assume that certain preventative measures, which appear obvious, should be carried out, though, in fact, such measures may be impracticable.

FUNERALS: The cost of burying air-raid victims is a serious hardship to many poor people. As a certain amount of ostentation is thought to be essential, some people are running into debt to provide their relatives with what they consider 'a decent burial'.

4. REGISTRATION OF WOMEN

Confusion among women workers about what are to be regarded as essential industries is causing some of them to make 'panic changes' in their employment. Workers, managements and welfare officers would all like to be given guidance on this point.

The fear of being sent far away from their homes is also troubling a good many girls. Others are afraid, as are their parents, that they may be sent to work in vulnerable areas.

Middle-aged and older women who want to get work in munition factories complain of difficulties in doing so. Some say that when applying for jobs they have been made to feel that their services are not wanted.

5. NURSERIES

There is a considerable demand for more day nurseries. The shortage of them is said to be a hardship to women who would otherwise be ready and willing to do war work.

'Child-minders' are not popular and seem generally to be regarded with a good deal of suspicion.

There are many mothers of children under five, who want to go into industry, but will not do so unless their children are evacuated. Wives of men in the Forces who would like to feel that 'they are doing their bit' are said to be particularly anxious that the present evacuation scheme shall be modified, so that they can take up war work.

6. FOOD

The difficulties of shopping seem to be increasing. There is a good deal of grumbling about shortages, but queues are now faced more or less philosophically.

The high prices of fish and salad vegetables are causing many complaints. So, too, is the reduction of the milk ration, which is resented as being 'unfair'.

Among housewives and small fruit growers the jam scheme is very strongly criticised.

7. TOBACCO

The shortage of tobacco appears to be becoming more acute, particularly in the North and the Midlands. Many people seem to consider it no less serious than the food shortage, and there are continual complaints from all parts of the country.

APPENDIX

THE PLYMOUTH RAIDS, APRIL 1941

The following summary is based on a report from the RIO, South-Western Region.

After the recent heavy blitzes on Plymouth, the RIO visited the town and inspected the damage to civilian and public property. He met large bodies of citizens, and watched all the ameliorative services in action. Though he has been in the Bristol area for all the raids, and has worked upon all post-blitz efforts, his experiences at Plymouth were not only a shock but were acutely distressing.

A concentrated blitz lasting for five nights has created new aspects of old problems for the Regional organisation of the Ministry of Information. When air attacks develop in this way, with heavy casualties in homes and among the Civil Defence services when damage is incalculable, and distress and shortages are widespread, the public, for a few days, is unable and unwilling to listen to or comprehend official announcements from loud-speakers, or to read printed directions. At Plymouth, therefore, we evolved, with the co-operation of the WVS and the social services, a scheme whereby visitors went round from door to door in the worst areas, explaining, comforting, and helping.

Following the decision to evacuate the hospitals, the children, the aged and others, experienced broadcasters with loudspeaker vans were sent out into neighbouring towns and villages with appeals to citizens to improvise arrangements for the reception of evacuees. Though the prospects of its success were poor, this effort was essential because all the areas are already saturated with evacuees, voluntary or otherwise, from London and Bristol, and even from Southampton and Portsmouth.

Our experience showed that it is vitally important in blitzed areas that an experienced and responsible officer from the Ministry of Information Regional Headquarters should be available at once for consultation with high authorities, and should have the power to make immediate decisions, and to sanction expenditure. Telephonic and other communications with headquarters is often quite impossible for days.

Another lesson to be learnt from these continuous blitzes is that Rest and Feeding Centres are apt to disappear, and routes to the new ones are often deflected by the closing of roadways and by unexploded bombs. Improvised signposts are, therefore, essential. An innovation suggested by the press department was to have signposts printed with the wording: 'Follow the MOI green (or blue) line to the Rest and Feeding Centres', and with a big arrow to show their direction.

As has been pointed out in previous reports, after heavy raids throughout the hours of darkness, the local organisations of fire-fighting and civic administration are apt temporarily to collapse. There is consequently great need of such information services as we can create. Post-blitz rumours, especially about casualties, and other distortions may not be started by enemy agents but may be merely the work of neurotic people. The effect on public confidence is the same, however, and as the war months lengthen the necessity for dealing with these problems may become even more acute.

For the present, Plymouth as a business and commercial centre of a prosperous countryside has ceased to exist. The children from two-thirds of it, the aged, the infirm, and the great army of pensioners who always live in dockyard towns and naval ports will, for the time being, dwell in the countryside around. Given a few weeks, however, all will, no doubt, recover their poise, and the absence of further continuous raids will enable the city to improvise arrangements and resume its shaken life. It would be wrong to assume that the people are broken. But equally it would be suicidal to ignore the implications and symptoms of the actual state of affairs, and to avoid probing the disturbing causes of the aftermath of some of the fiercest raids yet made upon a provincial centre.

In addition to the RIO's report there is evidence of a good deal of defeatist talk, and such expressions as 'What have we to lose?' and 'We cannot be worse off' are frequently heard. It is suggested that 'judicious plugging by the BBC of stories from occupied countries might have some effect in stopping the rot'. A high percentage of the Plymouth victims are among the families of men in the Naval or Merchant Services, whose morale, it is thought, may be affected.

It is felt that the Government should reconsider its 'stay put' policy for towns like these western ports, where raiding is likely to continue. Many of those who 'stayed put' after the first big raids have now been killed.

Nightly evacuation has become a settled practice and involves thousands of people, but except for one or two enterprising local efforts it is still unorganised.

There are reports of sailors' children catching pneumonia through sleeping under hedges while the owners of big houses are refusing permission for sheds and garages to be used as temporary refuges by homeless and exhausted people.

There have also been complaints about a lack of human consideration among municipal officers and those responsible for evacuation arrangements.

NO 32: WEDNESDAY 7 MAY TO WEDNESDAY 14 MAY 1941

GENERAL COMMENTS

1. GENERAL MORALE AND THE RECENT BLITZES

It is now possible to postulate some general if tentative conclusions about the spirit of the public under the Air War. In the past months it has become increasingly noticeable that the morale of the civilian population depends more upon material factors, acutely involving their lives, than upon the ebb and flow of the events of war beyond these islands. Good or bad news produces, as it were, only ripples on the surface of morale, though these ripples may sometimes gather into an appreciable peak or trough.

The operating factors for the civilian much resemble those operating upon troops in the field. They are as follows:

1. A SECURE BASE: It now seems certain that the way civilians stand up to continuous night raiding depends largely on their having the feeling that there is a safe refuge *somewhere* for themselves and their families. They are willing to put up with the discomforts and dangers of the present, if they can look ahead to a few good nights' rest in the future – just as, in the last war, the troops in the trenches could always look forward to security in 'Blighty'.

In the London raids, this factor is less important than in the provincial towns. Raids on their present scale destroy only a relatively small number of London homes, and there are still millions of houses standing where the homeless can make new, if temporary, 'bases'. But in the smaller provincial towns (e.g. Plymouth), not only does the proportion of homeless following a series of severe blitzes exceed the capacity of the rest of the town, but the homeless themselves often do not regard the rest of the town as a 'secure base'. The picture is greatly complicated by the fact that the potential 'secure bases' in the countryside are already fully occupied by evacuees from London and elsewhere.

As a rough and ready guide, it can be said that whenever or wherever the civilian population is becoming short of 'secure bases' as a result of enemy action, a situation dangerous to morale is arising, because the people certainly become uneasy and tend to become hopeless.

2.   FATIGUE: A prime feature of each provincial blitz, where repeated raids have occurred, has been physical fatigue. As raid succeeds raid, night after night, not only does the general population become 'stunned', but Civil Defence and other key personnel, who have day as well as night duties, decline in efficiency. This is, in the great majority of cases, a purely temporary phenomenon, and after a few nights of unbroken sleep, there is a considerable recovery. Complete recovery, however, seems to take about a fortnight or three weeks.

3.   'CONDITIONING': Other things being equal, populations which have been subjected to gradually increasing raids take heavy raids better than those who experience a sudden heavy raid without previous 'conditioning'. Familiarity breeds not contempt, but a certain philosophy. London's first heavy raid after the long lull produced a much more marked result than the second serious raid last Saturday – though in both cases the restorative services functioned well.

4.   PERSONAL BLITZ EXPERIENCES: The sight of severe casualties or sudden death, the loss of friends or relatives, 'near misses', temporary entombment, or the loss of one's home, have a definite 'unnerving' effect, often delayed for a few hours or a day – and usually temporary. This was well shown in the London hospitals last September and October: patients who came in for illnesses did not mind the raids; on the other hand, those who came in as raid casualties begged to be moved out into the country at the earliest possible moment.

5.   FOOD: In the maintenance of the morale of blitzed populations, food is of equal importance to the 'secure base'. Hot cooked food is much more valuable than tea, cold bully beef and bread and butter.

The less material factors which help to determine civilian morale operate alike in raided and non-raided areas. In heavy raids, however, their importance may be suddenly exaggerated, either by concrete illustration, or by the increased sensitiveness of the blitzed population. These factors are:

1.   BELIEF IN EQUALITY OF SACRIFICE: As long as people believe that all classes and sections are suffering and enduring equally, they will put up with very great hardship. It is 'unfairness' that people resent. This requires one justification. There is little indignation against the 'top dog' if the 'underdog' sees a chance of getting even a slightly larger bone than he has at present. Thus, feeling against car owners (as 'joy-riders' and 'petrol wasters') has grown as people have seen the chances of even a third-hand car fading from them. Indignation against 'the unrationed rich at the Ritz' has remained within bounds while there is still an occasional 'cut off the joint' at the public house.

2.   TRUST IN LEADERSHIP: Leadership includes not only the Government, but also the administration – local and central, and the managerial classes generally. In badly blitzed provincial areas, the feeling that local leadership (the Local Authority) has broken down has been a serious factor. Similarly, loss of confidence in national leadership has been engendered where the public has thought that the news was 'doctored' or withheld; where local events were, to the eyes of the local inhabitants, misrepresented by official communiques; or where the public thought there were unnecessary muddles over food.

3.   ASSURANCE OF ULTIMATE VICTORY: Thanks to the British traditions of 'always winning the last battle', loss of confidence in ultimate victory is to be regarded as a *sign* of bad morale, rather than as a *cause*. Where there is evidence of such feelings, the underlying causes must be sought for.

4.   BELIEF IN A BETTER WORLD AFTER THE WAR: It must be admitted that a large section of the population has no such belief, yet its morale is quite sound. The question of 'peace aims' only assumes importance in the public mind when there is a lull in major war events.

2. THE PUBLIC'S REACTION TO NEWS

A preliminary note only is possible on the reactions of the public to the news of the arrival of Hess. Amazement at what was regarded as the most astonishing event of the war was the outstanding feature. Strangers spoke to one another with animation in trains and buses on the way to work. The romantic, unexpected and comic elements of the situation alike caught the public fancy. About half the people spoken to failed to offer any explanation of Hess' behaviour. Among the rest, the most popular supposition was that Hess had fallen out with Hitler or was afraid of 'being bumped off'. A party split was commonly mentioned. A few people regarded the whole thing as a plot or trap and feared that Hess might attempt to get back again. The majority thought he would be interned as an ordinary prisoner; a few (mainly women) feared he would be given a big house and 'the best of every-thing'. There was speculation as to 'who would rat next', and generally speaking Hess was regarded as a harbinger of better times ahead. At the same time, there is, as yet, no clear thought about the full significance of his action. There is eagerness for an official explanation.

Already rumours are cropping up – such as that he was brought down on the way to southern Ireland, where he was to be instrumental in stir-ring up revolt.

Apart from the Hess news, the events making for optimism or depression have been roughly equal in number and strength. The Premier's speech in Parliament had a cheering effect, removing much of the belief that people were being kept in the dark deliberately; but this was offset by the heavier shipping losses. (With a few criticisms, the issue of figures monthly instead of weekly appears to be quite acceptable; it is, however, suggested that if news of our losses is no longer useful to the enemy after this delay, it should be possible to include some news of U-boat destruction at the same time.)

The rise of the toll of raiders taken by our night-fighters has been con-trasted with the fact that, so far, very heavy damage has always been reported on the night when the toll was highest. Here, however, the balance was in favour of optimism, except in the worst-bombed areas. The growing belief that America will soon be in the war, with her Navy protecting our convoys, has been paired off with the equally growing belief that all our expeditions have been short of equipment, we have nothing like enough tank or anti-tank guns even now, and we cannot stand up to the Germans on land.

The idea that we were too quick for the Axis in Iraq – that for once we were on the offensive ourselves – has been seized on with much joy, after preliminary forebodings. It has given the campaign such significance that if serious reverses should be reported in the near future, the lowering of public spirits may be out of proportion to the actual losses involved. It now seems to be generally accepted without very much ill-feeling that Turkey is going to let us down, although there was some adverse comment on the fact that the Prime Minister's Anzac Day address dwelt so much on our battles against the Turks, in view of what is still called 'a delicate situation'.

3. THE RECENT AIR RAIDS

Reports suggest that spirits in Belfast were considerably more shaken by the raids there than they would have been in an English town. This is partly because the first attack on Belfast was on a big scale, so that the people had no gradual hardening, and the Belfast civil authorities no testing period in which to discover weaknesses. There is a feeling that the civic authorities relied too much on the military, for fire-fighting and 'clearing up the mess', and there is a good deal of criticism of ARP personnel. Postal Censorship quotes letters stating that 'out of 26 wardens, about six are left to do all the work', and that 'there were ARP personnel on the refugee trains'. After the blitz of April 15/16, the Minister of Public Security urged people to return to their homes if these were undamaged; but many feel this to be a mistaken policy in view of the probability of more heavy attacks. The nightly trek from Belfast now amounts to some thousands, and officially organised evacuation is desired. Feelings of discouragement in Belfast are also attributed to the influence of southern Ireland, where the idea that we have already lost the war appears to be growing. Two extracts from Postal Censorship are typical of its general tone: 'The idea of England's ultimate defeat is being thrown about here as a matter of time only' – 'Everyone here thinks we have already been beaten.'

Despite the heavy raids on London on May 10th/11th, less depression is evident here than during the early part of last week. The raid on 16th April, with its severe damage, came as a shock after a comparatively quiet period; Saturday night's raid was not unexpected, on account of the full moon. The fact that it came at a weekend gave most people a chance to make up lost sleep before returning to work, and there was little outward sign of stress on Monday. The restorative services worked well. Further details of the Plymouth and Merseyside situations will be found in Appendices I and II.

4. REPRISALS

The demand for the bombing of German towns continues in Leeds, Belfast, the Bristol region, the Inverness area, Glasgow, Reading, and Southampton; and is reported, though less strongly, from other parts of the country. It is still noticeable that on the whole the demand tends to come from people who have not themselves suffered from severe raids. Only a few people have violent feelings on this subject, and many more, while expressing them-selves in favour of reprisals, are content with words and not action: thus Mass Observation reports, in the Kings Norton by-election enquiry, that 37% of the voters favoured reprisals, with 23% against, and 40% with no opinion. But the Reprisals candidate forfeited his deposit, polling 1,696 votes, against 21,573 for the Conservative candidate.

5. RUMOURS

There have been rather more rumours this week, to which Hess is already adding his quota. Haw-Haw rumours are reported from Tunbridge Wells, Barrow-in-Furness and Oxford. Casualty figures were greatly exaggerated in many districts. From Northern Ireland and Wales come rumours that Liverpool was completely gutted after the last raid; epidemics were raging because the sewage system was damaged, and the military had been called in to take charge of the town. In Manchester, the Merseyside raids were attributed to the arrival of the 'biggest convoy ever'.

Another variant has appeared of the story that we do not bomb the Rumanian oil wells because British capital is behind them. This is that the RAF have the exact position of an important dam in Italy, supplying the elec-tricity for many war factories, but that this is spared for the same reason.

Yet another variation on an old theme is the story of a mysterious red fluid dropped from our own planes during practice. This fluid is said to be indelible.

A story of 'explosive fountain-pens', dropped by the enemy, caused considerable excitement in Belfast.

6. BROADCASTING

There are still many reports of increased listening to enemy broadcasts, because of the scarcity of information in our own news services. It is, however, impossible to discover the actual volume of Haw-Haw listening; many reported cases may be merely garbled versions of what other people say he said.

A good deal of indignation still exists about the reticence of British communiques. A small minority felt that it was not reassuring to learn that the Government was not much better informed than the public about what was happening in Greece during the evacuation.

7. CONDITIONS IN WALES

The suggestion that a booklet, 'Growth of the Empire Commonwealth', should be distributed throughout Wales, as well as in England and Scotland, drew the objection that it would only increase the opinion, in Welsh-speaking Wales, that justice was not being done to this part of the Empire. It appears that any stressing of the consideration received by other distinct national cultures within the Commonwealth would lead to unfortunate contrasts with the grievances of Wales. Among these are the facts that Welshmen cannot give evidence in their own language in the Courts of Law in their own country, and that conscripted Welshmen are scattered among the regiments of Scotland and England, while the Welsh regiments are filled with other nationalities. Dislike is also expressed for the idea of Welsh children being evacuated outside Wales, away from their country traditions, when the rural areas of Wales have expressed their readiness to receive them. There is reason to suppose that these views are held only by a minority.

SPECIAL COMMENTS

8. SPECIAL RAID PROBLEMS

WAR DAMAGE ACT: Little interest in this Act is reported, but it is stated that men are asking what will happen when they are called up and are unable to continue the payments of their premiums.

FUNERALS OF AIR-RAID VICTIMS: Detailed evidence has been received in connection with the funerals of air-raid victims, in which reference is made to 'one of the most unconscionable ramps'. The close relatives are usually too stunned with grief to bargain with the undertaker, but in one case where a distant relation took a firm line, the estimate of 35 guineas was promptly reduced to 22 guineas.

Another form of 'funeral ramp' is believed to be prevalent, though this is impossible to prove. If the relatives of an insured person agree to use the undertaking service of the insurance company, the insurance is paid within a few days. This 'service' invariably costs almost exactly the amount of the insurance. But if the relatives go to an independent undertaker there is sometimes a delay of three or four weeks before the payment is made.

9. REGISTRATION OF WOMEN

A well-qualified authority suggests that in many cases the objection to the girls' being sent away from home comes not from the girls themselves, but from the parents. Various reasons are mentioned:

(1) If the girls are away from home, they might not contribute to the family budget.

(2) The husbands are often out in the evenings, and the mothers would be very lonely if their daughters were away.

(3) In many cases a fear and a prejudice on the part of the parents which they found very difficult to explain.

From the same source comes the suggestion that propaganda should be directed *at the parents* to make them see the importance of their girls doing war work. It is added that compulsion as to staying in the same job should not be stressed, as this evidently causes some apprehension.

It is reported that there are complaints from girls who registered recently for National Service, that they were given no choice of jobs, but were told that they must go where they were needed. Young women registering for National Service are described as still dreading being sent to munition factories. 'They seem to think the work would be very heavy and dangerous.'

10. FOOD

There are many complaints about the unequal distribution of unrationed foodstuffs, particularly in country districts, and an increased demand for all-round rationing so as to avoid unfairness. The rationing of sweets is suggested.

The high price of fish continues to be a subject of numerous complaints, particularly from the poorer classes. The shortage of eggs in London also continues to cause much comment, particularly as it is felt that there are plenty of eggs in the country and that it is the distribution that is at fault.

Workers in one factory canteen expressed annoyance at Major Lloyd George's recent speech. There is still a feeling of unfairness in regard to restaurant meals. The workers contrasted their own canteen with its two meatless days a week. Dissatisfaction continues to be reported among the poorer classes in other areas concerning the supply of rationed goods in hotels and restaurants. The Ministry of Food are urged to take more drastic action about the milkless day, which continues to cause a good deal of annoyance.

11. TOBACCO

The shortage of tobacco continues, and the extension of rationing to cover cigarettes is a common plea in one Region.

12. EVACUATION

Evacuation continues to be a chronic sore, exacerbated as each new provincial blitz adds to the difficulties in the reception areas. The old and infirm and the 'under-fives' still constitute an unsolved problem. It is reported that even those old people who are willing to go into country institutions are held up through lack of accommodation.

The high rents charged in the safe areas up and down the country are the subject of a good deal of discussion, and it is reported that in Northern Ireland evacuees from Belfast are being charged as much as 12/6 a week to sleep on the floors of farmhouses. 'Fabulous prices' are mentioned as being charged in the Portsmouth and Plymouth areas. There is a suggestion that there should be a fixed scale of rents throughout the country.

APPENDIX I

REPORT ON CONDITIONS IN PLYMOUTH FOLLOWING THE SEVERE RAIDS

1. INTRODUCTORY NOTE

On May 5th, 6th and 7th, on the instructions of the Director of the Home Division, the Regions' Adviser and the Head of the Home Intelligence Branch visited Plymouth to study post-blitz conditions. A large number of local and regional officials were interviewed. In addition, the blitzed parts of the city were visited; and Communal Feeding Centres, Queen's Messenger Canteens, Rest Centres (including a peripheral Rest Centre at the Tavistock Town Hall) and parts of the dockyard were inspected. No likely occasion for conversation with members of the general public was missed.

It is possible for us to compare the situation in Plymouth with that in the other blitzed cities, inasmuch as one of us has visited many of these cities within the past months, while the other has analysed all the Home Intelligence reports of these raids.

2. GENERAL SCALE OF THE DAMAGE

Plymouth is an amalgamation of three towns, Plymouth proper, Devonport and Stonehouse. While all parts are severely damaged, the devastation is largely to the dockyard workers' residential area in Devonport, to the shopping centre in Devonport and Plymouth proper, and to the Civic Centre in Plymouth proper. In these parts, whole streets are completely flattened. The exact amount of damage is not known, but two estimates given were 15,000 houses damaged in Plymouth as a whole, and 50% of the houses in Devonport. Certainly the damage is on an enormous scale, though there are a few parts of the city which are still almost entirely intact. The exact number of casualties for the 5 raids is also unknown, as there may still be bodies buried under the debris. Both the Regional Commissioner and Paymaster Captain Ayre put the total fatalities at 1,200, though the former said there were not many dockyard casualties, while the latter spoke of two direct hits, one causing the death of 100 Naval ratings, and the other the death of 80.

3. THE PEOPLE OF PLYMOUTH

The morale of the people as a whole appeared to be good. They were making a slow but steady recovery from their harassing experiences and were showing a high degree of courage and individual adaptability. But it was stressed that they still had some way to go before they could again face a 'repeat performance' with anything approaching confidence. On all sides, there was evidence that those with air-raid duties to perform had performed them with great courage. But one factor was in the end beginning to tell against them – *physical fatigue*. As raid succeeded raid, the powers of adaptability and concentration and the individual efficiency of the personnel declined. Those on duty all night often had full days of work to tackle. And the effects of the fatigue were most disastrous where many offices were concentrated in a single person.

Each night a number of people were trekking out of the city to sleep somewhere in the comparative safety of the countryside. The official estimate of 6,000 nightly trekkers seemed to us to be on the large side. The people were travelling out by bus, Army lorry, private car, or on foot. Some were sleeping in lodgings, others in tents, others in emergency Rest Centres (public buildings, dance halls or chapels), and some on the moors surrounding the city. What we saw seemed to be on a far smaller scale than the trek out of Boulogne in the Spring of 1918, when whole families, with old people, babies, and possessions, walked 8 kilometres each night to sleep in the Forêt de Boulogne. The trekkers from Plymouth were of all social classes – the individual and not the family group. Those we saw in the Rest Centre at the Tavistock Town Hall were the kind which takes shelter nightly in the London Tubes. They probably represent that section of the population which either from age, fatigue or poor mental constitution feels it can in no circumstances endure 'another night of it'. Many of the nightly trek-kers were, in fact, not homeless, and returned daily to their undamaged houses in Plymouth. The volume of the nightly trek was stated not to be decreasing, as a fair volume of gunfire and a few bombs were still Plymouth's nightly ration while we were there. There was no sign of the roads being blocked by the trekkers.

4. THE LOCAL MINISTRY OF INFORMATION

The local sub-office had continued to function in the centre of Plymouth (the Regional Commissioner had established his sub-office at Tavistock, 14 miles from the city). We gained the impression that our Plymouth sub-office had done excellent work. After the raids, the fatigue of the population was so great that loudspeaker announcements and notices giving lists of places where help for the homeless was available made little impression. This situation was solved partly by the use of bold posters (printed in green and blue) with arrows pointing the way to Rest Centres and Feeding Centres, and partly by the use of voluntary women workers, who went round with the loudspeaker vans to give individual help and instruction to the people in the blitzed areas. It was suggested that it would be a great help if some form of armlet (indicating that the wearer was an MOI Adviser) could be devised and issued. The first instructions about help for the homeless (issued to the MOI by the Municipal Authorities) were in some cases incor-rect; as a result the MOI was blamed by the public for disseminating false information. These mistakes were put right as soon as correct information could be obtained from the local authorities.

The broadcast news of the Plymouth raids was taken by the public to min-imise the severity of the situation, and this naturally led to much criticism. The RIO issued a formal notice in the local paper pointing out that the MOI and BBC were merely disseminating agencies for official communiques by other ministries. In fact, the remarks complained of were BBC comments, and not part of the official communiques themselves, though listeners failed to make this distinction. The leader of public complaint on this matter was Lady Astor. We talked with her and hope that we left her with a more friendly feeling towards the MOI. The matter is now dying a natural death.

5. THE LOCAL AUTHORITY AT PLYMOUTH

The pre-blitz preparations of the Plymouth Local Authority appear to have envisaged nothing on the scale of what actually did happen. The Authority was carrying on, on an expanded peace-time basis, rather than on the expectation of being a front-line battle headquarters. The Emergency Committee of the Council consists of the Lord Mayor and three Aldermen (civic leaders by virtue of long and faithful political service) – of whom two are over 70. The Town Clerk directs the activities of all the municipal officers (engineer, surveyor, and MOH) and is also ARP controller and officer in charge of post-blitz welfare services. The Chief Constable is also chief of the fire-brigade. As a result of this situation, we had a vivid impression of lack of directive in the blitzed areas, of absence [The remainder of this appendix appears to be missing.]

APPENDIX II

THE RAIDS ON MERSEYSIDE, 2–6 MAY

The following is a summary of the reports received from the Regional Information Officer, North-Western Region.

1. BOOTLE

There was a severe concentration of raids on Bootle where the big docks are situated. From the beginning, the Town Clerk, who is ARP Controller and Emergency Information Officer, kept a grip on the situation; he asked each morning early for the exact number of loudspeaker vans required. The largest number of vans used here was five. Half-way through the period, the Town Hall was put out of action through an unexploded bomb, and the large Ministry of Information van was used as a mobile Information Centre. Appropriate Municipal Officers went out with it, and issued VOW1 forms and travel vouchers, and also allotted people to billets. Queues of people wishing to make enquiries gathered quickly. The Mayor of Bootle went out with one of the vans and broadcast his thanks to the population for their steadiness, and generally gave out reassuring statements.

2. LIVERPOOL

In Liverpool conditions were more difficult. On Saturday (May 3) the chief problem was to get people home from the city in the middle of the day and the Transport Manager used vans for this purpose. On Saturday night the city was much more seriously damaged and the Regional Commissioner set up advance headquarters and held a conference, but the local authority representatives appeared to resent what they regarded as intrusion by Government departments.

Our Emergency Information Officer and his Deputy did not appear and owing to the breakdown of telephone communication it was very difficult to make any enquiries.

On Monday (May 5), when the city returned to work, the transport problem was acute. Only a very small number of buses could run and there were no trams. Several important railway routes were knocked out. Large numbers of private motorists parked their cars on both sides of main streets.

The Regional Commissioner held another conference and the Ministry of Transport urged strongly that private motors should be stopped a mile from the centre of the city. The Chief Constable showed reluctance to take this step and because of the congestion the Transport Department had difficulty in routing the services and could not get wrecked tram cars out of the centre of the city.

It was found possible, however, to use our vans for transport announcements and for notices from the Ministry of Labour. Our Emergency Information Officer and his Deputy turned up and said that the Town Clerk had not put into effect the emergency arrangements. He had not sent them either warning that the emergency had arisen or transport to bring the Emergency Information Officer into the city as promised. They said the Town Clerk had stated that the emergency provided for had not arisen and that there was no need for loudspeaker vans to operate. Reports from our vans showed that wherever they went with the meagre notices supplied, they were mobbed by members of the public wanting information. They gave what help they could but had not nearly time or knowledge enough to deal with the situation properly.

A Staff Speaker was put in charge of the vans and he made all possible contacts. On Tuesday (May 6) the Ministry of Pensions asked for notices to be put out. Again, vans were besieged by people wanting information. To make any progress at all, it was necessary to use the loudspeakers to tell people that they had had all the information available from the van; that there were people in the next street who had not heard the announcements; and that the van would come back if there was any further information to give them.

Attempts were made to contact the Town Clerk and eventually the Emergency Information Officer's Deputy found him and persuaded him of the importance of having information and notices emanating to the public from the Municipal Authority. The Town Clerk said that if six vans were available on Wednesday he would have notices and announcements ready for them. Six vans were supplied and two local vans were held in reserve.

Van drivers reported a big trek of people out of Liverpool, particularly after the second night's raid. They were hailed by people wanting lifts and not going to any special destination, but just anxious to get out of the city for the night.

Van drivers also did useful work by bringing out of the city messages from people who wanted to let relatives in other towns know that they were all right. Owing to the breakdown of telephone communication this would have been difficult by any other means. Our own messages to and from Liverpool and Bootle were transmitted by police wireless through the good offices of the Regional Commissioner.

3. USE OF WOMEN WORKERS TO ASSIST VANS

In Liverpool, the Emergency Information Officer had made an arrangement with the Personal Service League to lend him staff, and it was therefore possible to send out CAB workers with most of the vans. They had a very busy time, and adequately answered the many questions put to them in the course of the tours. The Officer in charge of the vans says: 'The questions we received were so many and varied that I could not possibly have dealt with a tithe of them had not the ladies been with us.'

4. FATIGUE AND REST

The bulk of the enquiries dealt with were on one point only – how to get out of Merseyside for at least one night's rest. There was very little interest in how to get repairs done to houses or money to pay for replacement of furniture and belongings. Already Merseyside has had experience of the machinery for billeting, rehousing, etc., and so it may be that the public generally has a fair knowledge of the appropriate action to take.

The fact remains that the enquiries made and the general behaviour of enquirers showed *loss of sleep* to be the important factor. Again and again people in responsible positions in the town asked, 'Do you think we shall get a rest tonight?'

There was a general disinclination on the part of enquirers to listen to explanations. People wanted a straightforward statement of what help they could get. Fatigue seemed to affect them in one of two ways. Either they had become apathetic and listened to instructions without really observing the information or their tempers were short and they showed an inclination to argue and grumble about trivialities.

Particularly in Bootle it was noticed that a high percentage of those making enquiries at the vans were of Irish extraction, but there was no evidence of bad morale in the sense that no one was ever heard to suggest that the war should be stopped. In fact many people remarked to the effect that if only the town could have about a fortnight's respite it would be quickly straightened out again, and able to carry on.

Vans became more and more important during the week in the efforts to care for the homeless, and at one time there were nine operating in Liverpool and six in Bootle.

5. REST CENTRES

In Bootle general information among the public about Rest Centres was very small; it was with difficulty learned that as a result of the inability to use nine of the twelve Rest Centres in the town, an Emergency Centre had been opened for feeding purposes only at the Junior Technical College. Conversations with the staff, who were most helpful, showed that the only food available up to May 4 had been soup, bread and tea. This, it was said, was due to the breakdown in supplies. It appeared that the opening of this Emergency Centre had not been properly publicised, as the number of people using the centre for lunch on that day had been small. On the other hand, many people in and around were complaining of the lack of proper feeding facilities for themselves and those who had suffered in the blitz on the previous night.

Visits to the other Rest Centres on May 4 suggested that the feeding arrangements were equally inadequate. A good deal of time was spent in particular at the St. Matthew's Rest Centre, where in the evening people were being supplied with tea and bread and butter. Enquiry as to whether a proper meal would be served elicited the information that no such meal was available or was likely to be available, but they intended to continue to serve tea and bread and butter at intervals. The Rest Centre was filled, and a fair number of people were also resting in the church. No attempt was being made to interest the people, the only activity being on the part of the billeting officers, who were interviewing in an attempt to find billets for as many people as possible before darkness fell.

The sufferers in the blitz were being left almost entirely to their own devices. It is suggested that an attempt should be made to build up an organisation which can help, advise and encourage the people who use Rest Centres, who are obviously dispirited as a result of their experiences.

6. THE NIGHTLY TREK

On Stanley Road, on May 4, it was apparent that large numbers of people were attempting to evacuate themselves from the city. Beside the Stanley Hospital there were some hundreds of people with children and bundles of clothing, moving about, and in addition there were numbers of people passing out of Liverpool on lorries and other vehicles.

These movements were uncontrolled, and during the whole of the evening there was no obvious person attempting to advise the people concerned or to control their movements in any way. A good number of them had been to Daisy Street School, where they said people were being evacuated to Walton village, but they had been turned back from there because of the congestion of the school and because they had been told that evacuation was impossible. Some, therefore, were making their way to their homes and others were attempting to board outgoing vehicles.

At the Daisy Street School, the playground was filled with people waiting for buses to take them to Walton village. The official in charge said that he was satisfied they would be evacuated before dark.

Later in the evening, on the Huyton Road, there was evidence of the same uncontrolled evacuation. People were passing out both on foot and on any vehicles available. Again there was no evidence of persons to advise or control.

7. RUMOURS

A story about Bootle, which was entirely without foundation, was circulating in some parts of the Region, though not in the town itself. People here were said to be parading through the streets demanding peace.

There were also reports equally without any truth, that there had been serious riots in Liverpool, as a result of which martial law had been declared.

NO 33: WEDNESDAY 14 MAY TO WEDNESDAY 21 MAY 1941

GENERAL COMMENTS

Attention is drawn to a special review of some of the factors of industrial absenteeism with special reference to those possibly remediable by propaganda (see subsection 10 of this report).

1. GENERAL STATE OF CONFIDENCE AND REACTION TO NEWS

The main features of the reaction of the public to the week's news have been:

1. A growing anti-French feeling, coupled with a fear that our slowness to take action in Syria is due as much to lack of equipment as to excess of scruples.

2. A strong belief that Hess is being treated with excessive kindness.

3. An increasing demand for reprisals, possibly associated with the relative freedom of the country from night raids. (It has often been noted previously that the demand for reprisals decreases during and immediately after severe raids, and vice versa.)

4. Many reports of increased listening to the German radio, attributed to our own delays in announcing war news.

On the subject of the Near East, and especially on the attitude of France, there is considerable anxiety. The question is frequently asked: 'Why do we not invade Syria, before the Germans have established themselves there, especially as we are told that we have an army of half a million men under General Wavell?' The old cry: 'Britain is always behind', silenced for once over Iraq, is now being heard over Syria. Many people are reported to be saying: 'We are always too late in taking action, too poor in numbers and material, and have too much respect for convention.' Great uneasiness is also expressed about our position in Palestine.

It seems to be generally felt that we should 'drop our kid-glove attitude to the Vichy government and substitute something much more active'. Indeed, the most remarkable single manifestation of public feeling this week has been the outburst of anger against France, and the dissatisfaction with our 'apparent tenderness' towards the Vichy government. It is felt that our very existence is now endangered by 'sticking to a punctilio which other people are not sticking to'. The suspicion is expressed in one quarter that the Free French forces do not seem to be very popular in their own colonies.

The tendency, recorded last week, to 'write off' Turkey as a potential ally continues.

About Iraq, there is still uncertainty, the general impression being that we have control of the country only at local points; there appears to be considerable confusion in the mind of the public as to the importance or otherwise of the Iraq pipe-line. In one newspaper, it was described as 'a main source of the fleet's fuel supply', while on other occasions the cutting of the pipe-line has been presented as a matter for no great anxiety. In this, as in other connections, it has been suggested that anxiety is synonymous with uncertainty, and that the public would rather know the truth, however disagreeable.

A legend of German 'invincibility on land', referred to some weeks ago, is once more slowly forming in the minds of some people, and is becoming something of a superstition; it is expressed by remarks of this kind: 'Don't think we'll ever get the better of Jerry, certainly not on land; their equipment's so efficient.' Such a feeling is, however, limited, and is entirely confined to land operations.

It is now possible to describe in greater detail the public's reaction to the arrival of Hess. Incredulity soon turned to jubilation. No theory has been too fantastic to put forward, from the idea that he was in love with Unity Mitford and had flown here to see her, to the fear that he had come to assassinate the Prime Minister. There are very few exceptions to the view that Hess is being treated too kindly. He is regarded as personally responsible for 'some of the most repulsive features of Nazi brutality', and the theory that he is an incorruptible idealist does as little to make him attractive in English eyes as the *Daily Mirror*'s description of his polished toe-nails. 'Press reports of Hess enjoying a light diet of fish, chicken and eggs have caused widespread disgust and indignation, especially in view of the difficulty experienced by housewives in obtaining these kinds of food.' This is general, as it is mentioned by a number of Regional Information Officers.

It was felt from the first that Hess was the 'answer to the propagandist's prayer'. Now, several days later, the view is being expressed that the news might have been handled with greater effect.

No criticism of the Duke of Hamilton has been received.

Some connection has arisen in people's minds between the arrival of Hess and the postponement of President Roosevelt's speech. This speech is awaited with intense interest. Speculation is divided; some fear that the delay means postponement of American convoys and the possible entry of America into the war, while others hope that, when the President's speech does come, it will be a declaration of war against the Axis Powers. The speeches of American politicians are read with a certain amount of impatience, and some people are saying that 'the Americans are a long time about it. It's all Big Talk with them.'

2. BROADCASTING

The public's reaction to broadcast news is still characterised by a 'distrust of news bulletins and of the official communiques as a source of full and reliable news'. Many people continue to complain of the 'repetition of unimportant items, the reiteration of individual aerial combats and the repetitive, boring phraseology of communiques'. But it is the lack of news, and the suspected mitigation of bad tidings, which seem to dissatisfy people most. 'We want the news, even if it is bad.' 'There must be many like myself cursing this country for the want of news. We could bear anything; only not to know is undermining our courage.'

Once more from a number of sources come reports of an increase in listening to enemy broadcasts, and a growing tendency to believe them. Of 22 Police Duty Room reports from Chief Constables, 6 mention continued listening to German broadcasts, and Regional Information Officers make similar observations. 'Nothing but a prompter, more comprehensive explanation of what has happened will reduce the amount of listening to German broadcasts, which has undoubtedly increased during the past month.'

3. REPRISALS

The demand for reprisals is steadily increasing. It now comes usually from 'bombed' and 'unbombed' areas (whereas previously the unbombed have always been the more vocal).

There is also a demand for the publication of photographs showing the effects of our bombing on German cities: 'nothing is said to give greater satisfaction'. But a certain discretion is evidently desirable in the description of our exploits. A recent statement on the wireless about the creation of a '*beautiful*' bomb has been received by many people with repugnance, as it is felt that 'no bomb which destroys homes and families can be described as beautiful, though this does not lessen the desire for us to bomb Berlin and Rome'.

4. RUMOURS

If a mass of phantasies about Hess is excluded, the week's rumours are mostly concerned with the Merseyside raids. It is alleged that there was to be a scheme of compulsory evacuation; that there had been 15,000 deaths, rioting, martial law, and also a heavy daylight raid; but most persistent of all, that there had been petitions for 'peace at any price', and processions with peace banners and 'Stop the War' posters. These were all without any foundation.

Connected with the subject of rumour is the recurrent fear that if a certain place is singled out for praise in a speech or visited by royalty or a distinguished statesman – or merely visited by Hess – it will then be badly blitzed by the enemy. Reports of this anxiety come from Belfast, whose dockyards were visited by Mr. Menzies; from Norwich, which was visited by the Duke of Kent; and from Glasgow.

SPECIAL COMMENTS

5. SPECIAL RAID PROBLEMS

WAR DAMAGE ACT: There has been a sudden awakening of interest in this subject. Concern is felt over the widespread ignorance of the provisions of the Act, and over the apparent shortage of forms. This shortage applies not only to the public, but to the insurance agencies as well. Companies drawing no commission from this type of insurance often seem unwilling to co-operate. In view of the shortness of the time left for registering for extra compensation, there are suggestions that press publicity should be intensified, and that more forms should be issued at once with the simplest possible instructions attached.

FIRE-FIGHTING: It is widely believed that there has been a falling off in voluntary fire-watching, and in many urban areas there is a growing demand for compulsion. This is desired not only as a safety measure, but also so that public-spirited people do not feel, as at present, that others are sheltering unfairly behind their willingness. The announcement that fire brigades are to come under Government control has been welcomed, but it is felt that fire-watchers should be taken over in the same way. Already some are reported as saying 'The only people who get a decent night's sleep are soldiers, all in bed by 10 p.m.' In places where military help in civil defence has been available, for example Belfast and Avonmouth, it has been very greatly appreciated, and the rumour that the military assistance at Avonmouth was to be withdrawn caused much dismay; the Battle of the Ports, it was said, was a soldiers' battle, well as a people's battle.

6. EVACUATION

The problem of evacuation from Merseyside, where the neighbouring reception areas are already overcrowded, is complicated by the insistence of the dockers that their families, though out of the target area, must be within nightly reach. The idea of camps just beyond the range of the city is under discussion. (A special report from the RIO, Bristol, says that a single camp there has already enough applicants to fill it for two years; and suggestions are reported that more camps of this kind in all the congested areas would meet a real demand.) A scheme for dockers' hostels, in the town where they work, has not met with their approval. A similar suggestion, that their families should be moved and the dockers themselves be left to sleep in deep shelters, has been criticised because of the opposition of the men, and because few suitable shelters have sanitation and washing facilities.

Billeting steps taken in the Liverpool area include schedules of all vacant rooms, empty houses and other available accommodation, such as buildings taken over by the military and now relinquished. But there is still great reluctance on the part of mothers to let their children go if they cannot accompany them, and evacuation in this area is said not to be progressing as fast as it should.

The approach of the holiday season has given rise to many complaints that landladies in the 'safe' areas, such as rural Wales and the Lake District, are turning away evacuees to make room for holiday-makers. There is increasing support for the view that the taking over of large country houses for evacuees is the only solution to the problem of bitter personal hostilities between hosts and evacuees, town and country populations, etc.

7. FOOD

The desire is still expressed that rationing – or at any rate registration – should be extended to cover all scarce commodities. It is felt that registration would at least prevent people who can afford to lay in a stock of household goods from going from shop to shop, buying up whatever is becoming scarce.

Fear is expressed that price control without rationing is worse than useless, unless both wholesale and retail trades are better organised, if possible under centralised rather than local control. At present it is thought that price control merely tends to drive goods off the market altogether.

There are still many complaints about the milkless day, and of the fact that food distribution plans do not take sufficiently into account the movement of populations due to evacuation. (Incidentally this leads to much ill-feeling against evacuees in the reception areas – 'They come like locusts and eat up everything.')

8. REGISTRATION OF WOMEN

One of the greatest discouragements to women in registering for war work is still the number of stories of those already in munition factories, standing idle for want of adequate organisation. Women are also reluctant to give up lucrative jobs while rich people can still employ several domestic servants. Registration has brought home the inequalities of pay under which women suffer. Those who know they are taking men's places in industry or in civil defence tend to resent this differentiation. The lower compensation for air-raid injury is much criticised; and dissatisfaction is felt over the question of married women's employment and income tax – there are several cases reported in which, by taking a war-job, a wife actually finds herself out of pocket on account of increased income tax and additional expenditure at home for domestic help. Many women's services are said to be lost to the country because of this, and suggestions are being made of adjustment in the assessment of income tax in such cases.

The scheme of taking on married women on a part-time basis has proved satisfactory in some factories where it has been tried as an experiment. The problem is to make suitable arrangements for the children. The idea of 'child-minders' has proved very unpopular, and day-nurseries attached to the factories are offered as a solution.

9. TRANSPORT

The desire for a general tightening-up of regulations affecting private motorists is apparent in many comments received this week. There are strongly expressed demands that petrol should no longer be wasted on pleasure-trips. Car-parties to races and football matches have aroused particular indignation; and complaints from the Midlands and Wales suggest that motorists in the towns are using their fuel allowances to reach farms, market-gardens etc., outside, where they can buy, above the fixed prices, the commodities which are scarce in their neighbourhood.

Lights on vehicles at night are said to be far beyond the regulation strength in many districts. From Belfast there is a report that 'the sound of sirens starts a stampede, and a stream of cars with bright head-lamps'.

10. ABSENTEEISM IN INDUSTRY

In the following short review (compiled from many sources), an attempt is made to assess the factors causing absenteeism in industry, bearing in mind particularly those which might be remedied by propaganda. Other more material factors must be mentioned, if only to clarify the picture.

Absenteeism is always much greater among women than among men. In war-time, absenteeism among women tends to increase out of all proportion to the increase among men; the greatest increase is among married women, who would not normally be working in factories.

It must be remembered that, in times of stress, absenteeism is not always necessarily a bad thing. With increased overtime, and holidays greatly curtailed, it may act as a natural safety-valve for the hard-pressed individual; and one voluntary day off may save several days of involuntary sickness.

Unpunctuality and slowness in starting work are almost as important as absenteeism itself in causing loss of production.

A study of the causes of absenteeism shows that it is an evil which cannot readily be cured by increasingly severe discipline.

The main causes of absenteeism are:

1. FATIGUE, due to
   (a) Domestic duties and home conditions. (This has been found to be the most important single cause among women.)
   (b) Long hours of work.
   (c) Travel difficulties.
   (d) Sleepless nights through raids, or fear of raids, or through doing Civil Defence duties.
   (e) Nutritional difficulties.
2. ILLNESS: The second most important single cause among women.

3. MATERIAL NECESSITIES:
   (a) Time taken off to do shopping.
   (b) Time taken for coping with immediate post-raid problems – salvage of property etc.

4. THE INCOME TAX SITUATION

5. MENTAL FACTORS:
   (a) The 'sheep for a lamb' situation. A worker is late; she feels that 'clocking in' will prove her to be at fault – so she might just as well take the whole day off and be hung for a sheep as a lamb. This is the third most important single cause among women.
   (b) Lack of incentive to work, due to:
      (1) Ability to 'afford a day off now and then', on account of high wages.
      (2) Lack of a feeling of active participation in the war effort.
      (3) Inability to enjoy the relative high wages, owing to the shortage of luxuries, the curtailment of entertainment, and the 'lack of colour' in war-time provincial life.
      (4) A feeling (often a misapprehension) that 'the bosses are incompetent'.
      (5) Lack of ambition, particularly among women and youths.
      (6) A belief that the 'Lease-and-Lend bill will do it all for us'.
   (c) The prestige of married women. This tends to influence the behaviour of single girls, and as a result, the high absentee rate among married women may prove infectious.

DETAILS OF THE MAIN CAUSES

DOMESTIC DUTIES AND HOME CONDITIONS: By the social etiquette of the manual worker class, from which most married women in factories are drawn, a man cannot help in the domestic work at home without being looked down on by his mates. This applies particularly to the North. Certain things a man may do to help his wife, such as lighting fires; but all cleaning and washing up (the bulk of the housework) must be done by the woman, either before or after she leaves the factory – even if the man is out of work and the woman is supporting the family. The same applies to shopping.

Now that rationing and scarcity of various commodities have made shopping more complicated, it has been found that much absenteeism is due to time spent in buying food, and other household supplies. Absenteeism has been considerably reduced in factories which have added stocks of essentials to their canteens, so that the women may buy these in their lunch break. But there will always be husbands on leave, and children evacuated or at home for whom arrangements must be made.

LONG HOURS OF WORK: The Health of Munitions Workers Committee have recently found that a 12-hour day gives not only a lower hourly output than a 10-hour day but a lower gross output. They also found that a seven-day week gave less output than a six-day week. Evidence from all sources supports this observation.

Thus in one factory, at a time when high production was of the greatest importance, the employees were working 68 hours a week. These hours failed to maintain output, and it was decided to reduce the hours to 60 as an experiment. Not only did output per hour increase, but the total *daily* output increased by about 8%, and quality improved as well.

It was also found that women who worked 55 hours a week lost 13 more days in absenteeism per year than those working only a 48-hour week. The addition, twice a week, of two hours to an 8-hour day, reduced work to the slower tempo of a 10-hour day on *every* day of the week. Unfortunately, when hours are reduced the output does not usually rise immediately, but only over a long period of adaptation, which makes the conversion of old-fashioned managers to the reasonable shortening of hours particularly difficult. Similarly, longer hours do tend to produce more for the first few weeks; but after a period, output decreases rapidly.

THE INCOME TAX SITUATION: Reports from many sources have recently suggested that absenteeism is being caused by unwillingness to earn wages high enough to be liable to much taxation. This has apparently been occurring ever since the deduction of tax from wages. On the other hand, it is also suggested that this is not a serious cause, because so many workers would feel hurt in their pride if they thought their friends knew their work had failed to reach income tax proportions.

LACK OF FEELING OF PARTICIPATION IN THE WAR EFFORT: There is a tendency for many workers to underrate their individual responsibility for output. Even in the blitzed areas, they have only a temporary feeling of being 'in the war' as fighters. In the last war there was plenty of hustle and bustle at home, bright lights etc. This time there is considerable 'dullness', and to many life seems to 'have no flavour'. They only partly realise that the Fighting Forces rely on them for munitions and that lack of effort is 'letting the Forces down'. More contact and explanation between the Services and the munition workers might have a stimulating effect.

NO 34: WEDNESDAY 21 MAY TO WEDNESDAY 28 MAY 1941

GENERAL COMMENTS

1. GENERAL STATE OF CONFIDENCE AND REACTION TO NEWS

The continued freedom of the country from air raids has had two main effects:

1. In the severely bombed areas, recovery of spirits has slowly but steadily continued.
2. In the country as a whole, there has been considerably greater interest in the progress of the war outside Britain than even the dramatic nature of events might have led one to expect.

Preliminary reports indicate that the jubilation over the sinking of the *Bismarck* has more than outweighed the depression at the loss of HMS *Hood*. But there is considerable anxiety over the battle of Crete. It is suggested that 'should the Germans win it, the legend of their invincibility will have been increased to a formidable extent'. King George's flight from Crete is regarded as a strong 'indication that Crete is known to be doomed'. Reports agree that whatever happens we should hold on, 'if only for the prestige to be gained from a victory there'. It is felt that 'defeat or retirement would be a severer blow to confidence than Greece or Norway', particularly in view of the Prime Minister's words, which were taken as a promise that we would not withdraw from Crete.

'Critically minded people' ask how the Germans have been able to make large-scale use of the Greek aerodromes, 'seeing that only a short time ago our inability to give adequate air-support to our forces in Greece was ascribed to the lack of adequate aerodromes in that country'. It is also asked 'why, if the Germans are able to improvise so quickly, we should apparently still lack aerodromes in Crete after having been in the island for months'. It is suggested that a wireless talk on the physical features of the island and its position in the Mediterranean might help to dispel some of these doubts.

The attack on Crete is widely (but by no means universally) regarded as a 'full dress rehearsal for the invasion of this country in the near future'. The conviction appears to be growing that invasion will be attempted, and there is satisfaction at the policy of 'keeping a huge army here and taking no chances'.

A critical attitude over our apparent inactivity towards Syria is widespread. We are once more accused of 'letting the Germans get in first every time', and anger against France continues to grow. People wonder why 'official criticism of the Vichy government carries a hint of sentiment'. There seems to be a growing disinclination to distinguish between the French government and people, 'especially among ex-Service men who in the last war fought for France'. Many people feel that it would be better to have France our declared enemy, so that we could penetrate Syria and also seize Dakar. Darlan's recent words and actions 'have not changed the attitude towards France appreciably, simply because nobody any longer expects anything but the worst from France'. Some bitter feeling against Free French forces in this country is also reported, and they are regarded as a serious source of leakage of information to the enemy.

The absence of any official announcement about Hess is said to be causing uneasiness in more than one part of the country, and is coupled with the suggestion that he must have friends in high places. Sir Nevile Henderson's reference to him as a decent and harmless person has 'had a bad effect', and is represented as a 'particularly unfortunate line to take when speaking on behalf of the Ministry of Information'.

The Hess affair has revived the idea of an active Fifth Column in this country, composed of people in 'high Society' and even among those in important political positions. Some suspicion is now expressed of the Duke of Hamilton being a Fifth Columnist; it is pointed out that, when questioned about him, the Prime Minister said that the Air Ministry would answer all questions about him as the Duke is in the Air Force, and this is taken to mean that the Prime Minister knows all about him but does not want to have anything to do with it.

A general impression seems to be forming that 'our War Cabinet is not as strong as it should be', nor as resolute, and that 'apart from Mr. Churchill's speeches, little was being done by the Government to encourage belief that leadership is as resolute as the nation itself'. There is considerable criticism of the Ministry of Labour, a feeling that they are 'monkeying about with conscription for women' while there are still many men unemployed, and that, while we are 'desperately short of agricultural workers', still more young labourers are to be drafted into the Forces. Nor are these criticisms of muddle and indecision always confined to the Ministry machine itself.

Some uneasiness is being felt about the morale of foreign seamen who are at present in this country, Norwegian, Dutch, Polish, French and Belgian. There is said to be growing unrest among them, and a fear that Britain may not win the war, the Belgians in particular 'having reached the stage when they do not care a hoot for England'. There are requests for propaganda, literature and films emphasising the British point of view upon war issues.

Among British merchant seamen dissatisfaction is reported on the ground that they are not welcomed in Service men's canteens, that their casualties are never given, and that in general they are given insufficient recognition as compared with the attention lavished on the Forces.

There has been relatively little speculation about the lull in air raids on this country. In badly bombed parts of London, people are reported to show signs of nervousness at weekends, when heavy raids are thought to be particularly likely. Last Wednesday was also named as a probable date for a blitz. In Bristol, the resumption of heavy raids with the waxing of the moon is anticipated; at the same time, the hope that our night-fighters will inflict heavy losses is stated to outweigh the fear of the resumption of raids. The most popular explanation of the lull is weather conditions, but it is also suggested that Hitler is holding his hand until the Americans have made their attitude more plain; for there is a belief that nothing stimulates pro-British American public feeling as strongly as tales of horror from English blitzed towns.

From the badly raided areas, there are still some reports of apathy and physical weariness. Depression is said to be 'especially noticeable among women, who have to put up with all the petty, nagging annoyances of war'. The nightly trek from the raided towns continues to be a serious problem. At Barrow, one estimate says that 60% of the population are sleeping out of the town each night. On Merseyside, large numbers are said to be making arrangements to sleep outside during the next full moon period (June 2–16). At Wallasey there are complaints that a nightly exodus leaves hundreds of houses without fire-watchers. At Belfast, the nightly trek continues, and many are still sleeping in open fields and the hillsides. A special study of the situation has been made at Southampton and Portsmouth. The Southampton figure is believed to be about 20,000 people per night, including those who normally live outside or have homes 'for the duration' outside. About 12,000 of these nightly evacuees are said to have unsatisfactory accommodation, ranging from single rooms with no amenities, to barns and fowl houses. An unspecified number are sleeping in the open, or in the vehicles which take them out. At Portsmouth, the nightly trek is more obvious, as there is only one main road out of the city; in the town the trekkers are sometimes referred to as 'the Yellow Brigade', while outside they are spoken of as 'those dreadful blitzers', and are lodged on sufferance with a minimum of amenities. At Southampton, the general attitude of both public and authorities is that the town has had its share of raids and that heavy attack is now unlikely. In Portsmouth, on the other hand, renewed attack is expected. (Full reports on the general morale situation in Southampton and Portsmouth may be obtained on application to the Home Intelligence Branch.)

Those commenting on the apathy and depression in raided areas suggest that there is an increasing need for encouraging open-air activities, and for providing colour and distraction generally to take people's eyes and minds off depressing prospects. The processions and bands in connection with London's War Weapons Week are said to have aroused great enthusiasm, and there are many demands for brass bands and martial music. A limited survey of public opinion on this question showed that 68% of those questioned were in favour of military bands going round the streets; 20% thought it was undesirable; and 12% were undecided.

2. BROADCASTING

The public continues to be very critical of both the BBC and 'our news services'. One of the main causes of this discontent is still 'the absence of faith in our ability to face bad news'. Recollections of 'the optimistic stuff served out after Norway make listeners instinctively distrust the more encouraging items of news from Crete'. On the other hand the manner, if not the gist, of these items has met with some approval: 'the lively accounts of dramatic events are contrasted favourably with colourless reports of earlier campaigns'.

There is 'substantial agreement between the Chief Constables' in one Region that it is the 'unimaginative tardiness' of the news services that is turning listeners towards Haw-Haw and the New British Broadcasting Station. Chief Constables report that the recent change in the transmission times of the NBBS has brought enquiries as to what the new times were.

3. RUMOUR

Rumours are fewer. In the Merseyside area, the tales of rioting and peace demonstrations are dying down; this is attributed to their exposure by Lord Derby at a public meeting, to strong leading articles in several Lancashire newspapers, and to word-of-mouth dissemination of the true facts. In more distant parts of England, these stories are still reported, and Bristol, Barrow-in-Furness, and Newcastle are named as places where there have been peace demonstrations.

At Chesterfield, commercial travellers are accused of despondent defeatist talk. In other parts, Army officers in hotel bars are said to be the 'worst careless talkers'.

A rumour is circulating in some areas that Lord Nuffield is to be interned.

In view of the current fears that royal visits tend to be followed by blitzes, careful enquiries were made in the Chatham area, after it had been visited by the Queen. No evidence whatever was found of any fear that the royal visit would be followed by a raid.

4. REPRISALS

Considerable interest has been aroused in the South-Western Region by the Bishop of Bristol's suggestion that a night-bombing truce might be arranged. Discussion is described as being 'very evenly balanced', but the majority of people are said to take the attitude that they have had to endure the terrors of night bombing, and now that we are in a position to hit back strongly the Germans should be made to suffer in the same way.

Elsewhere the demand for reprisals is still considerable. At the same time, some reports suggest that there is a 'growing sense of the futility of mutual bombing'. The feeling is also expressed that 'sooner or later there would be an outcry about our reprisal raids on Berlin, as people do not believe that our raids on Germany approach in savagery their reprisal raids here'.

SPECIAL COMMENTS

5. FIRE-FIGHTING

There is considerable public feeling about the need for better organisation of fire-watchers. 'The present chaos allows some districts to have well-trained and well-equipped men on active service during raids, while other districts provide little more than plucky amateurs, short of their proper kit.' It is suggested that 'fire-fighting and fire-watching should be brought together under one control'.

The employment of troops in fire-fighting is urged once more, as fatigue and other factors are thought to be causing a falling-off in the civilian services. Particularly in Plymouth and Bristol, there is a growing feeling that the withdrawal of troops is 'short-sighted', as if the fire-damage is unchecked there will 'soon be little left for the military to defend with rifle and tank'.

Farmers report a recurrence of last year's anxiety in connection with crops. It is feared that there may be efforts to set fire to the fields. Already short of workers, they cannot supply the watchers themselves, and hope is expressed that some organisation will deal with this at once, as in another month or two it would be too late. It is urged that saving crops, in the present circumstances, is quite as important as saving buildings, and possibly more so.

6. FOOD

Complaints of maldistribution continue. The difficulties housewives experience in providing workers with 'packed' lunches is still a major complaint. Shortages of fish and eggs are also commented on. There is growing indignation at the alleged profits of the 'middle-men'.

Suggestions are made that the jam ration to households where there are young children should be increased. Working-class mothers are finding it more and more difficult to provide substitutes for this staple food, as the prices of other commodities rise, and tinned goods become scarcer. There is some criticism of the fact that multiple stores are liberally supplied with both jam and syrup, in districts where the latter is unobtainable in other shops.

Praise for newly opened 'British Restaurants' is widespread, and there are requests for more and bigger ones. Both food and prices are considered satisfactory, but it is thought that the organisation could in some cases be improved. It is alleged that some local authorities are not opening such restaurants 'because they doubt if they will run at a profit'.

7. THE RAT SITUATION

The unsealing of drains, through raid-damage, is thought to be responsible for an apparent increase in rats, who escape from the sewers and are reported to be doing serious damage in bakeries, etc. Firms who have always employed several men solely to deal with rats cannot get exemption for them and are now required to report any increase on their premises to the Borough Council, who then send a Rat Officer round to inspect. Many small firms refrain from doing this, knowing from experience that the Borough Council will probably refuse responsibility, claiming that it is not the sewer but their own arrangements which are at fault, and will then rec-ommend the firm to carry out alterations involving them in considerable expense.

8. REGISTRATION OF WOMEN

Suggestions have been received that, before the registration of the next age-group, it should again be made clear that expectant mothers and those with young children will not be called up for service; at present there is anxiety on this point. There are further requests for day-nurseries attached to fac-tories, where mothers who wish to work can feel that their children will be properly looked after. There is also evidence that many more mothers would be willing to evacuate their children, and take up national work, if residential nurseries in the country were provided. It is generally agreed that by the time a woman has done a day's work in a factory, she is too tired to give her children satisfactory attention, and the good done by a day-nursery is often undone when they are taken home at night.

As the registration age rises, a larger proportion of married women will be affected, and the problem of household shopping will become more urgent among factory workers, who are never free when the shops are open. This is already causing discontent and absenteeism; and it is given by many women, not yet eligible for calling-up, as their chief reason for not volunteering. In one West Midland factory, women are allowed to leave written orders to be collected by the local tradesmen, and the Welfare Department of another large firm has asked local shop-keepers to remain open late on one evening a week; both experiments seem to be working well.

9. LEGAL PROBLEMS OF THE POOR

A special report by the Secretary of a free legal advice centre, dealing with the people of Camberwell, Lambeth and Southwark, makes the following points:

1. As the law stands at present, there are many justifiable grievances among both tenants and landlords. Tenants have, for example, almost insuperable difficulties in finding out if their rents are legally excessive.

2. The Landlord and Tenant War Damage Act of 1939 is causing more grumbling at present than any other legal problem. Tenants fail to understand why they should pay full rent for a house which is damaged by enemy action, to such an extent that they can inhabit only one or two rooms (they only cease to be liable for rent if they cease to live in the house). Persons who buy houses on a mortgage fail to see why they should continue to pay instalments and interest when the house is completely destroyed.

3. Under the Courts Emergency Powers Acts of 1939–40, landlords cannot remove furniture from tenants' houses, unless a summons has been served, and leave of Court obtained. Where tenants evacuate, leaving no address, the summons cannot be served, and the landlord cannot even store the tenant's furniture and relet his premises.

4. There is a considerable increase in the number of people seeking divorce. This is stated to be due to hasty and ill-considered marriages, thanks to the imminence of calling up, or to one of a couple, who have lived apart for many years, now wishing to marry a member of the Forces. The number of Poor Persons' Lawyers is greatly reduced, and as a result, many people are having to wait over a year before their cases can be begun. Richer people who can afford the minimal cost of £50 can have their cases heard at once, and this naturally leads to much class ill-feeling. (Under the Herbert Act, divorce within three years of marriage is impossible, whether or not the marriage be 'hasty and ill-considered', except in special cases.)

A full report may be seen on request to the Home Intelligence Branch.

10. EVACUATION

The difficulty of evacuating old people and invalids is still an important problem in many places. The authorities will pay the railway fare and billeting allowance for a bedridden person, providing the invalid can find his or her own billet. This a priori is usually an impossible task. A special report on this situation at Portsmouth states that: '233 old people asked to be evacuated in the first half of May; during the same period 62 invalids also registered'.

The evacuation area behind Portsmouth has already reached saturation point, and 'over 2,000 other people are also seeking accommodation in the area'. As the plight of the old people 'is widely known and pitied, it has a depressing effect on public morale'. It is also pointed out that helpless persons impose a heavy responsibility on overburdened wardens.

NO 35: WEDNESDAY 28 MAY TO WEDNESDAY 4 JUNE 1941

GENERAL COMMENTS

1. GENERAL STATE OF CONFIDENCE AND REACTION TO NEWS

In the absence of severe raids, public attention has been largely concentrated on the Mediterranean. As the week went by the likelihood of a withdrawal from Crete was taken more and more for granted. By the time the news of evacuation came, it had been so clearly foreseen that there was little shock – rather a rapidly engendered wave of anger and disappointment. General feeling about the progress of the war is possibly more pessimistic this week than at any period since the fall of France. The cheering events – the sinking of the *Bismarck* and Mr. Roosevelt's speech – took place early in the week and were more than written off by the growing anxiety. There appears to be a 'growing sense of inferiority' in the face of repeated withdrawals, due, it is thought, to German thoroughness, efficiency, and speed.

In its almost unanimous outburst of criticism, the press seems not to have led public opinion but to have followed it. The evacuation of Greece had been accepted as inevitable; but there is strong feeling that the loss of Crete could have been avoided; once again 'our men's heroism' is thought to have been thrown away by lack of equipment, and unjustifiably inadequate preparation.

There is great anxiety about our losses. The German casualty figures are not widely believed, but their statement that eleven British warships have been sunk seems to have had some effect, and it is felt that 'half the tale has not yet been told'.

Three points are outstanding in public criticism of the Battle of Crete:

1. There are stated to be signs of a 'growing distrust of the high direction of our strategy on land and air'. (There is nothing but praise for the work of the Navy in evacuating the troops from the island.) More critical people are asking: 'Who is doing the thinking in this war?' For the

first time there is some criticism of General Wavell. He is said to be learning that 'it is one thing to chivvy the Italians, and another to fight the Germans'.

2. There is a large volume of dissatisfied comment on the lack of air-support for our troops. 'If the Hun could make air-bases in Greece in a month, why couldn't we in Crete in six?' And: 'We actually leave our air-bases for the Jerries to land their planes.' People are asking if our air strength has really increased as much as we had hoped – and been led to believe.

3. To many the gravest aspect of the battle is the success of what has been widely accepted as a dress rehearsal for invasion here. BBC and newspaper efforts to stress the different conditions which would operate against the enemy in Britain have apparently failed to dissipate the anxiety about what paratroops can accomplish as invaders of an island. Indeed, one effect of the episode has been to reawaken discussion of the invasion of Britain. (The invasion pamphlet, incidentally, has met with general approval.)

Other points which are stressed are: the fear that Cyprus will soon share the fate of Crete; that enemy paratroops in British uniforms should be shot when captured; and that more prominence should have been given to the British units in Crete. There has been little criticism of the way the news from Crete has been treated, apart from delays in announcing details of Naval losses, and RAF claims to have 'successfully' bombed aerodromes in Crete without apparently preventing a continuing influx of German troop-carriers. The use of the phrase 'adjusting our positions' as a synonym for 'withdrawal' is also remarked on.

Growing antagonism to Vichy is still reported from many districts. There are expressions of impatience that we do not invade Syria, but are 'waiting for the enemy to get ahead of us again'. This is considered all the more urgent since the fall of Crete, and also because of the belief that 'it won't be long before we are at war with France'. Now that Vichy is 'coming out into the open in support of Hitler', it is considered obvious that the French government must know that an allied victory would mean their complete obliteration.

The shock of the loss of the *Hood* soon passed in relief at the sinking of the *Bismarck*, and the swift release of the news by the Admiralty was appreciated. Among the majority of people the reaction was one of pleasure at a 'fine story of revenge', but the more critical were relieved on hearing at last that we had done something at sea – where we are supposed to be supremely competent – in a supremely competent manner.

Mr. Roosevelt's speech was eagerly awaited, and on the whole has given all the satisfaction that was expected, although a small section of the public hoped for more – even including a declaration of war. The feeling of 'It's all talk with the Americans' seems to be slowly dying, and the RIO South-Western Region reports: 'Previously many people regarded America as something to be seen on the films. Now they are seeing a different sort of America, and it is one which they admire.' It is suggested that the fact that full American help cannot arrive for at least six months is one cheerful consolation for the coming autumn (to which tired workers are already looking ahead with some dismay, as the herald of a tough winter).

2. SOME LONG-TERM TRENDS

The following results of surveys by the British Institute of Public Opinion have been received. They were carried out on samples of 2,200 people, just over a month ago (April 24th, 1941):

(a) 'Do you think that the new Budget spreads the cost of the war fairly?'

	Yes	No	Don't know
Total:	57%	24%	19%
Men:	60%	29%	11%
Women:	56%	19%	25%
Economic groups:			
Higher:	66%	23%	11%
Middle:	65%	24%	11%
Lower:	55%	24%	21%

It will be seen that the degree of concrete opposition remains remarkably constant in all groups, and that the highest degree of ignorance or uncertainty is among women, and the lower income groups (a usual finding on more or less abstract questions).

(b) On the subject of compulsory saving, the figures are similar, but with a higher degree of general approval.

'The new Budget will increase income tax, and return some of the money after the war. Do you approve or disapprove of this idea?'

	Approve	Disapprove	Don't know
Total:	72%	16%	12%
Men:	74%	18%	8%
Women:	71%	14%	15%
Economic groups:			
Higher:	80%	14%	6%
Middle:	72%	18%	10%
Lower:	72%	15%	13%

(c) Do you approve or disapprove of women being compelled to do war work?'

	Approve	Disapprove	Don't know
Total:	72%	23%	5%
Men:	72%	23%	5%
Women	72%	23%	5%

The percentages remained remarkably constant for all groups. The reasons given for disapproval were:

> Woman's place is the home;
> Women are not suited to war work;
> It isn't necessary if industry is organised properly;
> Compulsion is wrong.

(d) On the subject of reprisals, and feeling about the German people, the following results bear out the trend of opinion recorded in the Home Intelligence reports. (These questions were asked shortly before the Kings Norton by-election took place.)

'Would you approve or disapprove if the RAF adopted a policy of bombing the civilian population of Germany?'

	Approve	Disapprove	Don't know
Total:	55%	37%	9%
Men:	56%	37%	7%
Women:	53%	36%	11%

In other groups, similar figures were obtained. The most popular reason for approving was: 'Let the Germans have a taste of it.' Next came the view that it would end the war quickly and break German morale. The main reasons for disapproval were futility, a descent to Hitler's level, and a belief that reprisals were a waste of bombs.

It is pointed out that, at the moment, social pressure (in the form of the press, the cinema news reels, and the National Savings Campaign) favours an approval of reprisals.

A more subtle test of public feeling is the following question:

'Which of the following statements expresses most nearly your personal opinion of Germany and the German people?'

	The Germans are an evil and wicked nation; I hate them all.	Some Germans are not bad, but as a nation Germany is a danger to the world.	Only the German leaders are evil.
Total:	18%	52%	30%
Men:	15%	57%	28%
Women:	20%	49%	31%
Economic groups:			
Higher:	9%	74%	17%
Middle:	14%	58%	28%
Lower:	20%	49%	31%

Both extremes of opinion are most marked in the lower income groups, and least marked in the upper income groups. Many persons interviewed regarded the number of categories offered as inadequate.

3. AIR RAIDS

The recent lull in raids has been taken by many to mean that the Luftwaffe was fully engaged in the Middle East; and it was suggested that if our bombers could not save our own troops in Crete it was an opportune moment for them to 'pour destruction on to Germany's industrial plants and military concentrations'.

Slow recovery from the stunning effect of previous blitzes has been reported from most of the hard-hit towns. But there is also considerable concern that better advantage has not been taken of the respite to press forward with ARP improvements. Local authorities are still sometimes accused of treating each attack as an isolated disaster, and apparently believing that once a town has been devastated it is less likely to be raided again.

Nervousness in areas which are relatively immune from raids is causing some fatigue and 'agricultural inefficiency', because of the habit of sitting up through night alerts, whether a local attack is developing or not. (In Enniskillen, 90 miles from Belfast, there is a regular nightly trek into the surrounding country, although the place has not been bombed at all.) It is suggested that broadcasts intended for towns, stressing the importance of shelters and the advantages of ground-floors, etc., have been taken too literally in rural districts.

4. RUMOUR

There are few new rumours this week. An allegation that 'Peace at any Price' was chalked on walls in Liverpool is still current; but a counter-rumour now adds that the instigators have been discovered and interned. There are stories in both Cardiff and Swansea of plans to make those places 'great naval ports'. The fact that evacuation of school children has been proceeding in both has given colour to the rumours, and there is consequent alarm among some of the inhabitants lest developments should lead to further air attack.

5. CONSCRIPTION IN NORTHERN IRELAND

The decision not to enforce conscription in Ulster has been received with mixed feelings, vehement on both sides. The balance of opinion is considerably in favour of the Government's action in dropping the scheme, even among those who would have liked to see conscription applied if it could have been done 'without bringing a hornet's nest about our ears'. There is, however, some feeling that if the Government was prepared to give way to Mr. de Valera and the Catholics, their views might have been discovered before any question of conscription was raised, in order to avoid what has been described as 'this public exhibition of weakness'.

SPECIAL COMMENTS

6. CLOTHES RATIONING SCHEME

Only preliminary reports have been received so far on the public's reactions to the Clothes Rationing Scheme, which has aroused intense interest. There is 'smug satisfaction' on the part of those who have had enough money and foresight to lay in a good supply already, but in poorer families there is a feeling of slight dismay, though this has been to some extent lessened by a realisation that equality of distribution is the real object of the scheme.

On the whole, the scheme appears to have been favourably received, and to be regarded as 'sensible and businesslike'; people are willing to put up with it as being an essential part of the war effort. There is, however, a feeling that the advantage will tend to lie with those who can afford to buy a garment of good quality which requires the same number of coupons as a cheap article, but which will last twice as long. It is feared that women's stockings will provide the greatest difficulty, as their life is so short in relation to the number of coupons they take. Many people are asking what is going to be done about knitting wool for Service comforts, and the proposal to use the WVS as a distributing agent has caused strong feeling among rival knitting groups.

Three practical problems which have already emerged are as follows:

(a) Members of the forces who are discharged after many years of service have no civilian clothes whatever. For a moderately complete outfit, 161 coupons are needed. Soldiers are already seeking help on this point at Citizens' Advice Bureaux.

(b) Foster parents of evacuated children often cannot buy children's clothing in the country. Yet if they send the ration books to the parents in the towns, postal and other delays may prevent their getting the children's food rations.

(c) Parents of children evacuated to America are, at present, allowed to send up to £10 worth of clothing out of the country. Since these children have no ration books, the parents are asking about the position, and whether any special arrangements are going to be made.

7. FOOD

The food situation shows little change. Prices and distribution, rather than actual shortages, are still matters of general complaint; in some parts there is a growth of feeling against the Ministry of Food. Appeals to Local Food Committees are thought to carry the 'risk of being penalised by the tradesmen' while the Ministry of Food 'takes no notice of the representations of the Local Food Committees'. There is considerable feeling that the Ministry does little to help the mothers of young children, who are too busy to stand in queues to get eggs and other necessities. The reservation of oranges for invalids and young children is held to be the only fair method of distribution. A larger jam ration for families with small children is still much in demand, and it has also been suggested that a special sweet should be packed and sold only for children, on whom the shortage is particularly hard.

The prices of vegetables and fish still cause many complaints; there is some disappointment that these are not to be controlled, since it is considered that 'the rationing and controlling of perishable food stuffs is the only fair solution'. At the same time, the feeling persists that when prices are fixed, the articles disappear and that 'the maximum price at once becomes the minimum price'.

Extra rations for heavy workers are continually asked for. Particular difficulty is still being experienced in providing 'packed lunches' – a constant source of anxiety to the wives. The shortage of eggs in urban districts still causes some bitterness, since they are reported to be quite plentiful in the country; and people are said to be hoarding them when they can get them.

There are reports of queues from many parts of the country; apart from inconvenience, they cause considerable waste of time and contribute to absenteeism. There are also more comments on the difficulties of house-wives and war-workers in contending with evacuees when it comes to shopping for scarce goods, since the latter have leisure to 'corner supplies'.

There are still many vigorous protests about the Ministry of Food's jam-making scheme.

8. EVACUATION

Two factors which may cause difficulty in the event of further large-scale evacuation are reported:

1. HOLIDAY LETTING: In some areas local people are said to be turning out evacuees because they cannot pay the high prices usually charged for accommodation in the holiday season; it is said that 'anyone with a big house and more room than they need is willing to let rooms cheap, rather than have evacuees'. There are still reports of excessive charges being made to evacuees.

2. THE BILLETING OF WAR-WORKERS: There are indications of great alacrity to provide billets for war-workers, as their billeting allowance is said to be higher than that of evacuees. The raising of evacuees' bil-leting allowances is suggested, but there appears to be a tendency for the rents to increase with the allowances.

9. HIGH WAGES FOR JUVENILES

Social workers are disturbed about the high wages given to boys who are replacing men. Where labour is short they can often command far higher wages than those paid to skilled adults before the war. Saving is naturally unattractive to them, and it is felt that a glut of money in a dead-end job will leave them permanently unfitted for normal conditions of work.

10. TRADE

TOBACCO: There is only one report of any improvement in tobacco sup-plies, and several complaints that the position has deteriorated. This is par-ticularly resented since the Tobacco Controller's broadcast, which was regarded as a promise of better supplies.

COAL: Complaints of coal shortages come from 'almost every part of the Midland Region', from the Southern Region and from elsewhere, and there is said to be a prospect of a great shortage of coal in Bradford next winter. The lack of coal is still said to be accounting for a shortage of beer at Reading.

11. FIRE-WATCHING

Dissatisfaction about fire-watching continues. There is still unwillingness to undertake fire-watching duties; and there are reports of shirkers and of shortages of equipment. Compulsory registration of all men between 16 and 60 is advocated as the only reasonable solution. There are still many complaints about houses being left unguarded by people who leave the badly raided towns every night.

12. HORSE RACING

A special report from the RIO Cambridge on public reactions to racing at Newmarket makes the following points:

1. Of 876 private cars and 28 charabancs in the car-park on the second day of the May meeting, the majority had come from considerable distances (e.g. London and the Midlands).

2. The type of person predominating was described as 'the worst variety of well-to-do race-goer'. Although members of the Services were admitted at half price, very few were seen. The number of working men enjoying an afternoon's relaxation was negligible.

3. The number of race-course staff, including jockeys, stewards, gatemen, car attendants, totalisator operators, and groundsmen, as well as police officers and bookies, appeared to be very high indeed.

4. Oranges were on sale from a van, without restriction as to numbers purchased, and above the maximum prices. Quantities of sumptuous foods were on sale at the buffet and snack bar at exorbitant prices.

5. It was suggested that the meeting attracted the kind of crowd likely to cause public resentment, and that it represented a serious wastage of food, man-power, and petrol.

Indignation at the wastage of petrol by visitors to sporting events is reported from other sources.

APPENDIX

The following summary is based on a long report from the Public Relations Branch, St. Andrew's House, Edinburgh.

SCOTTISH MINERS AND THE PRESENT EMERGENCY

GENERAL SITUATION

THE NEED FOR MORE COAL: After the fall of France, the coal mining industry lost a substantial part of its labour force – partly to the Services and partly to munitions industries. The decline in coal production has been relatively greater since these workers included a high proportion of productive workers as against on-cost (maintenance) workers. The result is that there is now a problem of production. Increasing demands from the home market, particularly the expanding munitions industries, have more than compensated for the loss of most of the overseas markets.

The success of the present production drive depends largely upon the active collaboration of the miners. At first sight the prospects of this collaboration are not bright. Absenteeism in Scotland has increased from just under 4% in 1939 to over 5%. Production per man-shift has dropped considerably, and this decline in output, as in the last war, seems to be progressive.

The object of this report is to enquire into the main factors in the decline in production, with particular reference to the miners' attitude to the war and to the present emergency. Some suggestions are made at the end of this report for measures to improve the situation.

FACTORS IN DECLINE IN PRODUCTION

LOSS OF MAN-POWER: The workers lost to the Forces and to the munitions industries are probably the best and most hard-working men in the industry: the younger men who went into the Army, either those who were Territorials or Naval Reservists, or those others who secured dismissal by fair or foul methods and then volunteered for the Services, and the older men who went into munitions or other work.

Many of the older miners, hard and steady workers with families, went over to munitions work in the slack period after June 1940. They were losing one or more shifts a week and decided that the industry could not afford to keep them. Even today, as the figures show, the higher-paid munitions industries are attracting miners away. They find that even though they work many more hours' overtime the work is lighter and better paid than in the mines.

MECHANISATION: In Scotland the majority of mines are mechanised to a greater degree than those in England and Wales. A small increase in absenteeism or the loss of one or two key workers will, therefore, affect production seriously, and will cut down production for the whole shift, thereby cutting down the average output per man-shift.

Another factor which affects production is the shortage of wagons. It is no longer practicable to stock coal at the pithead, as the storage space is generally full of duff (waste). When there are no wagons at the pithead, therefore, this involves a stoppage of work underground. The shortage of wagons is said to be now less serious than it was from New Year until Easter, but there are difficulties of supply of haulage ropes, pit props, etc.

FRICTION BETWEEN MEN AND MANAGEMENTS: There is probably more friction between workers and employers in the coal industry than in any other heavy industry. 'Some of my best and most reasonable managers,' says a general manager, 'are in despair about the obstructive attitude of the men.' On the other hand, miners and miners' leaders say that the owners, always arbitrary, have become even more arbitrary since the outbreak of war.

This lack of good industrial relations is exemplified in two major issues: non-unionism and ARP arrangements.

NON-UNIONISM IN THE MINES: Attempts to set up a system of national and district arbitration in Scotland have been held up for over a year by reluctance on both sides. We understand that steps are now being taken to expedite these arrangements. But a major condition put forward by the miners is that the owners should co-operate with the unions in abolishing non-unionism among mine-workers.

At a meeting in Glasgow in March 1941, the Secretary of Mines pressed both sides to accept an agreement that the owners on the one hand should urge all their workers to join the approved Miners' Union, and that the men on their side should agree to cessation of strikes. It was made clear that the owners should regard refusal to join the union as sufficient reason for dismissal, but this the owners were not prepared to do, though the miners' leaders were prepared to accept the proposed agreement. This was, therefore, left as a recommendation to both sides. This 100% unionism is, of course, a major national issue and in Scotland there is also the special difficulty of the Deputies' Union, which the Scottish Mineworkers wish to amalgamate with themselves.

ARP ARRANGEMENTS: The question of fire-watching is now the subject of detailed discussion between the Regional Commissioner, the owners and the Scottish Mineworkers' Union. In September last the owners agreed that full-time roof spotters should be appointed for each group of pits. Later experience proved throughout the country that this kind of arrangement was not the most effective, and the owners, therefore, offered an alternative scheme whereby roof spotters would take up their positions on receipt of the alert. The miners, however, stood out for the original agreement, and as a result surface workers stopped whenever the alarm sounded. The men appeared to be holding their ground on the principle that an agreement, once arrived at, should not be broken by one side, irrespective of the wisdom of the practice embodied in the agreement. This is borne out by recent conversations with the Deputy Regional Commissioner. When the Industrial Alarm Scheme was explained to both sides, both owners and men admitted that the new scheme was both practicable and desirable.

MINOR DISPUTES INVOLVING STOPPAGES: In the first three months of 1941, 65 disputes took place in Scotland. (The number for the corresponding period of 1940 was 57.) 58 of the 65 occurred in Lanarkshire and West Lothian. Of this total, 30 lasted for only one day, and 26 lasted for two, three or four days.

Reasons for the stoppages were – in 25 cases working conditions – in 21 cases wages and wage rate disputes – in 10 cases dismissal or transfer of workers – and in 9 from miscellaneous causes. Work was resumed on the old conditions in 33 cases, and pending negotiations in 16 cases.

The frequency of these short and apparently meaningless stoppages is an index to the general bad feeling on both sides, particularly in Lanarkshire. Most of the disputes, according to an experienced negotiator, could be settled in a very short time, given effective *local* conciliation machinery. The present practice of pit committees, composed entirely of representatives of the men, affirming their case before the management, tends rather to exacerbate the disagreement. It is therefore the more unfortunate that the incipient moves towards the creation of adequate local arbitrary or conciliation machinery should be held up by failure to agree on preliminary issues.

The answer to this problem, so far as the men are concerned (the owners are equally a problem) demands a closer examination of the miners' attitude to the war and of the effects of the war on the miners' way of life.

MINERS AND THE WAR

The great majority of miners are apparently unaware of the main issue of the war and of the dangerous situation the country is in. Mining villages are self-contained, closed communities, largely inaccessible to outside influences, and this isolation produces the same general unawareness of the war as is to be detected in some rural villages and small country towns. 90% of their talk is 'shop', 5% is sport, and the remainder is devoted to social affairs, including the war.

More important is the deep-seated hostility to the management or 'owners', and the suspicion of all the latter's recommendations. 'The owners wouldn't be for the war if it didn't pay them' is a common remark, and many of the younger and relatively irresponsible men are much more bitter against the 'class enemy' than against the Nazis.

Most important of all is the general ignorance of the present and prospective shortage of coal. After a recent heavy raid, five hundred miner-ARP wardens in Fife remained on duty in the morning after the all-night warning. They were paid compensation for the loss of their work on the early shift. To avoid the considerable drop in coal production which this causes, instructions were given to each Chief Warden that in the case of future all-night warnings 50% of their miner-wardens were to be released for work in the pits. This caused considerable discontent among the miner-wardens. The ARP sub-controller, a local editor who knows the miners very well, then went round every ARP station in his area explaining that it was not a case of the County Council trying to avoid paying 10/- a man; nor had it anything to do with pressure by the coal owners to maintain their profits. It was done entirely to avoid an abrupt drop in coal production owing to miners being on air-raid duties.

This explanation was new to the miners. *They did not consider the coal situation to be serious.* The articulate ones pointed out that since most of the overseas markets had been lost there was surely no need for extra production. They had had bitter experience in the past of producing so much coal that they rendered themselves partly or wholly unemployed. But when the situation was fully explained to them they agreed with a good grace to accept the situation. The sub-controller explained to us that the miners as a whole do not read the newspapers; in any case the coal emergency has been relatively little featured in the press. On the other hand, they would attend well-conducted meetings, even in the summer, if they thought that besides such meetings a general effort was being made to improve conditions in the industry.

EFFECTS OF WAR – SHORTAGE OF ESSENTIAL FOODS: The most important material factor in the present situation is the shortage of essential or customary food-stuffs. After the shift the miner needs and demands a good square meal and a few hours' rest; during the shift he needs sandwiches of meat, cheese or something equally nourishing, and washed down by sweet tea. He is denied these things to a great extent by the meat and sugar ration, and up till recently by the small allowance of cheese. The effects are disastrous. It is suggested, therefore, that pit canteens should be issued with special supplies of cooked meat to enable them to serve meat sandwiches to miners going down the pit.

ABSENTEEISM AND ALLEGED SLACKING: So far as can be gathered from miners and managers, roughly about 20% to 25% of the miners practice regular absenteeism. The remainder work regularly, though on rare occasions a shift will ca'canny deliberately, to force the management's hand in a dispute.

The war-time increase in absenteeism is probably due almost entirely to the greater strain put on the miners, coupled with the drop in the consumption of essential or customary food-stuffs. As one miners' leader pointed out, the miner used to work less in summer than in winter, because of the drop in demand. This gave him the opportunity to recover his energies in the slack period. But for the last two or three years, according to this leader, there has been little, if any, drop in summer work. Now the effects are beginning to tell.

LACK OF SPENDING OPPORTUNITY: In recent months most miners have been earning relatively steady wages; but the shortage of supplies, the Purchase Tax, etc., have made it more difficult to find anything on which to spend any extra money there may be. This situation has added to the small proportion of miners who, once they have made a certain wage, don't see the point of working any more. This is also bound up with stories about miners who stop work when their wages reach the point at which they become liable to income tax. Most of those in a position to know hold that there is not very much in these stories. Many miners who have absented themselves without apparent good reason (perhaps, unknown to themselves, malnutrition) give their reluctance to pay income tax as a good excuse.

MINERS' LEADERS AND THE ESSENTIAL WORK ORDER: Although the majority of miners may be unaware of the present emergency, their leaders are fully alive to the dangers of the situation. A delegate conference met on 8th and 9th May to discuss the Order. The conference opened with the intention of pressing for a National Joint Board to discuss wages and other conditions, a demand for the abolition of non-unionism in the mines, and a minimum weekly wage. But the delegates, being informed of the present situation, agreed to leave it to the Executive to accept the Essential Work Order on the promise that national negotiations respecting wages should be entered into at once with the support of the Government.

The working of the Order will not be easy, however. Three districts, including Scotland, voted against the majority decision at the conference, and unless some agreement on a guaranteed *weekly* wage, satisfactory to the miners, is arrived at, it is unlikely that the Essential Work Order will be applied without friction, particularly in Scotland. The example of the dockers' £4.2s.6d is frequently cited. But there the resemblance ends. 'Don't imagine,' we were warned, 'that the Government can impose a date for the acceptance of the Essential Work Order and get away with it as they did with the Glasgow dockers and their guaranteed week scheme.'

Informal discussions in Fife show that some leading coal companies are beginning to think seriously of a *minimum* weekly wage with a special war bonus sufficient to attract back to the mines workers who are now earning good money in munitions. Generous treatment of the miners in the present situation would not only get these essential workers back without trouble; it would also, in the opinion of the miners' leaders, go far to alter the miners' habitual attitude of hostility and end suspicion of the owners and the Government.

COMMUNIST INFLUENCE: Communists and near-communists, acting on broadly political or revolutionary grounds, are working hard and with success at exploiting grievances in the mines. Not only are they successful in confirming and rendering articulate the miners' distrust of the owner class and in spreading a general cynicism about the war. They are also successful in confirming and encouraging the miners' existing habits of demonstration stoppages so as to hamper production, particularly in the districts of Cowdenbeath in Fife, and Blantyre and Shotts in Lanarkshire. The Lanarkshire Miners' Union was the only important working-class body in Scotland to send delegates to the People's Convention. At the recent annual conference of the 26 Scottish Mineworkers' Federation a cleverly worded resolution praising the 'Soviet Union's policy of peace' was passed by 37,000 to 12,000 votes in spite of opposition from the chair and platform.

In the mines these men do not act as communists. They are genuinely, in almost every case, miners with a grievance; their communism being a clear-cut set of dogma which give an impressive and inspiring background to the particular grievance. They act, not only against the miners' leaders. In the name of working-class unity and 100% trade unionism, they encourage stoppages condemned by the union and withhold particulars of local disputes from the miners' agent.

It would be a mistake to attribute the miners' attitude of hostility to the owners and indifference to the war to communist machinations. On the contrary, these disruptive elements are relatively more effective among the miners than among other industrial workers precisely because wages, working conditions and industrial relations give them more scope. Many miners are still unaware of the present emergency, and the great part they can play in the country's defence. They are, therefore, liable to influence by the quasi-defeatism and cynicism of communist propaganda, the more so because the condition of the industry up till recently has been slack.

RECOMMENDATIONS

NEED FOR ADEQUATE CONCILIATION MACHINERY, FOOD SUPPLY ETC: Better industrial relations, an adequate *local* machinery of conciliation, and a guaranteed *weekly* wage are necessary material and institutional conditions of improvement. If the three parties, Government, owners and men, can operate the Essential Work Order harmoniously, this will effect the necessary improvements.

An adequate food supply is needed also to reduce absenteeism and the general exasperation which fosters minor disputes. It would help matters if the owners could assist in the institution of new pit canteens and with any special issue that may be found possible, of meat etc. for sandwiches to be sold to workers going underground.

FAVOURABLE OPPORTUNITY FOR PROPAGANDA AND PUBLICITY: Several influential miners' leaders have expressed the hope that effective publicity will be undertaken by the Government on positive lines. 'We will welcome any assistance you can give us,' said one leader, 'to bring home to these younger irresponsible chaps why they've got to get down to winning this war. But you'll need to have a good straightforward case. The miners have no use for mere exhortation.'

We think it would be unwise to embark on any loud or widely advertised campaign of propaganda. The general method should be to secure the collaboration of some leaders among the owners and the men for a quiet and intensive effort at persuasion. It has been suggested to us in various quarters that the Secretary of State for Scotland commands the confidence of the miners and that he and Mr. Joseph Westwood, MP, Under-Secretary of State, could play a very influential part in securing the goodwill of the miners' leaders in a well-planned campaign of persuasion.

The general policy should be to attempt to identify the miners with the struggle against the common enemy. 'It must be explained that the extra output required has nothing to do with the owners' profit. Tell the miners that the *country* is in danger and that their best efforts are needed to save their sons and brothers on active service from the grave danger they are in.' This is the gist of the advice given us.

We are reluctant to set down anything that would look like a cut-and-dried plan of action, because, in our view, we should proceed tentatively, taking local circumstances into account. Careful preliminary work would be necessary in each district.

Meetings are the best method of getting the miners' attention. The speakers should, as far as possible, be known to the men, and the co-operation of local Coal Production and Pit Production Committees, and in particular local miners' leaders, should, therefore, be sought.

These meetings should be held at the pithead or in the village in the open air, preferably with a loudspeaker van. Indoor meetings might also be successful, especially if preceded in previous weeks by Ministry of Information films.

We are already co-operating with miners' welfare clubs in the showing of films, and many of the Ministry's films usefully subserve the purpose of the proposed campaign. But it would be worthwhile making other films, and we should be prepared to make suggestions for suitable subjects.

In several mining districts War Commentary meetings have already been instituted, and those are being extended as rapidly as possible. They are held usually in cinemas on Sunday evenings and provide an informed exposition of the progress of the war. In Kilmarnock and Hamilton they are attended by between 1,500 and 2,000 people each week.

In industrial areas the organiser of informal discussion groups, which have been successful in combatting communist influence, is co-operating with voluntary workers and is preparing to extend these discussions to the mining areas.

Leaflets by themselves will arouse little interest. But leaflets distributed at effective local meetings would be read and marked. One leaflet should state clearly the facts of the situation. Others might follow the model of the leaflet 'Workers under Nazi Gangsters', e.g. 'Miners under Nazi Bosses'.

The co-operation of the newspapers (including local weeklies) which circulate in the mining areas, and of the BBC for feature items and the handling of news to help in this effort, should also be sought. The model generally should be the quiet and unobtrusive work done on the Industrial Areas Campaign during the past few months.

PUBLIC RELATIONS BRANCH
ST. ANDREW'S HOUSE
EDINBURGH
21 May 1941

NO 36: WEDNESDAY 4 JUNE TO WEDNESDAY 11 JUNE 1941

GENERAL COMMENTS

1. GENERAL STATE OF CONFIDENCE AND REACTION TO NEWS

(NB: No reports on the state of public feeling have been received *since* the Parliamentary debate on Crete.)

The most striking feature of public feeling during the week has been a decline in expressed confidence in the Government – both national and local. The trigger which fired off this feeling was the evacuation of Crete, and the events leading up to it; but the loss of confidence does not confine itself altogether to those responsible for actual Service operations. On the home front, and in the sphere of local government, there are many who say that more should be done than is being done. There are, too, reports of an increasing separation between the leaders and the led. In particular, there is a growing number of people who say that speeches, however good, are not enough. Nevertheless, all available evidence goes to show that the country as a whole is still steadily behind the Prime Minister's leadership, and determined to 'see the war through'.

On the subject of the Battle of Crete, public feeling has changed since last week. Then, although there was no surprise, and consequently no shock at the news of evacuation, people were still too close to events to apportion blame in detail. Now there is anger as well as apprehension; the main line of criticism is that 'we were seven months in the island; what were we doing? Why were our airfields not properly defended?' (It is noticeable that this criticism is voiced in almost identical words from district after district.) More particularly, there are requests that fullest information should at once be given as to why it was impossible to render our airfields useless to the Germans before the evacuation.

The view seems to be widely held that evacuation was forced on us 'through lack of foresight and initiative, rather than the superiority of the enemy'. Acute concern is expressed lest we are far behind Germany in our actual war technique. The alleged inadequacy of our preparations to defend Crete is compared with 'the rapid re-conditioning of the Greek airfields and their effectiveness when in German hands'. A feeling exists that 'someone has blundered, and that air co-operation with the other Services requires careful consideration and reorganisation'. It is also said that the separation of Army and Air Force Commands was much to blame for what is described as 'the disaster'.

There is now some dissatisfaction at the manner in which the news of the Battle of Crete was given out. 'Communiques have been found irritating, particularly the excuses, and the minimising of Crete's importance.' The public is said to be 'increasingly critical of optimistic official spokesmen who have persistently under-estimated our dangers'.

In the earlier part of the week the anger and distress over Crete were frequently coupled with expressions of fear lest we should be 'too late again' in Syria. There is great satisfaction that we have taken the initiative. Anti-French feeling, which was rising sharply, is held in suspense until it is known whether there will be strong opposition from the French Colonial troops. Hopes are expressed that many may desert to the side of de Gaulle.

Markedly different reactions to our reverse in Crete are found among two special sections of the community:

1. The more mentally energetic people tend to think that our national energies are not yet fully engaged in the war effort. They call for a

drive in production, and for strengthened appeals to the patriotism of the workers.

2. Factory workers, housewives, and those with relatives who have been in the various evacuations etc. are said to take less and less interest in war news of any kind. 'It is becoming increasingly difficult to arouse them to any urgency, or to re-stimulate them to effort. The effects of appeals, slogans, broadcasts, headlines, is becoming slighter.' There is evidence too that among them 'there is growing the idea that we are fundamentally inefficient, as opposed to Germany's efficiency'.

Talk on the lines of 'What have we got to lose if Hitler comes?' is reported less among the working classes than among the middle class and the small capitalist. It has been suggested that the BBC should again devote some of its propaganda talks to those who still feel that a Fascist regime 'would safeguard a small bank balance'. In this connection, there is much praise for W. J. Brown's recent broadcasts.

Invasion is again a very live subject of discussion. In mid-May, according to Mass Observation figures, only 19% of a London sample expected invasion. This figure had risen to 39% by the beginning of June, and there are indications that the figure is still rising. Unshaken confidence remains, however, in the strength and courage of the RAF; those who believe invasion is coming, but take an optimistic view of the outcome, base their faith on the result of the Battle of Britain last September. 'We beat them then; we can do it again as long as we've got the airfields.' On the other hand RIO Cambridge reports 'growing lack of confidence in the ability of the Army to withstand invasion', and specifies considerable concern over alleged apathy and deficiencies in the Home Guard.

After dying down, the interest in Hess has reawakened, apparently because the public statement has not been given. Disappointment is expressed that not even a photograph of him in England has yet been published, and various rumours are once more circulating. Some capital is being made of this by the Communist Party, and on the part of the general public there appears to be a certain amount of feeling that 'the Hess business has been bungled'.

2. THE TREATMENT OF NEWS

The public takes strong exception to certain methods of treating news, and to particular phrases which are apt to occur in official communiques and the utterances of Government spokesmen:

1. 'Adjusting our positions' is taken as synonymous with retreat.

2. 'Retiring to prepared positions' is interpreted as retiring to positions which will shortly have to be vacated.

3. 'Strategic withdrawal' is regarded as retreat with the abandonment of equipment.

4. 'We will fight to the death', or 'we will hold at all costs' is held to imply probable withdrawal with great sacrifice.

5. 'The enemy is sustaining heavy casualties' is taken to mean that in spite of this he is advancing.

6. The fact that our bombs produce fires, columns of smoke, and the upset of lorries is now fully realised by the public, and the constant reports of these trivia produce irritation and cynical comment rather than satisfaction.

7. There is doubt as to the meaning of the word 'successful'. Thus, during the battle of Crete there were frequent references to the 'successful' bombing of Crete aerodromes. The public asks why it was possible for the Germans to continue using these successfully bombed bases.

8. The constant repetition, in slightly different guises, of a single piece of good news – in an apparent attempt to offset it against a larger volume of bad news – causes great irritation. In particular, the many and various accounts of the sinking of the *Bismarck* which 'covered' the bad news from Crete caused considerable feeling.

3. RUMOUR

Rumours this week have not been numerous.

There is a belief that balloon barrages are an indication to the enemy of the presence of a target town, and may, therefore, be more danger than they are worth. In support of this it is suggested that Leeds, 'the only sizeable town without a barrage', is one of the few towns of any consequence which have not been very heavily raided. Minor rumours deal with the imminence of various new forms of rationing, particularly soap. Haw-Haw is said to have promised 'a serious raid on London this week'. Ipswich and Southend have both been reported 'about to be evacuated entirely'.

SPECIAL COMMENTS

4. CLOTHES RATIONING SCHEME

General reactions to the scheme continue favourable. The only criticism of the scheme as a whole comes from Northern Ireland, where it seems to be strongly opposed on general grounds, and also because it is feared that it will have an unfavourable effect on trade with Eire.

There has been considerable praise for the way in which the secret was kept, and for the fact that the announcement was made on a Sunday. The scheme has given people something of immediate personal interest on which to focus their attention, and they seem to have been glad of an opportunity to exercise humour, ingenuity and speculation.

This general expression of approval has not prevented a tendency for people to think of themselves as belonging to some category which merits special concessions. It is widely considered, for example, that some allowance should be made in connection with certain occupations which make a heavy demand on clothes, or which require special clothing. Nurses are particularly mentioned. Overalls are thought to be too highly rated, as they are required in a great number of occupations. Doctors and medical students working in hospitals have to provide themselves with white coats, and in many factories and shops overalls are issued to employees free, or at much reduced rates; yet it is claimed that in all these cases the use of overalls does not mean that the wearers need to buy fewer clothes than other people. It is particularly hoped that the WVS will not be supplied with uniforms coupon-free, unless all occupational clothing and civil uniforms are also to be obtained in the same way.

It is asked that special concessions should be granted for trousseaux, layettes, maternity wear, mourning, clothes lost in the laundry, and particularly for children's shoes which wear out, or are grown out of, so rapidly.

One point, it is believed, will cause great hardship. If a woman can afford to buy ready-made clothes for an infant she can do so without coupons; but if she makes them herself, while expecting the child, she must use her own coupons to buy wool, flannel and other materials.

The question of second-hand clothes is felt to be full of difficulties and to present opportunities for evasion and dishonesty. It is feared that stocks of new clothes which remain unsold in the shops will be dumped on second-hand shops, after being sprayed with a little scent or camphor, and sold without coupons.

It is said that many poor people never buy new clothes at all. After a time the second-hand stocks may become exhausted owing to people making their clothes last longer, and the poor who rely on second-hand shops will suffer.

Several methods of evading the payment of coupons are mentioned as being possible, or already in operation, particularly in connection with the fact that soft furnishing material by the yard needs coupons, but that made-up curtains (a term that can be very loosely interpreted) do not. A scarf needs two coupons, but with a few stitches it can be transformed into a hat and sold coupon-free.

Many difficulties are prophesied for the shops, and in particular it is felt that present stocks of light summer clothes will not be much in demand as women will save their coupons for winter buying; as a result the shops will be very short of coupons with which to obtain their winter stocks.

A considerable amount of the knitting that is done in air-raid shelters, wardens' posts, ambulance depots etc., has the effect of calming nerves and occupies the many idle hours which have to be passed in strained and uncomfortable circumstances, often in a bad light. It is suggested that if the supply of knitting wool is cut, the greater part of this soothing and useful activity will be at an end.

5. FOOD

QUEUES: The question of growing food queues is reported to be causing much 'unrest and discontent'. Considerable evidence has been received to suggest that queues are becoming more frequent, and more widespread, and that they are being formed for a far greater number of commodities than before. There are queues for saccharine, cakes, sweets, biscuits, eggs, sausages, cooked meats, dog and cat food, and tobacco, and for rationed goods such as butter and meat. In one place they are said to start at seven in the morning.

There is a feeling that 'food queues are unnecessary, and reflect Government and other inefficiency'; some people express 'disgust' at seeing them, as a 'reflection on national prosperity'; indeed queues seem to cause more annoyance to those who see them than to those who stand in them. For a number of people, mainly women, standing in a queue has become a 'war-time sport', and there are still reports of people who join queues without knowing what they are for.

Besides the general reduction of supplies, various causes for queues are suggested:

1. Increased population (evacuees, billeted troops, etc.) with no pro-rata increase of supplies. It is suggested, for example, that in Cambridge, 'where there are well over 5,000 official evacuees alone', shops are still only receiving what was their quota in March 1940.

2. Diminution of supplies generally available to public because of early morning purchases by evacuees, leisured women, etc.

3. The habit of some shop-keepers not to open till a long queue has formed and then to do all the day's business in a few hours and close early to let the assistants go home.

The main result of queues is that only those who have plenty of time on their hands derive any benefit from them, while war-workers, mothers with babies, and the old and infirm are unable to compete. A typical case is that of a bus-conductress who works 8 to 10 hours a day and has her housework to do, and asks how she is to feed her children.

Absenteeism is another widespread result, and it is stated that 'full-time war-workers and part-time Civil Defence workers are apparently so discouraged by their catering difficulties that some of them have had to resort to housekeeping as a full-time job and give up their war work'.

OTHER FOOD DIFFICULTIES: The demand for an extension of rationing continues. People are still hoping that if any more oranges become available, they should be distributed to children through the milk-in-schools scheme, and to hospitals. There are some questions as to how it is that, if shipping space really is so precious, parcels of food from America can be sent to individuals in this country; it is asked why this food should not be pooled, and it is pointed out that most of this is sent to people who can already afford to buy luxury foods.

There is still a strong feeling that agricultural and farm labourers are unfairly placed as regards food. It is thought that 'they suffer from isolation, are denied assistance by employers, and are yet expected to do a day's work on the minimum amount of food'. They are not, moreover, in a position to avail themselves of canteens or communal feeding.

Complaints continue that canteens catering for the troops are often 'full of chocolate and slab cake'. The legend of the Army wasting masses of food dies hard, and it is pointed out that soldiers get four square meals a day. Children are still considered to have first claim on any available sweet-stuffs.

It is said that in many country districts the cafes and tea shops are full of soldiers, even in the mornings, consuming the supplies of cake, sweets and cigarettes intended for the civilian population; and it has even been suggested that such places should be put out of bounds for the Forces till late afternoon so that the public, who do not have access to canteens, may have better opportunities.

6. EVACUATION

There is a good deal of comment this week on mothers taking their children back to badly bombed places like Bristol and Liverpool soon after they have been evacuated. It is asked 'why public money should be spent on taking them to safety when they are allowed to return for no good reason'. Although there are many cases in which the children themselves want to return, because the country is so quiet (and even 'because of the sweet shortage'), the mothers are generally blamed.

Overcrowding is reported from many places – among them Oxfordshire, Berkshire, and Canvey Island. Bombed-out people from Plymouth complain of bad conditions in halls where they are accommodated, and huts in the neighbourhood of Petersfield in which refugees are living have been severely criticised. The situation is said to call for 'a more comprehensive

and constructive treatment of the evacuee question'. Complaints about scabies continue to be widely reported from one Region.

The question is again raised of large country houses which have either no
evacuees or too few. The position of the billeting officer in country districts
is said to be a peculiarly difficult one. To do his work properly he should be
an established resident and know the locality intimately; yet if he uses his
powers of compulsion he becomes extremely unpopular and is faced with
the problem of 'living it down afterwards'.

There are still reports, particularly from Blackpool, of excessive charges
being made to evacuees and workers now that the holiday season has
begun, and of evacuees being turned out to make way for people who are
prepared to pay more for the rooms.

7. COAL

It is suggested that the bad summer is accentuating complaints about
the coal situation; reports of shortage continue, particularly from the
Birmingham district, where coal is to be rationed, from Rugby where
the position is described as serious, and from the north of Scotland. In one
Region it is said to be 'a long time indeed since a grumble has been so sustained and widespread'. The shortage is described as being particularly
puzzling for people in the Midlands where there are so many pits.

It is claimed that thousands of miners need to be brought back into the
Yorkshire coalfields to make good the present shortage and build up stocks.
Absenteeism is said to be causing an 'avoidable loss of 2½ million tons a
year' in Yorkshire alone.

One report says that miners are excusing absenteeism on the grounds
that their meat ration is entirely inadequate to give the necessary stamina.

8. LABOUR

There seems to be a feeling among middle-aged women, and particularly
among those of the professional classes, that there is no demand for their
services; they have great difficulty in getting employment. The impression
is that the Labour Exchange officials are more interested in their birth certificates than in any qualifications they may have. At the same time there is
a great shortage of female staff in the large stores, and it has been sug-

gested that the solution of the labour problem for middle-aged women might be found if it could be represented to them that it is a form of war-work to take the place of younger and more active women who are leaving to make munitions.

The feeling persists that we are not making sufficient use of foreign refugees, particularly professional people.

9. THE RAT SITUATION

In spite of the fact that there is little public interest or concern on the subject of rats there is some evidence that the rat situation is fairly serious. Rat catchers are not reserved. Before the war, there were very few of them, and their number is decreasing. Local authorities have great difficulty in dealing with the rat problem; in Bristol, for example, they have appealed to the Regional Commissioner for help. It is suggested from several areas that administrative action rather than publicity is needed for dealing with the main aspects of the rat situation, and that, until local authorities are in a position to take effective action, publicity will do little to help. Rat weeks are sometimes described as excuses for doing nothing during the remaining fifty-one weeks of the year. At the same time, there are some requests from rural areas for more guidance for farmers. The situation with regard to rat-destroying agents is complicated because red squill, the standard rat poison, comes from Algiers and is now unobtainable.

In urban areas subjected to heavy raids, the number of rats seen about has increased. High explosive bombs kill rats, whereas fires due to incendiaries tend to drive them to new homes, so that the increase may be apparent rather than real. At Bristol, the situation has been serious because of a large amount of contaminated food which was not worth salvaging from damaged warehouses; these stores have provided both food and breeding grounds. In several urban areas, an increase in mice is reported, and this is attributed to blitzing of mouse-infested houses.

In rural areas, rats continue to be a serious problem, particularly rick infestations, though there is little evidence of an increase in numbers. In some parts, a decrease is reported since the recent drive. There are fears that new rural food stores may soon become infested.

NO 37: WEDNESDAY 11 JUNE TO WEDNESDAY 18 JUNE 1941

GENERAL COMMENTS

1. GENERAL STATE OF CONFIDENCE AND REACTION TO NEWS

This week, public feeling in the country is at a slightly more cheerful and optimistic level. The factors making for this improvement appear to be:

1. A measure of satisfaction at the Prime Minister's explanation of the evacuation of Crete.

2. The advance into Syria.

3. The continued absence of heavy raids in weather which does not prevent our raiding Germany vigorously.

4. Increased hopes of American aid.

5. The absence of any obvious impending disaster.

6. An apparently trivial but nevertheless important factor in determining public feeling – the belated arrival of summer.

On the other side of the picture are the following:

1. Continued criticism of lack of news and of its presentation.

2. A hang-over of doubts about Crete, and associated with this a desire that there should be strengthening changes in direction on the Home Front.

3. A fear that it is the French rather than the Germans whom we are beating in Syria.

4. An even stronger fear that our industrial organisation is far from perfect.

5. Uneasiness over the Battle of the Atlantic – in particular a desire for some information about U-boat losses, to counteract Roosevelt's statement about our shipping losses.

Public opinion is still considerably disturbed over Crete; but where, last week, criticism was detailed and outspoken, it has now turned into uneasiness, embracing many aspects of our war effort. It is felt that the Prime Minister, in the debate on Crete, answered most of the specific charges against our conduct of the campaign as fully as the circumstances permitted. But there is a tendency to regard the debate on Crete as more of a personal triumph for the Prime Minister than a reassurance to the public; the reply to Mr. Hore-Belisha is thought in some quarters to be severe, if not harsh.

While belief and trust in Mr. Churchill as a man and a leader remain firm, this week there has been more adverse comment on his choice of advisers than at any time since he became Prime Minister. The 'Fight to a finish' declaration before the allied statesmen at St. James's Palace, though well received as a whole, brought back to public memory French and British statesmen pledging themselves last year that there would be 'no separate peace'.

The Syrian campaign, with the initiative entirely on our side, continues to be a source of great satisfaction; although in accordance with the present temper of the people, it is now accompanied by considerable foreboding. 'Where are the Germans?' 'We are only doing well because we are up against the French.' 'It will be a different story when we meet the Germans...' The conviction that 'they are everywhere more efficient than we are' is still considerable.

People have become afraid of believing good news.

The more thoughtful sections of the public regret that hopes of swiftly over-running Syria were fostered too early in the campaign, both by the press and the BBC. The news of stiffened resistance and heavy fighting in some sectors has caused anti-French feeling to rise again, after a short period when the main attitude was 'wait-and-see'. It is now said that 'no steps we could take to remove the menace of the French Fleet would be criticised'.

The absence of serious raiding, through the period of the full moon, was accepted, early in the week, as a sign of worse to come in some other direction, though a welcome relief in itself; later, the belief grew that the explanation was in our favour. The fact that night after night we brought down several bombers out of a relatively small number, scattered over the country, was taken as an indication that 'they are finding their losses too heavy to come in force', and 'we have the night bombing in check, though it can never wholly be stopped'. By many people this lull is regarded as 'a saving up for invasion', and Eire is once more the place mentioned as the most probable scene of attack. This view is usually connected with the recent bombing of Dublin, which occasioned such surprise, both in Ireland and this country, that opinion about it is only now crystallising – to the effect that it was a German try-out of Irish morale and resistance: 'If the Irish take this lying down, they know they can walk in.' In connection with the invasion of England, criticism of Home Guard equipment and personnel continues.

The conviction that all is not well with our war effort finds expression in demands for more equality of sacrifice everywhere. Signs of privilege, due to class or money, however small, are immediately resented; and any evidence of industrial mismanagement takes on additional symbolic importance.

2. PUBLIC FEELING ABOUT AMERICA

Over the past month, there has been a marked increase in the popularity of America, coupled with a growing belief in her ability and determination to fulful her promises. At the time of Mr. Cordell Hull's recent speech on the attitude of the United States to Vichy ('what we want are deeds and not words'), it was reported by RIOs that this comment embodied Britain's feeling towards America. While there is still much criticism and anxiety about the slowness of American aid, they now record a new appreciation, particularly in industrial centres, of the inevitable time-lag in gearing up to war-production. The astuteness of President Roosevelt 'in persuading the people to push him towards the path he wishes to take' is generally realised, and there is firm expectation that America will ultimately send us men as well as munitions. Though disappointment was voiced in some quarters over the President's recent speech, because it did not contain a declaration of war, other sections of the public express the view that America is at present more useful as a non-belligerent, neutralising Japan. The President, whose personal popularity here is said to stand second to Mr. Churchill's, is trusted to keep America 'on the borderline' until her deliveries of war material to this country have become so great that she can satisfy her needs as a belligerent without depriving us of vital supplies. It has been suggested that films showing the growing weight of American help, and others showing the American people at home, 'free of the idiosyncrasies of cinema types', would greatly enhance her prestige in this country and give 'much needed encouragement'. Broadcasters on America, such as Raymond Gram Swing and Alistair Cooke, are said to have an increasingly appreciative audience, and it is thought that more such American commentaries would be welcome. Ministry speakers report that, at the moment, America is the subject which produces much the largest volume of questions from audiences.

Reports of labour troubles and sabotage in US factories are viewed with considerable concern as 'Hitler's answer to Roosevelt'; and the President's prompt use of the military to deal with strikes was greatly appreciated. It is feared that accounts in British newspapers of slackness and incompetence in our own production drive may have an adverse effect on American goodwill.

3. PRESENTATION OF NEWS

A special study by Listener Research on the reaction of the public to the news confirms most of the points made in past Home Intelligence Reports. Twelve statements were submitted to a panel of Honorary Listener Correspondents, and they were asked to say whether each statement represented the opinion of the majority, the minority, or none of their contacts. The results were as follows:

Statements	Majority	Minority	None
Important news is not given quickly enough.	59%	29%	10%
Important news is too often withheld by the authorities.	58%	33%	7%
There is too much toning down of reverses and boosting of successes in news bulletins.	53%	37%	8%
The BBC Overseas News in English is better than the news bulletins in the Home Service.	48%	35%	11%
Whoever is responsible for releasing news seems to think we 'can't take it if it is bad'.	38%	42%	18%
News bulletins contain too many trivial items.	18%	50%	32%
News bulletins are often badly arranged: the news most wanted sometimes comes too late in the bulletin.	15%	45%	39%
Listening to Haw-Haw is increasing, but this is not caused by any dissatisfaction with BBC news.	10%	28%	58%
Some news readers let their personal feelings colour the way they read the news. This is objectionable.	6%	33%	61%
Dissatisfaction with BBC News is causing an increase in listening to Haw-Haw.	5%	20%	74%
Too many words and phrases which the ordinary listener cannot understand are used in news bulletins.	3%	26%	70%
Sometimes news bulletins contain deliberate lies.	3%	22%	74%

(Where figures do not add up horizontally to 100%, this is due to small percentages of Correspondents not replying.)

In addition, Correspondents were asked to say whether confidence in the news was decreasing, increasing, or unchanged. The result was:

Decreasing	Unchanged	Increasing
12%	75%	12%

These figures are less informative than the previous ones, since they indicate the extent of change of opinion rather than the level of opinion. Thus, among the 'unchanged' group there may be many who think well or ill of the news, but who have merely held their particular opinions over an unspecified time.

The high degree of dissatisfaction with the news, exemplified in the first table, shows that the criticisms reported in the Home Intelligence reports are not confined to the vocal section of the community. The withholding of news and the toning down of news are the outstanding complaints. Criticism of arrangement and the inclusion of trivialities are large minority opinions. The phraseology of the bulletins and the tone of announcers are little criticised. The wisdom of not treating circumstantial reports of an increase in Haw-Haw listening as evidence of a genuine increase is once again exemplified.

This week, our own material follows the familiar lines:

1. Irritation at the disproportionate time given in BBC bulletins to trivial events.

2. Appreciative comments on the 'conciseness and balance of the Overseas news, particularly to Canada and North America'.

3. Criticism of reiteration of our successes long after they have occurred.

4. A desire for brief unpadded bulletins when there is little news.

5. Objection to the minimising of our losses; in particular, there is feeling about the port of Benghazi, which now apparently 'needs so much attention from our bombers', although it was 'said to be unimportant when we gave it up'.

On the subject of the *Scharnhorst* and *Gneisenau*, there is some speculation about how badly they have been damaged, and requests for further news – 'as in its absence, there is doubt as to the accuracy of our bombing'. News of Hess is still awaited.

4. PUBLIC FEELING ABOUT THE SERVICES

While confidence in the Navy and the RAF remain at a high level, there is a tendency to single out the Army as a scapegoat for public criticism. The reasons for this appear to be:

1. The absence of spectacular Army successes against the Germans.
2. A belief that the casualty rate is relatively lower in the Army than among the other Services.
3. The presence of large numbers of troops at home who do not share the civilians' dangerous duties in civil defence and fire-watching.
4. Certain doubts about the efficiency of the Army as compared with the other Services – in particular, doubts about the Home Guard in some areas as an effective agent against trained invasion shock-troops.
5. Complaints of delays in the payment of the allowances to wives. The remedy, a visit to the Assistance Board, is considered to have a certain stigma for a woman whose husband has always earned a good wage. Where deductions are unexpectedly made, appeals to the Regimental Paymasters are said to involve long delays.
6. As long as he remains in England the soldier is thought to have few worries and no shortages. It is still resented that he is able to get chocolate, cake and cigarettes in Service canteens, and that he should still be seen buying these and other commodities in the shops.

The relative unpopularity of the Army is said to be shown by the high proportion of conscripted men who express preference for the Navy or RAF; it is alleged that many of those who express preference for the Army are in reserved occupations.

5. RUMOUR

There are few rumours this week which have more than local currency. Haw-Haw is said to have warned Eire that the bombing of Dublin will be repeated if men from the south of Ireland continue to join the British forces. Hess is reported to have brought over a proposal to limit the night bombing on both sides. He is also said never to have been here at all, and to have been sent back to Germany, having failed to persuade the British Government to declare war on Russia. Russia is the subject of contradictory rumours – that she has either agreed or refused to let Germany take over the Ukraine.

SPECIAL COMMENTS

6. FOOD

EGG DISTRIBUTION SCHEME: The proposed scheme is having a mixed reception. There has long been a demand from a large section of the public that eggs should be rationed. The urban population approves the scheme in general; the criticism comes largely from the country districts, particularly from people who have made some arrangement whereby they are already obtaining sufficient supplies. There are suggestions that a large 'subterranean trade' has been taking place. It is suggested that a 'wholesale massacre of fowls' will ensue from the order that flocks of more than 12 birds will be subject to the scheme; it is pointed out that the small poultry-keeper sells to friends any eggs he does not consume, and that this type of producer is unwilling to fill up forms to dispose of a couple of dozen eggs a week. There is still resentment at motorists touring the countryside in search of eggs, and certain people are said to be buying fowls from poultry-keepers who will continue to look after the birds and will pass on the eggs to the new owners. It is suggested that 'if the regulations are obeyed, a *fresh* egg will no longer be obtainable'. There are some reports that shops are discouraging people from registering as 'they do not expect to have the eggs to supply them with'.

QUEUES: Reports of queues continue to be received from many parts of the country, and there is no evidence of any decrease. Sheffield gets the prize for the earliest queue, starting at 6 a.m.; and shredded suet is now added to the list of commodities for which people queue up. It is suggested that certain shops regard a queue as a good advertisement. Much police time is said to be occupied with the control of queues, and the extra travelling done by shoppers has led in some districts to congestion in the transport system. Women come into Leeds on the workmen's trains, with a cheap workman's ticket, so as to attack the shops in good time.

It is frequently pointed out that it is the idle who profit, while the industrious suffer. The difficulties of married workers in getting their shopping done are once more stressed, as the shops shut at 6 and by Saturday afternoon most unrationed goods are sold. Great appreciation has been expressed at the action of a Deptford store which stays open late on Saturdays and reserves large stocks for factory workers, which they can obtain only by producing a chit signed by the factory to say that they are employed on essential war work and cannot shop at normal times. It is suggested that, while such a scheme is open to some abuse, it could be properly organised and extended on a nation-wide basis.

GENERAL FOOD MATTERS: Complaints of uneven distribution continue, particularly from the 'refugee-ridden districts'. In the protected areas of Scotland the shortage is said to be aggravated by the influx of families of Service personnel and civilian workers, who, with more money than the 'natives', clean up the shops.

The price of fish and vegetables continues to cause indignation. There is still talk of the heavy worker, both agricultural and industrial, not getting sufficient food. In the Derbyshire industrial area the heavy workers are said to be obliged to eat the greater part of the rationed food in the home, with the result that it is the children who go without. For the first time, there are definite suggestions that the very poor may not be getting enough to eat, partly on account of high prices and partly because of the gradual disappearance of ordinary commodities. 'Even the price of a meal at a Communal Feeding Centre is beyond their means.'

There is still a steady demand that sweets should be reserved for children, and that oranges should be kept for hospitals, nursing mothers and children.

Criticism of the jam-making scheme continues unabated and on familiar lines; it is now suggested that while the scheme, applied to the larger towns, possesses real merit, jam-making 'is to country folk, in humble homes and castles alike, a great annual event involving the pride of the kitchen and the services of all the household'.

The shortage of beer is reported from Yorkshire, Berkshire and elsewhere, and there is talk among licensees of some kind of registration of regular customers.

7. INDUSTRY

From many parts of the country, there is evidence of talk among the public about alleged slackness in factories engaged on war work, and especially on aircraft production. This talk appears to be generally believed, and is said to be having a serious effect on public confidence. The criticism takes two forms:

1. ALLEGATIONS OF ADMINISTRATIVE MISMANAGEMENT: There are many reports of workers being kept idle for days at a time, and being told to 'kill time' because of shortage of material. The workers as well as the public complain of this. Thus, in an aircraft factory near Leeds, workers are said to have been given a week's holiday without pay when, 'in the men's opinion', there was plenty of material to keep the factory busy. Another case, which is reported to have caused 'strong feeling in the district', is that of a precision tool factory at Brighton, working on Admiralty contracts, where wholesale dismissals of men and women have taken place following the completion of a contract. Strong criticisms are alleged for allowing a fully equipped factory and staff to be without work at a time when there is an urgent need for tools.

   There is said to be a real need for 'propaganda work in the factories telling men who are temporarily slack, why it is so, in order that harmful discussion should be stopped'.

2. ALLEGATIONS OF SLACKING: Complementarily, it is suggested that the workers themselves are apathetic, and that this arises from an insufficient sense of the desperate urgency of the struggle. Other suggested causes of this half-heartedness are the 'evidence which workers see of time wasted in many factories; of the petrol waste; the outcry about cigarette shortage; the chocolates in Army canteens, with few for the children; the idle troops who could share fire-watching and fire-fighting with civilians who have to do this as well as their ordinary work; and able-bodied people in safe areas who should be working'.

   It seems increasingly to be felt that there is some 'real defect in industrial organisation', that 'there are glaring social injustices' and that there is no real equality of sacrifice. It is even stated that the conscription of labour as a whole would be welcome as being more effective and also more fair.

8. CLOTHES RATIONING SCHEME

There are few new aspects of the public reaction to clothes rationing. The chief topics of anxiety are still socks, stockings, knitting wool, baby-wool, specialised occupational clothing, non-military uniforms, clothes for expectant mothers and growing children, the coupon value of handkerchiefs and collars, and clothes for the Merchant Navy. It is hoped that something can be done to check the unofficial statements appearing in the press since they lead the public to expect concessions (like coupon-free summer dresses) which do not always materialise.

From Northern Ireland comes the suggestion that people are 'flocking to neutral Eire to buy without coupons', that smuggling on a large scale is taking place, and that 'worried British Revenue Authorities say it will be the biggest racket Ireland has known for years'.

9. PETROL

The effects of the new petrol restrictions are beginning to be felt. Some doctors in Leeds are now said to be making their rounds on foot, as requests for supplementary rations are not always met. In parts of the Nottingham district it is said to be 'impossible to carry on important work in connection with local government administration because adequate supplies are not available'.

There are many demands for a considerable cut in the ordinary basic ration, if not its total abolition, and for the restoration of the Supplementary Allowance. It is pointed out that commercial firms, doing useful work like removals, food distribution, etc., have had their ration cut while the allowance for pleasure motoring continues uncut. People observe that there always seems to be plenty of petrol for taking parties to race-meetings, and also for long journeys in search of eggs and other food.

10. TRADE AND COMMERCE

TOBACCO: The tobacco shortage is still mentioned in many reports as 'causing resentment and concern'. In particular, there is feeling about uneven distribution; for example, there are said to be plenty of cigarettes at

Brighton, but a great shortage at Tunbridge Wells; the opportunities of the Forces for buying both at canteens and at shops are also still resented. From Orkney come complaints that supplies are very short and that only the wrong kind of tobacco is obtainable; seafaring communities require hard cake and thick twist – not expensive mixtures.

COAL: 'Considerable dissatisfaction' about the coal situation is still reported, chiefly from the Midland and South-Western Regions and from London. Householders are said to be unable to get enough coal to do any stocking and in some cases they cannot got enough for current needs; coal queues are reported in the poorer parts of Birmingham. The public does not yet seem to understand 'why there should be any real shortage, especially since we have lost our foreign market'. The situation in North-West Scotland, which has been reported throughout the winter as being bad, is said to be due to:

(1) Public indifference in the early stages.

(2) Lack of convenient and adequate storage dumps.

(3) Transport difficulties and costs.

11. EVACUATION

The question of evacuation and particularly the difficulties connected with billeting are still causing considerable uneasiness. It is hoped to present detailed evidence on this subject next week.

12. INSTRUCTIONS TO LOCAL AUTHORITIES

From a number of sources, there are bitter complaints that local authorities still receive insufficient warning of new Government legislation. As a result, immediately after press or radio announcements, Local government officials and enquiry bureaux are besieged by members of the public, before these officials have received any instructions from Government departments. The public have to be turned away, and inevitably blame the local authorities for incompetence. A practical suggestion which has been made is that the BBC should devote a short but regular period once a week (not a time of peak listening) to announcements specially for local authorities, so that they may be forewarned of impending circulars.

NO 38: WEDNESDAY 18 JUNE TO WEDNESDAY 25 JUNE 1941

GENERAL COMMENTS

1. GENERAL STATE OF CONFIDENCE AND REACTION TO NEWS

In the earlier part of the week there was again a slight rise in general confidence. The factors making for greater cheerfulness were, in the main, the same as those of last week: the freedom from heavy raids, increased hope of American aid, and the absence of any obvious impending disaster. Added to these there was the fresh tale of RAF successes (in daylight sweeps, night raids on Germany, and against enemy night bombers) and the fact that the announcement of radiolocation was taken by many people as a proof of our growing superiority in the air. In this connection, the RIO North-Western Region reports that 'press prominence given to radiolocation, coinciding with Mr. Bevin's statement about the conquest of night bombing and the lull in raids, has produced an unfortunate reaction. There is a widespread tendency to infer that night bombing is now likely to disappear. It is said that relief in some cases is as great as if people had been told the war was over. This attitude is felt to be bad for morale, as optimism is likely to deteriorate when the next heavy night raids are experienced.' Though the attack on the Sollum area was considered a failure in some quarters 'in spite of official reassuring statements', RIOs report that on the whole 'the operations in the Western Desert caused satisfaction'; and our withdrawal at their close 'was not accompanied by cynical comment such as has marked the reception of this kind of news in the past; this is probably because we took the initiative in attacking the enemy'. It is also reported that 'the allied progress in Syria is contributing to the rise in confidence, though there is considerable anxiety that we should hurry'. Yet another factor making for cheerfulness was 'President Roosevelt's action in closing the German Consulates and agencies in the USA; this is welcomed as further evidence that America means business.'

On the other hand, there were still 'some residues of the Cretan agitation, chiefly in the form of a conviction that we do not appear able to beat the

Germans on land'; distrust in our Higher Command; grave concern about the state of industry; and in the background a fear summed up by the feeling, 'Hitler is saving up for something.' A new cause of anxiety this week was 'the signing of the pact between Germany and Turkey, which was regarded as a further serious diplomatic set-back'. There has been comment on the Government's apparent anxiety to find every excuse for the Turks, and to 'play down the significance of the pact'. But on balance, before the announcement of the German attack on Russia, it was said that morale was 'rather higher than it had been for some time'.

The reception of the news that Germany and Russia were at war has been reported as 'jubilant, with a strong under-current of caution', and as having a further 'tonic effect on the morale of those who had previously shown signs of war-weariness and apathy'.

Reactions so far seem mainly to be:

(1) A belief that Germany has been forced into this attack, since the time chosen – before the harvest – is generally regarded as unpropitious.

(2) A feeling of relief that Hitler, engaged in the East, 'will not have much time for us, and will lose equipment and men, while we strengthen our resources'.

(3) Satisfaction at what is called 'a final demonstration to the world of the complete worthlessness of any pact into which Germany may enter'. It is added that 'the public have been told many times that no agreement with the present rulers of Germany will ever be possible, but the latest development has brought that fact home with a force which no other means could have achieved'.

The disinclination to believe in good news, recorded last week, seems to be responsible for a certain amount of vague foreboding which has been expressed. Actual reasons given for regretting the news were:

(1) An unprovoked attack must be taken as 'a mark of German strength'. Hitler's 'cheek' in attacking Russia while we are still unconquered is commented on.

(2) 'Hitler has always known what he was doing up till now.'

(3) Our position would be adversely affected if the German onslaught were successful, 'since the enemy would then have much larger resources to draw on, which would do much to offset American aid to Britain'.

There is little confidence in Russia's military capacity, which is judged by her performance against Finland, and a large section of the public feel that the most that can be hoped for is that she will be able to hold out long enough to give us some real advantage. It is accepted by many people that the true object of the attack is not the Ukraine and its riches, but Hitler's desire 'to make 100% sure that he would not be stabbed in the back while attacking England'. There is eagerness that we ourselves should, in some way, 'strike now, while the Nazis are tied up, before it is too late for us to strike at all'. Unless we do this, it is feared we may have to 'sit down for defence when we are still more savagely attacked'.

Mr. Churchill's pledge, on the part of the country, to give aid to Russia has been 'generally accepted as both a practical and logical move', and it is felt that he 'discharged a difficult task well when he spoke of our support for Russia, after he had for many years voiced his contempt, and at times his abhorrence, for the Bolshevik regime'. His speech was greatly admired, and has more than offset the recent fear that his touch was not quite as sure as it had been.

2. PUBLIC OPINION ON RUSSIA BEFORE THE NAZI ATTACK

Two months ago, the British Institute of Public Opinion put the following question to a sample of 2,200 people:
'Would you like to see Great Britain and Soviet Russia being more friendly to each other?'

The results were as follows:

	Yes	No	Don't know
Total:	70%	13%	17%
Men:	76%	13%	11%
Women:	63%	14%	23%
Economic groups:			
Higher:	61%	26%	13%
Middle:	69%	15%	16%
Lower:	70%	12%	18%

The question is admittedly so worded that it carries a slight bias in favour of friendship with Russia. However an analysis of the spontaneous comments shows that definite reasons were usually advanced for the opinions held:

44% of spontaneous comments followed these lines:
'It would help us...Russia is powerful...The more friends we have, the better...Better for us than against us...It would be one in the eye for Hitler.' Frank self-interest is the keynote of this group.

19% followed these lines:
'It's our own fault it hasn't happened before...They're progressive, or go-ahead, or Socialist.'
These are the rather more ideological comments.

18% were antipathetic:
'Don't like Russia...Don't trust them...They were never any good...No truck with communism.'

19% were miscellaneous noncommittal comments:
'Don't know anything about Russia...I'm not interested in politics... I would agree if they kept communism out of it.'

3. PUBLIC FEELING ON INVASION PROSPECTS

There is still much discussion of possible points for many landings. In the South-Western Region, fear is reported that the overcrowding of the coastal districts with evacuees and summer visitors might considerably hamper military efforts in the event of invasion from the west. In Wales anxiety about our defences is again expressed, especially in connection with the defence of aerodromes. It is thought also that there may be 'successful land-ings from Eire by air-borne forces strong enough to establish themselves'; and that invasion of Wales from Eire is not unlikely. In this connection, although Eire's desire for neutrality seems to have been strengthened by the bombing of Dublin, the feeling that 'the time has come for action' appears to be increasing both in England and among pro-British elements in Eire. 'Unless we can be sure the Hun won't get the ports, we should take them now'...'If you knew how we (Southern Irish) despise you for not tak-ing them!' A report, quoted by RIO Northern Ireland, says, 'There is a grow-ing opinion that America could save us by occupying the Eire ports, as Eire would not (and could not) fight her own kith and kin.'

4. SYRIA

There is now some disappointment that our progress is not 'overwhelming and rapid, in the grand German manner'. Two theories are widely held to explain its slowness:

(1) That Britain is not hitting as hard as she might for fear of offending French susceptibilities.

(2) That the strength of the Vichy resistance is greater than had been expected.

The daily repetition of the news that we were nearing Damascus resulted in 'people becoming a little impatient, with no capacity for enjoying the final occupation of the city'. The statements that 'some captured French soldiers were not aware of German penetration, and did not know against whom they were fighting' is held to be a reflection on our propaganda.

5. PRESENTATION OF NEWS

'Pungent criticism about the nature and quality of official news is still prevalent,' but there is 'some appreciation of the lack of "frills" of which there were formerly many complaints'. The public is as insistent as ever on hearing 'the whole truth as far as war news is concerned', in so far as this will not 'give the enemy any actual advantage'. It is frequently reported that public confidence mounts 'when plain facts are plainly expressed, even though the news may not be wholly encouraging'. There are again comments that the 10 a.m. European news bulletins in English are much better than the Home News bulletins. From those who listen to our foreign broadcasts, there are suggestions that the compilers of the Home News have much to learn from the 'Les Français parlent aux Français' service.

Vernon Bartlett's Sunday *Postscript* (standing very high in popularity compared with those of Mr. Herbert and others) has been eclipsed in general appreciation by Mr. W. J. Brown's *Postscript* on the Polish slave in Germany. This is described as 'the most consummate piece of defensive oratory yet heard'.

6. THE BATTLE OF THE ATLANTIC

The Prime Minister's insistence that the debate on shipping must be held in secret was considered 'a bad omen', coming at a time when public confidence in our war effort as a whole was still 'considerably shaken by our losses in Crete'. Much anxiety was felt, especially after the postponement of the announcement, lest our Atlantic losses for the month should prove to be appalling. Due partly to the fact that they were lower than was feared, and partly, it is thought, to the general improvement in spirits, there is now some belief that secrecy was necessary 'because of the increasing success of our counter-measures'.

7. WAR-WEARINESS

Reports of apathy in industry continue to come in, but there are also reports of some apathy among other sections of the general public. 'Indifference, and reluctance to discuss the war', are alleged. 'People are not listening so closely to BBC bulletins, and confess to being fed up with eternal specula-tion'...'In some districts indifference to war news is associated with a growing fear that the war will last much longer than earlier estimates indicated'...'This lack of interest, and the absenteeism and slackening of effort which is widely thought to prevail in factories' seem, to some people, 'to indicate a degree of war-weariness' in the whole country. It is added, however, that 'it may be attributable in part to the excessively long hours of work, and the need for recreation and holidays'.

8. RUMOUR

Russian soldiers are already reported to have landed at Dover; and from Wales come rumours of 'suspicious characters in British uniforms, who speak poor English and wear no distinctive badges'. It is also said that 'Jehovah's Witnesses' are suspected of encouraging conscientious object-ors, and are on the staff of the Ministry of Food at Colwyn Bay.

SPECIAL COMMENTS

9. BILLETING DIFFICULTIES

Although billeting systems are much the same in all areas, they operate less efficiently in some places than in others. One of the chief difficulties is the frequent reluctance of the billeting officer (who may be the Town Clerk, the Sanitary Inspector, or some other local official) to enforce his powers. If he himself lives in the neighbourhood, he may fear the annoyance of other residents, particularly if they have 'influence' which may prejudice his position with the local council. If the council is a supine body, he may hesitate to take steps in which it may not give him adequate support.

The responsibility for the reception of evacuees is vested in local authorities, to whom the Ministry of Health has delegated its powers in this matter. Complaints about billeting must, therefore, be made to local authorities, and only if they remain inactive can a direct appeal be made to the Ministry of Health. But sometimes when such an appeal has been made, the Ministry is said to have been reluctant to override the decision of the local authority.

Although there is a fairly general feeling 'that billeting should not be left in the hands of the local agents' (this is very strongly felt in some areas), there is no agreement as to what might be a better arrangement. Some think the power to appoint billeting officers should be transferred from local authorities to the county councils. Others think that they should be responsible to, and appointed by, a Government department.

It is frequently suggested that the owners of large country houses are shirking their billeting responsibilities. This is said to be the 'cause of perpetual minor grievances in many districts'. Stories are told of billeting officers who say: 'If this goes on, I shall have to start on some of the big houses.' In another case the officer is alleged to have discouraged a man who was anxious to take evacuees by telling him that, in doing so, he would be 'letting down' owners of other large houses in the neighbourhood.

Complaints, however, are by no means confined to large houses. Enquiries in one area suggest that 'there is far more persistent difficulty and resentment regarding the 5–7 bedroom type of house, where the occupant is a person of some local consequence whom the billeting officer or local council do not wish to offend'. A reliable report states that, in one area, out of twelve billeting officers, 'only two would face up to the occupant who was unwilling to accept evacuees'.

The following is a summary of complaints mentioned in recent reports from the London, Eastern, Southern, South-Western, Welsh and North-Western Regions, and also from Northern Ireland, and other sources. Districts mentioned by name include: Cornwall, Cheshire, Lancashire,

Cumberland, mid-Wales, North Bucks, the Thames Valley, Horsham, Welwyn and Budleigh Salterton.

1. Many large country houses are already used as hospitals, hostels etc., or are earmarked for future use as such by one of the Services or the Red Cross, etc. In one area the bigger houses are said to have been reserved for the Air Ministry for 18 months and the bulk of them are still unoccupied.

2. In some cases old houses have inadequate water and sanitary arrangements for the number of available rooms.

3. Householders, though obliged to provide water and sanitary arrangements, are not required to give cooking facilities and may prevent the local authority from putting in cooking stoves and heating arrangements, etc., by objecting to structural alterations. There are said to be cases of evacuees being 'frozen out of country houses through lack of comfort'.

4. The hostility of owners who do not refuse evacuees, but who make them feel unwelcome. The case is quoted of a house in the Thames Valley which 'has repeatedly had evacuees pumped into it; they have regularly retired, beaten by the unsympathetic attitude of the owner and his wife'.

5. The difficulty of accommodating children in houses where an elderly couple have been looked after by two or three maids, and who are now reduced to making do with one. Cases are known of old servants threatening to leave, and actually doing so, on the arrival of evacuees.

6. Problems also arise from the billeting of war-workers; e.g. the shift system, which dislocates the domestic time-table of a household.

7. Responsibility is sometimes said to be evaded by securing exemption on medical grounds.

8. Some householders have taken the precaution of filling the house with relatives and friends, not necessarily from bombed areas, so as to leave no room for evacuees.

9. The isolated position of some houses, remote from urban amenities, such as fried fish shops, cinemas, and public houses, is such that many evacuees will not remain in them.

10. EVACUATION

There are still reports, particularly from the Bristol Region, of evacuated children being brought back to blitzed areas. Various reasons are suggested:

1. A wave of optimism caused by the radiolocation announcement, and the resulting confidence, felt among certain sections of the public, that night bombing will have been overcome by the winter.
2. The extra cost of keeping children's clothes mended and repaired.
3. The distance separating children and parents – particularly in the case of Bristol evacuees in Cornwall.
4. Children's homesickness, or local billeting maladjustments.

11. FOOD

BLACK MARKETS AND ILLICIT TRADING: Although the existence of black markets seems to be taken for granted by a large section of the population, evidence that they do exist is scanty and unreliable; and it is thought that talk about them is in most cases little more than an emotional outlet, and that they are a scapegoat for difficulties in obtaining goods. Few people, however, seem to doubt that illicit trading is extensively practiced, and there is a 'strong undercurrent of public resentment at all manifestations of the food racket'. This discontent tends to link up with feeling about the war effort as a whole. It is pointed out that 'people are ready to accept the "guns before butter" system of rationing, but object to being swindled either by profiteers or by those who can pay any price'. This feeling is expressed by the remark 'We all know you can get plenty of butter in the West End, if you like to pay for it': but criticism is somewhat vitiated by the 'fact that so many people appear to have no moral scruples if the chance to get a little extra comes their way'.

There is said to be a good deal of trafficking in eggs by motorists visiting outlying farms, and one case is mentioned of a dealer getting 60 dozen eggs a week in this way, by paying a slightly higher price. There appears to be a certain amount of 'bartering'. People in agricultural and rural districts feel certain shortages, and have little opportunity to shop in the towns, and they are glad to barter eggs or pigs or rabbits for tinned produce which may be unobtainable in the shops. The practice of illegal slaughter is said to 'obtain throughout the Region', according to the Bristol RIO, the meat being distributed to various butchers.

A certain amount of illegal retail trading is admitted, and is excused on the grounds that if a shop-keeper were to adhere strictly to the law he would go out of business. Thus, a greengrocer maintains that, unless he is prepared to pay enhanced prices at Spitalfields and Stratford, he could not supply his customers. In Manchester recently, on the day when the maximum price for gooseberries was announced as 5d per lb, the greengrocers complained that they could only buy them in the market at 1/8d. There is some feeling that the wholesalers are often responsible, but that the retailer is blamed.

The public appear to welcome any signs of action being taken to stop illicit trading and to punish profiteering. Great satisfaction is said to have been expressed in Leeds at the magistrate's decision in sending a man and wife to prison for a month for profiteering in eggs and jam, and there is a wide hope that Lord Woolton will be able to carry out his promise to stop food racketeering.

There is thought to be a certain amount of trafficking in cigarettes. People ask how it is that hotels often have such large supplies. Some tobacco wholesalers are said to be selling all their supplies retail, and a man on duty at a shelter, largely used by Jews from Bow and Poplar, said that he was offered practically anything he wanted, including 500 Players.

EGG DISTRIBUTION SCHEME: Criticism still tends to come more from the country than from the town, though in both it is from the 'small man'. The fact that a shop must have a minimum of 50 registered customers before it can sell eggs is taken in some quarters as 'further evidence of Lord Woolton's supposed animosity towards small traders'. People with a small flock of hens are said to resent the scheme 'as being a kind of encroachment on their personal liberty'; and to regard the taking of their eggs as being 'like taking the cabbages out of their garden'.

There have been complaints of misleading information in the press. An article in the *Daily Sketch* of June 14th is said to have given the impression that people need not register for eggs, as the scheme had been shelved.

QUEUES: The position appears to be unchanged. Queues for unrationed goods, mostly cooked meats, sausages, tinned goods, biscuits and cigarettes, and even green-groceries, are still reported from a number of towns. There continues to be strong criticism against the responsible authorities for not taking sufficient account of the 'influx and deflux of population caused by war emergencies'. It is suggested that the billeting of Service men and women has not been allowed for in the population figures. Shops are still blamed for encouraging queues for advertising purposes.

GENERAL FOOD MATTERS: There appears to be no lessening of the demand from dockers and other heavy manual workers for an increase in rations. Miners are still said to be very 'dissatisfied with the amount of foodstuffs available for taking down the pits', and railway men 'continue to grumble because so little is available for sandwich meals which they need when out working long journeys, etc.'.

There is a feeling that the sedentary worker does not need as much as the physical worker.

The beer shortage appears to be on the increase, and consternation is reported at the closing of public-houses in some towns for certain periods. In Rugby three out of four 'pubs' are said to close one night a week. It is suggested that, psychologically, this shortage appears to have more effect upon the factory workers than any naval disasters; they 'interpret this shortage to mean that we are in a worse position than is being disclosed'. Shortage of coal, labour and transport are suggested as causes of the beer shortage.

Before the new announcement about sugar for home jam-making, there was still widespread dissatisfaction about the jam scheme, and most housewives were said to be 'saving their sugar so that they will be able to make their own jam with their own fruit'; those without sugar were said to be preparing to bottle their fruit. This possibility, and the dubious prospects of the fruit harvest, might, it was feared, make something of a fiasco of the scheme. There was also the feeling that much fruit would be wasted because of transport difficulties and the 'impossibility of running to the jam centre with each few pounds of fruit as it ripens'.

BRITISH RESTAURANTS: There is continued praise for British Restaurants, and a demand for even more of them. It is hoped that they will be better advertised because it is often very difficult to find them. There is some talk of local authorities, with suitable buildings commandeered, and anxious to begin, being held up by endless correspondence and delay until given the permission to start. The question is raised as to how British Restaurants can get enough supplies to have a meat meal every day, while some factory canteens are only allowed enough for one meat meal a week.

12. COAL

That the coal shortage is causing less comment this week is said to be due to the warm weather, but it continues to be reported from several places and is still said to 'agitate every part of the Midland Region'. It is continually urged that there are not sufficient stocks to enable people to lay in supplies for the winter. There are still protests against 'draining man-power from the mining industry for munitions work and the armed forces, especially in view of the serious coal shortage'. The miners themselves are said to be 'very upset at the use being made of the figures for absenteeism, pointing out that this is common in every industry and that it is unfair to make use of this against men who are as patriotic as any'. The attendance bonus proposal is reported to be meeting with strong criticism from the miners and their organisation, and to be regarded as a slur on them.

13. TRANSPORT AND HOLIDAYS

Feeling about so-called 'joy-riding' seems to be growing, and the Government's appeal to people not to travel long distances during the holidays has led to increased resentment at the amount of pleasure motoring, particularly in connection with the recent race-meeting at Newmarket. In the Midland Region, 'holidays at home' is said to be 'honoured more in the breach than the observance'. At one holiday resort resentment is apparently felt at so many young people taking more than two weeks' holiday and using their cars so much. Strong criticism has been made lately of people who drive out of Bristol every night to sleep in the country, thus taking advantage of those who have no cars or who are too patriotic to use petrol in this way. This contrasts with the reports of crowded conditions in trains and buses and the 'inadequate transport facilities for war-workers'. Criticism continues of people who motor round the countryside looking for eggs.

Resentment at the 'bad and selfish driving' which is said to 'characterise the officers and men of the Army' has not been altogether allayed by the recent War Office statement on the subject. In a 'heavily militarised region', where 'few people have not had unpleasant adventures owing to the rottenness of khaki-clad drivers', the statement is described as 'the sort of thing which discredits official "hand-outs"'.

APPENDIX

HOME INTELLIGENCE SPECIAL REPORT
ON CONDITIONS IN PORTSMOUTH

From May 19th–24th, 1941, post-blitz conditions were studied.

A list of persons interviewed is appended. As the time was short it was not possible to check all statements made or make a full study of official figures. The report therefore gives an impression rather than a comprehensive account of conditions in Portsmouth.

This report has been examined by the Regional Information Officer, Southern Region, and has been submitted by him confidentially to the Regional Commissioner's Office. Many helpful criticisms from both these sources have been embodied.

I DESCRIPTION OF CITY AND DAMAGE

(1) Portsmouth city, which includes the pleasure resort of Southsea, is built on a peninsular, bounded by the Isle of Wight, Hayling Island and Gosport, with the Portsdown hills to the north. The main route out of the city runs over these hills. Portsmouth continues to be an important naval base, the main activity being refitting and repair.

(2) The city has had alerts by day and night almost continuously since August 1940 and 58 bombing attacks in which about 800 people have been killed. It is said that the Isle of Wight is used as a pointer for incoming and outgoing enemy aircraft, so there is a lot of gunfire. The barrage is reported to be of such magnitude that it is impossible to sleep but our visit coincided with the first lull since the Autumn and we did not hear a shot. There have been 3 major blitzes, in January, March and April. Most of the damage in the first was caused by fires which numbered over a thousand. Many of these could not be tackled as the water supply failed; gas and electricity services were also interrupted. The dockyards were not attacked in this raid but have suffered since. High explosives and landmines caused most of the damage in the last two blitzes and there was again interruption of the utility services, but not for long. The scale of the damage is enormous, particularly in the south and in the poor Portsea area by the docks. Both the main shopping centres have been destroyed as well as many public buildings, including the Guildhall. Portsmouth is proud of its reputation as 'No. 1 Blitzed Town'.

II THE LOCAL AUTHORITY

The local authority appears more progressive than in some other towns. With one or two exceptions, we found them not only conscious of the major problems but willing to admit short-comings. There is a genuine wish to co-operate both internally and externally, and the personnel is good. One of the main reasons given for this happy state of affairs is that most of the officials have now faced the fact that the city is 'broke'. This has relieved the tension which existed when they were still trying to balance their budget and has also impressed them with the need for area organisation. They are fortunate in having an energetic Lord Mayor and Lady Mayoress, an exceptionally efficient Chief Constable and excellent co-operation for voluntary agencies and the naval authorities. We felt, however, that many of those in authority were inclined to be rather too paternal in their attitude to the public, instead of encouraging them to help themselves.

III INFORMATION SERVICES

(1) The Secretary of the Information Committee welcomed the enquiry and made useful suggestions. As Deputy Chief Warden, he is in personal touch with people of importance and has first-hand knowledge of local conditions. The Committee itself is held in poor repute by various other officials, who say it does nothing, and that many of its members are people who should not be trusted with important information. Closer co-operation between this Committee and the CAB and Welfare Committees would seem desirable, though possibly hard to achieve. The Ministry itself is said to be on good relations with the local authorities, in spite of the Local Information Committee.

(2) A new Emergency Information Service is being organised. The Secretary is the Chief Librarian who is working night and day to get his plans in working order. He is making every attempt to follow Regional instructions. He will be responsible for circulating posters and notices and the loudspeaker vans and is hoping to get voluntary helpers to accompany them to give oral instructions and advice. There will be branch offices in each of the six libraries.

(3) The CAB is one of the features of Portsmouth. Under the vigorous if somewhat autocratic direction of Miss Kelly, CBE, JP, who is also Hon. Secretary of the Council of Social Service, it has been operating effectively since the beginning of the war. The outstanding features are the registers of addresses of all casualties and homeless people who have passed through Rest Centres, and the arrangements for friendly visiting. The registers meet an important need, for much distress is obviated when people are able to get news of relatives in hospital and those who have moved away. The system is simple and might well be copied in other places. The friendly visiting of people who have been rehoused or discharged from hospital also helps their recovery. It has been noticed before that people in the semi-shocked condition that follows a bad raid need more than anything to feel that they matter as individuals and that they still have a place in the community. A criticism of this organisation is that it is over-centralised. A branch office is, however, soon being opened on the outskirts of the city

and other offices in neighbouring country towns are being started. It is hoped that permission will be given to advertise in the buses.

IV EMERGENCY ORGANISATION

(1) The planning of Rest Centres, known here as Emergency Centres, appears to have been good and there is excellent co-operation between the Public Assistance authority and the voluntary agencies. The PA arrange transport to collect people from the scenes of incidents and, at the same time, arrange for the opening of appropriate Centres. Two potential dangers are the apparent dependency on the telephone as a means of communication and the insufficient number of centres. At present, there are 20 centres with room for only 3,500 people or 5,000 'at a pinch'. Twice as many are contemplated but suitable buildings are scarce. The area organisation of voluntary helpers, a scheme evolved by Miss Kelly's agency, has proved of great value. Each area has a supervisor and is capable of functioning as a self-governing unit in an emergency. Among other tasks, they staff the Emergency Centres. After the work is done, a full report is made and problems are discussed in committee. The Centres have been cleared after each incident with commendable speed, reaching a peak of 1,000 in one day after the last blitz.

(2) Feeding in Emergency Centres has sustained a high standard, the Lord Mayor insisting on the provision of roast joints every day, where possible. Catering has been complicated by people drifting away from the Centres without notifying the Supervisors and by others, not living in the Centres, turning up for meals. While feeding in Emergency Centres was good we were told there had been a breakdown in supplies for firemen and demolition workers drafted in from other districts. Many of these had no food for as long as 24 hours. It appears that available WVS canteens were not summoned.

(3) The sick in Centres are attended by Red Cross nurses. The difficulty of getting ambulances to take patients from the Centres to hospital is reported, also the fact that ambulances cannot be used to take the infirm beyond the city boundary, 'a piece of red tape which causes unnecessary

suffering'. Another complaint made was that an infirm person cannot be admitted to hospital unless they become a casualty. The MOH says his greatest problem is the clearance of EMS hospitals which become 'cluttered up with chronics'. We were also told that civilian sick got insufficient attention and there was some criticism of doctors, many of whom are said to leave the city at night. All these things have a bad effect on morale as they are not only painful to the sufferers but distressing to the public who must stand helplessly by.

(4) No description of emergency organisation would be complete without mention of the Navy, which has risen to the occasion in every emergency. Naval ratings are detailed to help with the rough work in Emergency Centres, others are drafted to the scene of incidents where they assist in rescue and demolition and do such odd jobs as minding babies and carrying suitcases. They have been of immense help in repairing electric cables, etc.

(5) Provisions against fire have now been improved with the installation of water tanks throughout the city. The digging of pits has been advocated as water is said to be only a few feet below the surface. This would ensure an endless supply but it may be technically impossible. If so, we feel the fact should be announced, in order to allay criticism.

V   PRESSING PROBLEMS

A.   FLIGHT TO SAFETY

(1) TREKKING: By 6 p.m., an observer will see that all traffic is moving northwards. The movement begins at about 3.30 p.m. and continues until dusk; at the peak period, there are long queues at every bus stop along the route. The people are making for the bridge on the main road out of Portsmouth, in order to sleep in the northern suburbs, the surrounding hills, or in towns and villages within a radius of 20 miles. On one night after a bad blitz, it was estimated that 90,000 left the city and now, after a raid-free period, there are said to be still some 30,000 trekkers, half of them being men. This figure takes no account of other thousands who move from the city centre to the outskirts but do not cross the bridge. It is interesting to note that most of the trekkers do not get far enough away to escape the

terrific noise of the bombardment and that many who sleep in unprotected halls in what should be regarded still as target areas are less safe than they would be in shelters in the heart of the city. But they feel safer because there is open space around them and something other than houses for the bombs to hit. They crowd into houses and halls in the villages, into shelters and holes in the hills, into stables and hop-pickers' huts. Some sleep under hedges and some in the vehicles that drove them out. On a round with Messrs Fry's cocoa van, a new and popular institution, we saw people lying on open banks and a colony of 120 in some disused stables without water or sanitation. For such quarters, some families pay as much as 17/- a week in bus fares. It is perhaps significant that the trekkers are known as the 'Yellow Brigade' by people who remain in Portsmouth and as 'those dreadful blitzers' by the country folk.

(2) SHELTERS: There are over 40,000 shelters of all types. Many of them are good but they are not much used since the trekking habit took hold, except those in the comparatively unblitzed north. On the Portsdown hills and along the London Road, the shelters are still crowded, though the numbers have decreased considerably with the recent quiet nights. A count in the London Road shelters revealed that, out of 700 people, only 19 came from local towns and all the rest from Portsmouth. There are no bunks in public shelters, due to the official policy of 'discouraging' their use and 'encouraging' the use of Andersons by bunking them. We saw people propped up on narrow benches or lying on the floor of public shelters, though we were told later that they were 'not supposed to' as the shelters 'were not meant for that'. There are no shelter marshals and no attempts at organisation. The urban district authorities say that the shelters are left in an indescribably filthy condition and that people will not use the Elsan lavatories, where these are provided. They have to employ special men to clean them out. A story was told of some children found at mid-day in a shelter who declared, 'We live here.' It appeared their parents left them during the day while they worked and shopped in Portsmouth. Lack of sleep is one of the main dangers of shelter life in these conditions. No shelterers questioned by us admitted to more than 2 or 3 hours.

(3) TRANSPORT: The huge daily movement of population makes transport a major problem, especially for workers. Over 6,000 men from the

dockyard alone sleep out of the city. All available buses are crowded on to the roads but the service is still inadequate. At the same time, the trains are not used to capacity, due to the higher fares and the comparatively few stopping places. A difficulty is that the demand increases with each new provision made. For instance, an early train put on for the benefit of 40 dockyard workers evacuated to Petersfield was soon carrying 400. 'This sort of thing makes planning impossible. We have no idea when saturation point will be reached.' Another difficulty is that the wives and children of workers accompany their husbands on the early buses, so keeping other workers off. This is said to be because few have amenities for cooking or feeding at their place of sleep, so they must come back to their Portsmouth homes for breakfast.

(4) FEEDING: The need for communal feeding both in Portsmouth and the surrounding areas seems largely unrecognized. Only three 'Municipal Restaurants' exist in the city and are used to capacity. There is a plan for a large number to be opened, but only in the event of 'dire necessity', that is, after a big blitz. We feel that this attitude is not in keeping with the Ministry of Food's conception of communal feeding and that more propaganda is needed. The attitude of the official in charge appears largely responsible for this policy. Apart from a personal horror of communal feeding, he expressed the opinion that it encouraged parasitism and laziness and he did not see why 'workers probably earning more than I do' should be 'subsidised by the Government'. From another source, we learnt that catering establishments in the city have been reduced to 15%, so the need for alternative provisions appears obvious. The feeding of dockyard workers is one of the greatest problems. Out of a total of 20,000, it is estimated that over 5,000 never have a hot meal. This is due in part to the bombing of existing dockyard canteens but much more to the huge number who join in the nightly trek and have no opportunity of getting their accustomed evening meal nor a satisfactory breakfast. After considerable pressure, 2 kiosks have been set up at the dockyard gates, providing tea and sandwiches. They open at 9 a.m. and close at 6 p.m., so are little use to the dockyard workers except between 12 and 1 p.m., during which time only a few hundreds can be served. We saw the scramble one day and noticed how miserable the dockyard workers looked in comparison with the cheerful soldiers also using the kiosks. In

this connection, we heard of some discontent among workers at being 'kept out' of canteens run for Service men, whom they feel get all the consideration. There is also much bitterness among women workers because of the shop hours and the difficulty of getting anything to put in their menfolk's sandwiches. It was also noted that the fact that it is 'customary' for dockyard workers to take sandwiches for their mid-day meal is being used as an excuse for failure to make other provisions.

(5) EVACUATION: Over 34,000 people, mostly children, have been evacuated since Sept. 1939; until the bad raids began, they were returning at an average rate of 103 a week. Further evacuation is felt to be a problem of the utmost urgency. Recently, the Lord Mayor called for a new registration and in the first three weeks of May 2,500 people responded. These included 233 old people as well as a number of invalids and babies. We were disturbed to hear that there appears to be no scheme behind this registration. There is vague talk of Dorset for school children but apparently no possibilities for the other classes. Thousands have already crowded into the surrounding areas, many of which are now overcrowded according to Ministry of Health standards. One hears of women spending all their money on fares to distant towns where they hope to find room and of soldiers getting 48 hours' leave to search for billets for their families. The most desperate cases are those of the very poor in Portsea, who are surrounded by dockyards and very nervous but cannot afford the nightly journey to safety, and of old people who are too feeble to seek for themselves and who cannot even, in some cases, reach a shelter. Two Salvation Army Hostels for old people are full and a residential nursery for babies has just been opened at Bishop's Waltham but we were told that more were needed. It is thought that many do not register because they feel it is hopeless.

(6) SUGGESTIONS: The various suggestions made to cope with the above problems include the following:

(a) The removal of London school children from nearby areas to make room for Portsmouth workers.

(b) Requisitioning of all available halls and large houses. For this purpose, medical certificates and pleas of hardship would have to be reviewed by an independent authority.

(c) The building of hut camps provided with shelters for use in a bad attack. It was suggested that the best method would be to build huts in the grounds of large houses, which would act as centres.

(d) The construction of a large shelter to hold several thousand, in units of 1,000, in the chalk hills. (The city engineer has already drawn up plans permitting of a high degree of organisation but was despairing of getting them passed in time to complete building before the autumn.)

(e) That people in houses near shelters might allow refreshments to be made in their kitchens by the WVS. (This would save the expense and petrol of mobile canteens.)

(f) That trains should lower their fares to correspond with road transport and that they should run non-stop to the more distant towns, leaving the buses to cover adjacent areas. (In this way, the buses would increase their capacity as they would return more quickly.)

(g) That travel vouchers be issued in cases of hardship, payment being assessed according to means.

(h) That the last trains taking people out should be equipped with bunks or hammocks and run into sidings for the night.

(i) That communal feeding be taken out of the hands of the local authority and run on national lines.

(j) That the Ministry of Food make arrangements for the mass production of a sandwich filling and popularise it by advertisement.

(k) That an appeal be made to retailers to extend their hours and remain open in the lunch hour.

B. LABOUR

(1) We were told the demand for male labour of all types, especially for skilled men, exceeds the supply. A sufficient number of women are available for factory work but there is a shortage of domestics and office staff.

(2) The general attitude to work appears to be healthier than in Southampton, doubtless because of the naval example and discipline. There is a complaint, however, that it is harder to enforce discipline now that the threat of dismissal is no longer immediate and because it is

difficult to keep a check on 'excuses' owing to abnormal conditions. Behaviour during alerts has improved. In the dockyards, work continues until the whistle blows, 'then it is a job to make them take shelter'. Absenteeism is noticed after Sunday work (the City Engineer has stopped Sunday work for this reason) and among married women. With the latter, it is often in order to shop. There is a complaint that women are jibbing at wearing the protective caps provided, or refusing to put all their hair inside. 'Gruesome descriptions of scalping make no difference.' We were told that the employment of women in the dockyard shops is satisfactory. 'Men are accepting them very well on the whole...their presence seems to be stimulating'.

(3) Difficulties of transport, feeding and accommodation have been noted. Unsatisfactory living conditions are thought to be taking their toll in an increased sickness rate with slower recovery and a tendency to septic conditions from minor injuries. There is a slow but steady fall in production which is causing alarm. Problems arising out of the policy of dispersal of certain units to other towns need more study, but no details were available.

C. FIRE-WATCHING

Since the nightly exodus from the city, fire-watching is very unsatisfactory. Large areas are uninhabitable but still inflammable. Adequate protection is thought to be impossible until compulsion is introduced. The men who trek out and 'leave the city to its fate' are much criticised and it is felt that if they are made to take their turn, it will be good for general morale as well as their own.

D. CIVIL DEFENCE

We were impressed by the excellent co-operation between police and wardens, not always evident in other towns. It is perhaps because the Chief of Police and Chief Warden are combined in one man, who is able and progressive. Since his appointment, he is said to have infused new life into a Force whose spirits were flagging. He and others are concerned about the welfare of the Civil Defence personnel. It was stated that the cumulative effects of exhaustion were being felt and that far too little was done to ensure that these key people got proper food and rest. It was emphasised that the spirit of the whole community depended on the good morale of these services. A scheme on a modest scale for giving the police a few days relaxation in a holiday home outside the city is being tried and it is hoped it may be developed. Proper accommodation outside the target area must also be ready for reinforcements – both firemen and police – called in for an emergency. In the past, they are alleged to have been neglected. A plan for a regular exchange of men from less vulnerable areas is under consideration. There is also a scheme for housing the city police in a suburban hostel where community living would ensure good food. A hostel in the city is considered far too dangerous and the men are dispersed in billets.

E. HOUSING

(1) There have been 55,000 claims for damage to houses (out of a possible 75,000) so it may be imagined that not all get immediate attention. There are the usual complaints about rain doing unnecessary damage – 'soaking bedding and soaking morale' – and also complaints that the system of allotting certain areas to certain contractors leads to absurdities such as the repairing of a deserted street whilst a neighbouring inhabited street is neglected. A grouse against the Government is that owing to the elaborate forms to be filled in before money can be claimed for repairs, local councils have to borrow and pay heavy bank charges. (Largely owing to this, the Gosport Council has an overdraft of almost £50,000 and complains of having to 'finance the Government'.)

(2) Over 7,000 people have been placed in vacant requisitioned houses and over 14,000 billeted. Rehousing becomes progressively more difficult. Homeless people are encouraged to look out for possible houses for themselves. These are then requisitioned and arrangements are made to adjust the rent, the offer made by the applicant being accepted. The help with rent is supposed to be temporary but, owing to understaffing and the need for a special enquiry into each case, it has sometimes continued for months. When rent adjustment is made, the Government pay the balance but will not do this until a report is made on each house by the overworked district valuer, so there are long delays. A case was cited of a man who let two houses and received no rent for so long that he had to apply for Public Assistance. This sort of thing kills co-operation and makes people refrain from offering

houses, as they did at first. It is suggested that it would be solved if the Town Clerk were empowered to pay immediate rent.

While the homeless are waiting to be rehoused, they are moved from Emergency Centres into temporary billets, for which purpose an up-to-date 'hospitality' list is kept. There are always some people too dirty or uncouth to billet and it is thought that some houses should be kept ready so that such people could be installed immediately. The Rehousing Officer would like to requisition 100 houses for this purpose, but has been refused permission. He has only 6.

F. CRIME

On all sides we heard that looting and wanton destruction had reached alarming proportions. The police seem unable to exercise control and we heard many tales of the wreckage of shelters and of stealing from damaged houses, and were told that some people were afraid to take shelter in an attack for fear of being robbed of their remaining possessions. This seems another illustration of the lack of community spirit. The effect on morale is bad and there is a general feeling of desperation as there seems to be no solution. Some of the trouble is caused by children, many of whom do not go to school, though attendance for a half day is again compulsory, but the worst offenders appear to be youths of 18 or 19, though it is difficult to judge as few are caught.

VI MORALE

The morale of the city may be summed up in a sentence often repeated, 'The spirit of the people is unbroken, but their nerve has gone.' That is to say, though they have been badly shaken by their experiences and are afraid, they do not want to give in. The ability to return to normal may be seen in the way cinemas begin to fill and shelters to empty as soon as there is a lull. A few factors that make for good morale are the following:

(a) Good leadership in the Lord Mayor and other public figures.

(b) The fact that neither the authorities nor the public are shutting their eyes to the gravity of the situation. They know there must be more attacks and are proud of their importance as a naval base.

(c) The presence of the navy, especially in an emergency.

(d) The friendly visiting carried out by the CAB and their businesslike register of addresses.

(e) The unflagging work of the clergy and Salvation Army in shelters and clubs and in a crisis.

The following are danger points:

(1) Neglect of the welfare of the Civil Defence services on which civilian morale depends.

(2) The cumulative effects of lack of sleep, bad feeding and comfortless quarters.

(3) The trapped feeling of people who cannot be evacuated or even escape at night. Concern over the plight of old people and children.

(4) The withdrawal of clergy on the destruction of their churches.

(5) Lack of home or school discipline for children.

(6) Widespread looting.

(7) The lack of community spirit, shown in this looting of bombed persons and also in the fact that no attempt is made by the people to organise shelters or appoint marshals, and in the reluctance to take fire-watching duty. The paternalism of the authorities may foster this and it may be, in part, temperamental. The danger should be recognised as, in a crisis, panic may spread amongst a collection of people where there is no group feeling and everyone acts for himself.

VII CONCLUSION

In face of these problems, we believe the time has come when talk of front-line defence must give way to action. The front line is no place for babies, invalids and old age pensioners; they and all unnecessary people should be cleared from the city; they put a strain on its resources and are a grave responsibility in an attack. The essential workers and defence services that remain should then come under front-line discipline, which would include proper provision for their feeding, safety and welfare, with an assurance of reasonable rest periods in base towns, for no soldier is left permanently at the front. If it proves necessary for these people to sleep outside the target area, it would mean that huts with shelters or else a large shelter in the chalk hills must be built. Work on building should start without delay in order that it shall be completed before the bad weather sets in. The best possible use of the railways as well as buses must be arranged and also compulsory fire-watching for the protection of areas that are derelict but still inflammable.

Such drastic action can only be taken by an authority with wide executive powers. It will be made easier because experience has already brought home the necessity to many of the present officials and also, in part, to the people of Portsmouth.

PORTSMOUTH REPORT   28.5.41

LIST OF SOURCES

I INTERVIEWS

1. Mr. F. Maxwell Wells, Sec. of the Voluntary Information Committee, Deputy Chief Warden.

2. Mr. Harry Sargeant, Emergency Information Officer.

3. Chief Constable West. Also Chief of Wardens & Fire Service.

4. Superintendent Inspector Baker.

5. Inspector Stratton.

6. Col. Duke, Deputy Town Clerk, ARP Controller.

7. Mr. Scott, Emergency Feeding Organiser.

8. Col. Williamson, MOH.

9. Mr. Birch, Rehousing Officer.

10. Secretary of Mr. Davison, Evacuation Officer.

11. Mr. Parkin, City Engineer.

12. Miss E. H. Kelly, CBE, JP, Hon. Sec. CAB and of Portsmouth Social Service Council.

13. Miss H. M. Kelly, OBE.

14. Mrs. Daly, Lady Mayoress.

15. Mr. Brogden, Deputy Public Assistance Officer.

16. Mr. Rose, Ministry of Labour Welfare Officer.

17. Mr. Hall, Labour Manager.

18. Miss Robbins, Labour Manager.

19. Mr. Knapman, HM Factory Inspector.

20. Mr. Chase, Dockyard Welfare & Safety Officer.

21. Miss Bradshaw, Dockyard Welfare & Safety Officer for Women.

22. Mrs. Valentine, Deputising for Mrs. Williams, WVS Organiser.

23. Canon Robins.

24. Brigadier Manning, Salvation Army.

25. Major Grace, Salvation Army.

26. Mrs. O'Rorke, Superviser, St. Jude's Emergency Centre.

27. Mr. Martin, Divisional Warden.

28. Messrs. Fry's Representative.

29. Sir Hugh Cocke, Chief Billeting Officer, Petersfield.

30. Mr. Fardell, Local Controller (Evacuation), Petersfield.

31. Mr. Ben Levy, MOI Secretary, Petersfield.

32. Mr. Burley, Clerk to Urban District Council, Petersfield.

33. Mr. Madgwick, Town Clerk, Havant.

34. Miss Bean, Evacuation Officer, Havant.

35. Mrs. Byde, CAB, Havant.

36. Mrs. Monkton, WVS Organiser, Havant.

II OTHER SOURCES OF INFORMATION

37. A day spent in Petersfield and a day in Havant to investigate problems in dormitory and reception areas.

38. Visit to dockyard.

39. Visit to badly blitzed parts of town, poor quarters and new shopping centres.

40. Meal in Communal Feeding Centre.

41. Tour of Cosham and Portsdown Hill at night, with Messrs. Fry's Van, to see shelters, huts, etc.

42. Conversations with members of the public, policemen, wardens, etc.

NO 39: WEDNESDAY 25 JUNE TO WEDNESDAY 2 JULY 1941

GENERAL COMMENTS

1. GENERAL STATE OF CONFIDENCE AND REACTION TO NEWS

The greatest single influence upon public feeling during the past week has been the Russo-German campaign, the effects of which seem to have been to encourage cheerfulness and hope. Other factors which have sustained this mood have been those mentioned last week: the day and night successes of the RAF, the continued absence of heavy raiding on this country, and the comparative lack of fresh ominous news.

Opinions on the war in Russia range from extreme reserve to complacent optimism. In most reports, however, there is a cautious and sometimes sceptical note. The quality of Russia's resistance up to date has, therefore, come as a pleasant relief.

The more thoughtful fear that if Russia is quickly defeated we shall receive 'the full onslaught of an enemy flushed with victory, with greater resources behind him than he had before', and that 'our position in the Middle East will have been rendered well-nigh untenable'. At the other end of the scale is the feeling that 'Germany is already beaten'. The majority compromise with the opinion that 'at worst, the Russian campaign will have a weakening effect on Nazi resources, and if Russia holds out, the war will be shortened'. There is a great deal of confusion about Russia's potential strength. Before her pact with Germany, she was often described in the press as 'a Colossus'; at the time of the Russo-Finnish war she was represented as 'being no match for a large and well-equipped power'; but now her armed might is again being played up. There is inevitably a desire for 'much more interpretive material about the campaign, to assist ordinary people to follow events'.

Many people hope that we shall soon begin more active hostilities on the Western Front; some even advocate a direct attack on Holland. It is feared that 'unless we can do something now, another golden opportunity will be lost'.

The Prime Minister's broadcast is thought to have given the public a rational approach to the political aspects of our collaboration with Russia. Doubts on this score seem to be 'entirely submerged in a feeling of relief that we have another powerful democracy at our side'. At the same time, there is some apprehension about 'the difficulties at any peace conference at which the British Empire and Russia may be allies'.

It is said to be the opinion of certain trade union leaders that Russia's entry into the war will have a remarkable effect on production, and that communists are now expected to cease their 'hindering manifestations', and to turn their energies in a more helpful direction. On the other hand, there is a fear in some quarters that increased optimism may lead to a slackening off in the war effort. Lack of reliable news from the Russian front is apparently taken by many people as a sign that 'the Russians are rather more than holding their own'. It is felt that we should 'immediately stress the tremendous importance of maintaining a *real* two-front war'.

Beneath the more or less cheerful tension caused by this latest development of the war, there is still evidence of some 'depression, weariness, and even gloom'. This may be accounted for by some of the following factors:

1. General anxiety about the future; not necessarily a doubt of victory, but anxiety over what we shall have to go through to achieve it, and also about what will be done after the war is won.

2. The feeling that, 'Churchill excepted, we are being badly led.'

3. 'Official muddles over transport, industry, factory management, agriculture, etc.'

4. Difficulties of obtaining food, tobacco and coal.

5. The need for holidays; indecision as to whether they are possible, or even permissible.

6. The lack of things on which to spend money.

7. 'Too many rules and regulations.'

8. Shortage of supplies, causing lack of trade, the shutting of small shops etc.

2. BROADCASTING AND PRESENTATION OF NEWS

Criticism of news presentation is on the wane. This is said to be 'because there is not much official news at present, rather than because people are satisfied with what they get'. Such complaints as there are follow the familiar lines – 'We can take bad news as long as we don't feel we are being misled.'

Mr. Churchill's broadcast on Russia was received with such warm approval that it is said to have 'quelled a rising tide of criticism and doubt of the higher direction of the war'. 'His use of the word "guttersnipe" appealed to almost all classes.' Appeals by other Cabinet Ministers are said to 'leave people cold'.

Quentin Reynolds's *Postscript* aroused 'exceptional interest and approval'; its 'tonic effect' is described as remarkable, and people ask 'why we cannot have more of this kind of thing'. A negligible minority is said to have found it 'cringe-making'.

There is still approval for the Empire News Bulletins, and the American who broadcasts from Ankara is listened to by some people because he is believed to give first-hand information on the Near Eastern and Russian situation.

BELIEF IN NEWS AMONG THE FORCES: An enquiry was made at the beginning of June by Listener Research into the attitude of the Forces towards presentation of news. This enquiry was on the same lines as that made into the civilian attitude to news presentation, the results of which were given in our Weekly Report No. 37 (11th to 18th June 1941).

114 reports were received from Forces Correspondents (72 from the Army, 10 from the Navy, and 32 from the RAF). The Forces Correspondents contributing these reports represent between them over 11,000 men.

The main interest of the enquiry lies in a comparison of the results received from Forces Correspondents with those received from Local

Correspondents working among civilians. Both results are shown below. On the question of general confidence in the news, the results were as follows:

Percentage of Correspondents who report that among those with whom they come in contact:

	Civilians	Forces
	%	%
Confidence in the news is *decreasing*	12	22
Confidence in the news is *unchanged*	75	65
Confidence in the news is *increasing*	12	9
	99	96
No reply	1	4
	100	100

The enquiry took the following form. Twelve common criticisms of the news were listed. Correspondents were asked to indicate whether each statement represented the views of a majority, a minority, or none of the men with whom they come into contact. In addition, they were asked to sum up the attitude of their contacts by saying whether confidence in the news was decreasing, increasing or was unchanged.

A detailed analysis of the answers to these questions showed that the general conclusions to be drawn from the enquiry are:

1. That men in the Services, like the general public, want news good or bad and resent any attempt to make it as palatable as possible.

2. That there is widespread belief among the Forces, as there is among civilians, that in the speed of its operation there is something wrong with the machinery for giving news, though it is realised, at any rate among the more thoughtful listeners, that it is not the BBC which must be held to account for this deficiency.

3. That there is not much criticism among the Forces of the way in which news bulletins are now arranged, though there is rather more feeling among the troops than among civilians that news bulletins contain too many trivial items.

4. The charges that announcers are open to criticism for letting their personal feeling colour their news reading receive little support among the troops. There is even less support for the view that news bulletins are not phrased simply enough.

5. That tardiness in the announcement of news acts as an encouragement to listening to enemy broadcasts, though there is no evidence of any widespread increase in this habit among the troops, or of any serious consequences of it.

6. That the view that the BBC overseas news in English is better than the news bulletins in the Home Service is fairly widespread among the troops, as it is among civilians.

3. RAF

Jubilation is reported at the RAF's sustained offensive over Germany and enemy-occupied territory. In some quarters this is regarded as a 'far more solid cause for satisfaction' than Russia's entry into the war. It is generally believed that 'we are exploiting a great opportunity', and there is satisfaction at our being able 'not only to hold the Germans successfully, but to carry the campaign into their own country'. There is, however, a call for 'more precise information as to the damage being inflicted', and the hope is expressed that 'we shall go right into the heart of Germany while she is still busy on her Eastern front'.

4. SYRIA

Although interest in Syria has been diminished by events in Russia, the slowness of our advance is causing comment and anxiety; there is talk of 'kid-glove methods', and of our being 'too easy-going'. It is suggested that, if General de Gaulle was right in saying that Vichy resistance was broken with the fall of Damascus, we must be showing undue gentleness in handling the enemy.

The resistance of the Vichy forces intensifies dislike and contempt for the French, and there seems to be little attempt 'to distinguish between Vichy and Frenchmen generally'. As a remedy for this, 'the need for intensive propaganda is stressed'. Incidents have been reported recently in which Free French sailors were assaulted because they were thought to be Vichy French.

5. RADIOLOCATION

The announcement of radiolocation has produced three reactions. The most marked is a fear that it may have helped the enemy. There is severe criticism that a secret invention should be revealed in such detail. It is even classed as 'loose talk'. The more cautious are said not to be putting too much faith in the idea, having had 'so many "let downs" in the past'. There are reports that the announcement has produced 'increased general confidence', and the feeling that we have 'got the bombers on the run'. The suggestion, apparently made by a newspaper, that people would 'shortly be as safe in their beds as they now are in the daytime', is said in some cases to be taken as an absolute fact. Cases are also reported of a decrease in fire-watching as a result of the announcement.

6. RUMOURS AND CARELESS TALK

Soldiers returning from East Coast manoeuvres are reported by Northamptonshire canteen workers to be talking loudly of important schemes, and declaring that an attack on the Belgian coast is imminent. Rumours of an impending land attack on enemy-occupied territory is also mentioned by two RIOs.

SPECIAL COMMENTS

7. FOOD

PRICE CONTROL: The fact that price control seems to be 'invariably followed by shortage' is the main grievance this week. It is reported from almost every district; the shortage of tomatoes has brought the matter into even greater prominence than usual. A report by the RIO South-Eastern Region is typical of many: 'Greengrocers closed on the eve of tomato control price day with a good stock on their hands. At opening time on Monday, there was no sign of tomatoes in stock. Obviously they had not been destroyed, and were being sold over the controlled price to customers well-known to the shop-keepers.' In the North Midland Region, it is said that a firm of canners made a lightning tour and bought up all stocks. In the North-Eastern Region it is argued that price control 'operates at present in favour of the south of England, as the northern crop is late. Southern growers do not find it an economic proposition to send tomatoes to the north at the present price.' It is feared that price control will affect fish in the same way; from mid-Wales come reports that 'people there have already forgotten the taste of it'; and there is apprehension that 'it will be the same with eggs soon'.

It is hoped that the Ministry of Food will 'broadcast or publish an explanation of control and its consequences, and what is being done to ensure supplies to people at a distance from the source of origin'.

JAM: There is great satisfaction over the announcement of the new sugar concession to private jam-makers; the co-operative jam-making scheme for the Women's Institutes continues to be sharply criticised.

ILLICIT TRADING: Although the evidence suggests that 'black markets' exist as much in imagination as in fact (the public is showing a tendency to suspect them everywhere), illicit trading appears to be on the increase as more and more commodities come under control. It is believed that retailers are still reluctant to report offending wholesalers to the authorities for fear of having their supplies cut off in revenge. It is, therefore, urged that those who come forward with information should be guaranteed alternative sources of supply.

CONCESSIONS FOR LORRY DRIVERS: Drivers of heavy lorries are frequently away from home for several days at a time, and must depend for food on wayside cafes. It is said that the food served there is quite inadequate for the strenuous work they are doing. The staple diet seems to be sausages. Not only are these much below the pre-war standard, but the men are surfeited with sausages, and some complain that they cannot eat them any more. The only alternatives are tea and cakes, though of these there is often a shortage. Concessions are hoped for, so that these men 'can get some kind of decent food'.

8. INDUSTRY

Further criticism, 'some very bitter', has been received from several sources about the management of our war factories. It is again said that 'men, keen to get on, are kept idling'; workmen in a Bristol aircraft plant have protested against this, and also against the alleged employment of skilled labour for the carrying out of simple jobs 'which could be done far quicker by trucks'. On the other hand, there are still complaints from managements that the workers themselves exploit the system of double pay on Sundays by working then and absenting themselves later. A widespread feeling that something is radically wrong with our war industry is said to be a grave and growing discouragement to the country's morale.

9. CLOTHES

No public reactions have yet been received to the revised list of coupon-charges published on Tuesday.

The smuggling of clothes across the border into Northern Ireland from Eire is now said to be 'becoming quite an important local industry'.

It is reported that in the mining district of Lanarkshire, where the excuse of 'no boots' is already used for absence from school in the winter, women cannot afford strong shoes for children. They buy sand-shoes in the summer, and some have already used ten coupons on these for one child alone. At this rate coupons will be exhausted before the cold weather, and before the need for real boots is felt.

10. INCOME TAX

On the whole, 'even those to whom it is an innovation' are said to pay the tax quite cheerfully 'once they understand the necessity', but there is said to be a good deal of confusion on certain points. It is suggested, therefore, that the tax authorities should make the demand in simpler language, and that further publicity should be given to the need for tax on incomes which have hitherto been immune. There have been some complaints that income tax authorities have shown a lack of courtesy and sympathy when consulted on difficult points. Also, lack of privacy in their offices is an embarrassment to some people who are compelled to discuss intimate affairs in the presence of others.

DEDUCTION AT SOURCE: Among factory workers in Coventry, recurrent irritation is said to result from the insertion in the weekly pay envelope of a slip saying that such-and-such a sum has been deducted, without explanation.

It is suggested that a more acceptable method would be to include a reminder, not more than once a quarter, that too much clerical work would be entailed by a detailed explanation of each pay envelope, and then giving the figures for the whole three months. This would avoid 'constantly rubbing it in' that the worker really gains very little from his overtime pay.

11. HOLIDAYS

There is a demand for 'more direction' on this subject. It is regretted that 'there is so much asking people to do things and so little compulsion'. Complaints have been made in many districts that although the Government has recognised the need for one week's holiday for workers, people have been asked to spend their holidays at home, but no restraint has been placed on holiday travel for those on whom such appeals have no effect. It is felt that this method of restraint 'penalises only the patriotic'. It is felt that 'there is a definite need for a national campaign directed to keeping the middle class at home, and especially those people who are still striving to keep up the traditions of an annual holiday for themselves and their families at some pleasure resort'.

12. SALVAGE

The feeling is growing that 'salvage is collected from houses to keep the public quiet, and then left to rot'. Dumps of tins are said to be 'assuming enormous proportions' at St. Ives, and in the Grimsby district many of them remain uncollected. From Eastbourne there are complaints that 'tons of metal, in the shape of tins, cycle frames, bedsteads, etc., are thrown on the public tip and left to be buried under a mass of rubble'. Cottagers in Northamptonshire were asked to collect salvage 'on the understanding that local councils would take it away; but lack of help from local authorities is a continuous cause of complaint and irritation'. Great quantities of waste paper are said to have been found on a dump in a Kent village, 'unsorted, covered by other rubbish, and soaked with rain'; and from the North-Eastern Region there is a report that the waste paper which the Youth Squad had been collecting for months 'has merely been littered about'. There is doubt 'whether the National Salvage Campaign is really to be taken seriously'.

13. CONSTANT COMPLAINTS

No considerable change has been reported in public concern on the following points:

COAL: Widespread anxiety still exists about the coal situation, especially as to how it will develop before next winter; there is a feeling of resentment that 'so little foresight should have been shown by the authorities'.

RECRUITMENT OF LABOUR: Disappointment and dissatisfaction continue to be expressed by women of about 35 who are told that they are 'too old when they volunteer for war work'. Discourtesy at Labour Exchanges is reported; one in Lambeth is said to be particularly unhelpful, and many complaints of rudeness have been received.

QUEUES: These are said to be increasing in number, and with them the complaints of busy women that they cannot compete with the leisured ones in standing to wait for food.

BEER AND TOBACCO SHORTAGES: It is said that 'a plain statement of the position would clearly be welcomed'.

APPENDIX I

HOME INTELLIGENCE SPECIAL REPORT
ON CONDITIONS IN MERSEYSIDE

I INTRODUCTORY NOTE

A special study was made in Liverpool from June 3rd–10th 1941. A day in Birkenhead and a day in Bootle were included in this period. The welfare of the civilian population was investigated and special attention was paid to labour problems (Appendix II). The report has been submitted to the Regional Information Officer, North-West Region, and many helpful criticisms have been embodied.

It should be noted that this report gives an impression and does not pretend to be comprehensive. It was not possible to see all officials concerned nor to check every statement. Detailed descriptions of emergency measures have been omitted.

A list of persons interviewed and other sources of information is appended.

II DESCRIPTION

To the visitor, Liverpool has a depressed and sordid atmosphere. This is partly due to its blackness and the number of very poor seen in the streets, and is enhanced by the blitz debris. (The atmosphere in Birkenhead is strikingly more cheerful.) The population, about 850,000 before the war, is thought to have increased slightly, owing to increased activity in the docks and shipyards and the expansion of factories, mainly engineering and aircraft works. The mixed population of the city is a special feature. There are small colonies of Chinese, Arabs, Greeks and West Indians, transient seamen of all nationalities and a large settlement of Irish, reported to be of a poor, even primitive type. The feud between the Catholics and Orangemen has raged hotly in the past but has somewhat abated since the war.

Raids on Liverpool started in June 1940 and gradually increased in intensity. There was a heavy attack in December but the worst period was from the 1st to the 8th of May, when there was a blitz every night. 1,435 of the total of 2,549 deaths occurred in this week. 700 water mains were hit and electricity and gas affected. The telephone is still out of action in the city centre, and it is unlikely that the city will have more than a skeleton telephone service while the war lasts. The docks suffered severely and half the houses have been damaged. In Bootle, 14,000 out of 17,000 houses were damaged and all utility services put out of action. There is still a considerable feeling of neglect because these raids were not at first given sufficient publicity. Liverpool dislikes being disguised as a 'North West town', while London raids are described in detail, and the suppression of casualty figures and the extent of the damage is resented.

III INFORMATION SERVICES

(1) The Liverpool Information Committee Secretary is the Town Clerk, who appears too preoccupied with other responsibilities to give much time to the work. A complaint from various members of the Information Committee was that they were not themselves given sufficient authoritative

information with which to combat rumours. The Ministry of Information was blamed.

(2) In Liverpool, the Emergency Information Service has been reorganised. The new system, as we understood it, is as follows: the ARP Controller decides when an emergency has arisen and informs, first, the RIO (who sends the loudspeaker vans); secondly, the Emergency Information Officer; and thirdly, the Chief Constable. Heads of Departments, such as the Assistance Board officer and the MOH, send typed copies of instructions to be broadcast and two Civil Defence cadets act as dispatch riders. In the last raids, the Emergency Information Officer appears to have had difficulty in getting information, and there was a complaint that inaccurate instructions were broadcast. In spite of this, the vans proved their value and were appreciated. It was remarked that small cars fitted with loudspeakers were more useful than vans, which are too large to negotiate back streets and debris, and increase the traffic congestion.

Large advertisements in the news columns of local papers were found to be a good way of distributing information, but we were told that publicity in general was not good, that people did not know about emergency measures and that printed instructions on Help for the Homeless issued to officials were not kept up to date. We spoke to a woman who had been referred to four different offices to make a claim for furniture removal. Each visit involved a long journey, and, with tears in her eyes, she said that no one seemed to know where she should go. There were other cases of this sort, which produced the feeling that it was only people who spun a good tale who could get help.

In Bootle, public offices were destroyed and we were told that confusion and distress would have been lessened if more effort had been made to make known their emergency quarters. Actually the offices were rapidly blitzed out of one building after another, until finally the large MOI van became the main information centre. In Liverpool a central information bureau for changed business addresses would have been much appreciated.

(3) The CABs are said to have functioned well, in spite of the fact that the Municipal Information Bureau in the Museum was hit, as well as many CABs. Regional Assistance enabled certain deficiencies at the time of the blitz to be covered, by allocating CAB workers to MOI vans. The Regional

Information Officer considers this to have been most helpful. The CABs are run by the Personal Service Society, which is well known and respected. At the Municipal Information Bureau, queries are answered which do not need special investigation of a case-work nature.

IV THE LOCAL AUTHORITIES

The local authorities are aware that renewed attacks are likely but, in Liverpool, they appear rather too easily satisfied with the provisions made and are inclined to ignore public opinion and psychological factors. Their attitude was indicated in the way in which they replied to questions by quoting praise for past efforts instead of detailing future provisions. Their reception of the enquiry was friendly but not welcoming. They were inclined to be defensive and unwilling to discuss difficulties. As an instance, not one official mentioned the reorganisation of the fire-fighting service, undertaken by a Whitehall official, and, considering the subject outside our sphere, we did not press for details. (We observed that pipes have now been laid from the Mersey; from unofficial sources, we heard that when the water gave out firemen stood idle instead of helping to save furniture and prevent sparks catching new buildings.) Apparently Regional officials are having great difficulty in persuading Liverpool to begin the provision of static water tanks on blitzed sites, as has been done extensively in Manchester. There is some resentment because the Whitehall official is said to be getting masses of equipment which the deposed fire chief is said to have pleaded for in vain.

The difficulties in emergency [provisions] appear to have been increased by the fact that Liverpool, Bootle, Wallasey, Birkenhead, and also outlying suburbs such as Huyton, are separated, rather artificially, each under its own authority. This complicates the organisation of billeting and Rest Centres and leads to situations such as the overcrowding of hospitals in one area when those adjoining had room. The need for further co-ordination is felt by the public and acknowledged by certain officials. Thus, the exodus problem is now being handled in a comprehensive way, which includes the County authorities.

There seems also a regrettable lack of co-operation between the authorities and voluntary bodies in Liverpool, and between police and wardens. The

Emergency Committee of three, which meets daily, is considered to be unreceptive of ideas and unwilling to delegate powers. The authorities in general are described as 'apathetic and moribund' – a phrase often used, though not always deserved. The Birkenhead authorities appeared more alive to public feeling. They have appointed a woman Welfare Officer who administers the Lord Mayor's Fund and makes each applicant feel he is receiving personal consideration. She has organised teams of workers for after-care visiting following raids, a system which might well be copied elsewhere.

V EMERGENCY MEASURES

Emergency measures have been gradually improved and the authorities feel it was fortunate that the mild early raids acted as a rehearsal. The official attitude, as stated to us, is that the safety of the people matters more than their comfort; there is little sympathy for those that have been frightened rather than hurt. As we were not in the city during a raid it was hard to gauge the effect of this on morale.

Distress after the blitz is alleged to have been caused by the enormous crowds of sightseers (one town is supposed to have run 7/- bus trips for the purpose); the Regional Information Officer states that the 'sightseer trips' were probably a myth based on the fact that pleasure coaches, drafted in to replace blitzed buses, were seen going through the city. The large number of private cars brought into service also fostered the idea of sightseers. A genuine cause of distress were the sights in over-filled mortuaries. The main mortuary at Bootle was itself destroyed, along with a large number of bodies. City hospitals also became crowded; when one was blitzed no note was kept of the destination of hastily evacuated patients. People are still touring country hospitals in search of relations. Some of the people from Rest Centres are also untraced, and it is evident that the problems of record keeping need further consideration.

There are an adequate number of Rest Centres run on a well-organised, decentralised system, and a policy of rapid dispersal by billeting was carried out to the satisfaction of officials. They were able to deal with the large number of 37,000 people in a week, since there was a survey of all available accommodation, and arrangements for an emergency staff (drawn from various departments of the corporation) who used compulsory powers when necessary. There were hostels for difficult types, such as old people or very large families. From unofficial sources we heard that ill-feeling had been caused by the bullying manner of same billeting officers, and it was also said that the people were not really dispersed, as they congregated unorganised in halls on the outskirts of the city and beyond. In these the standard of behaviour and cleanliness rapidly deteriorated. Volunteers in charge said conditions were indescribable; people would not even make use of the lavatories provided (a suggested explanation was that some slum lavatories are so dirty that parents forbid their use). PAC officials in city centres were able to exercise more control and made the people help with scrubbing and cleaning. It was felt that their discipline was sometimes unsympathetic, but it is evident that if volunteers are to take charge of halls they should have preliminary training and rehearsal. It was remarked that good lighting and somewhere to lie down were important factors in keeping up morale.

Feeding arrangements had been carefully organised and worked more or less according to plan. The Rest Centres are supplied from PAC central kitchens and the Education Authority has charge of other emergency Feeding Centres, mobile squads and the British Restaurants, which are popular, though not, strictly, an emergency measure. There is ample provision for alternative cooking should any or all of the first centres fail. In spite of planning, there was some confusion; stories were told of people in Rest Centres waiting till 3.00 p.m. or later for a meal, and the mobile canteens were said to be badly directed; some demolition workers and others were without food for long periods. It was suggested that it would be better if all Rest Centres had, at least, facilities for making tea, which should be given to people as soon as possible. Besides the PAC and the Education Authority, the Dock and Harbour Board has a hand in organising feeding where dockers are concerned. It is thought that arrangements could be improved if they were co-ordinated by a single controller. On the docks, Cadbury's Canteen, sent from Birmingham during the emergency, first gave free cocoa and later charged a nominal sum, which undersold other canteens and caused dissatisfaction. Similar complaints have been noted in other areas.

In Bootle an organiser from the Region took over the feeding. His work, later handed on to a London official, was praised, but some local people complained, apparently with little justification, that he had a superior, academic manner and did not appear to appreciate the strain they had undergone. This is probably a typical reaction to outside help, and one which regional officials should be prepared to meet.

An Assistance Board officer pointed out the importance of feeding the people waiting for immediate relief. Delay is inevitable, and unless applicants are made as comfortable and happy as possible they exert a depressing effect on each other. The Assistance Board was universally praised, though a few of its officers were unprepared to deal with what seems the unreasonable touchiness of people not accustomed to apply for relief. There were not many complaints of money given for relief being misused, though some people spent most of it on funerals and there were people who got a grant for clothes and then applied to the WVS for a free issue. One WVS office was mobbed and had to close down. The Lord Mayor's Fund has had many appeals for help with funerals, as it seems that Government aid is still connected in the minds of the people with the idea of a public funeral or pauper burial.

VI TREKKING, EVACUATION, AND REHOUSING

After the blitz there was a nightly trek from the city. It is supposed by some of the authorities to have been small, and they discount as a myth the tales of sleeping in the open. There is reason to think they under-estimate the movement. The maximal figure for the nightly exodus, given by the Regional Information Officer, is 50,000. Some officials say the 'wind-up cases' should be made to stay put and are critical of certain country folk who 'opened their arms to the people, irrespective of if it were necessary'. This is said to encourage panic. In Liverpool it was said that if trekking facilities were made 'everyone would go and it couldn't be done'. The Regional Information Officer describes the official policy as doing nothing to encourage the nightly exodus, but to be ready to deal with it if it should recur. In Bootle so few houses were left that the nightly movement had official sanction and help was given with fares to work.

Records of permanent evacuation were destroyed, but it is known that most of the original evacuees returned. There has been a new movement out since the blitz, but only school children and expectant mothers come under an official scheme. Others are paid allowances if they can find their own billet, and there were cases of mothers and babies and old people who could not manage this. The billeting of Catholic children in Wales has proved especially difficult; one priest even urged them to return on the ground that spiritual was more important than bodily safety. There is an unusually strong desire for family unity, and the phrase 'We'll all die together' is often heard regardless of the fact that bombs do not respect family groups. It was felt that more women would go away and stay away if better arrangements could be made for their husbands and adolescent children in their absence. After seven nights of blitz many were at the end of their tether and begged to be sent out. It was felt that another seven nights would have emptied the city. Even after this experience people who found billets are drifting back, and in some quarters there is a feeling that the most dangerous areas should be compulsorily cleared. The area immediately behind the city is said to have reached saturation point and there were reports of 20 people living in one council house and other instances of overcrowding.

Over half the Liverpool houses have been damaged. Houses, both furnished and unfurnished, are now requisitioned, but it is obvious that rehousing will become increasingly difficult, and some sort of building seems imperative. The rehousing officer has plans for bungalows of a semi-permanent nature. They are divided three-room houses or huts, with kitchenettes and showers and a shelter between every two. They could be built of salvage materials (except for the shelters) and would be arranged in groups round the perimeter of the city, in touch with existing transport, shops and public houses. Each might have a community centre. The plan was not at first sanctioned by the Ministry of Health, possibly on the grounds that bungalows of this type would be used as a substitute for proper rehousing after the war.

In Bootle the housing situation is even more acute. At present people can only be offered street shelters for sleeping, with the prospect of a billet in the town later. This is not what they want and the authorities recognise the necessity of establishing colonies of people outside the area.

VII SCHOOLS

Most schools reinstituted a full-time programme six months ago, but many have now been damaged and attendance is poor owing to the long distances that must be travelled and the fact that in practice Catholic children cannot be made to attend non-Catholic schools.

VIII SHELTERS

Since the last blitz people are said to be more in favour of the smaller surface shelters, which stood up well. Those built with unsatisfactory cement are being demolished. A nightly movement from the suburbs into large basement shelters in the city has abated but not ceased. At midnight we saw some shelters with as many as 500 occupants, though there was no alert. The station of the Mersey Tunnel was crowded. It was adopted as a shelter in spite of official discouragement and the warning that it might be in danger of flooding, and a marshal and nurse are now provided and lavatories have been installed. There is no canteen and no alternative lighting system, though there have been as many as 2,000 shelterers. People sleep on the platform. Workmen were seen cooking an evening meal on spirit lamps. There are groups of Greeks and Chinese and occasional soldiers and sailors, sometimes drunk. Children were seen running about at midnight, and as the station is cleared by 5.00 a.m. for workmen's trains one supposes they must suffer from lack of sleep.

Shelter inspectors make a round every night. Public shelters are clean, and usually well ventilated and well lit. Where bunks have been installed they have been put in bays, leaving a clear passage. In the large shelters marshals have been employed, and are said to be most effective when they are corporation officials in uniform. Hot water urns are being fitted so that people can make their own tea, as it is felt that canteens encourage those who are not genuine shelterers. The Liverpool authorities would still prefer people to shelter at home and have advocated the use of Andersons and strengthened rooms. It may be for this reason that little entertainment has been organised in public shelters.

There were the familiar complaints of immorality in shelters, and the women Police Patrols have a difficult task in a city where there are many seamen and foreigners. They report that young girls in their early teens run away from home and are sometimes 'lost' in shelters for weeks at a time. The Police Patrols had a shelter and hostel of their own, but both were damaged in the blitz.

IX OTHER PROBLEMS

Other problems included looting, and the now familiar demand for more cigarettes for 'blitzed' towns. The distribution of food is said to be bad, and we again came across the feeling that neighbouring towns did not realise or sympathise with the problems of the town that is blitzed.

Our attention was drawn to the numbers of Irish who come to Liverpool hoping to get a permit to go to Ireland. Those eligible may do so only if they are intending to stay for the duration, but it seems that it is common knowledge that it is safe to promise this, as the recruitment of labour in Belfast makes it easy to return to England should they wish.

The most pressing problem remains the need to do something about housing before the winter. There is, in some quarters, a demand for a special officer to take charge of civilian welfare, and there are people who feel that when a town is badly blitzed there should be a system by which emergency measures are taken over by officials from outside the area. The suggestion of a special welfare officer has never been formulated as a working proposal. Bootle might be ready to accept being taken over by outside officials but Liverpool is always resentful of any such action. Compulsory evacuation is also suggested and receives strong support from certain people.

X MORALE

The people seem fatalistic and there is an unusual family solidarity, encouraged by the Catholic element. Though they are dour by temperament and have not the Cockney resilience, they stood their eight-day ordeal with fortitude and seem able to readjust to normal conditions. As in Portsmouth, it was remarked that the morale of the 'near-bombed' suffered more than that of the bombed. It was also said that people were ready to help themselves until they realised there was official help available. They then expected everything done for them.

There seems some resentment against the authorities who are accused of trying to force people to stay in the city during bombing, by making it difficult for them to get out. Unless they can sleep where they feel safe, there is some fear that they might get out of control in a new crisis. The investigation of the cumulative effects of lack of sleep is also demanded. We noticed nervousness and increasing apprehension as the time of the full moon approached.

A symptom which may indicate fear is the distrust of foreign elements. Anti-Jewish feeling is said to be growing. Jews are supposed to be cowards who have fled to the best billets in safe areas and who avoid fire-watching duties. One restaurant recently refused to serve Jewish customers. Greeks are also disliked and there are occasional outbursts against the Chinese in shelters, though they give no trouble and are cleaner than the general shelter population. There have also been unfortunate incidents when Free French sailors were subjected to insults and rough usage. The same attitude was perhaps reflected in objections to members of the Peace Service Union who helped in a Rest Centre, and to the fear and distrust of communist activities. In brief there seems to be a need to have someone to blame, and someone to act as scapegoat to work off the people's own fears.

The prevalence of rumours, such as the story that 30,000 were killed in the blitz, and that incendiary envelopes were to be dropped, is another sign of weakness.

The conclusion is that morale in general seems good, but that it would be as well if the authorities were more alive to a strong undercurrent of anxiety that exists.

APPENDIX II

LABOUR PROBLEMS – MERSEYSIDE

3–10 JUNE 1941

I GENERAL

This appendix is concerned mainly with the working of the new scheme for dockers, and allegations of slacking and absenteeism in factories. Feeding and transport difficulties have arisen as the result of the blitz and there is a forecast of difficulties of accommodation for workers who will be imported to man new factories.

It is subject to the same reservations as the main report [Appendix I].

II IN THE DOCKS

(a) ATTITUDE TO WORK: There are 16,000 dockers on the new flat rate. 1,500 are said to have refused to take work offered in one week, the main reasons being unwillingness to go to other ports when they considered there was plenty to do at home, and delay in payment of men who have been away. Some difficulty appears to have arisen because men declared they had never been offered jobs, but there is evidence that these men were not in the appointed place and that many were, in fact, attempting to hide. Officials thought it unlikely that any genuine worker was included with those breaking their contract but a number of dockers' wives seem to have felt there had been a real injustice. Officials estimate that about 25% are unreliable or unsuitable and that perhaps 10% of these may have to be removed from the docks.

Men known to be good workers complain that they are employed continuously while slackers draw the same money for doing nothing. It is alleged that some men who do nothing all the week take Sunday work and make as much as a man who has worked hard for six days. Older men complain that they are not fit to do a full week's work but that they must do so, if asked, or break their contract. There appears to be some resentment among 'regulars' used to working for certain firms and handling a certain type of cargo that they are forced to take unsuitable work. Some complaints were heard of the new ruling that men must return to their own centres to have their cards stamped, as this may entail a walk of several miles.

(b) METHODS OF DEALING WITH PROBLEMS: Men refusing work are being suspended without pay or unemployment benefit. 600 have just been so treated with a threat that the period of two weeks may be extended. A plan is being made for the erection of compounds round the various centres which will make it impossible for slackers to hide or stand out of earshot. (We feel that these 'cattle pens' may have a bad effect on the morale of the decent dockers, especially as they are likely to be used by agitators as an excuse for 'slave' propaganda.) Work records and observations on individual dockers are being compiled. These were started three weeks before the blitz but were destroyed by fire. They will be used as evidence for the discharge of slackers and unsuitable workers and for more satisfactory allotment of different types of work. A separate pool of older dockers is contemplated but is said to present grave administrative difficulties.

(c) GENERAL ATTITUDE TO DOCKERS: Few officials or members of the public had a good word to say for the dockers, the tendency being to class them all with the worst. It was suggested that the only way of getting them to work was to conscript them into the Army and then force them to do the job for 2/- a day. Seamen appeared particularly bitter about them, due to their own observations of work dodging, the dockers' comparatively high rate of pay, and the fact that they could live at home. (This attitude is interesting in view of the unpopularity of Liverpool dockers on Clydeside as compared with the Tynesiders, who are great favourites, as also are the London dockers.) A police superintendent was sympathetic. He described them as 'nobody's children', with no leaders except the 'loud-mouthed subversive type'. He thought they would respond to good leadership if anyone would take the trouble. It is said that trade union leaders, though in favour of the new scheme, are not using their powers of persuasion sufficiently.

III INDUSTRY

(a) SUPPLY AND DEMAND: It appears there has been no necessity as yet for any large importation of labour, with the exception of demolition workers temporarily borrowed from other towns and a number of technicians from Jamaica. A serious shortage of skilled women for office work is reported. Allegations are made of the 'freezing' of skilled workers in certain shipyards and factories, while they are urgently needed elsewhere.

(b) ATTITUDE TO WORK: The general complaint is that the attitude to work is an entirely mercenary one. 'When we want to move a worker to another department, the only question they ask is, "What's the bonus?"' The bonus pool system is criticised as penalising the good worker who feels he is 'carrying' the slacker. Slackness is more apparent amongst the young workers, especially youths and girls without responsibilities. It is alleged that many rate-fixers are open to graft. Absenteeism is prevalent after

Sunday work. On the other hand, attendance after the blitz week is said to have risen remarkably rapidly after a sharp drop and it is not thought that blitz conditions are being used as an excuse for absence, except in a few cases. Much has been said about the causes of absenteeism, but little emphasis laid on what appears to us to be the main reason, the lack of organisation of rest periods and holidays. There is an apparent disregard of the many investigations into hours of work and the effect on output. It must be remembered that, as far as the dockers are concerned, they have been educated to the casual labour system. Holidays are unheard of in their ranks. There are no welfare traditions on docks – or in shipyards.

The 'costs plus' system in operation on Government contracts is said to be leading to uneconomic planning and to account for the 'freezing' of skilled workers already mentioned. An official in an aircraft factory stated that, in his opinion, more work could be turned out with two-thirds of the staff if it was properly organised. It is said that Government investigation at this factory has not yet resulted in any improvements. Smaller firms with some Government contracts complain that the Government is not paying up sufficiently quickly and that they are having to pay interest on overdrafts which they are not allowed to include in their costs. They are also having to borrow money at high interest in order to fulfil contracts which are not paid for until completed, and this extra cost is also disallowed. The Government is criticised for wasting money on unnecessary supervision.

The workers' idea (possibly distorted) of the employers' attitude to the war effort appears important. It seems their patriotism is overshadowed by their unwillingness to make profits for employers whom they regard as their natural enemies. Propaganda impressing workers of their importance, rather than encouraging their war effort, appears merely to incite them to use their increased bargaining power, whilst the recent publicity given to slacking in factories is regarded as an organised attempt by capitalists to throw blame on the workers to cover their own short-comings. Keen workers with too little to do are said to be suffering from a sense of frustration which is leading to the feeling 'What's the use?'

(c) WELFARE: Welfare traditions are said to be poor in many of the established industries, especially in the shipyards. The high standards set in some new factories is causing discontent among the less fortunate. We were told that many firms are dodging the order to set up canteens as long as they can or are providing 'token' canteens which are poor, and therefore not patronised, or else inadequate. Genuine difficulties are reported in getting equipment, and lack of organisation in distribution is resulting in one factory getting cooking utensils and no stoves, and another stoves and no cooking utensils. The value of good welfare officers has been proved in one factory, where bombed-out or distressed employees are helped to straighten out their affairs without the sacrifice of too much work time. The WVS are co-operating with rehousing and other problems and a member attends regularly at the factory.

(d) DAY NURSERIES: We heard that day nurseries under the local authority were closed some time before the war as it was said they did not pay. No new ones have been started under the Ministry of Health scheme. A limited investigation into the need reveals a demand from about 20% of working mothers and a much higher percentage who would use them in an emergency. Satisfactory data is, however, difficult to collect and the authorities do not seem inclined to experiment. (In Nottingham, the University conducted a house-to-house survey on behalf of the Council of Social Service and we suggest that Liverpool University might possibly help, if approached.) Opinions differ about the location of nurseries. Welfare officers favour small, well dispersed nurseries in working-class districts, as they say that transport services to the big factories are already overburdened and that, in any case, the immediate vicinity is not safe. A doctor in the Public Health Department thought this idea impracticable as the population is so scattered, and an enormous number would have to be set up to avoid a double journey, one to the nursery and one to the factory. Pending further enquiries, it seems that nurseries could at least be set up on Corporation housing estates and in other places on the outskirts of the city and beyond, to which large numbers of workers have moved. An increased demand is reported from Bootle, which is said to be partly due to the increase in illegitimacy.

The Regional Information Officer reports that the care of children is proving the greatest single obstacle in the way of the campaign to get women into war work.

IV CONCLUSION

Problems arising from the reorganisation of dock labour, and the recent airing of conditions in factories, have tended to raise public opinion against the workers without full appreciation of their point of view. In the factories, it would seem that the alleged attitude of employers to the war effort as it affects workers needs further consideration.

Difficulties caused by abnormal living conditions as a result of the blitz are general, and are discussed in the main report. It appears that the major problem in the future will be the accommodation of new labour for factories now under construction. Billeting of the homeless, already difficult, will clash with the needs of workers unless priority arrangements are satisfactorily made.

LIST OF SOURCES

FOR APPENDICES I AND II

LIVERPOOL

1. Town Clerk – Secretary of MOI Committee

2. Labour Member of Emergency Committee

3. Chief Constable

4. Police Superintendent, dock area

5. Emergency Information Officer

6. Official, Public Health Department

7. Officials, Education Department

8. Official, Evacuation Department

9. Official, Rehousing Department

10. Official, Billeting Department

11. Official, Public Assistance Committee

12. Officials, Assistance Board

13. Lord Mayor's Secretary

14. Secretary, Lord Mayor's Relief Fund

15. Chief Warden

16. CAB Secretary

17. Personal Service Society case worker

18. WVS Organiser

19. Council of Social Service Secretary

20. Catholic Council of Social Service Secretary

21. University Settlement Warden

22. Catholic Priest

23. Church of England Vicar

24. Salvation Army Canteen Manager

25. 3 Shelter Inspectors

26. Shelter Marshals

27. Nurse, Child Welfare Association

28. Psychiatric Social Worker, Child Guidance Clinic

29. Editor, *Daily Post*

30. Labour Exchange Manager

31. Dock Labour Manager

32. Port Director

33. Assistant Port Director

34. Ministry of Labour Welfare Officers

35. Women's Welfare Officer, Rootes Securities Ltd. (Aircraft)

36. Labour Manager, Rootes Securities Ltd. (Aircraft)

37. ARP Wardens

38. Managing Director, J. Foreman and Co., engineers

BOOTLE

39. Chief Constable

40. Police Superintendent

41. Town Clerk

42. CAB and Personal Service Society Secretary

43. Official, Assistance Board

44. WVS Organiser

BIRKENHEAD

45. Town Clerk

46. Municipal Welfare Officer

47. Labour Manager, Cammell Laird and Co., shipbuilders

MISCELLANEOUS SOURCES OF INFORMATION

Tour of shelters of various types at night, Liverpool

Meals in British Restaurants, Liverpool and Birkenhead

Visit to aircraft factory

Visit to church meeting, Garston, Liverpool

Conversations with members of public

LIST OF ABBREVIATIONS

AA	anti-aircraft
AFS	Auxiliary Fire Service
ARP	air-raid precautions
BBC	British Broadcasting Corporation
BIPO	British Institute of Public Opinion
CAB	Citizens' Advice Bureau
CO	conscientious objector
CP	Communist Party
EMS	Emergency Medical Service
GPO	General Post Office
HE	high explosive
HI	Home Intelligence
HMS	His Majesty's Ship
HO	Home Office
IC	information committee (see LIC)
ILP	Independent Labour Party
IRA	Irish Republican Army
LCC	London County Council
LIC	Local Information Committee of the Ministry of Information
LPTB	London Passenger Transport Board
LSF	Local Security Force (Irish auxiliary police force)
MO	Mass Observation
MOA	Mass Observation Archive
MOH	Medical Officer of Health
MOI	Ministry of Information
MP	Member of Parliament
NAAFI	Navy, Army and Air Force Institutes
NBBS	New British Broadcasting Station
NCSS	National Council of Social Service
PAC	Public Assistance Committee

PPU	Peace Pledge Union
RAF	Royal Air Force
RIO	regional information officer of the Ministry of Information
TNA	The National Archives
UAB	Unemployment Assistance Board
UK	United Kingdom
USA	United States of America
WVS	Women's Voluntary Service
YMCA	Young Men's Christian Association
YPI	Young People's Institute
YWCA	Young Women's Christian Association

GLOSSARY

Air Training Corps youth organization designed to prepare boys for service in the RAF.

Alexander, A. V. from May 1940, First Lord of the Admiralty.

aliens term chiefly applied to civilians of enemy nationality living in Britain. They included Jewish refugees from Nazi persecution and political opponents of the Hitler regime, as well as other long-established immigrants.

Anderson, Sir John from September 1939 to October 1940, Home Secretary and Minister of Home Security; from October 1940, Lord President of the Council.

Anderson shelter outdoor domestic air-raid shelter named after Sir John Anderson who, as Lord Privy Seal in 1938, initiated its development. It was erected by bolting together sheets of corrugated steel and covering them with earth or sandbags.

Andrade, Professor Edward Professor of Physics at University College, London, and Scientific Advisor to the Directorate of Scientific Research, Ministry of Supply.

Anzac Day an annual commemoration held on 25 April to mark the anniversary of the landing of Australian and New Zealand troops at Gallipoli in 1915.

Assistance Board provided public assistance to those in financial distress.

Astor, Lady society hostess and Conservative MP for Plymouth Sutton.

Attlee, Clement Leader of the Labour Party and, from May 1940, Lord Privy Seal.

Axis powers the powers – principally Germany, Italy and Japan – that opposed the Allied powers.

Axis–Japan pact military alliance between Germany, Italy and Japan in September 1940.

balloon barrages large balloons, tethered with metal cables, to defend against low-flying enemy aircraft.

Bartlett, Vernon journalist, broadcaster, and Independent Progressive MP for Bridgwater.

Battle of the Atlantic long-running naval battle, at its height between 1940 and 1943, during which German U-boats attacked Allied convoys traversing the North Atlantic in an effort to cut Britain's North American supply lines.

Battle of Crete in May 1941 the Germans launched an airborne invasion of Crete and within a matter of days the British and Commonwealth forces were forced to evacuate the island.

Battle of the Ports reference to the blitz on the ports.

Beable's 'bomb Berlin' posters the brainchild of J. M. Beable, these unofficial posters were displayed in London in October 1940 and featured the message 'Bullies are always cowards bomb Berlin and save London'.

Beaverbrook, Lord proprietor of the *Daily Express* and, from May 1940, Minister of Aircraft Production. In May 1941 he became a non-departmental Minister of State with a place in the War Cabinet.

Bevin, Ernest prominent trade unionist who, from May 1940, served as Minister of Labour and National Service. From October 1940, he was also a member of the War Cabinet.

billeting finding temporary accommodation for individuals, including evacuees, in private households.

Bishop of Bristol Dr Clifford Woodward.

Bismarck German battleship sunk 600 miles west of Brest in May 1941 after a pursuit by the Royal Navy. Some 2,000 crew members were lost.

black-coated workers clerical workers. The black coat of the mid-nineteenth century symbolised a middle-class status.

black market illegal trade in officially controlled commodities.

black-out civil defence measure under which lights inside buildings had to be obscured during the hours of darkness, and lights outside buildings extinguished (subject to certain exemptions in the case of external lighting for vital war work), in order to prevent them being seen by enemy aircraft during air raids.

'Blighty' an affectionate, informal term for Britain.

Blitzkrieg a term, literally meaning 'lightning war', generally used to denote the rapid German military victories in Europe in 1939–40.

Brenner meeting meeting between Hitler and Mussolini at the Brenner Pass on the Austrian–Italian border in October 1940.

British Institute of Public Opinion British affiliate of the American Institute of Public Opinion.

British Restaurants a network of communal feeding centres, run by local authorities, which were intended to provide nutritious meals at affordable prices.

Brooke, General Sir Alan from July 1940, Commander-in-Chief, Home Forces.

Brown, Ernest from May 1940 to February 1941, Secretary of State for Scotland.

Brown, W. J. General Secretary of the Civil Service Clerical Association.

Burma Road overland supply route from Burma to south-west China along which war materials were provided to Chinese forces fighting the Japanese. As a result of Japanese diplomatic pressure, it was closed from July to October 1940.

ca'canny a deliberate reduction of output by workers going slow.

catafalque structure on which a coffin is placed during a lying-in-state.

Chamberlain, Neville Prime Minister from May 1937 to May 1940; from May to October 1940, Lord President of the Council. He died in November 1940.

charabanc bus used for pleasure trips.

child evacuee ship in September 1940 a British passenger ship, *City of Benares*, was sunk by a German U-boat in the North Atlantic en route to Canada. Of the 260 lives lost, seventy-seven were child evacuees.

Christmas 'truce' in December 1940 it was reported that Hitler had intimated that no German bombing raids would be made on Britain at Christmas if the British would, in turn, suspend their attacks. No official truce was said to have been agreed, but there was little air activity over the period.

Churchill, Winston from May 1940, Prime Minister and Minister of Defence. He succeeded Chamberlain as leader of the Conservative party in October 1940.

civil defence services services to protect the public against the effects of air attack. They included such personnel as air-raid wardens, fire-fighters, first-aid parties, heavy rescue squads, and decontamination teams.

Cockney nickname for a native of East London.

compulsory saving from 1941 the extra income tax that was to be paid through a reduction of personal allowances and earned income allowance was to be offset by a credit given to taxpayers after the war in the Post Office Savings Bank up to specified levels.

co-op cooperative societies.

Cooke, Alistair US-based journalist and broadcaster. British born and raised, he was granted US citizenship in December 1941.

corporation municipal government.

Cosgrave, W. T. Leader of the Irish political party Fine Gael.

costs plus a system under which government contracts were awarded on the basis that contractors would be paid reasonable costs plus a specified payment to allow for a profit. This payment could either be a percentage of costs or a fee fixed in advance which did not vary with the costs of a project.

coupons ration books were issued to individual members of a household. These books contained coupons and when rationed commodities were purchased the retailer extracted or crossed off the appropriate coupons.

cowl hood.

Craigavon, Lord Prime Minister of Northern Ireland. He died in November 1940.

Daily Worker communist newspaper. In July 1940 the newspaper was warned by the government about its editorial line and in January 1941 was banned on the grounds of 'systematic publication of matter calculated to foment opposition to the prosecution of the war to a successful issue'.

Dakar expedition by British and Free French troops in September 1940 to secure the Vichy-controlled West African port of Dakar. The operation ended in failure and had to be abandoned.

Dalton, Hugh from May 1940, Minister of Economic Warfare.

Darlan, Admiral François Vice-Premier and Foreign Minister of the Vichy government.

De Valera, Éamon the Taoiseach, head of the Irish government.

Deputies Union an association of miners in supervisory roles.

Derby, Lord Lord Lieutenant of Lancashire. He was known as the 'uncrowned king of Lancashire'.

Dickensian crone a withered elderly woman reminiscent of characters in the novels of Charles Dickens.

Dill, General Sir John from May 1940, Chief of the Imperial General Staff.

dividends a regular payment made by a company to its shareholders out of its profits.

docker dockyard worker.

Duncan, Sir Andrew from October 1940, Minister of Supply.

Dunkirk French port from which the British Expeditionary Force was evacuated back to the UK in May–June 1940.

Dutt, (Rajani) Palme communist journalist and theoretician. He also served for a period as General Secretary of the Communist Party of Great Britain.

East Africa in January 1941, British and imperial forces advanced from Anglo-Egyptian Sudan into Italian Eritrea. Meanwhile, operations were launched from Kenya to harass Italian Somaliland and Italian Abyssinia. By May the Italian empire in east Africa had been overrun and the Viceroy, the Duke of Aosta, surrendered.

Eden, Anthony from December 1940, Secretary of State for Foreign Affairs.

egg distribution scheme in June 1941 it was announced that the supply of eggs would be controlled. As part of this, all private poultry keepers with more than twelve hens were required to sell their excess eggs to an authorised packing station or approved buyer. This was subsequently amended to more than fifty hens.

Egypt in September 1940 columns of Italians troops under the command of Marshal Graziani advanced some sixty miles across the Libyan border into Egypt where they occupied Sidi Barrani. In December British and Commonwealth forces counter-attacked and pushed the Italians back into Libya. In April 1941 the tables were turned when Axis troops under General Rommel captured Benghazi and laid siege to Tobruk.

Eire Gaelic name for Ireland.

Elizabeth, Princess George VI's elder daughter and later to become Queen Elizabeth II.

Elsan lavatories portable chemical toilets.

Empress of Britain Canadian passenger ship en route to Britain set on fire by the Luftwaffe, and then sunk by a German U-boat, off north-west Ireland in October 1940. Forty-five lives were lost.

Essential Work Order under this order of March 1941, specified industries were classified as essential to the defence of the realm, the efficient prosecution of the war effort and the life of the community. In these scheduled undertakings the right of the management to sack employees, and of the employees to leave of their own volition, were strictly controlled and in general subject to the special permission of the Ministry of Labour and National Service. All workers in a scheduled undertaking were to have a guaranteed wage, contingent on certain conditions and obligations.

excess profits tax a tax on the wartime profits of trades and businesses in excess of the profits made at a specified pre-war level. In 1940 the tax rate was set at 100 per cent.

Exchange Labour Exchange.

Fifth Column term originating from the Spanish Civil War to denote those within a country who were thought to be sympathetic to, or working for, the enemy.

Fire of London probable reference to one of the most destructive nights of the blitz, 29–30 December 1940, when some 1,500 fires were started in London.

'fire-crowing' presumably a reference to fire-watching. 'Jim Crow' was a nickname given to roof-top aircraft spotters. It was said to have been coined by

Churchill who associated it with a ship's 'crow's nest'. There was no connection to the 'Jim Crow' race laws in the USA.

fire-watchers those called upon to watch over business premises and residential areas in order look out for, and when practical extinguish, incendiary bombs dropped by enemy bombers before they took hold of buildings.

foot-and-mouth disease a contagious viral infection that affects cattle and sheep.

Formby, George music-hall entertainer and film star.

Franco, General Francisco Spanish dictator.

Free French Forces French military units under General de Gaulle that continued the fight against the Axis powers after the capitulation of France in 1940.

Gandhi, Mohandas Karamchand (known as Mahatma Gandhi) Leader of the Indian independence movement.

Gardner, Charles BBC war correspondent.

Gaulle, General Charles de Leader of the Free French.

George Cross/Medal decorations intended to reward men and women for civilian gallantry. The George Cross was to rank next to the Victoria Cross; the George Medal more widely distributed.

Gilbertian humorous and improbable, in the style of the comic operas of Sir William Gilbert and Sir Arthur Sullivan.

Girl Guides female scouting organization.

goodwill the brand name, reputation and customer base of a business as an intangible asset.

Greece in October 1940 Italian forces invaded north-west Greece from Albania. This attack was quickly repulsed and Greek forces advanced into southern Albania. In April 1941 German forces invaded Greece. British and Commonwealth forces sent from Egypt to aid the Greeks were swiftly forced to evacuate. By June Greece was under German occupation.

Greenwood, Arthur from May 1940, Minister without Portfolio and Chairman of the Production Council.

Greenwood, Professor Major Professor of Epidemiology and Vital Statistics at the London School of Hygiene and Tropical Medicine.

guaranteed week in order to ensure a quicker turnaround of vessels, the government decreed that from March 1941 dockers in selected ports would henceforth be employed by the Ministry of Transport and guaranteed a certain number of shifts per week and a minimum wage, subject to certain conditions, such as the stipulation that they would turn their hand to any work that needed to be undertaken at the ports. Many Glasgow dockers, however, wished to preserve the principle of casual labour.

Halifax, Lord from February 1938 to December 1940, Secretary of State for Foreign Affairs; from January 1941, British Ambassador in Washington. He was a prominent Anglo-Catholic.

Haw-Haw, Lord nickname given to William Joyce, former member of the British Union of Fascists, who broadcast German propaganda to Britain.

Henderson, Sir Nevile British Ambassador in Berlin from 1937 to 1939.

Hendon bomb in February 1941, seventy-five people were killed when a single 2,500kg German bomb destroyed 196 homes in West Hendon in north-west London.

Herbert, A. P. author and Independent MP for Oxford University. He steered the Matrimonial Causes Act through the House of Commons.

Herbert Act the Matrimonial Causes Act of 1937.

Hess, Rudolph Hitler's deputy who, on 10 May 1941, set off from Augsburg in Germany in a long-range Messerschmitt Bf 110 on a secret freelance peace mission to Dungavel House in Lanarkshire, Scotland the residence of the Duke of Hamilton. With the attack on the Soviet Union imminent, it seems that he hoped to enlist the help of the duke (who had never met Hess and knew nothing about the peace mission) in negotiating an end to British hostilities with Germany in order to avoid a two-front war. Hess failed to land at Dungavel and was forced to bail out near Eaglesham where he was swiftly apprehended by a local ploughman and escorted under guard to Maryhill barracks in Glasgow. He was incarcerated in Britain for the rest of the war.

Hickey, William byline pseudonym of Tom Driberg, the *Daily Express* columnist.

Hitler, Adolf Leader of Nazi Germany.

Hoare, Sir Samuel British Ambassador in Madrid. In 1935, whilst serving as British Foreign Secretary, he and the French premier, Pierre Laval, had drawn up a plan to partition Abyssinia in order to end the Italian–Abyssinian war. The plan was leaked to the press and denounced as a sell-out of the Abyssinians. Hoare and Laval were forced to resign.

holidays at home a government campaign to encourage workers to take their holidays close to home in order to reduce wartime travel. Local authorities and voluntary bodies were to provide local amusements and entertainments for holidaymakers.

Home Guard local part-time defence force composed of those who were ineligible for call up to the armed forces, often as a result of age. Affectionately nicknamed 'Dad's army'.

Hood Royal Navy battlecruiser sunk during a clash with the German warships *Bismarck* and *Prinz Eugen* in the Denmark Strait in May 1941. Of the 1,418 crew members, only three survived.

Horder, Lord prominent physician who in September 1940 was appointed chairman of a government committee to investigate the effects of the use of air-raid shelters on public health.

Hore-Belisha, Leslie Liberal National MP for Devonport and Secretary of State for War from May 1937 to January 1940.

hospital almoner hospital social worker.

Hull, Cordell US Secretary of State.

Hun nickname for Germans.

Huxley, Professor Julian zoologist and member of a small advisory committee on Home Intelligence set up by Mary Adams in April 1940.

Illustrious Royal Navy aircraft carrier attacked by the Luftwaffe off Malta in January 1941. The ship was badly damaged and 126 crew members killed.

In Town Tonight popular Saturday-night BBC radio programme.

Industrial Alarm Scheme a scheme whereby industrial concerns developed air-raid alarm systems linked to information provided by the Royal Observer Corps about the path of attacking bombers. This was then used in tandem with their own roof spotters. Such a scheme often gave them warning of attack in advance of the public air-raid warnings.

Iraq in April 1941 there was a military coup in Iraq that led to the installation of a pro-Axis regime. In May, British and imperial forces intervened and restored a pro-British administration.

Irish ports question neutral Ireland refused to allow the Royal Navy access to its ports in the south and west of the country to help combat the U-boat campaign in the North Atlantic. This was condemned by Churchill as 'a most heavy and grievous burden and one which should never have been placed on our shoulders'.

jam scheme in March 1941 it was announced that no extra sugar allowance would be given to housewives for making their own jam from soft fruit. Instead, they were urged to sell their spare fruit to a common pool from which jam would be produced by such organisations as the National Federation of Women's Institutes. In June some sugar concession was made for the making of jam out of the stone fruit crop.

Jehovah's Witnesses Christian religious movement founded by the American evangelist Charles Taze Russell.

Jerry nickname for Germans.

Jervis Bay British armed merchant cruiser sunk by the German pocket battle-ship, *Admiral Scheer*, in November 1940 whilst on convoy escort duty in the North Atlantic. As a result, 190 crew members were lost. During the action the captain of the *Jervis Bay*, Edward Fegen, steamed straight towards the enemy and brought his ship between the *Admiral Scheer* and its prey to allow the convoy time to scatter and escape. He was awarded a posthumous Victoria Cross for his gallantry.

jibbing unwilling to do something.

Joubert, Air Marshal Sir Philip Assistant Chief of the Air Staff.

Kent, Duke of fourth son of George V.

Kindersley, Sir Robert merchant banker and President of the National Savings Committee.

King George VI.

King George George II of Greece.

King-Hall, Commander Stephen writer, broadcaster and National Labour MP for Ormskirk. In June 1940 he had joined the Factories Defence Section of the Ministry of Aircraft Production.

Koritza in November 1940 this city in south-east Albania was abandoned by the Italians in the face of the advancing Greek forces.

Krupps German armament manufacturer.

Laval, Pierre Vice-Premier of Vichy France.

layettes clothes for a newborn child.

Lease-and-Lend Bill a bill signed into law by President Roosevelt in March 1941 that allowed the US, which was then neutral, to provide war materials to the Allies. It permitted the president to 'sell, transfer title to, exchange, lease, lend, or otherwise dispose of, to any such government [of a country whose defence the president deemed vital to the national interest of the US] any defense article.' The terms and conditions of such aid to foreign governments were to be those the president deemed 'satisfactory'. Under Lend-Lease, Britain effectively gained free access to the powerhouse of the US economy and eventually received approximately $30 billion in war supplies. There was also some 'reverse' Lend-Lease through, for example, the provision of military goods and facilities to US forces in the UK.

lily-livered timid and cowardly.

Limitation of Supplies Order measure introduced in June 1940 to restrict the supply of consumer goods to the home market by imposing quotas on the production of various non-essential articles, such as pyjamas, umbrellas, cigarette cases and lawn mowers.

Lloyd George, Major Gwilym from February 1941, Parliamentary Secretary to the Ministry of Food.

Local Food Control Committees committees of local people, including representatives from both consumers and retailers, that enforced rationing regulations in their areas. Some 1,500 were established across the country.

Lofoten Islands raid in March 1941 these German-occupied Norwegian islands were raided by British commandos in order to destroy fish oil factories (the glycerine from which was used in munitions production).

London Bridge arches in February 1941 sixty-eight people were killed when a German bomb hit an air-raid shelter at Stainer Street railway arch near London Bridge Station.

Luftwaffe German air force.

Lymington, Lord landowner, environmentalist, and former Conservative MP for Basingstoke. He had been prominent in pro-German circles in 1939.

M&B 693 a sulphonamide anti-bacterial medication.

Madame Tussaud's waxworks museum on Marylebone Road in London.

Margaret Rose, Princess George VI's younger daughter, later to become Countess of Snowdon.

Mass Observation an independent social research organization founded in 1937 by Tom Harrisson and Charles Madge.

Maximum Prices Order in order to discourage speculators, in January 1941 an order was issued which made it an offence for any manufacturer, wholesaler, retailer, or other dealer to sell certain specified foods at a price higher than that charged in December 1940.

means test an intrusive official investigation into a person's financial circumstances to determine whether he/she was eligible for welfare payments or other public funds.

Menzies, Robert Prime Minister of Australia.

Messerschmitt German fighter aircraft.

miners' agent local union official who handled disputes between miners and pit managers.

Mitford, Unity Nazi sympathiser. Fourth of six daughters of Baron Redesdale.

Molotov, Vyacheslav Soviet Foreign Affairs Minister.

Morrison, Herbert from October 1940, Home Secretary and Minister of Home Security.

Mosley, Sir Oswald leader of the British Union of Fascists. In May 1940 he had been interned as a security risk.

mother and children scheme in October 1940 the government extended its official evacuation scheme for mothers and children to cover the whole of the Greater London area.

multiple stores a chain of shops owned by one company and selling the same merchandise.

Munich the Munich conference of 1938, regarded as the high-water mark of the British government's appeasement of Nazi Germany.

Mussolini, Benito Italian dictator.

Napier engineering firm.

National Milk Scheme under this scheme, which was introduced in July 1940, nursing or expectant mothers and children under five years of age could obtain a daily pint of milk at a reduced price, or free of charge if they could not afford it.

New British Broadcasting Station German radio station broadcasting 'black' propaganda to Britain. It was aimed at mainly middle-class listeners.

Norway in April 1940 British and French troops landed in Norway in order to assist the Norwegians after the German invasion. The campaign ended in failure and a few weeks later the British and French were forced to withdraw.

Nuffield, Lord motor manufacturer and philanthropist. He had been persuaded by Oswald Mosley to put up £50,000 to help found the latter's short-lived 'New Party' in 1931 (from the ruins of which the British Union of Fascists emerged). Once Mosley's fascist aims became clear Nuffield withdrew his support.

Orangemen members of the Orange Order, a protestant unionist organization based primarily in Northern Ireland.

paratroops in Italy in February 1941 British paratroops destroyed a key aqueduct at Tragino in southern Italy. They were captured and became prisoners of war.

People's Convention a communist-inspired 'people's parliament' met in London in January 1941. Its programme included the creation of a 'people's government', the safeguarding of workers' rights, the defence of their living standards, the organisation of production in the interests of the people, the provision of adequate air-raid shelters, the promotion of friendship with the Soviet Union, the freeing of British colonies, and the achievement of a 'people's peace'.

People's Vigilance Committees communist-inspired groups which campaigned for practical measures, such as improvements to air-raid shelters, as well as promoting broader political aims, such as a 'people's government' and a 'people's peace'.

Personal Service League philanthropic organization set up in the early 1930s to work in distressed areas.

Pétain, Marshal Philippe head of state of Vichy France.

Phillips, Frank BBC broadcaster.

Picture Post photojournalistic news magazine.

piece-work work paid according to the amount produced.

Players make of cigarette.

Ploughing Orders in an effort to increase crop production, the government ordered farmers to plough up grassland.

poor persons' lawyers lawyers who gave their services free of charge to those who could not afford to pay for legal advice.

Pope Pius XII.

Postscripts series of talks broadcast on the BBC, usually after the 9.00 p.m. news on a Sunday night.

preserves fruit preserved in sugar, such as jam.

Priestley, J. B. novelist, playwright and wartime broadcaster. His *Postscripts* were broadcast after the 9.00 p.m. news on Sunday nights and ran from June to October 1940.

Pritt, D. N. lawyer and Independent Labour MP for North Hammersmith. He had been expelled from the Labour party in March 1940 and was closely associated with the Communist Party.

proselytise attempt to convert.

protected areas designated areas in which non-residents had to have a permit in order to remain or visit.

'pull off a double' betting term for selecting winning horses in consecutive races.

punctilio a strict attention to etiquette.

Purchase Tax from October 1940 a tax was added to the price of certain goods sold to consumers. This was set at thirty-three-and-a-third per cent for luxury goods and sixteen-and-two-thirds for goods in more common use.

purple warning night-time air-raid warning issued to premises with external lighting that was exempted from black-out regulations, as an order to extinguish their lights.

Queen Elizabeth, consort of George VI. Later styled Queen Elizabeth, the Queen Mother.

radiolocation radar.

ramp a swindle.

reception areas areas of the country that were believed to be relatively safe from air attack and to which those from the evacuation areas were sent to escape the bombing. There were also neutral areas that were neither to be evacuated nor serve a reception purpose.

Red Cross international humanitarian organization founded in 1863.

'red tape' unnecessary bureaucracy. So named after the red tapes traditionally used to bind and secure official documents.

Region VI Southern Region.

Regional Commissioners officials who coordinated civil defence measures across the various regions of the country.

registration of women under the Registration for Employment Order of March 1941 married and single women of specified ages (which eventually came to include those born between 1893 and 1926) were required to register at local offices of the Ministry of Labour and National Service and, if their circumstances permitted, they could be directed into appropriate war work.

Reichswehr designation of the German armed forces from 1919 to 1935. Renamed the Wehrmacht in 1935.

reserved occupations under a Schedule of Reserved Occupations, workers deemed vital to the war effort on the home front had their call-up to the armed forces deferred.

Reynolds, Quentin American journalist and war correspondent.

Ribbentrop, Joachim von Nazi Foreign Minister. He was hanged in 1946.

rick infestations infestation of corn ricks.

roof cranny narrow opening or space in a roof.

Roosevelt, Franklin D. President of the USA.

roundsmen traders' employees who made regular rounds in order to take orders and deliver goods.

Rumania in October 1940 it was reported that German troops were moving into Rumania. The following month it joined the Axis powers, as did Hungary and Slovakia. Bulgaria joined the Axis powers in March 1941.

Russo-Finnish War Soviet–Finnish War fought over the winter of 1939–40. The Soviet Union invaded Finland in November 1939 but, despite the odds, the Finns resisted until March 1940 when they were forced to sue for peace. The Soviet losses were heavy.

Sabbatarians those who strictly observe Sunday as the Sabbath.

salvage superfluous or waste materials useful to the war effort.

scabies a contagious skin condition.

Scharnhorst* and *Gneisenau German battle-cruisers. Over the spring and summer of 1941 it was reported that the RAF had repeatedly attacked the docks at Brest in north-west France where these ships were anchored.

Secretary of State for Scotland from February 1941, Tom Johnston, Labour MP for West Stirlingshire.

shop stewards local trade union officials who represent their members in discussions with management.

Sinclair, Sir Archibald from May 1940, Secretary of State for Air.

Sinclair, W. A. Lecturer in Philosophy at the University of Edinburgh and wartime broadcaster. Between December 1939 and May 1940 he gave a series of radio talks on Nazi propaganda.

slab cake a large, flat, rectangular-shaped cake.

Smith, Malcolm managing editor of the *South Wales Evening Post*.

Sollum harbour on the Egyptian–Libyan border occupied by the Italians in September 1940. It was recaptured in December but lost again in April 1941.

Somaliland in August 1940 the Italians had invaded British Somaliland and the British were obliged to evacuate this East African protectorate. In March 1941 British and imperial forces conducted an amphibious landing at Berbera and the protectorate was soon recaptured.

Southampton Royal Navy light cruiser attacked by the Luftwaffe off Malta in January 1941. Eighty-one crew members were killed. The ship was subsequently scuttled.

Spitfire funds public subscriptions to raise money for the production of new Spitfire fighter aircraft.

stirrup pump a portable water pump operated by hand.

summer time in March 1941 it was announced that the clocks would be set two hours ahead of Greenwich Mean Time over the summer months in order to increase the hours of daylight at the end of the day. This, it was calculated, would, among other things, aid war transport and munitions production.

supine inactive.

Swing, Raymond Gram American journalist and broadcaster.

Syria in May 1941 the Vichy French granted the Germans the use of military facilities in Vichy-controlled Syria. In response, British, Commonwealth, imperial and Free French forces were sent into Syria–Lebanon in June in order to prevent the Germans creating a base from which an attack on

British troops in Egypt could have been launched. Damascus was captured later that month.

Taranto in November 1940 Swordfish biplanes of the Fleet Air Arm, flying from HMS *Illustrious*, attacked this southern Italian naval base and inflicted severe damage on the Italian fleet.

Tenants' Defence Leagues communist-inspired organizations which advised tenants on such matters as rents, repairs, evacuation and ARP issues, and campaigned for better conditions for tenants.

The Great Dictator a 1940 Hollywood film, starring Charlie Chaplin, which parodied Hitler and Mussolini.

tocsin alarm bell or signal.

totalisator an automated betting machine.

treating buying a round of alcoholic drinks in a pub.

trousseaux bridal clothes.

Tube informal name for the London underground railway network.

Turko-Bulgarian agreement in February 1941 Turkey and Bulgaria signed a non-aggression pact.

U-boat German naval submarine.

Vichy government term for Pétain's French collaborationist regime based in the city of that name.

VOW1 form form used for making a claim for war damage.

War Commentary BBC programme that provided weekly analyses of the events of the war, mostly by military experts.

War Damage Act legislation of March 1941 which included, among other things, free compensation up to specified limits for war damage to furniture, clothing, and other personal effects, together with contributory insurance schemes to cover other losses.

War Production Executive Committees in January 1941 new government committees were set up to oversee production and regulate imports.

war service grants grants to supplement the ordinary allowances paid to families and dependents of men serving in the armed forces in order to prevent serious financial hardship.

War Weapons Weeks a week of military displays, exhibitions, and other activities in towns and cities as part of the national savings campaign to raise money for the war effort.

wardens air-raid wardens.

Wartime Social Survey a government-sponsored social survey organization set up in 1940 under the auspices of the National Institute of Economic and Social Research.

Wavell, General Sir Archibald from July 1939, commander-in-chief in the Middle East.

Weygand, General Maxime Vichy's Delegate-General in French North Africa.

whist drive a social gathering at which the card game, whist, is played.

white paper on evacuation the report of a committee, presided over by Geoffrey Shakespeare, Under-Secretary of State for the Dominions and Chairman of the Children's Overseas Reception Board, into the welfare of evacuated and homeless people in the reception areas.

Willkie, Wendell defeated Republican candidate in the 1940 US presidential election. He visited Britain in January 1941 as a personal representative of Roosevelt.

Women's Land Army a female civilian organization whose members undertook wartime agricultural work, often in place of male farm workers called up for war service. Its members were popularly known as 'land girls'.

Wood, Sir Kingsley from May 1940, Chancellor of the Exchequer; from October 1940, member of the War Cabinet.

Woolton, Lord from April 1940, Minister of Food.

Workers' Challenge German radio station broadcasting 'black' propaganda to Britain. It was aimed at working-class listeners.

Yugoslavia in March 1941, following the Yugoslav government's decision to join the Axis powers, air force officers staged a coup and overthrew the regime. In April German forces invaded Yugoslavia and quickly forced the country into surrender.

INDEX